PERSPECTIVES ON MAIMONIDES

THE LITTMAN LIBRARY OF JEWISH CIVILIZATION

Dedicated to the memory of
LOUIS THOMAS SIDNEY LITTMAN
who founded the Littman Library
for the love of God
and in memory of his father
JOSEPH AARON LITTMAN
יהא זכרם ברוך

'Get wisdom, get understanding:
Forsake her not and she shall preserve thee'

* The Library records with sorrow the death of Vivian D. Lipman since this work went to press.

Perspectives on Maimonides

Philosophical and Historical Studies

EDITED BY

JOEL L. KRAEMER

With contributions by Lawrence V. Berman, Joshua Blau, Gerald J. Blidstein, Joseph Drory, Andrew S. Ehrenkreutz, Ithamar Gruenwald, Steven Harvey, Warren Zev Harvey, Arthur Hyman, Alfred L. Ivry, Tzvi Langermann, Ralph Lerner, Jacob Levinger, Aviezer Ravitzky, Isadore Twersky, and Michael Winter

PUBLISHED FOR
THE LITTMAN LIBRARY
BY
OXFORD UNIVERSITY PRESS
1991

Oxford University Press, Walton Street, Oxford OX2 6DP
Oxford New York Toronto
Delhi Bombay Calcutta Madras Karachi
Petaling Jaya Singapore Hong Kong Tokyo
Nairobi Dar es Salaam Cape Town
Melbourne Auckland
and associated companies in
Berlin Ibadan

Oxford is a trade mark of Oxford University Press

Distributed in the United States by
B'nai B'rith International
1640 Rhode Island Ave., N.W.
Washington, D.C. 20036, U.S.A.

British Library Cataloguing in Publication Data
Perspectives on Maimonides: philosophical and historical studies.
1. Jewish philosophy. Maimonides, 1138–1204
I. Kraemer, Joel L. II. Berman, Lawrence V. III. Littman Library
181.06092
ISBN 0–19–710071–6

Library of Congress Cataloging in Publication Data
Perspectives on Maimonides: philosophical and historical studies / edited by Joel L. Kraemer with contributions by Lawrence V. Berman . . . [et al.].
p. cm.—(Littman library of Jewish civilization)
Includes bibliographical references.
1. Maimonides, Moses, 1138–1204—Congresses. 2. Philosophy, Jewish—Congresses. 3. Philosophy, Medieval—Congresses. I. Kraemer, Joel L. II. Berman, Lawrence V. (Lawrence Victor) III. Series: Littman library of Jewish civilization (Oxford University Press)
B759.M34P37 1990 296.1'72—dc20 89–72156
ISBN 0–19–710071–6

Set by Hope Services, Abingdon
Printed in Great Britain by
The Alden Press, Oxford

TEL AVIV UNIVERSITY

The Kaplan Chair in the History of Egypt and Israel: The Study of Egyptian History and its Relationship with Israel

This volume is the proceedings of a colloquium held at Tel Aviv University in June 1982 under the auspices of the Kaplan Chair.

Other Publications of the Chair and its associated Project

Shimon Shamir (ed.), *Self-Views in Historical Perspective in Egypt and Israel*, Tel Aviv, 1981.

Anson F. Rainey (ed.), *Egypt, Israel, Sinai: Archaeological and Historical Relationships in the Biblical Period*, Tel Aviv, 1987.

Shimon Shamir (ed.), *The Jews of Egypt: A Mediterranean Society in Modern Times*, Boulder, Colo., 1987.

Acknowledgements

THIS book would not have been come into being without the help and support of a number of friends and colleagues, and the efforts of a great many other people. In this regard it is my pleasant obligation to thank first of all Professor Shimon Shamir, distinguished incumbent at Tel Aviv University of the Kaplan Chair in the History of Israel and Egypt, founder of the Israeli Academic Centre in Cairo and now Israel's ambassador to Egypt, under whose auspices the colloquium on 'Maimonides in Egypt' from which this volume originated came into existence. Professor Shamir was actively involved at every stage of the way, and it was his lively concern that moved the project along to fruition.

At Tel Aviv University, Ms Amira Margalit organized the colloquium with her usual efficiency and courtesy, and Mr Joseph Abraham helped graciously and efficiently with all the photocopying. I am specially grateful to Mrs Edna Liftman, Administrator of the Dayan Centre, who tended the volume through its many vicissitudes (*habent sua fata libelli*) with devoted solicitude.

Finally, my thanks are due to the Littman Library and Oxford University Press. In particular, I should like to thank the late Louis Littman for believing in the project, and for concerning himself with it even in the last days before he died. From his hospital bed he entrusted responsibility for the manuscript to Dr Albert H. Friedlander and Dr Louis Jacobs, and I should like to acknowledge their own contribution to its publication. At Oxford University Press, Anne M. Ashby and Vivienne Smith made much appreciated efforts on behalf of this volume. Finally, my gratitude and esteem go to Connie Wilsack, whose professional expertise and eagle eye, first at Tel Aviv University and now at the Littman Library, were invaluable in preparing the volume for publication.

J.K.

Tel Aviv
March 1989

Contents

Abbreviations ix

Contributors x

Introduction
JOEL L. KRAEMER 1

I PHILOSOPHY: ETHICS, POLITICS, METAPHYSICS

1. The Ethical Views of Maimonides within the context of Islamicate Civilization
LAWRENCE V. BERMAN 13

2. Maimonides' Governance of the Solitary
RALPH LERNER 33

3. Maimonides in the Sultan's Palace
STEVEN HARVEY 47

4. Maimonides on the Philosophic Sciences in his *Treatise on the Art of Logic*
JOEL L. KRAEMER 77

5. Why Maimonides was not a *Mutakallim*
WARREN ZEV HARVEY 105

6. Neoplatonic Currents in Maimonides' Thought
ALFRED L. IVRY 115

7. Maimonides' Quest beyond Philosophy and Prophecy
ITHAMAR GRUENWALD 141

8. The 'True Perplexity': The *Guide of the Perplexed*, Part II, Chapter 24
TZVI LANGERMANN 159

9. Maimonides on Religious Language
ARTHUR HYMAN 175

II. JEWISH LAW

10. Maimonides' *Guide of the Perplexed* on Forbidden Food in the light of his own Medical Opinion
JACOB LEVINGER 195

11. Holy War in Maimonidean Law
GERALD J. BLIDSTEIN 209

12. 'To the Utmost of Human Capacity': Maimonides on the Days of the Messiah
AVIEZER RAVITZKY 221

13. Maimonides on Eretz Yisrael: Halakhic, Philosophic, and Historical Perspectives
ISADORE TWERSKY 257

III. HISTORY

14. 'At Our Place in al-Andalus', 'At Our Place in the Maghreb'
JOSHUA BLAU 293

15. The Early Decades of Ayyūbid Rule
JOSEPH DRORY 295

16. Saladin's Egypt and Maimonides
ANDREW S. EHRENKREUTZ 303

17. Saladin's Religious Personality, Policy, and Image
MICHAEL WINTER 309

Index 323

Abbreviations

AJS Review	*Association of Jewish Studies Review*
b.	ben, ibn (son of)
HUCA	*Hebrew Union College Annual*
HTR	*Harvard Theological Review*
IOS	*Israel Oriental Studies*
JA	*Journal asiatique*
JAOS	*Journal of the American Oriental Society*
JJS	*Journal of Jewish Studies*
JQR	*Jewish Quarterly Review*
JSAI	*Jerusalem Studies in Arabic and Islam*
MGWJ	*Monattsschrift für Geschichte und Wissenschaft des Judentums*
MPP	R. Lerner and M. Mahdi (eds.), *Medieval Political Philosophy: A Sourcebook* (New York, 1963).
PAAJR	*Proceedings of the American Academy for Jewish Research*
REJ	*Révue des études juives*
Révue . . . d'Ankara	*Révue de la Faculté de Langues, d'Histoire et de Géographie de l'Université d'Ankara*
SI	*Studia Islamica*
TB	*Talmud Bavli* (Babylonian Talmud)
TY	*Talmud Yerushalmi* (Jerusalem Talmud)

Contributors

Lawrence V. Berman, Stanford University (deceased)
Joshua Blau, The Hebrew University
Gerald J. Blidstein, Ben-Gurion University
Joseph Drory, Bar-Ilan University
Andrew S. Ehrenkreutz, University of Michigan
Ithamar Gruenwald, Tel Aviv University
Steven Harvey, Baltimore Hebrew College
Warren Zev Harvey, The Hebrew University
Arthur Hyman, Yeshiva University
Alfred L. Ivry, Brandeis University
Joel L. Kraemer, Tel Aviv University
Tzvi Langermann, The Hebrew University
Ralph Lerner, The University of Chicago
Jacob Levinger, Tel Aviv University
Aviezer Ravitzky, The Hebrew University
Isadore Twersky, Harvard University
Michael Winter, Tel Aviv University

Introduction

AFTER an evening of lectures in Berlin in 1935 to celebrate the 800th anniversary of Moses Maimonides' birth, the admiring audience went home with different names on their lips. Secular Jews wondered at the philosophic acumen of the great 'Maimonides', author of the *Guide of the Perplexed.* Orthodox Jews were awed by the erudition of 'the Rambam'—Rabbenu Moshe ben Maimon—author of the *Mishneh Torah.* And academic cognoscenti paid homage to the great physician and servant of the Ayyūbid royal court, 'Mūsā b. Maymūn'. Abraham J. Heschel, one of those present, had the impression that they were commemorating different people.

These various viewpoints reflect Maimonides' amazing versatility as legal scholar, communal leader, physician, and philosopher. But there is more than personal versatility involved in Maimonides' complexity; his literary production is highly enigmatic, saturated with ambiguity, inconsistency, even contradiction. There are various exegeses of this intricacy. Leo Strauss, for instance, taught that Maimonides wrote on different levels, conveying an esoteric message by subtle suggestion. Others have said that Maimonides changed his mind; or that contradictions were deliberately paradoxical, as Ithamar Gruenwald writes here. Some, like Isadore Twersky, have pointed to tensions in his thought. To be sure, all would agree that Maimonides' writings require careful deciphering. But the arduous hermeneutic task is carried on in distinct ways by different scholars.

This volume is called *Perspectives on Maimonides* because its papers represent contrasting viewpoints and interpretations. It is divided into three sections: philosophy, law, and history. The complexity of Maimonides' discourse is exemplified by the various issues treated here. The authors discuss the contrast between Maimonides' ideal of human perfection as intellectual fulfilment achieved in solitude and his extolling a virtuous life pursued within society. They address the disparity between Maimonides' staunch support of reasonable moderation and his commendation of the austere demands of ascetic piety. They treat the conflict between the rationalist notion of human reason as capable of achieving scientific understanding and the sceptical doctrine of human knowledge as vastly limited; the variance between the concept of language as a means of knowledge and communication and the view of language as a mode of obfuscation and distortion; the encounter between the doctrine of the supremacy of human reason and the claims of revelatory prophecy; the clash between a universal vision and the particular demands of national existence and survival.

For Maimonides, was the ideal of human perfection ('What do we live for?') theoretical or practical? In our modern world, the *vita activa* is acclaimed. *Homo faber*, man as doer, producer, and user of instruments, is applauded; and happiness is hailed as a cheerful hedonism and genial bonhomie. But in medieval thought—Jewish, Christian, and Islamic—happiness was regarded as primarily a function of the *vita contemplativa.*

The ultimate point of departure for discussion of human perfection was Aristotle's *Ethics*. Aristotle had raised the question of what is the good for man. By common consensus, he said, the good is happiness. Happiness, he contended, emerges from the exercise of virtue; and supreme happiness is activity in accordance with reason (*nous*), which is man's highest virtue and the best thing in him. Theoretical reason, he taught, is the divine element in man, and it above all else *is* man. Supreme human happiness cannot reside in the exercise of ethical virtue, justice, courage, liberality, or temperance; for the human activity that is most felicitous is that most akin to the divine activity, and this is necessarily contemplative.

This élitist and intellectualist formulation of the *finis ultimus* as a life of pure contemplation contrasts with another formulation in the *Ethics* which defines the aim of human existence as the organization of the broad range of human activity in a well-ordered and comprehensively planned life in accordance with ethical virtue and practical wisdom (*phronēsis*). In one place Aristotle ranks the two aims: while a life lived according to reason is best and pleasantest and happiest, a life in accordance with the other kind of virtue is happy in a second degree (*deuterōs*). In so far as the philosopher is human and lives among people, he chooses action in accordance with virtue. The virtuous life, the life of practical wisdom, then, is second-rate; it is the life of the philosopher not *qua* philosopher but *qua* human being who must live and function in society. Aristotle's promotion of the *bios theorētikos* above the *bios praktikos* created a number of difficulties for exegetes and ethicists. For one, it stresses the value of the rational aspect of man at the expense of his composite nature as a rational, sentient, physical being. In addition, his intellectualist view confines true human perfection to the happy few. What, then, is the fate of the many? Are they barred from happiness, perfection, and immortality?

For Maimonides, it appears, the ultimate vision vouchsafed man is not a union with the active intellect, nor with the spiritual forms; it is contemplation of God's governance in the world, of the orderly structure of the universe. The supreme vision is apprehension of God's attributes, that is, of God's actions in the world. The divine actions that one should know and imitate are loving-kindness, judgement and righteousness. True human perfection, then, is achieving, according to one's capacity, apprehension of God and knowledge of his providence as expressed in creation and in his governance of the world. Having attained this apprehension, the way of life of this person will be assimilation to divine actions, and this comes about by always pursuing loving-kindness, righteousness, and judgement. The *Guide* ends on this motif of assimilation to divine actions. Is perfection for Maimonides, therefore, theoretical or practical, contemplative or active?

Several of our authors (Berman, S. Harvey, Lerner) tackled the question of tension between the quiet life of contemplation and the engaged life of public activity, touching upon the lyrical finale of the *Guide* (Part III, chapters 51–4) and the very paradox of Maimonides' life: he cherished solitude and meditation but was engrossed in the tumult of public affairs and professional activity—about which latter, incidentally, he complained bitterly and often.

Thus, the pursuit of human perfection is optimally sought in solitude, away from the madding crowd, as Maimonides teaches in the finale of the *Guide* and in the parable of the palace which prefaces it (iii. 51). True worship is realized in solitude and detachment. But, as Ralph Lerner stresses, the solitary one, by imitating divine wisdom, which orients itself to what is beneath it, becomes involved in the affairs of mankind—as Maimonides did by governing the community and extending his care to the perplexed. Or, as Steven Harvey puts it, Maimonides felt compelled, in keeping with the Platonic–Alfarabian tradition, to return to the cave and to guide its dwellers to the happiness that lies within their capacity. Solitude, Harvey says, is necessary for the attainment of perfection, which is intellectual, but this cannot be achieved in pure isolation; as Alfarabi and Avicenna taught, the philosopher needs society in order to survive. The solitude is 'incomplete external solitude', not solitude that is anti-social or anti-political. Thus, Steven Harvey stresses that while perfect individuals can emerge from the cave at will—that is, ascend or descend in their theoretical activity and mystical vision—the descent does not belong to man's ultimate perfection.

Maimonides' own descent to the cave, if I may pursue the metaphor, took the form of communal service and literary enteprise. The *Guide*, for instance, as my own article points out, is a book of political governance which conveys true and correct beliefs that are necessary for the happiness of the political community. In Maimonides' own terms, the *Guide* is basically a dialectical (or Kalām) work, in the sense in which Aristotle and the Islamic philosophers understood dialectic—that is, as a stepping stone to philosophy proper and a means of establishing its first principles, and as the way by which the philosopher participates in society and conveys to the masses accepted beliefs and necessary opinions that are beneficial to them. The *Guide*, fundamentally, is therefore not a philosophic book, but rather (as Leo Strauss maintained) a Jewish book.

Warren Harvey takes issue with the view that Maimonides was a *mutakallim*, or practitioner of Kalām, in the *Guide*, and that it may be said to be a Jewish book *simpliciter*. In his view the *Guide* is a Jewish book exoterically and a philosophic book esoterically. It was written by a philosopher playing the role of a theologian, and thus the product is a Kalām work for the unsophisticated reader and a philosophic book for the sophisticated reader.

As a philosophic book, the *Guide* was indebted to the Aristotelian current in Islamic thought (as regards logic, physics and metaphysics, and ethics) and to the Platonic (–Alfarabian) tradition in political philosophy. But both skeins, the Aristotelian and Platonic, were filtered through the prism of late antique thought and are thus heavily tinged by Neoplatonism. Like his Muslim predecessor Alfarabi, Maimonides found an Aristotle who was quite Neoplatonized. Alfred Ivry argues that it was specifically through Shī'ī, Ismā'īlī literature that Maimonides was exposed to Neoplatonic themes, and that the product is a 'Neoplatonized Aristotelianism', which, Ivry claims, is closer to Plotinus than Aristotle. He cites, for intance, Maimonides' notion of the deity and emanation, which are reminiscent of Plotinus' One, and his concept of providence and the notion that ignorance of God is a mode of knowledge, which is also called devotion and love.

The presence of Neoplatonic motifs may suggest, but does not entail, a mystical orientation. Alfarabi, as I have said, was Neoplatonic, but he was not a mystic, and he carefully discriminated his notion of access to the active intellect from mystical notions of ecstasy and union with the divine. To what extent does Maimonides exhibit mystical traits? It is significant, perhaps, in this context, that Jewish mystics, such as Abraham Abulafia, and Muslim mystics, such as Ibn Sab'īn and some followers of Ibn 'Arabī, consulted the *Guide*. Furthermore, Maimonides' son Abraham was a mystic close to Ṣūfism, as his *Kifāyat al-'Ābidīn* (Sufficiency of the worshippers) shows; and some have maintained that he was inspired in this respect by his father. Note has already been taken of an ascetic strain in the *Guide*. S. Harvey and Ithamar Gruenwald place Maimonides in the environment of Jewish Merkavah mysticism. Gruenwald suggests that Maimonides was familiar with the works of the Merkavah mystics, and regarded metaphysics as an intellectual activity combining the Graeco-Islamic philosophic heritage with the mystical skein in the rabbinic tradition. He uses this insight to understand the relation between philosophy and prophecy and the contradiction between divine transcendence and immanence. He sees Maimonides' exposition of these themes as paradoxical and as representing a dialectical play of alternate positions. Gruenwald thus rejects a resolution of the contradiction by either a Straussian postulate of esotericism or by apologetic harmonizing.

Others have preferred to stress Maimonides' use of dialectic and rhetoric to address different audiences and to accommodate abstract philosophic language to the understanding of the common man who is limited to sense and imagination, just as 'the Torah speaks in the language of men'. Thus, Arthur Hyman's discussion of the close link between Maimonides' concern for language and his overall philosophic enterprise shows how different levels of discourse—exegetical for the masses and discursive for philosophers—convey Maimonides' views on the nature of the deity.

Levels of discourse are naturally bound to types of literary genre and target audience. Thus, the *Mishneh Torah* and the *Guide* are different in mode of address. Between the two compositions contradictions are evident. One of the more fascinating variances between the two works pertains to the physical configuration of the heavens, about which Maimonides is much more certain in the Code than in the *Guide*, where he expresses considerable scepticism about our ability to know.

In Maimonides' time there was a severe crisis with regard to the Aristotelian paradigm of celestial physics. As Tzvi Langermann stresses, the 'true perplexity' according to Maimonides, stems from the conflict between the basic principles of Aristotelian cosmology, which posits a uniform, circular motion of the celestial bodies about a fixed centre, and the artifices of Ptolemaic astronomy, which breach these postulates. An adherent of the Spanish Aristotelian school of the twelfth century (which included Ibn Bājja, Ibn Ṭufayl, Ibn Rushd (Averroes), and al-Biṭrūjī), Maimonides could not quell his disagreement with the Ptolemaic theory, which posited epicycles and eccentrics. Yet unlike his famous contemporary and fellow Cordovan Ibn Rushd, Maimonides could not simply embrace the ancient Aristotelian cosmology. In the *Mishneh Torah*, Maimonides actually affirmed the existence of Ptolemaic epicycles, despite the well-known difficulties these entailed. Langermann suggests that Maimonides may have taken a sceptical position in the *Guide* for tactical, religious motives, as enigma enhances piety.

While the *Guide* and philosophical excurses in the *Mishneh Torah* and in other works pose exegetical conundrums, Maimonides' halakhic works—The *Mishnah Commentary*, *Sefer ha-Mizwot*, *Mishneh Torah*, and his Responsa—are far more homogeneous, although even here shifts and inconsistencies abound. The division between the philosophical and the legal in the present volume is justified by the divergence of literary genres, but this is not intended to suggest that Maimonides' legal works lack philosophical themes. And likewise, there are legal materials in his more philosophic works, as Part Three of the *Guide* attests.

In his legal writings, Maimonides evinces now and again a certain amount of independence *vis-à-vis* his rabbinic sources, and there is considerable evidence that he actually believed in a progressive divine revelation, such that the Talmud was superior to Scripture, and post-talmudic notions transcended the rabbinic understanding (as, for instance, regarding providence). When justifying the prohibition of forbidden foods in the *Guide* (iii. 48), Maimonides gives a medical rationale, namely, that they are physically detrimental. But Jacob Levinger contends that this argument actually conflicts with Maimonides' assertions in his medical works, where he instead recommends non-kosher animals (such as the hare and onager) as beneficial for one's health. Yet it turns out that these are endorsed not as food but rather as remedies, and the discussion in the *Guide* is declared as substantially consistent with opinions expressed in his medical works. But it is of interest that Maimonides' medical opinions, while complying with the dietary laws of the Torah, do not always follow those of the Talmud; he approves the milk of camels, for instance, although it is prohibited by talmudic law.

There is also a tension between the talmudic rulings that Maimonides embraced and recorded in his Code of Law and his own ideology regarding holy war, as Gerald Blidstein points out. In his Code of Law, Maimonides sets forth a doctrine of universal holy war—the only just (or justified) war—by which the Jewish people coerce mankind to adhere to the universal Noahide laws. But this stipulation of an ideological motive does not appear in his talmudic sources, and in fact conflicts with rabbinic norms, Blidstein says. For in talmudic terms, there are two types of legitimate warfare: commanded war, pertaining to national–territorial goals; and permitted wars, having material aims.

The universal scope of holy war ties in with the spiritual and utopian pole in Maimonides' theory of redemption. In his discourse about redemption, says Aviezer Ravitzky, Maimonides speaks on two levels. He envisions redemption in the first place as political and as concerning the salvation of Israel; but he also sees it as apolitical and embracing the universal redemption of mankind. Beyond these two, Ravitzky notes, is personal redemption; for the ultimate aim of final human redemption is personal salvation, which is achieved by the eternity of the intellect. Although personal salvation was available to individuals before the Messianic era, spiritual realization will then be available to all.

The political redemption of Israel by restoration of a sovereign state in the Messianic era and the initial loss of political independence with the destruction of the Second Temple mark the two crises in Jewish history. But the political aspect of Jewish history—destruction of the state and its restoration—are not the only dimensions that concerned Maimonides. For him the factor of the settlement of the people in its land, 'the demographic–territorial situation', is related to national independence and the existence of the Temple, as Isadore Twersky shows. The dispersion of the people thus becomes an important concept in Maimonides' legal disquisitions, and his vision of the Messianic era in *Hilkhot Melakhim* (ch. xi) stresses the ingathering of the people.

Maimonides' vision of Jewish history was informed by a sense of pathos and tragedy. He lived at a time when, as he says in his *Epistle to Yemen*, 'our hearts are weakened, our minds are confused, and our strength wanes because of the dire misfortunes that have come upon us in the form of the religious persecution in the two ends of the world, the East and West' (trans. A. S. Halkin). By West, he meant the Almohade persecutions in Spain and North Africa, from which he had himself fled, and by East he meant in particular the Yemen. Maimonides was born in Cordova, Spain, in 1138, but the Almohade invasion in 1148 forced him and his family to leave there. They arrived in Fez, Morocco, in about 1159, and remained until 1165, when they were again forced to escape persecution. They sought refuge first in the Land of Israel, where the Crusaders were fighting the Muslims for hegemony, and then in Egypt, where Maimonides settled and spent the rest of his life, about forty years. (His is thought to have died in 1204.) He was called by his contemporaries al-Andalusī (in Hebrew, ha-Sefardi), but this is a typical toponymic gentilic and does not in itself betoken any special attachment to his homeland. He was wont to recall legal practice and linguistic usages from areas in which he lived, in particular the West. He would refer to a custom or idiom, for example, 'at our place in al-Andalus' or 'at our place in the Maghreb'. Joshua Blau explains that whenever Maimonides speaks of 'our place in the Maghreb' he uses it in the broad sense to include Spain. And when he says 'the Western countries', Spain is also meant. This observation has importance for dialects, as linguistic usage of the Maghreb would have to be regarded as reflecting Spanish Arabic.

Maimonides' coming to Egypt and his accession to the position of communal leader there (*ra'īs al-yahūd*, or 'head of the Jews') corresponded with the end of Ismā'īlī (Shī'ī) Fāṭimid rule and the rise of the Sunnī Ayyūbid dynasty under Ṣalāḥ al-Dīn (Saladin). We may recall that the Qāḍī al-Fāḍil, Saladin's right-hand man, was Maimonides' friend and patron, and it is conceivable that the fortune of this ascending star bode well for his Jewish colleague. Andrew Ehrenkreutz discusses this transition in power from the Shī'ī Fāṭimids to the Sunnī Ayyūbids, and the coincidence of Maimonides' rise to prominence at this juncture. The first decades of Ayyūbid rule, which corresponded with Maimonides' early years in Egypt, are taken up by Joseph Drory. And Michael Winter treats the religious personality, policy, and image of Saladin, stressing his piety and his reputation as a holy warrior. His last sentence is an apt conclusion to our volume:

'Maimonides' rather sympathetic view of Islam . . . owes much to the fact that he met Islam in Egypt at its best in large measure because of Saladin's dynamic leadership and vision.'

PART I

PHILOSOPHY: ETHICS, POLITICS, METAPHYSICS

I

The Ethical Views of Maimonides within the context of Islamicate Civilization

LAWRENCE V. BERMAN*

THE ethical views of Maimonides are the subject of this paper. However, it seems to me that Aristotle's *Nicomachean Ethics* (hereafter *Ethics*) had a decisive influence on Maimonides' views, as did concepts found in biblical, talmudic, and post-talmudic literature. It is therefore important to have an idea of the contents of the *Ethics* in order to determine the framework out of which Maimonides is working. This position is of course in accordance with my belief that Maimonides accepted the basic Alfarabian assumption that the various religions represent theoretical thinking in popular form.[1]

Within the past few years, the important influence of Aristotle's *Ethics* on the thought of leading intellectuals within the high culture of classical Islamicate[2] civilization has begun to be realized widely. The text was translated in the heyday of translations from Greek into Arabic in the ninth and tenth centuries, along with an extensive Alexandrian summary not preserved in Greek.[3] Soon its basic thrust and contents were absorbed into the writings of some of the most well known names in the eastern Islamicate intellectual tradition, such as Alfarabi, Ibn Sīnā, Ibn Miskawayh, and Abu l-Ḥasan al-ʿĀmirī. In the

* The editor is sorry to have to record the untimely death of Professor Berman in 1988 while this volume was being prepared for publication.

[1] See L. V. Berman, 'Maimonides, the Disciple of Alfārābī', *IOS* 4 (1974), 154–78.

[2] For the use of 'Islamicate', see M. Hodgson, *Venture of Islam* (Chiago, 1974), 57–60.

[3] See Aristotle, *Kitāb al-Akhlāq*, ed. Badawī (Kuwait, 1979). Comparison of selected passages of his edition of *Ethics* with the unique Arabic manuscript in the Qarawiyyīn Library of Fez reveals the need for corrections. The Hebrew and Latin translations of Ibn Rushd's *Middle Commentary on the Nicomachean Ethics* would also be useful in case of doubtful readings since Ibn Rushd worked from a manuscript similar to that in Fez; I have recently completed an edition of the whole of the original Hebrew version of the translation. See also L. V. Berman, *Hebrew Versions of Book Four of Averroes' Middle Commentary on the Nicomachean Ethics* (Jerusalem, 1981), Introd.

west of the Islamicate world, the text was the subject of reflection in works of Ibn Bājja, Ibn Rushd, and Maimonides.[4]

It is important to realize that from the Aristotelian point of view, ethics is considered a part of political science. Therefore, considering the end for man determines what the goal of the state should be, for the state is looked upon as an instrument providing the full realization of the man's potential for happiness. Accordingly, a major topic discussed in the *Ethics* is the goal for man, in general and in particular, aside from the importance of this subject for determining the kind of life the individual should pursue. A second major theme of the *Ethics* is the nature of the excellences or virtues of man in relation to practical activity and thinking.[5] These excellences are possible only in the organized political realm, for man is a political animal in addition to being a rational animal. The function of the state, as mentioned, is to ensure the practical and intellectual flourishing of each of its citizens. An underlying theme of the *Ethics* is that the happiness of the individual is ensured by proper laws which habituate the individual to proper behaviour in accordance with man's nature.

Maimonides' principal works are his *Commentary on the Mishnah*, his Code of Jewish Law (*Mishneh Torah*), and his *Guide of the Perplexed*. In these works, which span Maimonides' productivity over the course of his lifetime, the influence of the *Ethics* is marked. Thus, we see how a central figure of Islamicate civilization, heir to the best in that civilization of an intellectual cast, was none the less receptive to the important influence of the *Ethics*. In the *Commentary on the Mishnah* we perceive the influence of the *Ethics* both in the Introduction to that work, in the *Introduction to Avot*, and in the body of the commentary to *Avot*. To this day, of course, Maimonides' *Commentary on the Mishnah* is included in the vulgate edition of the Talmud, thus weaving an important thread of philosophic ideas into the very fabric of traditional Judaism, a result doubtless congenial to Maimonides. In the *Mishneh Torah*, the most obvious influence of the *Ethics* occurs in *Hilkhot De'ot* in the *Sefer ha-Madda'*. But I would argue that the very organization of the body of the law which the *Mishneh Torah* represents shows the influence of the basic conceptions of *Ethics*.[6] Thus, indirectly, the *Ethics*

[4] See L. V. Berman, 'Ibn Rushd's Commentary on the Nicomachean Ethics in Medieval Literature', in *Multiple Averroes* (Paris, 1978), 288–91.

[5] The practical virtues are discussed in *Ethics*, bks. ii–ix; see trans. M. Ostwald (Indianapolis, 1975).

[6] See L. V. Berman, 'The Structure of the Commandments of the Torah in the Thought of Maimonides', in S. Stein and R. Loewe (eds.), *Studies in Jewish Religious and*

has had a tremendous influence upon traditional Jewish circles. The third of Maimonides works which shows the profound influence of the *Ethics* is his *Guide of the Perplexed.* We see this notably in Maimonides' concept of the structure of the religious law and the function and goal of the religious teaching of Judaism.

The study of the ethical views of Maimonides in the light of *Ethics* and traditional Jewish ethical material in modern times began with David Rosin's study *Die Ethik des Maimonides*, published in Breslau in 1876. It is still useful, but needs to be incorporated into a larger study utilizing texts published since his time and the results of the research of modern scholars on various aspects of Maimonides' ethical thought. In this paper I should like to lay the foundations for such a study by discussing Maimonides' concept of the ideal man in the light of the *Ethics*, taking into account modern scholarly literature on the interpretation of the *Ethics* and the ideas of Maimonides.

THE 'IDEAL MAN' IN ARISTOTLE'S *NICOMACHEAN ETHICS*

The *Ethics* begins with the question of what is the end for man:

> Every art and every investigation and likewise every practical pursuit and undertaking seems to aim at some good. Hence it has been well said that good is that at which all things aim. (1094*a*1–3)

Aristotle then goes on to establish the existence of a supreme good for the conduct of life. But what is this supreme good? Here Aristotle, depending on received opinion, introduces the term 'flourishing' (*eudaimonia*, *sa'ādah*, *felicitas*, *hazlaḥah*), or 'happiness', as the usual translation has it. But, again, what is happiness? What does it mean to be flourishing?

Intellectual History Presented to Alexander Altmann (London, 1979), 53–6. Although I have not taken up the question of the influence of the *Ethics* on the schemes of organization of the commandments in the *Mishneh Torah* and the *Guide*, it seems obvious that the basic division of the commandments into theoretical and practical, with the practical being subdivided into the ethical and the political, stems from the *Ethics* or from thought patterns which serve as a basic motif of the *Ethics*. It would be instructive to compare the structures of other codes of law with the Maimonidean scheme as a touchstone of philosophic penetration. For the possible influence of Alfarabi's *Virtuous City* on the first book of the *Mishneh Torah*, see J. L. Kraemer, 'Alfarabi's *Opinions of the Virtuous City* and Maimonides' *Foundations of the Law*', in *Studia Orientalia Memoriae D. H. Baneth Dedicata* (Jerusalem, 1979), 125–53. Of course, Alfarabi is one of the great conduits by which thought based on the *Ethics* passed into Islamicate civilization and thence into medieval Western European thought.

In investigating the function (*ergon*) of man, Aristotle comes to the following conclusion:

> The good of man is the activity of his soul in accordance with virtue, or if there be several human virtues, it is conformity with the best and most perfect among them. (1098*a*16–17)

He proceeds to state:

> But inasmuch as happiness is a certain activity of the soul in accordance with perfect virtue, it is necessary to examine the nature of virtue (*peri aretēs*). (1102*a*5–6)

Books II–IX of the *Ethics* are then devoted to a examination of the nature of virtue or excellence (*aretē*). In the course of the discussion the moral and intellectual virtues are examined, analysed, and defined.

In the tenth and final book Aristotle takes up the question of *eudaimonia* again. Here we learn:

> If happiness consists in activity in accordance with virtue, it is reasonable that it should be activity in accordance with the highest virtue and this will be activity in accordance with the best part of us. . . . This activity is the activity of contemplation. (1177*a*12–18)

Happiness, then, consists in theoretical activity in accordance with wisdom (*sophia*), the highest intellectual virtue. If this is so, what is the relationship of this definition of happiness, which emphasizes the importance of philosophical theorizing as an end in itself, to the previous treatment of moral excellence or virtue in the body of the *Ethics*?

Modern commentators have understood the interpretation of Aristotle's understanding of the relationship between intellectual and moral perfection in different ways.[7] The view that I favour takes the position that one must take Aristotle literally when he talks about the supreme importance of the life of contemplation. In fact, this life 'is too exalted to suit a human being. For it is not *qua* human that one lives in this way but insofar as there is in one something godlike' (1177*b*26–28). The contemplative life is that which is most akin to the divine, and it is that which constitutes the truly human—that which makes man, man. The highest ideal is therefore one in which intellectual

[7] See Aristotle, *L'Éthique à Nicomaque*, ed. and trans. R. A. Gauthier and J. Y. Jolif (Louvain–Paris, 1970), ii. 851–66; J. M. Cooper, *Reason and Human Good in Aristotle* (Cambridge, Mass., 1975), 149–77; A. Kenny, *The Aristotelian Ethics* (Oxford, 1978), chs. 7–8; W. F. R. Hardie, *Aristotle's Ethical Theory*, 2nd edn. (Oxford, 1980).

contemplation of the truth plays a paramount role. However, Aristotle does not imply, I think, that the man of the highest intellectual perfection may perform actions which are immoral for the sake of his own gratification.[8] Thus, the ideal posited by Aristotle in the tenth book of the *Nicomachean Ethics* is akin to that of the *Eudemian Ethics*, except that the intellectual element is more emphasized and the distinction between the theoretical and practical use of reason is sharpened.[9] When Aristotle, however, speaks of the life of moral virtues as being 'flourishing (or happiness) in the second degree' (1178*a*8), it seems to me that he is describing the life controlled by practical reason (*phronēsis*), rather than the life of theoretical contemplation whose leading motif is wisdom (*sophia*) in the sense given to these terms in the sixth book of the *Ethics*.

THE 'IDEAL MAN' IN THE WORKS OF MAIMONIDES

The first place to look for a discussion of the ideal man in the works of Maimonides is the last chapter of his *Guide*, where he mentions the four perfections of the philosophers and then seems to add a fifth perfection which he calls the imitation of the actions of God. The first four perfections are the physical, the economic, the ethical, and the intellectual; in this, it seems quite clear, he depends upon his Arab predecessors, particularly Ibn Bājja, since the precise concept of four perfections does not occur in the works of Aristotle.[10] As I have pointed out elsewhere, the idea of the imitation of God and the imitation of the actions of God as a goal of philosophy was popular in philosophic circles before and contemporary with Maimonides. Here, it seems to represent a special interpretation of this idea and to go beyond the ideal for man as set down in the *Ethics*.[11]

[8] Here I differ from Kenny, *Aristotelian Ethics*, 214, as well as from Cooper, *Reason and Human Good*, 164, if I understand him correctly.

[9] See Hardie, *Aristotle's Ethical Theory*, 426–9.

[10] See A. Altmann, 'Maimonides' "Four Perfections" ', *IOS* 2 (1972), 15–24, *passim*.

[11] See L. V. Berman, 'The Political Interpretation of the Maxim: The Purpose of Philosophy is the Imitation of God', *SI* 15 (1961), 53–61; id., '*Ibn Bājjah and Maimonides: A Chapter in the History of Political Philosophy* (Heb.), (Tel Aviv, 1977), ch. 1. See also I. Twersky, *Introduction to the Code of Maimonides (Mishneh Torah)* (New Haven–London, 1980), 510–14, esp. 511 n. 390, with its discussion of S. Pines's changing views; and cf. Twersky, *Introduction to the Code*, n. 391, with its reference to Wolfson.

What is the content of the fifth perfection? It would seem to be practical in nature, referring either to the founding and maintenance of the political state, as I have argued and would still maintain, or simply to a heightened sense of moral action, as is the view of the others.[12] Perhaps both interpretations can be maintained. In case it is impossible to found and maintain a political state, the focus shifts to the only possibility left, which is moral. In any case, the content of the fifth perfection consists of the imitation of the actions of God as they are displayed in nature.

What, then, is the relationship between the fourth perfection and the fifth? Different answers have been given to this question. According to some, the positing of the fifth perfection marks a radical break with the Aristotelian ideal as laid down in the *Ethics*. Here the final end is taken to be concerned with practice rather than being theoretical in nature.[13] A second view is that the fifth perfection does not constitute the end for man in any final sense. It is a by-product. According to this view the fifth perfection is something like pleasure, which according to Aristotle is not the goal of the development of man's intellectual potential but a by-product of it.[14] A third understanding is that here Maimonides' Platonizing tendencies come to the fore. The

[12] See Altman, 'Four Perfections', 24; D. Hartman, *Maimonides: Torah and Philosophic Quest* (Philadelphia, 1978), 202–12; and Twersky, *Introduction to the Code*, 510–12.

[13] See S. Pines, 'The Limitations of Human Knowledge According to al-Fārābī, ibn Bājja, and Maimonides', in I. Twersky (ed.), *Studies in Medieval Jewish History and Literature* (Cambridge, Mass., 1979), 100: 'The only positive knowledge of God of which man is capable is knowledge of the attributes of action, and this leads and ought to lead to a sort of political activity which is the highest perfection of man. The practical way of life, the *bios praktikos*, is superior to the theoretical.' This position would seem to be a revision of his previous position as expressed in the introduction to his translation of the *Guide*, p. cxxi: 'As Maimonides points out in the last chapter of the *Guide* (iii. 54), man should endeavour to imitate him. . . . This statement has sometimes been interpreted as meaning that—in contradiction to the whole trend of his thought and to many definite assertions occurring in the *Guide* and even in the chapter in question—Maimonides at the end adopted the quasi-Kantian idea that the ordinary virtues and moral actions are of greater importance and value than the intellectual virtues and the theoretical way of life. It seems to me that this explanation is completely false.' What Pines is disagreeing with in this passage is the idea that ordinary moral virtues and moral actions are of greater importance than the intellectual virtues. Actions undertaken to create and preserve the highest possible type of community might be of greater importance. In his later work, Pines seems to agree with the Kantian analogy to Maimonides' position at the end of the *Guide*. Thus Pines seems to waver on the issue of the proper interpretation of the relationship of the theoretical life to the practical life for Maimonides. See also L. V. Berman, 'Maimonides on Political Leadership', in *Kinship and Consent* (Ramat Gan, 1981), 116–17; and cf. n. 11 above.

[14] See W. Z. Harvey, 'Political Philosophy and Halakhah in Maimonides', *Iyyun*, 29 (1980), 211–12.

end of man consists of both intellectual perfection and practical perfection. This would be in line with the views of Alfarabi as expressed in his *Attainment of Happiness* and other works.[15]

In any case, Maimonides' position at the end of the *Guide* would seem to differ from that of Aristotle at the end of the *Ethics* as we understand it. In order to get a better idea of the way in which the theoretical and the practical life relate to one another, it would be helpful, I think to look at Maimonides' understanding of two types which he conceives to be paradigmatic.

ADAM AND MOSES

Maimonides takes the story of Adam as an allegory of man's dilemma in the world.[16] Adam represents the ideal for man, the philosopher[17] who is in control of his appetites. Thus for him life is a paradise. However, he is convinced to change direction—to be concerned with material goods and to become a political leader. Fallen man is thus man for whom political life is the principal preoccupation. In fact, it seems clear that Adam before the fall is the exemplar of the fourth perfection of the philosophers. What is the cause of his fall? Quite clearly, it is imagination, the enemy of intellect.[18] It has been remarked that throughout the *Guide* practical reason is not mentioned, and it has been suggested that Maimonides turns away from this concept. I suggest that there is no evidence of such a fundamental shift. However, an emphasis on the imagination as a dangerous element in human personality if not properly guided by intellect is to be found in the *Guide*.[19] This tendency is something we do not see in Maimonides' earlier works.

[15] See Berman, *Ibn Bājjah and Maimonides*, 7–12, and the literature cited there.

[16] See L. V. Berman, 'Maimonides on the Fall of Man', *AJS Review*, 5 (1980), 1–15 for an extended treatment of Maimonides' understanding of the fall. See further S. Klein-Braslavy, *Maimonides' Interpretation of the Story of Creation* (Heb.), (Jerusalem, 1978), 199–217.

[17] Although Adam is not called a philosopher explicitly by Maimonides, I think that he can be safely called one since he was 'in his most perfect and excellent state, in accordance with his inborn disposition and possessed of his intellectual cognitions' (*Guide*, i. 2; trans. Pines, 256–8).

[18] See Berman, 'Fall', 11.

[19] There is no study of Maimonides' attitude to the imagination encompassing all his works. For a good indication of the danger that Maimonides sees in the imagination, see *Guide*, i. 73, Tenth Proposition (trans. Pines, 206–12), as well as Ivry's perceptive study,

Moses, on the other hand, as Maimonides remarks, is someone for whom imagination does not play a role in his prophesying.[20] He remains the philosopher who is the opposite of Adam. Thus, he is able to follow the ideal of the imitation of the actions of God as understood by Maimonides. The figure of Moses is clearly related to the philosopher-king of the *Republic* and the Athenian stranger of the *Laws*, and is compatible with a harmonizing interpretation of Aristotle's *Ethics* and *Politics*. According to Maimonides, it is a perfect man on the lines of Moses which the Torah intends to create. In other words, he is the man who is in complete control of his imagination and, having achieved theoretical knowledge in so far as possible, goes on to act in a manner which utilizes that knowledge for the amelioration of the political life of himself and mankind. He is a man who combines the fourth and fifth perfection.

SELF-CONTROL AND MORAL STRENGTH

It seems appropriate here to remark on the difference Aristotle makes between self-control and moral strength, and their discussion by Maimonides in his *Introduction to Avot*, vi, and then to remark on their relationship to Maimonides' concept of Adam and Moses. In the *Ethics*, Aristotle distinguishes between the self-controlled man (*sōphrōn*) and the morally strong man (*enkratēs*).[21] The self-controlled man for Aristotle—and here we are dealing with a technical term given a technical meaning—is the man who has been brought up in such a way that he feels no desire to perform actions in the domain of pleasure which may be considered evil. The morally strong man is the man who feels desire for non-virtuous things but through force of character is able to restrain himself. For Aristotle the self-controlled man is quite clearly superior to the morally strong man. It is important to remark that the man of practical intellect (*phronimos*) is a self-controlled man, according to Aristotle.[22]

which points out Maimonides' ambiguous relation to possibilities conceived by the imagination (A. L. Ivry, 'Maimonides on Possibility', in J. Reinhart *et al.* (eds.), *Essays in Jewish Intellectual History in Honor of Alexander Altmann* (Durham, 1982), 67–84).

[20] See *Guide*, ii. 37 (trans. Pines, 373).

[21] See for *sōphrosynē*, Aristotle, *L'Éthique à Nicomaque*, ed. and trans. Gauthier and Jolif, ii. 236–8 (trans. Ostwald, 313–14).

[22] See *Ethics*, vi. 5, 1140*b*11–30.

Maimonides, who quotes this position as adopted by the philosopher through Alfarabi,[23] asks whether this is also the position of the Jewish tradition. In the course of his discussion Maimonides quotes Prov. 21: 10, 'The soul of the wicked man desires evil,' and Prov. 21: 15, 'The joy of the righteous is in doing justice, but it is a torment to the wicked.' This seems to coincide with the position of the philosophers according to Maimonides. However, Maimonides quotes texts from post-biblical literature which seem to indicate the opposite. The first text which he cites is 'The greater someone is than his fellow, the greater is his evil inclination' (*Sukkah*, 52*b*). Another quotation is 'according to the pain is the reward' (*Avot*, v. 23), which indicates, according to Maimonides, that involved in every commandment is some pain which is the thwarting of desire. This implies that there is pain in every case of performing a righteous deed, which according to the philosophers should not be the case. Even more striking according to Maimonides is the following statement:

> Rabbi Simon b. Gamliel says: Let a man not say that I cannot eat meat with milk or that I cannot wear garments made out of a mixture of wool and linen, that I cannot have incestuous or adulterous relations, but let him rather say that I can, but what can I do? My father in heaven has forbidden me. (*Sifra* to Lev. 5: 26)

Here, again there seems to be a clear implication that for the talmudic Sages, the ideal man is he who has desires and overcomes them. A question imposes itself: is there a conflict between the philosophers and the talmudic Sages on this topic? Which is the ideal for man—the man with desires who overcomes them or the man who is virtuous without overcoming desires, who is wholly turned toward the good?

Here Maimonides introduces a distinction in the commandments of the Torah. There are those generally accepted (*mashhūrāt*) in human society as evil, such as killing, stealing, deceiving, repaying good with harm, damaging someone who has done no harm, and insulting one's parents. Concerning these commandments the sages have said 'even were they not written, they should have been written' (*Yoma*, 67*b*).[24] The other class of commandments consists of those not generally recognized in human society as being wrong; these are the command-

[23] See Davidson, 'Maimonides' *Shemonah Peraqim* and al-Fārābī's *Fuṣūl al-Madanī*', *PAAJR* 31 (1963), 40, 43–5. The distinction ultimately derives from the *Ethics*, but in the schools the topics discussed there were elaborated and distinctions emphasized.

[24] See A. Lichtenstein, 'Does the Jewish Tradition Recognize an Ethic Independent of Halakha?' in M. Fox (ed.), *Modern Jewish Ethics* (Columbus, Ohio, 1975), 62–6.

ments of the Torah which are ceremonial in nature. Here Maimonides suggests a solution to the apparent contradiction between the statements of the talmudic Sages and those of the philosophers. The text did not state that a person should not say that it is impossible for me not to kill, it is impossible for me not to steal, but what shall I do, my father in heaven has commanded me not to do them. Rather, all its remarks are directed to the ceremonial commandments, which are not universally accepted. Of course, Maimonides is suggesting that even the Rabbis agree with the philosophers that the ideal is a man who does not desire evil. This refers to those commandments which are recognized as being evil independently of the Torah. The talmudic Sages, however, when they say that one who is attracted to evil is superior to one who is not, are referring to those things which are not universally recognized as being evil, such as the ritual commandments peculiar to Jewish society.

Thus we see that in the *Introduction to Avot*, Maimonides takes the Aristotelian position as a given and tries to reconcile it with contradictions he finds in Jewish traditional literature. Whether we think his answer is adequate or not is not especially pertinent. What is pertinent is that the ideal of repentance is not held up as supreme, and this immediately throws new light on the inclusion of the laws of repentance in the *Mishneh Torah*.[25]

In the *Mishneh Torah*, Maimonides seems to have preferred a simpler interpretation of the rabbinic point of view—perhaps because he is giving a summary of rabbinic literature, and repentance plays an important role in rabbinic thought. This is another indication, if proof is needed, that the *Mishneh Torah* is not directed to a philosophic élite. In any case, we also need to take into account Maimonides' reluctance in the period after the *Commentary on the Mishnah* to reconcile rabbinic thought with philosophic thought.[26]

In the *Guide*, Adam is described as a master of theoretical philosophy, and thus presumably a self-controlled man; a man of practical wisdom, since complete control of the appetites is a condition of the highest intellectual perfection; yet nevertheless he falls. Thus it would seem that the emphasis in the case of Adam on the imaginative faculty is meant to explain the reason for the fall. It also seems to indicate to me

[25] See Twersky, *Introduction to the Code*, 455–6, which points out the contradiction between the *Mishneh Torah* and the *Introduction to Avot*; cf. E. Schweid, *'Iyyunim bi-Shemonah Peraqim la-Rambam* (Jerusalem, 1965), 105–19.

[26] See *Guide*, Introd. (trans. Pines, 9–10).

the more highly nuanced stance of the later Maimonides toward the black-and-white categories of the philosophical tradition he espoused at the time of the writing of the *Commentary on the Mishnah*.

Moses, who certainly comes closest to fulfilling Maimonides' ideal, is not someone who is in complete control of his emotions, at least as he is portrayed in the Bible. In the *Mishneh Torah*, his character serves as a model for departing from the mean, or middle way.[27] In the *Guide*, the defects in his personality are not mentioned, and he seems to be a figure set apart. The *Guide* seems to idealize Moses as a paradigm. Accordingly, he would seem to be a man of self-control (*sōphrōn*) rather than a morally strong man (*enkratēs*). Perhaps this is a reaction to a similar tendency within later forms of Islam to idealize Muḥammad as the perfect man.[28]

THE NATURE OF THE THEORETICAL LIFE: HUMAN KNOWLEDGE AND ITS LIMITATIONS

In two recent articles, Pines has discussed attitudes toward the limitations on human knowledge of Alfarabi, Ibn Bājja, Ibn Rushd, and Maimonides.[29] With respect to Maimonides his conclusion, despite contradictory tendencies within the *Guide*, is that Maimonides seems to have a more limited conception than his contemporaries of man's abilities to master traditional metaphysical subjects. Man's ability to grasp God and immaterial entities is severely circumscribed. This is in line with reports of Alfarabi's position in his commentary on the *Ethics*.[30] A major problem, however, lies in defining exactly what the scope of metaphysics is for Maimonides. On the face of it, the scope of traditional metaphysics in the definition laid down by Alfarabi in his *Catalogue of Sciences* would be limited to the study of being *qua* being, and the investigation of the principles of the various sciences.[31] One can speculate, obviously, about the nature of immaterial beings, but one can come to no clear demonstrable knowledge about them directly.

27 See *Hilkhot De'ot*, ii. 3 (*Book of Knowledge*, trans. Hyamson (Jerusalem, 1965), 48*b*).

28 See R. Arnaldez, 'Al-Insān al-Kāmil', *Encyclopaedia of Islam*, 2nd edn. (Leiden, 1971), *s.v.*

29 See S. Pines, 'La Philosophie dans l'économie du genre humain selon Averroès: Une response à al-Fārābī?', in *Multiple Averroes* (Paris, 1978); id., 'Limitations'.

30 See id., 'Philosophie', 187–90.

31 Ibid.

In his *Treatise on the Art of Logic*, Maimonides follows Alfarabi's *Introductory Epistle on Logic*,[32] stating that divine science includes (*a*) the investigation of every existent being that is neither a body nor a force in a body, and (*b*) the investigation of the ultimate causes of everything that the other sciences include. Thus in this early work, Maimonides is following the conventional wisdom. In the *Guide*, however, we have conflicting statements with respect to the knowability of the first of these two subjects. In fact, Pines argues that Maimonides' own position would seem to agree with Alfarabi's radical stance as expressed in his *Commentary on the Ethics* that there can be only political happiness. Talk of any kind of immortality is only 'old wives' tales'.[33]

Clearly, for Maimonides there is a theoretical sphere of human activity, but it seems to be much more circumscribed than in the systems of Ibn Sīnā, Ibn Bājja, and Ibn Rushd. The only theoretical knowledge open to man would seem to be terrestrial physics. Accordingly, as I have mentioned above, Pines comes to the conclusion that Maimonides might consider the fifth perfection as the end for man.[34] I hope to examine this whole question in greater detail separately.

THE NATURE OF THE PRACTICAL LIFE: THE SOURCE OF ETHICAL NORMS AND THEIR AUTHORITY

Maimonides never gives up the idea that theoretical ideas, however limited, can be founded upon demonstration of the most rigorous sort. Thus, the sphere of the theoretical is the sphere of truth. However, the sphere of the practical, he states repeatedly, is not essentially rational. The sphere of the theoretical in his view is characterized by apodictic truth, whereas the sphere of the practical is founded on those things which are generally accepted. (By apodictic I mean what has been demonstrated to be true by use of the principles of Aristotelian logic, not merely the bare statement of the conclusions.)[35]

[32] See Maimonides, *Treatise on Logic*, ed. I. Efros, in *PAAJR* 34 (1966), 155–60, ch. 14; D. M. Dunlop (ed. and trans.), 'Al-Fārābī's Introductory *Risalāh* on Logic', *Islamic Quarterly*, 3 (1956), 224–35.

[33] See Pines, 'Limitations', 84–5; cf. Berman, 'Disciple', 165 n. 38.

[34] See n. 13.

[35] For a different use of the term 'apodictic', see Twersky, *Introduction to the Code*, 490.

In Maimonides' *Introduction to Avot*, vi, already discussed in general above, Maimonides gives examples of those things which are well known (*mashhūrāt*), such as killing, stealing, deceiving, and so forth. These are what 'some of our modern scholars who became sick with the sickness of the [Muslim] theologians called rational commandments', a judgement with which he obviously disagrees.[36]

The reason that Maimonides disagrees with this statement is not that he thinks that all commandments are rational, as Twersky has recently claimed,[37] but rather that the Mu'tazilites conceive of the conventional, non-ceremonial commandments to be rational in some absolute sense.[38] Maimonides objects to this since he thinks, along with Alfarabi, that the concept of intellect in the Mu'tazilite sense is much less rigorous than that held by the philosophers of the school to which Alfarabi and Maimonides belong.[39]

In the *Guide*, i. 2, in speaking about his conception of Adam, Maimonides distinguishes between theoretical truths which are apodictic, the fruits of rigorous demonstration, and statements which are generally recognized as true (*mashhūrāt*). And in speaking about the Ten Commandments he divides them into the rational, those which are generally recognized (*mashhūrāt*), and those which are based upon traditions (*maqbūlāt*), the ceremonial commandments.[40] Thus throughout Maimonides' scholarly lifetime we see him holding on to this distinction. However, this basic concept of Maimonides seems to contradict the notion of a divine commandment, and it has been suggested to the contrary that the function of revelation for Maimonides is to provide the certainty that human reason is unable to provide. This point of view is difficult for me to accept.[41]

First of all, I find no evidence in the works of Maimonides that he advocates this concept. Of course, it has been argued that 'ground for obligation and authoritativeness is unquestionably the divine command

[36] See Maimonides, *Commentary on the Mishnah, Seder Neziqin*, ed. and trans. J. Kafiḥ (Jerusalem, 1964), 392, col. 2, ll. 15–23.

[37] Twersky, *Introduction to the Code*, 458; cf. S. C. Schwarzschild, 'Moral Radicalism and "Middlingness" in the Ethics of Maimonides', *Studies in Medieval Culture*, 11 (1977), 65–94; and W. Z. Harvey, 'Review of Twersky, *Introduction to the Code*', *Journal of the History of Philosophy*, 20 (1982), 200–3.

[38] See G. Hourani, *Islamic Rationalism* (London, 1972), 20–6.

[39] See Alfarabi, 'Introductory *Risālah*', beginning.

[40] *Guide*, ii. 33 (trans. Pines, 344).

[41] See M. Fox, 'Maimonides and Aquinas on Natural Law', *Dine Israel*, 3 (1972), pp. xxii–xxiii; id., 'The Doctrine of the Mean in Aristotle and Maimonides: A Comparative Study', in Stein and Loewe, *Studies in Jewish Religious and Intellectual History*, 114–15.

—no Jewish thinker would dispute this or introduce distinctions concerning source and validity, authenticity and normativeness—but philosophers of the Maimonidean kind will try to how that the laws *per se* are rational'.[42] But this attitude does not seem to me to connect directly with the dilemma of the perplexed individual who is concerned with the relationship between the source of authority for philosophy and revelation. Thus, small comfort is offered to the person for whom the *Guide* is intended. In other words, the perplexed individual is trying to understand the commandments of the Torah on philosophic grounds. In such a case, one has, as it were, to suspend one's belief in order to make the demonstration rigorous.

The solution that appeals to me, and that I think is more consonant with the understanding that Maimonides has of the nature of reality, is essentially philosophic. Moses is the man of practical wisdom (*sōphrōn/phronimos*) who has the best-modulated temperament and knows the truths of theoretical philosophy in so far as it is possible to know them. It is he who serves as the measure for man. It is his judgement which confers authority in those matters which are not the result of apodictic judgement. The realm of action is not a realm of truth, but rather of good and evil. In this area the most temperate man is the measure of ethical action.[43] This attitude obviously raises questions about the nature of revelation, but this must be left for another time.

The interpretation which understands the ethical norms to be based on rational, apodictic grounds clearly seems to be rejected by Maimonides, as mentioned above. Naturally, the attitude toward the commandments as displayed in the *Guide*, iii. 25–50, must be discussed. In this part of the *Guide* Maimonides argues from the purposefulness of God's actions in nature that the commandments of the religious law also must be purposeful. He shows in detail the reasons for the commandments. Thus, it would seem that all the commandments are rational. In this connection, I should argue that Maimonides is trying to show how these commandments are in accordance with reason. This is obvious in the case of the traditional or ceremonial commandments, but it is also true with respect to the ethical and political commandments, in addition to those other commandments which Maimonides thinks are rational, such as the unity of God and his non-corporeality. It is the function of practical reason to justify the setting of norms and laws. These laws, however,

[42] Twersky, *Introduction to the Code*, 457.

[43] See Fox, 'Doctrine', 105–6.

are not rational in an apodictic sense. In his role as defender of the law, Maimonides is trying to divine the reasons behind the lawgiver's laying down the laws he has laid down. The overwhelming majority of laws are based upon generally accepted premisses rather than absolutely true ones, and therefore cannot be true in any apodictic sense.

In the organization of the commandments in the *Guide*, Maimonides clearly differentiates between the ethical and political commandments on the one hand and the traditional commandments on the other. He points out, as we have seen, that the ethical and political commandments belong to every human society, whereas the ceremonial commandments belong only to Jewish society and can be justified only after the fact.[44] However, the fact that the ethical and the political commandments are based upon premisses that are quasi-universal does not mean that they have the same epistemological status as the rational commandments in an absolute sense. The latter are based on premisses which are valid in themselves, not because they are the opinions of someone else.[45]

THE SCOPE OF THE MEAN

It now seems proper to discuss the concept of the mean that Maimonides employs and its relationship to the concept of the mean in the *Ethics*. The mean is discussed in the *Introduction to Avot* as well as in his *Hilkhot De'ot*. I shall concentrate on the latter with occasional references to the former. In *Hilkhot De'ot* the doctrine of the mean is outlined: the way which man should follow should be in the middle between two extremes, one of excess and one of defect. This is also Aristotle's doctrine in the *Ethics*, and the investigation of its ramifications in the various moral virtues occupies a substantial portion of that work.

When Aristotle speaks of the mean or middle path, he is not referring to a compromise between alternative ways to act. His mean is in constant tension between the two extremes of excess and of defect.

[44] Berman, 'Structure', 61.

[45] See Maimonides, *Guide des égarés*, trans. S. Munk, i. 39. The text of Averroes (Ibn Rushd) quoted by Munk has recently been published; see *Three Short Commentaries on Aristotle's 'Topics', 'Rhetoric' and 'Poetics'*, ed. and trans. C. Butterworth (Albany, 1977), 152. (Eng. trans. on p. 47.) See also for the same point of view D. R. Blumenthal, *The Philosophic Questions and Answers of Ḥōṭer ben Shelōmō* (Leiden, 1981), 291, l. 21. The English translation on p. 131 is flawed.

There is always danger that activity will tend towards one or the other of the extremes. Thus, an individual who follows the middle path must be constantly alert to the possibility of being enticed by one or the other. Maimonides states:

> The right way is the mean in each group of dispositions common to humanity. . . . Thus a man should not be of an angry disposition, easily moved to anger, nor be like the dead without feeling, but should aim at the happy medium; be angry only for a grave cause that rightly calls for indignation. . . . This is the way of the wise. Whoever observes the mean in his dispositions is termed wise.[46]

Aristotle devotes much space to the investigation of this topic in a thorough manner.[47] Maimonides mentions the doctrine in telegraphic fashion as is appropriate to the introductory volume of his Code of Jewish Law. When Maimonides says 'this is the way of the wise', I think he means that this is the way of the man of practical wisdom (*phronēsis*). The Hebrew term translated as 'sage' can have at least two meanings—'the man of theoretical wisdom', and 'the man of practical wisdom'—as Maimonides himself points out,[48] and it is the second meaning that is needed here.

In the very next section Maimonides continues:

> Whoever is particularly scrupulous and deviates somewhat from the exact mean in disposition in one direction or another is called a saint. For example, if one avoids haughtiness to the utmost extent and is exceedingly humble, he is termed a saint, and this is the standard of saintliness. If one only departs from haughtiness as far as the mean and is humble he is called wise and this is the standard of wisdom. And so with all other dispositions.[49]

Here we see Maimonides setting up a standard different from that of Aristotle, for we do not find a concept of saintliness in the *Ethics*. That is, we do not find a category of someone who as a matter of practice deviates from the mean set up as an ideal.

It seems to me that we have here a good example of the palimpsest in the transmission of culture. In the case of Maimonides, he is trying to sum up the whole of rabbinic literature concerned with religious law and its roots in the Hebrew Bible. On this tradition he is imposing another point of view, which is that of the philosophic tradition to which he is also heir. In terms of theory, he thinks that the philosophic approach is the fundamental approach to reality. But in any case, one

[46] *Hilkhot De'ot*, i. 4 (ed. Hyamson, 47*b*).
[47] Aristotle, *Ethics*, bks. iii–v.
[48] *Guide*, iii. 54, beginning.
[49] *Hilkhot De'ot*, i. 5 (ed. Hyamson, 47*b*).

has the distinct impression that one point of view is being superimposed on another with the layers still distinctly visible.

Maimonides adds: 'But we are bidden to walk in the middle paths, which are the right and proper ways, as it says, "And thou shalt walk in His ways".'[50] From here it seems clear that Maimonides is giving an Aristotelian interpretation to the biblical verse. The interpretation of 'thou shalt walk in His ways' is in terms of the Aristotelian doctrine of the mean, and Maimonides seems to be telling us that the way of the saint is not incumbent upon the individual Jew as a matter of law. He then goes on to quote the very famous statement of the Rabbis in explanation of this verse: 'Even as God is called gracious so be thou gracious and even as He is called merciful so be thou merciful.'[51] Here we see Maimonides quoting in explanation of the verse the well-known rabbinic statement about the imitation of God in an effort to reinforce his interpretation of 'thou shalt walk in his ways' as referring to imitation of the ways of God.[52]

Is this a non-philosophic element in the ethical theory of Maimonides, representing the Jewish side? This is the position of M. Fox, who has written: 'Perhaps the most significant single difference [between Maimonides and Aristotle] is that while Aristotle construes moral virtue as a case of imitating nature, Maimonides has as his stance the imitation of God.'[53] At first glance it seems to be true that this is a doctrine which is not Aristotelian. As I have already stated, in the introductions to Aristotle's philosophy current in the times of Maimonides, one of the definitions of the goal of philosophy is that it consists in the imitation of God.[54] Thus, Maimonides' Aristotle certainly accepted the concept of the imitation of the actions of God as applying to praxis. However, more importantly, the only way that God can be known is through his actions, that is, through the traces of the divine action in nature. Through an examination of nature the philosopher can understand what mercy is and how it is to be imitated. Accordingly, Maimonides would not have seen any difficulty in identifying the imitation of God of the Rabbis with the mean of Aristotle: imitating nature is the only way that one can imitate God, as one can only know God through nature.

50 Ibid.

51 See D. S. Shapiro. 'The Doctrine of the Image of God and *Imitatio Dei*', in M. M. Kellner (ed.), *Contemporary Jewish Ethics* (New York, 1978), 131–2.

52 *Hilkhot De'ot*, ed. Hyamson, 47*a*.

53 Fox, 'Doctrine', 110.

54 See n. 11.

It is appropriate to raise here the question of the relationship between the concept of the imitation of God as expressed in the *Mishneh Torah* and the *Guide*. In the *Mishneh Torah*, walking in the ways of God is defined in terms of the imitation of the actions of God and is identified with the Aristotelian mean. In the *Guide*, as we have seen, the imitation of the actions of God is identified with the fifth perfection, whereas the moral perfection discussed by Aristotle in the *Ethics* is identified as the third perfection.[55]

In the *Mishneh Torah*, we do find two types of activity mentioned positively: that of the sage and that of the saint. An apparently simple solution would involve identifying the way of the sage with the third perfection and that of the saint with the fifth perfection. This obviously is not satisfactory, for the way of the saint is never defined in terms of imitation.

A more satisfactory solution, perhaps, is to say that the thought contained in the *Mishneh Torah* represents a less sophisticated stage, and that over the years Maimonides developed a more profound understanding of practical activity expressed as a twofold stage of development in the *Guide*. Thus moral activity as a prerequisite to intellectual perfection is not characterized as an imitation of the actions of God since intellectual perfection has not been achieved. However, once intellectual perfection has been achieved, which entails knowledge of the ways of God, the practical activity performed is characterized as imitation of the ways of God. And this kind of imitation refers primarily to the political activity of the philosopher concerned, I would argue.[56]

CONCLUSION

In conclusion, I should briefly mention two subsidiary questions: the 'soft' hierarchical concept of gradations among men in so far as it impinges on the concept of the ideal for man according to Maimonides; and, secondly, the relationship of the religious law to the Maimonidean ideal for man.

A 'soft' hierarchical conception of mankind is a fundamental axiom of Maimonides' thought. This is obvious throughout his writings, but most especially in his parable of the flashes of lightning with which he

[55] See Berman, 'Political Activity', 118.

[56] See n. 12.

begins the *Guide*,[57] and, towards the end, in his parable of the castle. Here we see a hierarchical ordering of men according to their capacities of understanding. I call this a 'soft' hierarchical ordering in contrast to that of Judah Halevi which I call 'hard' because in Halevi the differences between the levels of individuals and groups of individuals are differences of kind rather than of degree,[58] whereas in Maimonides' thought all men are one—except perhaps for Moses—but there are differences in degree according to their natural capacities. He never states that there are differences in kind between different kinds of human beings. This kind of hierarchical thinking contrasts, on the other hand, with non-hierarchical thinking characteristic of Abū Bakr al-Rāzī[59] and most forms of Near Eastern religion that are not of a mystical or philosophic cast.

Thus when we speak of the ideal for man, we are talking about the higher levels of human capacity. Maimonides, in conformity with Aristotle, I think, does not deny that there are different ideals of perfection according to varying human capacities. The ideal we have considered is for an élite; this is the way that I think Maimonides understood the intellectual ideal for man as contained in *Ethics*, much in the same way that Ibn Rushd, his great Muslim contemporary, understood the relation between the ideal for man sketched out in Book I and Book X of the *Ethics*. Essentially, the third perfection is that to which most men can aspire, the fourth and fifth perfections are available to a relatively small number of men.

Finally, in light of the point just mentioned, I should like to sketch out the relationship of the ideal of the practical life to the religious law. Constant vigilance is needed to see that society continues to imitate the 'ways of God' as expressed in the physical universe. After achieving theoretical perfection, Moses imitates the actions of God by founding a political community which is an imitation of the physical universe. Those who come after Moses are intent on seeing that the provisions of the founder are implemented and adjusted to emerging situations. As a response to this, Maimonides composes his *Mishneh Torah* which includes both the written and the oral law. The *Mishneh Torah* itself is not something static. Thus we see Maimonides in his Responsa answering questions which are asked with respect to the adjustment of

[57] With possibly the exception of Moses; see Pines, 'Limitations', 89–90.

[58] See S. Pines, 'Shī'ite Terms and Conceptions in Judah Halevi's *Kuzari*', *JSAI* 2 (1980), 165–7 and *passim*.

[59] See Abū Bakr al-Rāzī, *Opera Philosophica*, ed. P. Kraus (Cairo, 1939), 296.

the religious law to changing social circumstances. The prescriptions of the law need constant attention in order to ensure that they fulfil their function, which is to allow all who can to reach their highest potential. Therefore, for Maimonides as for Aristotle, the end of the political realm supplies the proper conditions for the flourishing of human potential, with the constant attention and supervision of those who are the most qualified in terms of their intellectual and practical achievements.

2

Maimonides' Governance of the Solitary

RALPH LERNER

MOSES Maimonides' *Guide of the Perplexed* ends as it begins, on an intensely personal note. Never are occasion and theme more visibly joined than when Maimonides addresses the individual's concern for his perfection. The pursuit of that goal is necessarily private, though quite how radically private—even ascetic—does not become altogether clear until the final section of the *Guide* (iii. 51–4). To speak in the language of exaggeration, we might declare that according to this account, man can become fully human only by drastically separating himself from others and from their concerns. At his highest, man is not so much a political animal as a transpolitical animal. With good reason, then, did Shem Ṭov's commentary to the *Guide* refer to the highly negative contemporary reactions to this discussion (ad loc. iii. 51, 64*b*, Warsaw edn.), underline its rejection of 'political perfection' (ad loc. iii. 54, 70*a*), and designate the whole section as Maimonides' 'governance of the solitary' (ad loc. iii. 51, 68*a*; ad loc. iii. 54, 71*a*).

In this final section, Maimonides addresses a theme of great sensitivity and importance, one touched upon earlier by him in the *Guide* and elsewhere, as well as by his notable Muslim predecessors. The pursuit of perfection is necessarily the pursuit of the few—so few perhaps as to be numbered on one's fingers.[1] Their relations to the run of mankind are problematic at best. What the properly disposed and trained individual needs most is to be left alone to tend to his all-consuming purpose in life. If others figure at all in his consideration, it is in the respect in which 'they are indubitably either like domestic animals or like beasts of prey', and accordingly to be used for his advantage or warded off.[2] In an insistently imperfect world, the best

[1] *Dalālat al-Ḥā'irīn* (hereinafter cited as *Guide*), i. 34 (39*a*, 41*a* Munk; 51. 4, 53. 28 Joel). See also Ep. Ded. (2*b*; 1. 26), and i. Introd. (9*b*; 11. 2–6).

[2] Ibid. ii. 36 (79*b*; 262. 22–27). The translation of Shlomo Pines is followed throughout: *The Guide of the Perplexed* (Chicago, 1963).

course of action is association with the just and the wise and avoidance of the wicked; and where a tolerably decent city is beyond reach, solitude is the preferred way of life, if need be even a retreat to the wilderness.[3]

In this bald form neither the theme nor its formulation is peculiar to Maimonides. The relations of the citizens of the virtuous city to the subpolitical others (whether within or outside the walls) had already been cast by Alfarabi in terms of possible domestication and exploitation as beasts of burden or, alternatively, as requiring the treatment accorded all other harmful animals.[4] Ibn Bājja, in his *Governance of the Solitary*, had discussed at length the stance that ought to be taken by an isolated individual who finds himself beset by the imperfect governance prevailing in imperfect cities. Addressing himself to the isolated 'Weed' (a term that Ibn Bājja, unlike Alfarabi, limited to deviants holding *true* opinions), Ibn Bājja had proposed an unnatural remedy for an unnatural situation. To those who had already in their minds travelled far from home, physical and psychic isolation might indeed make good sense.[5] Similarly, the education of Ibn Ṭufayl's Ḥayy in the ways of mankind leads to his coming to comprehend that the majority are like irrational animals, and beyond that to his acting on that lesson by returning to his desert island—and with no regrets.[6] Finally, Ibn Rushd's paraphrase of the *Republic* clearly points to the exposed position of a true philosopher who happens to grow up in 'these cities,' likening his position to that of a man come among perilous beasts. Isolation and living the life of a solitary are his best security against being compelled to either commit or suffer injury. That such a retreat from the world was characterized by Ibn Rushd as

[3] *Mishneh Torah, Hilkhot De'ot*, 6. 1 (54*b*10–23 Hyamson). But cf. *Eight Chapters*, ch. 4. See the English translation in *Ethical Writings of Maimonides*, ed. Raymond L. Weiss with Charles E. Butterworth (New York, 1975), 69–70.

[4] *Kitāb al-Siyāsa al-Madaniyya* (87. 7–17 Najjar). See the English translation, 'The Political Regime', in *Medieval Political Philosophy: A Sourcebook* (hereinafter *MPP*), ed. Ralph Lerner and Muhsin Mahdi (New York, 1963), 42.

[5] *Tadbīr al-Mutawaḥḥid* (10. 9–11. 2, 11. 9–12. 16, 78. 6–79. 8 Asín Palacios; *MPP* 127–8, 132–3). The parallelisms between Ibn Bājja and Maimonides have been much remarked on; see e.g. Lawrence V. Berman, 'Ibn Bājjah and Maimonides: A Chapter in the History of Political Philosophy' (Ph. D. thesis, Hebrew University, Jerusalem, 1959), (Heb. with Eng. summary); Shlomo Pines, 'Translator's Introduction' to *The Guide of the Perplexed*, pp. ciii–cvii, cxvi n. 96, cxviii–cxxiii; Alexander Altmann, 'Maimonides' Four Perfections', *IOS*, 2 (1972): 15–24; Harry Blumberg, 'Al-Fārābī, Ibn Bājja, and Maimonides on the Governnance of the Solitary: Sources and Influences' (Heb.), *Sinai*, 78 (1976), 135–45.

[6] *Ḥayy Ibn Yaqẓān* (147. 8–9, 153. 5–6 Gauthier; *MPP* 158, 160).

inferior to living in Plato's city constructed in speech would have struck few of his intended readers as an argument against separating themselves from their immediate contemporaries.[7]

And yet for all these parallels and prefigurations, the conclusion of Maimonides' *Guide* remains striking and even disturbing. It is in the *Guide*, after all, that the Law's prescribed forms of worship are praised, among other things, for the absence of such useless burdensome distractions as monastic life (ii. 39 (84*b*; 269. 12–13)). It is in the *Guide* that the Law is presented as undertaking the collective transformation of an entire people sunk in idolatry into a kingdom of priests and a holy nation (iii. 32 (69*b*; 384. 13–14)). And, finally, it is there that Maimonides proclaims the fraternal caring of the descendants of a common ancestor to be 'the greatest purpose of the Law' (iii. 49 (113*a*; 442. 2–4)). Further, if one needed the example of a life most opposed to withdrawal and disengagement, what more telling instance could be adduced than the life and acts of the author of the *Mishneh Torah* and of those patient responses to the agitations of perplexed and endangered Jewish communities? If the message of the concluding argument of the *Guide* is indeed separation and withdrawal, Maimonides' own life seems inexplicable. Determining whether there is in fact such a gap between prescription and practice requires a closer look at that argument.

Maimonides' governance is presented as a guide toward the proper kind of worship; this in turn is declared to be the end of man. All human beings may be ranked in terms of their closeness to achieving this paramount human end. And as though to dramatize the great differences within our species in this respect and to facilitate our seeing what conduces to achieving this end, Maimonides begins his discussion with a parable of his own invention, a parable of a city constructed in speech. 'The ruler is in his palace, and all his subjects are partly within the city and partly outside the city' (iii. 51 (123*a*; 454. 23–25)). In this political image there are only ruler and subjects; nothing is said of rules that might be prescribed by the one for the others. Rather is the emphasis on the stance or position of the subjects: where they are, which way they face, what they seek. The gradient seems to run from those outside the city, subpolitical beings with the external shape of men, to those who are present in the ruler's council,

[7] *Averroes on Plato's 'Republic'*, trans. Ralph Lerner (Ithaca, 1974), 78 (64. 23–27 Rosenthal).

even (in the extreme case) 'speaking and being spoken to in that holy place' (iii. 51 (124*a*; 456. 11)). To penetrate into the innermost part of this city, to come closest to God, one must in the decisive sense leave the earthly city altogether.[8]

In this respect, Maimonides' characterization of those outside the city is somewhat puzzling. They are depicted as 'outside' in that they have no doctrinal belief whatever. Maimonides locates them somewhere between men and the apes, likens them to the irrational animals, and implies by their extra-political position that all cities now rest on some shared doctrinal belief.[9] This is not to say that these ape-men are utterly contemptible. Their profound ignorance is vastly preferable to the profound error of 'those who are within the city, but have turned their backs upon the ruler's habitation'—presumably for the same reason that 'knowing' about the non-existent is far worse than not knowing anything at all.[10]

Among those who at least have adopted correct opinions, the lowest rank is occupied by those who are facing in the right direction but have not come within sight of the wall of the ruler's habitation. These are 'the multitude of the adherents of the Law, I mean *the ignoramuses who observe the commandments*'. Maimonides dismisses their mouthings summarily.[11] Above them are those who are in the vicinity of the habitation but still circling around looking for its gate. Those are the jurists who eschew speculation about fundamentals, accept true opinions on the authority of tradition, and limit their legalistic inquiries to the practices of divine service. Of about the same rank are those, like the addressee of the *Guide*, Joseph b. Judah, who study mathematics and logic but have not yet mastered natural science.[12] Above them are

[8] Consider the discussion of spatial metaphors in Bernard Lewis, *The Political Language of Islam* (Chicago, 1988), 11–14.

[9] See *Maqāla fī Ṣināʿat al-Manṭiq*, end of ch. 14 (*MPP* 190). See also *Guide*, ii. 29 (63*a*; 240. 10–12), i. 71 (94*b*; 122. 16–17); *Averroes on Plato's 'Republic'*, 46, 68–9 (46. 19–20, 60. 4).

[10] *Guide*, iii. 51 (123*b*; 455. 113–18). See more generally on the need to discriminate between the professional literature on a subject and the true reality of that subject: *Guide*, i. 50, 71; iii. 5 (125*a*; 457. 10–12); Letter on Astrology (*MPP* 227–36); *Eight Chapters*, ch. 1 (*Ethical Writings*, 63).

[11] *Guide*, iii. 51 (123*b*, 124*b*; 455. 20. 456. 19–23), i. 59.

[12] Of the circumambulations of the mathematicians and logicians Maimonides repeats that they are searching for the gate. The jurists are only said to be circling, a hint that they are not even aware of this gateway to a closer approach; ibid. iii. 51 (123*b*–124*a*; 455. 21–23, 28–30), Ep. Ded. (2*a*; 1. 10–15). See Leo Strauss, 'Maimonides' Statement on Political Science', in *What is Political Philosophy? and Other Studies* (Glencoe, Ill., 1959), 165–6.

those who have entered the gate and walk about in the antechambers; they are the ones 'who have plunged into speculation concerning the fundamental principles of religion', those who have come to understand 'the natural things' (iii. 51 (124*a*; 455. 24, 456. 2)).

The sixth stage is achieved by those who 'have entered the inner court of the habitation and have come to be with the king, in one and the same place with him, namely, in the ruler's habitation'—yet even here they are not in the presence of the ruler, nor have they caught sight or sound of him. This is the rank of the men of science, those who 'have achieved perfection in the natural things and have understood divine science', those who have achieved demonstrative knowledge where that is possible or come as close to that as is possible (iii. 51 (123*a*, 124*a*; 455. 1–3, 25–8, 456. 2–4)). Here too there are significantly different grades of perfection; and it is indeed precisely at this exalted level that the few should make yet another indispensable effort, an effort that Maimonides presents as worship properly so called. This is the rank of the various degrees of the prophets, those who are present in the ruler's council chamber, who 'see him from afar or from nearby, or hear the ruler's speech or speak to him' (iii. 51 (123*a*–124*b*; 455. 3–6, 456. 5–19)).

Whether the addressee (singularly called in this chapter 'my son' (124*a*; 455. 28)) is capable of achieving such a level of worship, or whether prophecy is too great a thing for him too (cf. ii. 32 (73*b*; 254. 17–23)), is not our concern. It is enough to recognize that the point of the parable is to lay before the intended readers the path they must follow in order to prepare for such worship, just as the point of the chapter as a whole is to confirm qualified readers in 'the intention to set their thought to work on God alone after they have achieved knowledge of Him'. Through that single-minded focused thought on God and on 'the beings with a view to drawing from them proof with regard to Him, so as to know His governance of them in whatever way it is possible', the rare individual achieves the end of man (iii. 51 (124*a*–*b*; 456. 5–8, 16–17)).

The bulk of iii. 51 consists of Maimonides' guide to true worship. This makes it clear that worship strictly so called cannot be achieved in a haphazard manner, still less on the basis of vain imaginings or of tradition. The first step is intellectual apprehension of God and his acts, which is to say an apprehension based on what the men of science know about natural and divine things. The more intense and sublime this apprehension and the stronger the bond between individual and God ('that is, the intellect') the greater is the love of man for God and the greater is the likelihood of his achieving what the Sages called 'worship in the heart'. Maimonides opines that such worship 'consists in setting thought to work on the first intelligible and in devoting oneself exclusively (*al-infirād*) to this as far as this is within one's capacity'. With the preoccupation being well-nigh total, it is not surprising that the condition and result of all this should be separation from all others. 'Mostly', Maimonides adds, this worship is attained 'in solitude and isolation (*bil-khalwa wal-infirād*). Accordingly every excellent individual keeps to himself as much as possible and begrudges any necessity that comes between him and his thought of God' (iii. 51 (124*b*–125*b*; 456. 19–458. 1)).

All the practices of the worship ought to be viewed as so many devices for training the individual to turn his thoughts from this world towards God, from the world of affairs to the world of God's commandments. Hence the performance of those cultic practices ought to be informed by 'this great end'. Later on, in the following chapter, Maimonides draws a sharp distinction between the purpose of all the actions prescribed by the Law and the end of the opinions taught by the Law. Just as the passion of fear is the intended end of the actions, so is love the object lesson of the opinions. By repeated actions 'some excellent men' are trained so that they achieve human perfection, 'so that they fear, and are in dread and in awe of, God' and consequently act as they ought to. The fruit of prescribed action is right action. The fruit of instruction in correct opinions—Maimonides mentions here only 'the apprehension of His being and His unity', the apprehension of His being as He is in truth—is an all-consuming love. 'You know', Maimonides says to his addressee (citing Deut. 6: 5), 'to what extent the *Torah* lays stress upon *love*.'[13]

Right action might be said to be the path to right opinion, or at least to the possibility of understanding right opinion in something better than summary fashion. However, Maimonides' demand for the

[13] *Guide*, iii. 52 (130*a*–*b*; 464. 2–465. 5). The importance of the opinions taught by the Torah is not expressed fully or obviously by their prominence in the Torah (iii. 28). This can lead to some perplexity and calls forth a guide of quite different proportions so as to make the implicit explicit. See Leo Strauss, 'How to Begin to Study *The Guide of the Perplexed*', in *The Guide of the Perplexed*, pp. xi–xiii; and *Guide*, i. Introd. (11*a*–*b*; 13. 2–5), iii. 25, beginning. The science of jurisprudence begins from an understanding of the Legislator's intention as expressed through the prescribed actions and opinions; see Alfarabı, *Iḥṣā' al-'Ulūm*, ch. 5 (107 Amine; *MPP* 27). See also below, n. 28.

deliberate, undistracted, fully conscious performance of routine practices itself requires a long programme of training and habituation (for example, one ought to practice 'for years' how to recite the *Shema*' prayer with the proper attention and thoughtfulness); and this program he sketches in fairly brief order (iii. 51 (125*b*–126*a*; 458. 1–20)). He devotes much more space to overcoming the reader's resistance to this regimen. Although Maimonides does not state explicitly what the likely objections to his governance are, they may be divined from the arguments he offers.

In the first instance, Maimonides stresses that he has provided the addressee with 'many and long stretches of time in which you can think all that needs thinking regarding property, the governance of the household, and the welfare of the body'. Clearly the tacit concern of the aspirant to perfection is that he and his dependants will be undone should he devote himself to following Maimonides' governance of the solitary. Not so, says Maimonides, if you make effective use of the time you are obliged to spend on eating, drinking, bathing, and talking with your family and with the multitude. All the demands of wordly things can be satisfied handily in that time. What is more, one might aspire to follow the model of the Patriarchs and of Moses, whose economic and political activities (much stressed here by Maimonides) were performed 'with their limbs only, while their intellects were constantly in His presence' (iii. 51 (126*a*–127*a*; 458. 21–27, 459. 5–27)). One is tempted to say that the prosperity and success of those great models were the consequence of their *not* putting their minds to their worldly business,[14] or alternatively that in whatever they did—tending to their flocks and fields and households or governing—their single-minded intention was always to come closer to God. Their worldly success is proof not of their skill as husbandmen or statesmen, but of God's providence.

It is not enough, though, that thanks to Maimonides' providence the individual who aspires to perfection should be able to pursue that goal without entailing his economic ruin. There is a further possible objection that the game is not worth the candle, that in the end what befalls a human being differs in no important respect from what befalls a gnat drowned in Zayd's spittle. To steel the individual's resolve to

[14] See the beautiful interpretation of Song of Songs 5:2 at *Guide*, iii. 51 (126*b*; 459. 5–10), depicting joyful solitude in the midst of vanity fair. Far more precious, of course, are the times 'when you are alone with yourself and no one else is there and while you lie awake upon your bed', ibid. (126*a*–*b*; 458. 28–459. 3).

follow Maimonides' regimen, he must be shown that there is providence, that 'deliverance from the sea of chance' is perfectly proportionate to the kind of intellectual apprehension that is the object of Maimonides' regimen, and that the interruption or diminution or cessation of that providence is mostly of *our* doing. If, then, the evils that befell the prophets or the excellent and perfect men were owing to their being distracted from, or impeded in, their intellectual apprehension of God, there is every earthly inducement to put earthly concerns far behind (iii. 51 (127*a*–128*b*; 460. 6–462. 5)).

The greatest providence, then, is a necessary consequence of the greatest love, but love (as Maimonides has already explained) is proportionate to and consequent upon apprehension. Even so, there is love and love. The true human perfection is passionate love (*al-'ishq*), that 'excess of love' (*ifrāṭ al-maḥabba*) that leaves no thought directed to anything other than the beloved (iii. 51 (128*b*–129*a*; 462. 11–17)). However excessive, this all-consuming love is presented as only simple justice. If walking in the way of the moral virtues constitutes doing 'justice unto your rational soul, giving her the due that is her right', if this can be called *ẓedaqah*, how much more can one agree with Maimonides' Solomon that the righteous or just man (*ẓaddīq*), giving everything its due, rightly 'gives all his time to seeking knowledge and spares no portion of his time for anything else'.[15] For of the several perfections to be found in us, one and only one 'pertains to you alone, no one else being associated in it with you in any way'. On this point the ancient philosophers, the modern philosophers, the prophets, and the Sages all agree: not the perfection of possessions, or of the body, or of the moral virtues, but the acquisition of the rational virtues ('the conception of intelligibles, which teach true opinions concerning the divine things') is what gives the individual true perfection. Maimonides accordingly enjoins the rare individual to disregard the generally accepted opinion according to which the first three perfections 'pertain both to you and to others', for that is not so if by 'you' one means what belongs to man *qua* man. And lest you neglect what is truly and properly your own, you ought not to 'weary and trouble yourself for the sake of others'. The guide to worship properly so called becomes a call for the utterly private pursuit of true science, a pursuit indistinguishable from the passionate love for the Beloved.[16]

[15] Ibid. iii. 53 (131*a*–*b*; 465. 18–26); i. 34 (39*b*; 51. 16–52. 1).

[16] Ibid. iii. 54 (132*b*–134*b*; 467. 28–470. 11). In this context (134*a*; 469. 7, 13), Maimonides drums upon the theme of private perfection by citing Prov. 5: 17, 'They

The extraordinary chapter that brings this section and hence the *Guide* as a whole to a close (iii. 54) ends with a brief description of the way of life of the properly disposed and trained addressee. It is nothing less than an imitation of God through man's assimilation to God's actions. Maimonides prepares us somewhat for this shift from intellectual apprehension to action by his discussion in iii. 53. And yet the beginning of iii. 54—'The term *wisdom* is applied in Hebrew in four senses'[17]—can hardly be said to signal the reimmersion of the solitary in the affairs of ordinary folk. So once again Maimonides gives us the opportunity to take delight in the way he is able to exemplify the very thing he is analysing.

The Hebrew word *ḥokhmah* may apply to the apprehension of true realities aimed at apprehending God, or to acquiring some art or other, or to acquiring moral virtues, or to an aptitude for stratagems and ruses. In each instance, Maimonides cites two or three verses from Scripture meant to illustrate the particular usage. But he immediately adds that 'it is possible that the meaning of *wisdom* in Hebrew indicates aptitude for stratagems and the application of thought in such a way that the stratagems and ruses may be used in achieving either rational or moral virtues, or in achieving skill in a practical art, or in working evil and wickedness'. For this possible meaning in Hebrew, Maimonides cites no scriptural verse at all, leaving us to wonder whether he could not conjure up a tolerably apt verse (unlikely on the face of it), or whether that which has been proclaimed to be Israel's wisdom in the sight of the nations—that is to say, the Hebrew book *par excellence*—is not itself the instance of this fifth meaning of *ḥokhmah*.[18] Hard on the heels of Maimonides' list of the meanings of the term 'wisdom' comes his list of the meanings of the term 'wise', an apparent repetition noteworthy for its non-parallelisms. To be wise is to actually possess the rational virtues, or the moral virtues, or a practical art, or ruses for working evil and wickedness. In which of these senses can 'one who knows the whole of the Law in its true reality' be termed wise? The fourth is out of the question, and the third sense is equally remote. It is hardly far-fetched to imagine a knower of the Law as

shall be thine own' and so on (the verse ends: 'and not for strangers with you'), and Prov. 5: 9, 'Lest thou give thy splendour unto others, and thy years unto the cruel.'

17 None of the lexicographic chapters occurring in i. 1–70 so announces the number of meanings or begins in quite this way.

18 *Guide*, iii. 54 (131*b*–132*a*; 466. 15–27). See iii. 31 (68*b*; 383. 4–13), and iii. 32 *passim* (esp. 69*b*, and 71*b*–72*a*; 384. 22–23, 387. 14–15).

possessing the moral virtues mentioned in it, but other than referring to the possibility (iii. 54 (132*a*; 467. 2–5)), Maimonides does not deal further with this meaning of 'wise'. By exchanging the positions of the arts and the moral virtues in the first and second lists, Maimonides may be hinting that he views them as somehow interchangeable, as being alike in that they are instruments, not ends in themselves.[19]

That would leave only the possibility that the knower of the Law is wise in the sense that he actually possesses the rational virtues. But this Maimonides denies explicitly and at some length, for what is known through the Law is known through tradition, not through demonstration. Maimonides does not lack for scriptural and talmudic passages that conform to, and hence confirm, this sharp distinction between 'the knowledge of the Law . . . as one separate species and wisdom, in an unrestricted sense, as another species' (iii. 54 (132*a*–*b*; 467. 5–7, 12–14)). The rational matter received from the Law are the opinions taught on the authority of tradition: such is the knowledge of the Torah. In a class apart is wisdom in the unrestricted sense, by means of which rare individuals are able to demonstrate the opinions of the Torah. This wisdom may be equated with what Maimonides himself does in the *Guide*,[20] an activity that he characterizes as 'the science of Law in its true sense' (i. Introd. (3*a*; 2: 13–14)). The ascent of the qualified few from received opinion to demonstrated knowledge is followed by the precise definition and deduction of 'the actions through which one's way of life may be ennobled'; the drawing of such inferences falls squarely in the province of 'the legal science of the Law'.[21]

Thus far the assimilation, or drawing-near, of man to God expresses itself in man's wisdom attempting to imitate God's wisdom through an ascent to demonstrative knowledge of whatever can be demonstrated. In actually possessing the rational virtues—wisdom in the unrestricted sense—man becomes most perfectly man and comes closest to the king in his council chamber. His re-emergence from the chamber may also be said to imitate that divine wisdom which directs itself to

[19] See ibid. iii. 54 (133*b*, 134*a*–*b*; 468. 24–469. 1, 18–24, 469. 29–470. 3).

[20] Ibid. i. 1 (12*a*; 14. 14), 9 (19*a*; 23. 16–17), 18 (24*a*; 30. 7).

[21] Ibid. iii. 54 (132*a*–*b*; 467. 7–9, 18–22). Compare *Mishneh Torah, Hilkhot Talmud Torah*, 1. 11–12 (58*a*5–17, Hyamson). The methods and dangers of the ascent to the true science of the Law and hence the need for the subsequent descent are explained in *Guide*, i. 33. See, more generally, Leo Strauss, 'The Literary Character of the *Guide of the Perplexed*', in *Persecution and the Art of Writing* (Glencoe, Ill., 1952), 38–94.

something much beneath it[22] and speaks in the language of the sons of man.[23] Further, it permits the human imitation of those divine actions which exemplify the fifth possible meaning of *ḥokhmah*, the employment of gracious ruses to lead men to accomplish God's first intention: 'And I will be your God, and ye shall be My people' (Jer. 7: 23).[24]

The imitation of God's wisdom seems to slide imperceptibly into man's assimilating his actions and way of life to God's actions. In each case, it turns out (if one may compare the infinitely great and the very small), a superior being deigns to concern itself with something vastly inferior. Scriptural language applies a moral attribute to this form of action, but Maimonides insists that this means only that divine actions resemble actions that in us Adamites would proceed from moral qualities, not that God possesses moral qualities. So when God brings into existence and governs beings who have no claim upon him, he is called 'gracious' (*ḥanūn*). In similar fashion God's very act of bringing all this into being is a form of excessive beneficence to which the term 'loving-kindness' (*ḥesed*) is applied. In the case of divine *ḥesed*, the excess appears to consist less in the measure of the beneficence than in the fact that the beneficiaries have no right at all to claim such treatment.[25] The human analogy or imitation occasions the transition from a life of solitary contemplation to a life of human providence.[26]

It may well be that 'Maimonides accepts as a commonplace' the philosopher's *imitatio dei*,[27] but his characterizations of both divine model and human imitator seem anything but ordinary. Indeed, given Maimonides' principle that the way of God's governance can only metaphorically—hence only falsely—be ascribed to moral qualities,

22 *Guide*, i. 10 (19*b*–20*a*; 24. 12–19), 15 (22*a*–*b*; 27. 25–28. 7).

23 Ibid. i. 26.

24 Ibid. iii. 32. See also Pines, 'Translator's Introduction', pp. lxxii–lxxiv.

25 *Guide*, i. 54 (65*a*–*b*; 84. 23–5, 85. 3–17), 72 (103*b*; 133. 10–14), iii. 53 (131*a*; 465. 9–18).

26 In a much debated essay, Shlomo Pines has concluded that for Maimonides the inherent limitations of the human mind rule out anything higher than knowledge of God's attributes of action. Accordingly, the highest human perfection would be sought in a governance patterned on a properly understood divine rule. Granting the profound ambiguity of Maimonides on this issue, Pines none the less ranks Maimonides with Kant as according primacy to a life of action over the contemplative life; see his 'The Limitations of Human Knowledge According to Al-Fārābī, ibn Bājja, and Maimonides', in Isadore Twersky (ed.), *Studies in Medieval Jewish History and Literature* (Cambridge, Mass., 1979), 82–109, esp. 98–100.

27 Lawrence V. Berman, 'Maimonides on Political Leadership', in Daniel J. Elazar (ed.), *Kinship and Consent: The Jewish Political Tradition and Its Contemporary Uses* (Washington, 1983), 117.

what then can it mean to give the following counsel to flesh and blood? Just as God's providence extends over the heaven and the earth, so too ought man in his way of life to emulate that manifestation of divine loving-kindness (*ḥesed*), judgment (*mishpaṭ*), and righteousness (*ẓedaqah*). Clearly, the more faithful the imitation of a divine providence so conceived, the greater would be the psychic distance between human ruler and ruled.[28] More puzzling still must be that shift from utterly private, indeed voiceless, contemplation to political governance cast in the language of the sons of man. What could impel such a descent?

The suggestion that 'the philosopher needs, after intellectual perfection, to imitate God by means of his desire to found a more perfect society', indeed that 'it is his duty to found an ideal state and to preserve it', seems a plausible resolution of the difficulty.[29] It is compatible with Maimonides' interpretation (in *Guide*, i. 15) of Jacob's dream of the ladder reaching up to heaven. Further, it recalls to mind Maimonides' discussion of that great measure of divine overflow which may compel a man of science to go beyond private study and a prophet to go beyond perfecting himself. In the one case, an individual is moved 'of necessity to compose works and to teach'; in the other case, 'the prophetic revelation that comes to him compels him to address a call to the people, teach them, and let his own perfection overflow toward them' (ii. 37 (81*a*–*b*; 265. 1–7, 12–14)). None the less, it is striking that nowhere in the *Guide* does Maimonides characterize the solitary's involvement with others as a 'duty'.

Comparably plausible—and problematic—is the attribution to Maimonides of the view that prophets as a group represent 'a special class of philosophers with a mission not merely to "ascend" toward the apprehension of God but also to "descend" to the cave as it were "with a view to governing and teaching the people of the earth" '.[30] Strictly speaking, no one has a 'mission' to ascend, beyond the general injunction laid on all believers to come to some apprehension of God

[28] The imaginings that the Lawgiver invents for others have no place in his own soul. See Pines, 'Limitations of Knowledge', 108 n. 82. On the passionless exercise of beneficence or cruelty, see id., 'Translator's Introduction', p. cxxii; and id., 'The Philosophical Purport of Maimonides' Halachic Works and the Purport of *The Guide of the Perplexed*', in Shlomo Pines and Yirmiyahu Yovel (eds.), *Maimonides and Philosophy* (Dordrecht–Boston–Lancaster, 1986), 12.

[29] Berman, 'Maimonides on Political Leadership', 118, 123–4 n. 18.

[30] Alexander Altmann, 'Maimonides on the Intellect and the Scope of Metaphysics', in *Von der mittelalterlichen zur modernen Aufklärung: Studien zur jüdischen Geistesgeschichte* (Tübingen, 1987), 129. (The internal quotations are from *Guide*, i. 15.)

or of his wisdom as manifested in the whole of being.[31] True, reference is twice made to Moses' prophetic mission in the context of a discussion of the names of God (i. 63 (81*b*, 82*a*; 105. 28, 106. 9)), but the thematic discussion of prophecy in the *Guide* eschews such language. According to that studiedly naturalistic account, not even the Patriarchs (to say nothing of the post-Mosaic prophets) came bearing and flaunting divine licences. Rather, what they did and what they said followed from the measure of the overflow reaching each particular individual's rational and imaginative faculties. Their teaching or preaching was a matter of course (ii. 39 (83*b*–84*b*; 268. 10–269. 5), 37 (80*b*, 81*a*–*b*; 264. 3–9, 264. 27–265. 14)). Not some imposed duty, not even some proclaimed mission, but a profound human understanding leads the perfect one to re-enter the world of practice.

Yet that re-entry is in no case a reimmersion in human concerns; the perfect one may be in the world of affairs but is not of it. In the highest instances, Maimonides has pointed out, domestic and political governance were conducted by the Patriarchs and Moses 'with their limbs only', or as we might say, with their minds elsewhere, concentrating on what truly matters.[32] Knowing what they know, the perfect ones do not refrain from guiding those whom they hold at a distance and to whom they can barely be said to be beholden. It is on that pattern of divine rule that Maimonides claims Moses modelled his political governance of the Children of Israel. And it is that pattern too (for the most part) that Maimonides recommends to 'the governor of a city, if he is a prophet'.[33]

It is extraordinary in the light of Maimonides' emphasis upon solitary intellectual apprehension that he should characterize the practical worldly business of the Patriarchs and Moses as 'pure worship of great import', but the grounds for his doing so are not mysterious. Because the end in view in all their actions was 'to bring into being a religious community that would know and worship God', to spread the doctrine of God's unity in the world and to guide people to love Him, they deserved their privileged proximity to the King.[34]

[31] *Guide*, i. 39, end (46*a*; 60. 18–21); iii. 28 (61*a*; 373. 19–21), 52, end (130*b*; 464. 27–465. 4).

[32] See text above, at n.14.

[33] *Guide*, i. 54 (65*a*–66*a*; 84. 25–85. 2, 85. 17–86. 18), iii. 54 (134*b*–135*a*; 470. 13–471. 7).

[34] The Alfarabian political science that underlies this argument is well developed in Joel L. Kraemer, '*The Jihād of the Falāsifa*', *JSAI* 10 (1987): 288–324, esp. 319–20. See also the translated passage from Alfarabi's *Book of Religion* (65. 20–66. 10, Mahdi), in Berman, 'Maimonides on Political Leadership', 122–3 n. 7.

Then, in a sentence of studied ambiguity, Maimonides denies either that he can hope to achieve a comparable rank or that he can hope to guide others to achieve a comparable rank.[35] And yet it is incontrovertible that Maimonides promises to use his knowledge to point out the Way of Holiness (Prefatory Poem), and guides his reader in the ways of calling God truly and without distractions (Concluding Poem). His governance of the select few in the *Guide* and of the whole community in the Code, his providence towards the perplexed and the endangered whoever and wherever they might be, are alike instances of a most singular human *ḥesed*, one that might rightly be called pure worship of the noblest kind.[36]

[35] *Guide*, iii. 51 (126*b*–127*a*; 459. 18–460. 6).

[36] For discussion of a comparable problem posed by Aristotle's transition from the concluding part of the *Nicomachean Ethics* to the *Politics*, see Joseph Cropsey, 'Justice and Friendship in the *Nicomachean Ethics*', in his *Political Philosophy and the Issues of Politics* (Chicago, 1977), esp. 254–6, 272–3.

3

Maimonides in the Sultan's Palace

STEVEN HARVEY

THE PROBLEM

MAIMONIDES' life has been justly characterized as a 'profound paradox'.[1] The same thinker who taught that the true human perfection and the ultimate end of man is only achieved through solitude and isolation, and therefore that 'every excellent man stays frequently in isolation and does not meet anyone unless it is necessary',[2] himself lived an unceasingly active and incredibly public life as private and court physician, business man, and Jewish communal leader, judge, and rabbi[3]—a life which afforded little time

[1] See Isadore Twersky, *Introduction to the Code of Maimonides* (New Haven–London, 1980), 3, and id., *A Maimonides Reader* (New York, 1972), 1.

[2] *The Guide of the Perplexed*, iii. 51, trans. Shlomo Pines (Chicago, 1963), 621. Cf. iii. 54, p. 635.

[3] See the terse biographical statements in Twersky, *Introduction to the Code*, 3–5, and Abraham J. Heschel, 'The Last Days of Maimonides', in his *Insecurity of Freedom* (New York, 1972), 285. Twersky and Heschel both marvel at the incredible accomplishments of Maimonides. For Twersky, 'the record is simply extraordinary, almost surrealistic'; for Heschel, the name Maimonides seems more like the 'name of a whole academy of scholars than the name of an individual'. George Sarton, the encyclopaedic and masterful historian of science, likewise speaks of Maimonides' 'incredible' accomplishments, and Sarton was considering only Maimonides' literary activities! See his 'Maimonides: Philosopher and Physician', in Dorothy Stimson (ed.), *Sarton on the History of Science* (Cambridge, Mass., 1962), 80–1, 99. The prior wonder, in view of Maimonides' public and communal obligations, is how he had time for any literary activities. Cf. Maimonides' own plaints on this matter as expressed in his later letters (e.g. in Twersky, *Maimonides Reader*, 6, 7–8, 473, 481, and id., *Introduction to the Code*, 39). For references on Maimonides as a physician, see ibid. 2 n. 2. For Maimonides as 'head of the Jews', see the references to S. D. Goitein's Genizah studies pinpointed by Twersky, ibid. 2 n. 1, to which must now be added Goitein's, 'Moses Maimonides, Man of Action: A Revision of the Master's Biography in Light of the Genizah Documents', in *Hommage à Georges Vajda: Etudes d'histoire et de pensée juives* (Louvain, 1980), 155–67. This last study also brings to light a little known facet of Maimonides: his business acumen (see pp. 162–3; cf. Max Meyerhof, 'The Medical Works of Maimonides', in S. W. Baron (ed.), *Essays on Maimonides* (New York, 1941), 269 n. 5).

for food and sleep, let alone the privacy requisite for contemplation and the intellectual worship of God. The classic testimonium for Maimonides' extraordinary schedule comes from his own hand in his well-known and often-quoted letter of 1199 to Samuel b. Tibbon.[4] Here, Maimonides revealed that he spent the greater part of every day in the sultan's palace in his capacity as court physician, and that upon his return home he invariably found a mixed multitude of people in need of his advice and help, who daily consumed his remaining time and energy until he virtually collapsed of exhaustion late every evening.

Now what makes this paradox so intriguing is not simply that we have a great thinker who says one thing and does another. Consider, for example, the paradoxical life of the twelfth-century Muslim philosopher, Ibn Bājja. Ibn Bājja was the first of the well-known Muslim and Jewish philosophers to propound the life of the solitary, and there can be little doubt that his discussion of this topic in the *Tadbīr al-Mutawaḥḥid* influenced Maimonides' own thinking on this subject.[5] Ibn Bājja taught that the philosopher 'must keep away from men completely so far as he can, and not deal with them except in necessary matters and to the extent to which it is necessary for him to do so'.[6] For Ibn Bājja, man's ultimate happiness and final end was to have intellectual cognition of simple substantial intellects and thereby to achieve conjunction with the Active Intellect.[7] Given the imperfection of the cities and the extreme unlikelihood of the creation of the

[4] The section of the letter in which Maimonides described his daily routine was written in Hebrew (see Isaiah Sonne, 'Iggeret ha-Rambam le-Shemu'el b. Tibbon', *Tarbiẓ*, 10 (1939), 329–30). The Hebrew text of this section is extant in several versions. Two versions appear in Alexander Marx, 'Texts by and about Maimonides', *JQR* 15 (1935), 375–8, and a third version was printed by Sonne in his 'Iggeret ha-Rambam', 331–2. Translations of this section abound. For an English rendition, see Twersky, *Maimonides Reader*, 7–8.

[5] See Efodi's comments on *Guide*, iii. 51 (printed with other standard commentaries in the Warsaw, 1872, Heb. edn. of the *Guide*, 64*a*). For modern accounts of this influence, see S. Munk, *Le Guide des égarés* (Paris, 1856; rep. Paris, 1970), iii. 438–9 n. 4; S. Pines, 'The Philosophic Sources of *The Guide of the Perplexed*', in his *Guide*, p. cvii; H. Blumberg, 'Alfārābī, Ibn Bājja, we-ha-Rambam 'al Hanhagat ha-Mitboded', *Sinai*, 78 (1976), 135–45; and Ralph Lerner, this vol., ch. 2.

[6] *Tadbīr al-Mutawaḥḥid*, in Ibn Bājja: *Opera Metaphysica*, ed. Majid Fakhry (Beirut, 1968), 90 (partial Eng. trans. by Lawrence Berman in *Medieval Political Philosophy: A Sourcebook*, ed. Ralph Lerner and Muhsin Mahdi (New York, 1963), 132).

[7] *Tadbīr*, 79 (Eng. trans., 132). But was this conjunction really possible for man according to Ibn Bājja? See S. Pines, 'The Limitations of Human Knowledge According to al-Fārābī, ibn Bājja, and Maimonides', in I. Twersky (ed.), *Studies in Medieval Jewish History and Literature* (Cambridge, Mass., 1979), 86–9. Cf. Alexander Altmann, 'Ibn Bājja on Man's Ultimate Felicity', in his *Studies in Religious Philosophy and Mysticism* (Ithaca, 1969), 73–107.

virtuous or perfect city, man's happiness could not be bound up with the city, the chatter and actions of whose inhabitants could only serve to distract and divert the qualified from the path to wisdom. Indeed, for Ibn Bājja, true happiness, if it could exist in these cities at all, could only be the happiness of the isolated (*sa'ādat al-mufrad*). It is for this reason, he argued, that the philosopher must order his own life, devote himself to his studies and eschew the company of non-philosophers. The goal of Ibn Bājja's philosopher was to emerge from the cave and to see the light, but there was no obligation or even desire to return to the cave and concern himself with the life of the city.[8]

Now in light of this radical reworking of Alfarabi's political philosophy, we might well have expected Ibn Bājja to have been a social recluse. But, in truth, the same Ibn Bājja who inveighed against the desires and excesses of the corporeal (*jusmānī*) or base (*khaṣīṣ*) man,[9] and who championed the life of the solitary, was himself known as a shrewd hoarder of riches, a witty socialite, and an arrogant and outspoken rogue, who, far from being a recluse, was a dedicated vizier and statesman.[10]

There is, however, no great paradox about Ibn Bājja's life. A person's thoughts or intentions are not always reflected in his actions, and this is the case, as philosophers themselves admit, even among competent philosophers.[11] Moreover, much can be learned even from

[8] For Ibn Bājja's statement that the only true happiness for the 'happy ones' in our cities is the 'happiness of the isolated', see *Tadbīr*, 43 (English trans., 128). For Ibn Bājja's version of the allegory of the cave, see his *Ittiṣāl al-'aql bil-insān*, in *Opera Metaphysica*, 168–9 (cited in Hebrew by Shem Ṭov Falaquera in his *Moreh ha-Moreh* (Pressburg, 1837) on *Guide*, iii. 51, p. 312). Ibn Bājja's cave allegory is discussed by A. Altmann in 'Ibn Bājja', 86–8; S. Pines' 'Limitations of Human Knowledge', 87–8; and id., 'Shī'ite Terms and Conceptions in Judah Halevi's *Kuzari*', *JSAI* 2 (1980), 213. The 'happy ones' here do not simply emerge from the cave and see the light; they transcend that state, they become the light itself, they attain conjunction with the Active Intellect. The goal of Ibn Bājja's philosopher, at least in the *Ittiṣāl*, is thus something more than 'seeing the light'; see Pines, 'Shī'ite Terms', 214 n. 282, and the references in n. 7 above.

[9] See e.g. *Tadbīr*, 62–3, 68–9, 77–9 (Eng. trans. 130–1).

[10] See D. M. Dunlop, 'Remarks on the Life and Works of Ibn Bājja', in *Proceedings of the Twenty-Second Congress of Orientalists*, ii (Leiden 1957), esp. 191–5. On Ibn Bājja's social ways, see A. R. Nykl, *Hispano-Arabic Poetry* (Baltimore, 1946), 252–4. On his worldly interests and his hoarding of riches, see Ibn Ṭufayl, *Ḥayy ibn Yaqẓān*, trans. George N. Atiyeh, in *MPP* 138–9.

[11] See e.g. Maimonides, *Guide*, ii. 36, p. 371, and Averroes, *Long Commentary on the Physics*, Proemium, ed. and trans. S. Harvey, in *PAAJR* 52 (1985), 67, 77. Cf. Alfarabi, *The Attainment of Happiness*, trans. M. Mahdi, in *MPP* 80–1, and Maimonides, *Commentary on the Mishnah, Zera'im*, Introd., ed. J. Kafiḥ (Jerusalem, 1963), 42.

such intemperate philosophers. A few centuries before Ibn Bājja, the Muslim physician and philosopher al-Rāzī wrote an *apologia pro vita sua* in response, *inter alia*, to criticism levelled against him that he 'swerved away from the philosophic life' in his indulging in worldly pleasures.[12] Al-Rāzī pleaded not guilty to the charge of 'excessive indulgence', but then, admitting for the sake of argument his 'shortcomings on the practical side', concluded, citing an unnamed poet:

> Practice what I have preached; for if it be
> That in my practice lies deficiency
> Still thou canst profit of my theory.[13]

Great thinkers benefited from Ibn Bājja's 'theory' while not condoning his lifestyle. They realized that a philosopher's wayward behaviour is not the result of science or philosophy, but rather of that philosopher's inferior temperament and personal shortcomings. As the discerning thirteenth-century elucidator of medieval Islamic and Jewish philosophy Shem Ṭov Falaquera explained, there are philosophers who cannot control their desires and thus 'fall into bad ways', just as there are doctors who cannot control their desires and thus eat food that they know will harm them.[14]

The paradox of Maimonides' biography, of course, has nothing to do with questionable moral actions that belie theoretical teachings. Maimonides' exhausting daily schedule was governed by his reason, not dictated by his passions. The paradox here is far more challenging, and its solution, we can imagine, far more instructive. Simply stated, the problem is how can reason choose a *bios*, a way of life, that leaves little time for those things it considers most important? To be more explicit, if, as it certainly appears, Maimonides agreed with Aristotle that all things aim at the good, and that the good for man is the happiness which is acquired through cultivating the contemplative life,[15] how could he choose the public life of communal service over the private life of contemplation?

[12] *Al-Sīra al-Falsafiyya*, trans. A. J. Arberry, in his *Aspects of Islamic Civilization* (Ann Arbor, 1967), 120–30. [13] Ibid. 130.

[14] Falaquera's *Epistle of the Debate*, ed. and trans. S. Harvey (Cambridge, Mass., 1987), 45.

[15] *Nicomachean Ethics*, i. 1, 1094*a*3; x. 6, 1176*a*32–3; and x. 7–8; see L. V. Berman, this vol., ch. 1. This is not to suggest that Maimonides agreed with Aristotle on the nature of the contemplative life, although he may have and it is likely that he thought that he did. For various interpretations of the contemplative life in Aristotle, see Trond Berg Eriksen, *Bios Theoretikos: Notes on Aristotle's Ethica Nicomachea X, 6–8* (Oslo, 1976), 82 ff.

THREE POSSIBLE SOLUTIONS

There are three solutions to our paradox which are, at least at first blush, quite compelling.

1. Maimonides, as is well known, thought very highly of Alfarabi and was particularly influenced by his political teachings.[16] He simply lived his life, in the Alfarabian tradition of Plato's political philosophy, in accord with the *obligation* upon the enlightened to return, if possible, to the cave in order to guide its inhabitants to that happiness of which they are capable. According to this explanation, Maimonides returned to the cave and chose the active life because, as Plato explains, he was compelled to.[17] There is, of course, an internal contradiction in the allegory of the cave, but this contradiction can be easily resolved.

2. In any case, Pines has recently argued that for Maimonides, 'The only positive knowledge of God of which man is capable is knowledge of the attributes of action, and this leads and ought to lead to a sort of political activity which is the highest perfection of man. The practical way of life, the *bios praktikos*, is [therefore] superior to the theoretical.'[18] If Pines is correct, not only would the internal contradiction of the cave allegory be resolved for Maimonides, but so, it would seem, would the paradox of his life. If man, after all, by nature cannot fully emerge from the cave, he has little choice but to live within it.

3. Maimonides' son Abraham also sought the path of solitude (*khalwa*), although for reasons somewhat different from those of his

[16] On the influence of Alfarabi's political teachings on Maimonides, see Pines, 'Philosophic Sources', pp. lxxviii, lxxxvi–xcii; Leo Strauss, 'Quelques remarques sur la science politique de Maïmonide et de Fārābī', *REJ* 100 (1936), 1–37, and 'Farabi's *Plato*', in *Louis Ginzberg Jubilee Volume* (New York, 1945), 357–93; L. V. Berman, 'Maimonides, the Disciple of Alfārābī', *IOS* 4 (1974), 154–78; and Joel L. Kraemer, 'Alfarabi's *Opinions of the Virtuous City* and Maimonides' *Foundations of the Law*', in *Studia Orientalia Memoriae D. H. Baneth Dedicata* (Jerusalem, 1979), 107–53.

[17] *Republic*, vii. 519*c* 521*b*. See also vi. 499*b–c*; vii. 539*e*, 540*b*. On the political responsibilities of the true philosopher according to Alfarabi, see *Attainment of Happiness*, 76–81 (esp. 81, para. 62). See further, Pines, 'Philosophic Sources', p. lxxxvi n. 50, and Berman, 'Maimonides, the Disciple of Alfārābī', 170–1. Cf. Twersky, *Introduction to the Code*, 95–6.

[18] 'The Limitations of Human Knowledge', 100. For a completely different view of Maimonides' reaction to the limitations of the intellect, see Abraham J. Heschel, 'Ha-He'emin ha-Rambam she-Zakhah li-Nevu'ah', in *Louis Ginzberg Jubilee Volume*, Heb. sect. 159–88. Heschel writes, 'After wrestling with those problems and riddles that are most important and realizing that their solution was beyond the limit of human reason, Maimonides desired to transcend that limit' (172).

father. Abraham taught that the true sage must shun the multitude and their distractions, and that ruling and time-consuming communal positions must be avoided unless they are absolutely necessary for the 'interests of religion (*al-maṣāliḥ al-dīniyya*)'.[19] Yet, as Goitein's Genizah studies have made very clear, Abraham assumed even more communal responsibilities than his father![20] Perhaps Maimonides, like his son, chose the active life with great reluctance because there was no one else equal to the task of preserving the religious community.[21]

Now, if any one of these three solutions is correct—and there is much to be said for all of them—then Maimonides' life was not the profound paradox it appeared to be. But there is a lingering uneasiness with all three, for not one of them really confronts Maimonides' statement on solitude or fully appreciates his yearning for contemplation. Now, his statement on solitude and his fullest discussion of contemplation both occur in the *Guide of the Perplexed*, iii. 51. To do justice to the paradox of Maimonides' life, we must understand this chapter, but this cannot possibly be achieved apart from an understanding of the place and importance of this chapter in the book as a whole.

THE PURPOSE OF THE *GUIDE*

Maimonides begins the *Guide of the Perplexed* by stating that the first purpose (*al-gharaḍ al-awwal*) of the treatise is 'to explain the meanings of certain terms occurring in the books of prophecy'. After some explanation, Maimonides reveals a second purpose, namely, to explain 'very obscure parables occurring in the books of the prophets, but not explicitly identified there as such'.[22] Near the beginning of Part II, Maimonides restates his purpose in somewhat less precise but not very different terms as being 'only to elucidate the difficult points of the Law and to make manifest the true realities (*ḥaqā'iq*) of its hidden meanings'.[23] However, in ii. 29 Maimonides provides a more surprising statement of purpose. Here he writes that the first purpose

[19] *The High Ways to Perfection of Abraham Maimonides*, ed. and tr. Samuel Rosenblatt (Baltimore, 1938), ii. 399. See also ii. 263.

[20] See in particular S. D. Goitein, 'Abraham Maimonides and his Pietist Circle', in A. Altmann (ed.), *Jewish Medieval and Renaissance Studies* (Cambridge, Mass., 1967), 151–64, and id., 'A Treatise in Defense of the Pietists by Abraham Maimonides', *JJS* 16 (1965), 107–8.

[21] Cf. *Mishneh Torah*, *Hilkhot Sanhedrin*, iii. 10.

[22] *Guide*, i. Introd., pp. 5–6.

[23] Ibid. ii. 2, p. 253.

of his treatise is 'to explain what can be explained of the *Account of the Beginning* and of the *Account of the Chariot*'.[24] This statement of purpose is repeated in the Introduction to Part III where Maimonides writes: 'We have already made it clear several times that the chief purpose (*mu'ẓam al-gharaḍ*) of this treatise is to explain what can be explained of the *Account of the Beginning* and the *Account of the Chariot*, with a view to him for whom this treatise has been composed.'[25] Now there is a clear divergence (*ikhtilāf*) here in the statements of purpose, which suggests that Maimonides' intention is to conceal something.[26] Obviously he is not concerned with the unworthy reader's thinking that the 'first purpose' of the *Guide* is the explanation of equivocal terms, nor it seems would he be troubled if the same reader would think that his 'first purpose' is the explanation of the Account of the Beginning and the Account of the Chariot. However, if his 'first purpose' is to explain the Account of the Beginning and the Account of the Chariot through the explanation of equivocal terms, and if by pointing out and making known the figurative meanings of these terms and explaining explicitly that these are their meanings in the biblical Account of the Beginning and Account of the Chariot Maimonides would be revealing the secrets of the Law, then there would indeed be reason for concealing this purpose from the many and for hinting at it for the few.

There is good textual reason for thinking that Maimonides did not wish to spell out the specific usefulness of his explanation of equivocal terms for understanding the Account of the Beginning and the Account of the Chariot. While approximately one-half of the equivocal terms explained in Part I are, in fact, found in one form or another in the first chapter of Ezekiel, significantly only in one of the chapters of Part I, the first of the lexicographical chapters, are verses from Ezek. 1 (or, for that matter, Ezek. 10) given to illustrate the figurative meanings of the terms. Maimonides, it seems, did not wish to be too

[24] Ibid. ii. 29, p. 346.

[25] Ibid. iii. Introd., p. 415.

[26] See *Guide*, i, Introd. pp. 15, 17–20. See further, L. Strauss, *Persecution and the Art of Writing* (Glencoe, Ill., 1952), 68–74. Not all readers of the *Guide* take Maimonides' declarations concerning the contradictions in the *Guide* as seriously as Strauss. For a cynical reading, see Herbert Davidson, 'Maimonides' Secret Position on Creation', in Twersky, *Studies in Medieval Jewish History* 16–40. Davidson cautions that Maimonides' 'claiming to be above carelessness does not guarantee his being so', and that some contradictions may simply be 'instances of poor organization' (p. 17). For a simple explanation of the divergence in statements of purpose in the *Guide*, see Sarah Klein-Braslavy, 'On Maimonides' Interpretation of the Paradise Story', paper presented at the Maimonides Conference at Tel Aviv University, 1982. According to this understanding, there would be no esoteric reason for the contradiction.

explicit. However, neither did he wish to be overly subtle. Concerned that the qualified reader might forget his instruction to connect the chapters of his treatise one with the other and instead assume that the lexicographical chapters simply explain equivocal terms, Maimonides makes known that his purpose in explaining the terms is 'not only to draw your attention to what we mention in that particular chapter. Rather do we open a gate and draw your attention to such meanings of that particular term as are useful for *our purpose* (*gharaḍunā*).'[27]

According to Maimonides, then, his explanation of equivocal terms opens gates. Maimonides had previously indicated this in a somewhat ambiguous way at the end of his Introduction to the *Guide*:

> After these introductory remarks, I shall begin to mention the terms whose true meaning, as intended in every passage according to its context, must be indicated. This, then, will be a key permitting one to enter places the gates to which were locked. And when these gates are opened and these places are entered into, the souls will find rest therein, the eyes will be delighted, and the bodies will be eased of their toil and of their labor.[28]

The ambiguity concerns what 'this' modifies; thus it is not immediately clear in this passage what the key is, nor what gates to what places it unlocks. Strauss apparently understood the key to be the *Guide* itself,[29] but a more likely interpretation is that of the medieval commentators, Efodi and Shem Ṭov b. Shem Ṭov, who took the key to be the explanation of equivocal terms.[30] This latter interpretation is supported by a parallel statement earlier in the Introduction that refers to the understanding of the parables as the key to understanding the prophets,[31] and seems to be confirmed by a very important statement in i. 8, in which Maimonides explicitly says that his explanations of equivocal terms are 'the key to this treatise and to others'.[32] As an example of precisely what he means and what treatises 'others' might signify, Maimonides tells us that the term 'place (*maqom*)' in Exod. 33:

[27] *Guide*, i. 8, p. 34; see also i. 10, p. 35. Joseph b. Kaspi explains in his commentary ad loc. that 'the root of Maimonides' intention in mentioning equivocal terms in these chapters. . . . is to discuss one-by-one all the [equivocal] terms that appear in the Account of the Beginning and the Account of the Chariot'. See his *Maskiyyot Kesef*, ed. S. Werbluner (Frankfurt, 1848), 23.

[28] *Guide*, I. Introd., p. 20.

[29] See his 'How to Begin to Study *The Guide of the Perplexed*', in the Pines edn., pp. lvi, and xiii–xiv. Strauss, however, first identifies the key with the 'preceding passage', that is, with the passage of the *Guide* that precedes the end of the Introduction, and not, presumably, with the *Guide* as a whole.

[30] See Efodi and Shem Ṭov, ad loc. 11*b*.

[31] *Guide*, i. Introd. 10. Cf. iii. 7, p. 428.

[32] Ibid. i. 8, p. 34.

21 has the same figurative meaning as he explained that it has in Ezek. 3. The lesson is clear: a figurative meaning of a term explained in the *Guide* in the context of one prophetic text can and ought to be applied by the reader, when appropriate, in the context of a different prophetic text as well as, when appropriate, in the interpretation of the *Guide* itself.

To sum up, the main purpose of the *Guide* is the explanation of the Account of the Beginning and the Account of the Chariot, and this explanation is done primarily through the explanations of equivocal terms and obscure parables. The explanations in the *Guide* of terms and parables, it may be added, lead to explanation of the Account of the Beginning and the Account of the Chariot in two ways: (*a*) by providing the reader with keys for reading and correctly interpreting difficult biblical texts;[33] and (*b*) by providing the reader with the keys to understanding the *Guide*, which itself makes known the hidden meanings of these secret teachings.

We must now try to clarify what Maimonides understood by the Account of the Beginning and the Account of the Chariot.

MAIMONIDES' UNDERSTANDING OF THE ACCOUNT OF THE BEGINNING AND THE ACCOUNT OF THE CHARIOT

Maimonides was the first thinker to identify the esoteric doctrines of the Account of the Beginning and the Account of the Chariot with natural science and divine science respectively.[34] All the special rules and conditions for studying and teaching these secret doctrines, as well as the legends of their initiates and would-be initiates preserved in the talmudic and midrashic literature, immediately applied, by definition, to natural science and divine science. Thus, for example, we read that

[33] Towards this end Maimonides also provides illustrations of and exercises in textual interpretation. See esp. *Guide*, ii. 30 (on the Account of the Beginning); and cf. iii. 1–7 (on the Account of the Chariot); see also Ibn Kaspi's closing comment to ii. 30 in *'Ammude Kesef*, 112. Note that ii. 30 is preceded by the statement and exposition of 'two preambles of general import (*muqaddimatayn 'āmmatayn*)'; viz. (*a*) that 'not everything mentioned in the Torah concerning the Account of the Beginning is to be taken in its external sense as the vulgar imagine', and (*b*) that the prophets use equivocal and derivative terms (see ii. 29, pp. 346–8).

[34] See his *Commentary on the Mishnah*, *Ḥagigah*, ii. 1; *Mishneh Torah*, *Yesode ha-Torah*, ii. 11 and iv. 10–13; and *Guide*, i. Introd. 6, 9, and i. 34, p. 77. Shortly after Maimonides, this identification became a commonplace among philosophically inclined Jews.

R. Akiba, 'who entered in peace and went out in peace', achieved human perfection when he 'engaged in the theoretical study of metaphysical matters'.[35] But if the identification is to be taken literally, then the purpose of the *Guide* could be viewed as the explanation of natural science and divine science—that is, physics and metaphysics. And this, as Strauss has noted, leads to a contradiction.

For Strauss, the contradiction stems from Maimonides' explicit statement in ii. 2 that his purpose is not 'to compose something on natural science, or to make an epitome of notions pertaining to the divine science according to some doctrines, or to demonstrate what has been demonstrated in them'.[36] This statement, it would seem, contradicts the *Guide*'s purpose to explain natural science and divine science. Strauss's solution is that

> the intention of the *Guide* is to prove the identity, which to begin with was asserted only, of the Account of the Beginning with physics and of the Account of the Chariot with metaphysics. . . . Maimonides does not intend to treat physics and metaphysics; his intention is to show that the teaching of these philosophic disciplines, which is presupposed, is identical with the secret teachings of the Bible.[37]

Strauss's solution may have been influenced by a comment by Ibn Kaspi that 'Maimonides' whole intention is to explain that all the true realities found in the books of the philosophers are in the Holy Books and the words of the Rabbis',[38] but his own reasoning seems to be based on an imprecise reading of ii. 2. Strauss understands Maimonides to be saying that 'all physics and an unlimited number of metaphysical topics are excluded from the *Guide*'.[39] However, Maimonides does not say that these subjects are excluded from the *Guide*, but rather, as we have seen, that *it is not his purpose* to treat them. This does not mean that he will not discuss these subjects but rather, inasmuch as these things 'have been expounded in many books, and the correctness of most of them has been demonstrated', that he will not 'demonstrate what has been demonstrated in them' or simply 'transcribe the books of the philosophers'.[40] Thus, while Maimonides writes that his

[35] *Guide*, i. 32, p. 68.

[36] Ibid. ii. 2, p. 253. See Strauss, *Persecution and the Art of Writing*, 44, 71.

[37] Ibid. 45–6.

[38] Ibn Kaspi, *'Ammude Kesef*, on ii. 2, p. 90. For Strauss's evaluation of Kaspi as an interpreter of the *Guide*, see *Persecution*, 56.

[39] Strauss, *Persecution*, 44.

[40] *Guide*, ii. 2, p. 253, and ii. Introd., p. 239.

purpose is not 'to make an epitome (*ulakhkhiṣ*) of notions (*ma'ānī*) pertaining to the divine science', he adds, some lines later, that 'many knots will be unraveled through the knowledge of a notion (*al-ma'nā*) of which I give an epitome (*ulakhkhiṣuh*)'.[41] In fact, Maimonides considered his Introduction to Part II to be just such an epitome of demonstrative premisses and first notions of physics and metaphysics.[42]

Maimonides, then, does not exclude topics of physics and metaphysics from the *Guide*. He treats and, indeed, explains matters 'demonstrated in natural science . . . and in divine science'.[43] But Strauss's uncanny and unsurpassed sixth sense for uncovering contradictions has not led us astray. The contradiction that arises in the *Guide* from the identification of the two Accounts with physics and metaphysics manifests itself in Maimonides' explicit statement that any explanation in the *Guide* of a matter already demonstrated in natural science or divine science is made because

> that particular matter necessarily must be a key to the understanding of something to be found in the books of prophecy, I mean to say of some of their parables and secrets. The reason why I mentioned, explained, and elucidated that matter would be found [above all] in the knowledge it procures us of the Account of the Chariot and the Account of the Beginning.[44]

If we identify the two Accounts with physics and metaphysics, the passage says that Maimonides only explains matters of physics and metaphysics already demonstrated by the philosophers because they are keys to understanding the parables and secrets—that is, because they lead to a knowledge of physics and metaphysics. But such a statement is meaningless, or at best tautological. Moreover, it is contradicted by Maimonides' statement that the purpose of the *Guide* is the explanation of the two Accounts, i.e. physics and metaphysics.

The solution to this contradiction may be that Maimonides did not intend the identification of the two Accounts with physics and metaphysics to be complete. Rather, the Account of the Beginning stands for that part of natural science that has not been and cannot be demonstrated, while the Account of the Chariot stands for that part, or

[41] Ibid. ii. 2, p. 253.

[42] See ibid. ii. Introd., p. 239; also Harry A. Wolfson, *Crescas' Critique of Aristotle* (Cambridge, Mass., 1929), 1.

[43] See Maimonides' explicit formulation in *Guide*, ii. 2, p. 254.

[44] Ibid. Note the emphasis placed on the Account of the Chariot here in its unusual listing before the Account of the Beginning. See e.g. *Guide*, i. Intro. 6; ii. 29, p. 346; and iii. 1, p. 415. But cf. *Mishneh Torah*, *Yesode ha-Torah*, i–iv.

perhaps only some part, of divine science that has not been and cannot be demonstrated—in other words, the secrets of these two sciences.

There may be support for the above interpretation of a limited identification of the two Accounts with physics and metaphysics in a passage in i. 34. Maimonides, speaking of the young who have achieved 'tranquillity and quiet' and have extinguished 'the flame that gives rise to perplexity', writes: 'They then may call upon their souls to raise themselves up to this rank, which is that of the apprehension of Him, may He be exalted; I mean thereby the divine science that is designated (*al-'ilm al-ilāhī al-maknī 'anh*) as the Account of the Chariot.'[45] This passage may be read as signifying that the Account of the Chariot is that part of divine science that concerns itself, *inter alia*, with the apprehension of God; in other words, only a part of metaphysics.

A clearer indication of the subject matter of the Account of the Chariot is provided by Maimonides' explanation of the figurative meaning of *rakhav* ('to ride'), the grammatical root of *merkavah*, the word for chariot. *Rakhav* is the last of the equivocal terms explained by Maimonides in the lexicographical chapters of Part I.[46] According to Maimonides, 'it is used figuratively to designate domination (*istīlā'*) over a thing', and, we are told, 'in this sense it is said of God'. Thus, the biblical phrase 'the rider of the heavens' means 'He who dominates the heavens'.[47] Maimonides explains that just as the rider is the ruler of the beast he rides, makes it move and go where he wishes, 'for it is an instrument for him that he uses as he wishes, being at the same time free from any dependence on it and not attached to it', so God is 'the mover of the highest heaven, by whose motion everything that is in motion within this heaven is moved . . . [while He is] separate from this heaven and not a force subsisting within it . . . [heaven being] the instrument by means of which He governs (*yudabbir*) that which is existent'.[48] In short, the figurative meaning of *rakhav* is dominates or governs, and the Account of the Chariot would thus be the teaching of God's governance of the universe.

An allusion to this interpretation of the Account of the Chariot is found at the end of i. 40. After explaining a fifth sense of the equivocal term *ruaḥ* as purpose and will, Maimonides writes: 'Scripture says that

[45] *Guide*, i. 34, p. 77.

[46] See ibid. i. 70. There is no mention in this chapter of Ezek. 1 or 10 (where the term does not occur), or of the Account of the Chariot.

[47] Ibid. 171.

[48] Ibid. 172–3.

he who knows the ordering of His will or apprehends His governance of that which exists as it really is, should teach us about it—as we shall explain in the chapters that will deal with His governance (*al-tadbīr*).'[49] Efodi and Abrabanel among the medievals, and Munk and Kafiḥ among the moderns, list the reference to the chapters on governance as the chapters on providence in Part III, especially chapters 18 and 19.[50] Pines, however, provides the reference iii. 2, which can be proven textually to be the chapter Maimonides had in mind.[51] The real chapters on governance include iii. 2 and, it is tempting to conclude, consist of the first seven chapters of Part III, the section on the Account of the Chariot.

The view that the proper subject matter of the Account of the Chariot is, for Maimonides, God's governance of the universe is virtually confirmed in iii. 6. Here Maimonides informs us that, according to the Sages, the chariot apprehension grasped by Ezekiel was identical with that grasped by Isaiah. Ezekiel, however, had to go into greater details for the sake of his listeners. The Sages wrote: 'All that was seen by Ezekiel was [likewise] seen by Isaiah. Isaiah is like unto a city man who saw the King; whereas Ezekiel is like unto a villager who saw the King.'[52] Maimonides reports that the Sages explained this in a comparison with two men who saw the sultan while he was *riding*. One man wanted to relate what he saw to city people, who know how the sultan rides, and could therefore say simply, 'I saw the sultan riding.' The other wanted to relate the same to desert nomads, who do not know how the sultan rides. Maimonides tells us that this man had to describe how the sultan rides 'and the characteristic of the sultan's troops, his servants, and those who execute his orders'.[53] In other words, he had to give a complete account of how the sultan governs. This was the task of Ezekiel.

[49] Ibid. i. 40, p. 90.

[50] According to Efodi, the reference to the chapters on governance is to iii. 18–19 (ad loc. 60*b*); according to Abravanel, to iii. 13 and 19 (ad loc. 61*a*); according to Munk (above, n. 5), to iii. 18 ff. (i, p. 145 n. 2); according to Joseph Kafiḥ (ed. and Heb. trans. of the *Guide* (Jerusalem, 1972), i, p. 93 n. 18) and Judah Even Shemu'el (ed. of Ibn Tibbon trans. of the *Guide* (Jerusalem, 1981), 77 n. 9) to iii. 18–26.

[51] See *Guide*, p. 90 n. 21. The editor of the Warsaw edn. (above, n. 5) also gives this reference (pp. 60*b*–61*a*). For evidence that iii. 2 is indeed the chapter to which Maimonides was referring, see esp. his mention there of the equivocality of *ruaḥ* and reference back to the discussion in i. 40, and his 'wondrous explanation (*al-tabyīn al-'ajīb*)' of Ezek. 1: 12 and 20 (*Guide*, iii. 2, pp. 419–21). As for the chapters in *Guide*, iii provided in the above note, they are the chapters on providence (*al-'ināya*); see *Guide*, i. 44, p. 95.

[52] *TB*, *Ḥagigah*, 13*b*.

[53] *Guide*, iii. 6, p. 427.

To sum up, Maimonides, as is well known, identifies the Account of the Beginning with natural science and the Account of the Chariot with divine science. This identification, however, is incomplete. The Account of the Beginning represents that part of natural science that has not been and cannot be demonstrated, and above all the question of the origin of the world. The Account of the Chariot represents a part of divine science that has not been and cannot be demonstrated, and it treats God's governance of the universe.

THE PARABLE OF THE SULTAN'S PALACE, THE ACCOUNT OF THE CHARIOT, AND THE LIMITS OF KNOWLEDGE

An intriguing speculation has occurred to me that breathes meaning into a hitherto politely ignored and unaccepted teaching of Strauss. In a number of essays, Strauss has suggested that the real plan of the *Guide* is that it consists of seven sections, each divided 'wherever feasible' into seven subsections.[54] Now, a structure of seven parts each in turn divided into seven parts conjures to mind the seven heavens and seven heavenly palaces of the Hekhalot literature.[55] Might not Maimonides have included some images and terminology of this mystical *merkavah* tradition in his allusions and references to the Account of the Chariot? If so, Strauss's plan of the *Guide* would not be so eccentric, for it would hardly be surprising to find that a treatise whose purpose is the explanation of the Account of the Chariot is

[54] See Strauss, 'How To Begin To Study *The Guide*', pp. xi–xiii. See also id., 'Maimonides' Statement on Political Science', in his *What Is Political Philosophy*? (New York, 1959), 166, and id., *Persecution*, 60 and 87 n. 143. Strauss may have been convinced that he had uncovered the real plan of the *Guide*, but his readers are not. See e.g. the reviews of Pines's trans. of the *Guide* (to which 'How To Begin' serves as the introductory essay) by I. Twersky (in *Speculum*, 41 (1966), 566); L. Berman in *JAOS* 85 (1965), 410; cf. his 'The Structure of Maimonides' *Guide of the Perplexed*', in *Proceedings of the Sixth World Congress of Jewish Studies* (Jerusalem, 1977), iii. 12–13; G. Vajda in *REJ* 123 (1964), 211–12, 216; M. Fox in *Journal of the History of Philosophy*, 3 (1965), 270; and A. Altmann in *The Journal of Religion*, 44 (1964), 261.

[55] See Gershom Scholem, *Major Trends in Jewish Mysticism* (New York, 1946), 43–54; Morton Smith, 'Observations on *Hekhalot Rabbati*', in A. Altmann (ed.), *Biblical and Other Studies* (Cambridge, Mass. 1963), 144–9; and Ithamar Gruenwald, *Apocalyptic and Merkavah Mysticism* (Leiden 1980), 135–9, 146, 153–5, 163–7, 189–93, 210–11. The major text for the image of the soul's ascending through the seven heavens is the *Hekhalot Rabbati*, but this idea is very old (see Scholem, *Major Trends*, 54) and could have been known to Maimonides from any number of texts. A likely source for knowledge of the Hekhalot could have been the gaonic literature, esp. writings of Hai Gaon (see Twersky, *Introduction to the Code*, 55).

structured in accordance with the journey of the Chariot. When one who is worthy ascends and, as Strauss explains,[56] descends through the seven parts of the *Guide*, he will have seen the secrets of the Account of the Chariot, just as the adept who ascends or descends to the seventh palace in the *merkavah* tradition.

This dazzling thought, were it textually supported, would certainly help explain the mystery of the pre-eminence of seven in Maimonides' writings and especially in the *Guide*. And seven is an important number in the *Guide*, even apart from Strauss's plan and his 'strange excursions'.[57] There are, for example, seven chapters in explanation of the biblical narrative of the Account of the Chariot, and the explanation of the equivocal term *rakhav* does, in fact, as Strauss points out, occur in i. 70. Indeed, apart from the obvious seven causes for contradictions, the venturous reader can uncover a number of chariot-related sevens in the *Guide*. For example, Maimonides, it can be argued, considered the parable of Jacob's ladder to be a description of the Chariot.[58] In the Introduction to the *Guide*, Maimonides illustrates

[56] Strauss, *Persecution*, 90–2.

[57] On the importance of the number seven in Maimonides' thought according to Strauss, see 'Maimonides' Statement on Political Science', 165–6, and 168 n. 23; *Persecution*, 87 n. 143; and 'How To Begin', p. xxx. Strauss claimed that 'numerical symbolism is of assistance to the serious reader of the *Guide*' (ibid.). He admitted that 'considerations of this kind are necessarily somewhat playful', but added that 'they are not so playful as to be incompatible with the seriousness of scholarship' ('Maimonides' Statement', 165). His readers do not always agree. As Altmann predicted in his review of the *Guide*, 'few will follow in a credulous mood this kind of "Kabbalistic" exegesis'. The expression 'strange excursions' is borrowed from Altmann's review.

[58] That Maimonides considered the parable of Jacob's ladder to be a description of the Chariot is clear to me, and I believe quite important. See in particular Maimonides' interpretation of the parable in *Guide*, i. 15, p. 41. Maimonides writes in this chapter: 'How well put is the phrase *ascending and descending* (Gen. 28: 12), in which ascent comes before descent. For after the ascent and the attaining of certain rungs of the ladder that may be known comes the descent with whatever decree the prophet has been informed of—with a view to governing and teaching the people of the earth.' In i. 40 (discussed above), Maimonides similarly writes that whoever apprehends God's 'governance of that which exists as it really is, should teach us about it'. But Maimonides adds that he will explain this further in the chapters on God's governance, which as we have already seen are those of the Account of the Chariot. The message in i. 15 and i. 40 is the same: those who ascend to an apprehension of God and his governance are obligated to descend 'with a view to governing and teaching the people'. This, for Maimonides, is a teaching of the parable of Jacob's ladder and a teaching of the Account of the Chariot. It is, of course, also the teaching of Plato's allegory of the cave (see above, n. 17). It may be added that Ibn Kaspi's commentary on i. 15 explains that the account of Jacob's ladder is one of three Chariot texts in the Torah (p. 31; see also his *Menorat Kesef*, in *'Asarah Kele Kesef*, ii. ed. by I. Last (Pressburg, 1903), ch. 7, p. 91). See similarly Samuel b. Tibbon, *Ma'amar Yeqqawu ha-Mayim* (Pressburg, 1837), ch. 11, pp. 54–6; and G. Vajda, 'An Analysis of the Ma'amar Yiqqawu ha-Mayim', *JJS* 10 (1959), 143–4. For other

the kind of prophetic parable where each word has meaning with the account in Genesis of Jacob's ladder. Maimonides lists seven subjects (*ma'ānī*) in this parable.[59] Then in a very strange discussion in ii. 10 of a Midrash on Jacob's ladder which Maimonides mentions to show that 'the number four is wondrous and should be an object of reflection', Maimonides relates that according to the Midrash there were four steps in the ladder. He then adds that according to some manuscripts of the Midrash there were seven. This extra and totally unnecessary bit of information, which detracts from his point about the number four, can only make sense if Maimonides wished to draw attention to the number seven.[60] In a more speculative vein, in the lexicographical chapters of Part I there appear to be forty-nine equivocal terms, that is forty-nine keys to the understanding of the Account of the Beginning and the Account of the Chariot. In addition, the one statement in Isaiah that according to Maimonides (in iii. 6) epitomizes the Account of the Chariot clearly contains exactly seven equivocal terms that were explained in Part I and that can reveal its true meaning.[61]

All this seemed very dubious to me until I reflected upon the famous palace parable of iii. 51. If there were anything to the Hekhalot hypothesis, or in fact to Strauss's plan, there would have to be exactly seven ranks of people in the parable. There are!

Maimonides describes the following ranks of men:

1. Those outside of the city.
2. Those within the city with their backs turned upon the sultan's habitation.

identifications of the account of Jacob's ladder as a Chariot text, see A. Altmann, 'The Ladder of Ascension', in *Studies in Mysticism and Religion presented to Gershom Scholem* (Jerusalem, 1967), 22–6 (repr. in his *Studies in Religious Philosophy and Mysticism*, 61–6). On the ladder motif in Hekhalot literature, see ibid. 2 (p. 42), and Gruenwald, *Merkavah Mysticism*, 120, 160–1. Altmann, however, in his fascinating and instructive study, claims that Maimonides did not consider the account of Jacob's ladder to be a Chariot text. Rather, according to Altmann, it was Ibn Tibbon who 'initiated [this] interpretation' (ibid. 19). Altmann's conclusion seems to be based primarily on Maimonides' not explicitly identifying the account of Jacob's ladder as a Chariot text. Cf. further, *Mishneh Torah*, *Yesode ha-Torah*, vii. 3 (a text Altmann did not consider, see loc. cit. n. 76), where Maimonides lists the visions of Jacob's ladder and Ezekiel's living creatures (*ḥayyot*) as his first two examples of prophetic visions in which the parable is communicated to the prophet along with its interpretation. (Maimonides' midrashic explanation of the ladder here does not, of course, argue against his viewing the vision as a Chariot text.)

[59] *Guide*, i, Introd., pp. 12–13.

[60] Ibid. ii. 10, p. 272. Cf. Kaspi ad loc., 96.

[61] Ibid. iii. 6, p. 427. The statement is from Isa. 6: 1–2: 'And I saw [see i. 4] the Lord sitting [see i. 11] upon a throne [see i. 9] high [see i. 20] and lifted up [see i. 20], and his train filled [see i. 19] the temple. The seraphim stood [see i. 13], and so on.

3. Those who seek to reach the sultan's habitation, turn to it, but do not yet see its wall.
4. Those who walk around the habitation searching for its gate.
5. Those who have entered the gate and walk about in the antechambers.
6. Those who have entered the inner court of the habitation and have come to be with the sultan, but cannot see or speak to him.
7. Those who make another effort and are in the presence of the sultan, and can see and speak to him.

In Maimonides' interpretation of his parable:

1. Those of the first rank are all human individuals who have no doctrinal belief. They are like irrational animals.
2. Those of the second rank are those people who have adopted incorrect opinions. They are dangerous because they lead others astray.
3. Those of the third rank are the multitude of the adherents of the Law, the simpletons who observe the commandments.
4. Those of the fourth rank are the jurists who believe true opinions on the basis of traditional authority, but do not inquire into the principles of religion.
5. Those of the fifth rank are those who have inquired into the principles of religion.
6. Those of the sixth rank are those who in addition have 'ascertained in divine matters (*al-umūr al-ilāhiyya*), to the extent that it is possible, everything that may be ascertained'.
7. Those of the seventh rank are the greatest of the prophets.

Maimonides adds that those who have studied logic and mathematics are of the fourth rank; those who have studied natural things are of the fifth rank; those who have understood divine science are of the sixth rank; and those who make an extra effort after learning what they can of divine science are of the seventh rank.[62]

A hint of Hekhalot influence in iii. 51 may be provided in the problematic statement in the beginning of the chapter that the chapter is 'only a kind of conclusion'. The term Maimonides uses for conclusion is *al-khātima*. *Khātima* is an equivocal term that can also mean seal, and in the Hekhalot writings seals are what the adept needs

[62] *Guide*, iii. 51, pp. 618–20. Cf. Efodi's interpretation in *Ma'aseh Efod* (Vienna, 1865), 7–9 (cited approvingly by Shem Ṭov in his commentary to the *Guide*, ad loc., 64*b*–65*a*).

to journey safely and successfully through the heavenly palaces.[63] With this sense of *khātima*, Maimonides would then be saying that iii. 51 is the decisive clue to understanding his treatise.

My intention here is simply to suggest the possible influence of *merkavah* terminology and symbolism on Maimonides.[64] What is

[63] See Scholem, *Major Trends*, 50–1, and Gruenwald, *Merkavah Mysticism*, 106–9, 166–7, 174–5, 185.

[64] My suggestion is that the influence of *merkavah* terminology and symbolism on Maimonides may have extended beyond the Talmud to the literature of the Hekhalot texts and *merkavah* mysticism; on the relation between the Hekhalot texts and the rabbinic Account of the Chariot, consider David J. Halperin, 'Merkabah and Ma'aseh Merkabah according to Rabbinic Sources' (Ph.D. thesis, Univ. of Calif. at Berkeley, 1977), 335–41. Certain mystics may have assumed that the palace in *Guide*, iii. 51 is a Hekhalot symbol; see Joseph Giqaṭilla, *Ginnat Egoz* (Hanau, 1614), 54*b*–55*a*; see further M. C. Weiler, 'Iyyunim ba-Terminologiyah ha-Qabbalit shel R. Yosef Giqaṭilyah', *HUCA* 37 (1966), 26; M. Idel, 'Tefisat ha-Torah be-Sifrut ha-Hekhalot', *Jerusalem Studies in Jewish Thought*, 1 (1981), 61–2; and A. Farber, 'Qeṭa' Ḥadash me-Haqdamat R. Yosef Giqaṭilla le-Sefer Ginnat Egoz', ibid. 166–7. My suggestion that Maimonides may have intentionally used *merkavah* terminology and symbolism does not mean that I believe that he may have had mystical leanings. He did not; see A. Altmann, 'Das Verhältnis Maimunis zur jüdischen Mystic', *MGWJ* 80 (1936), 305–30. I emphasize this in response to the studies by David R. Blumenthal on Maimonides' 'philosophic' or 'intellectualist mysticism' (see esp. 'An Introduction to the Concept of "Philosophic Mysticism" from Fifteenth-century Yemen', in *Hommage à Georges Vajda*, 291–308, and 'Maimonides' Intellectualist Mysticism and the Superiority of the Prophecy of Moses', *Studies in Medieval Culture*, 10 (1977), 51–67), which cannot be discussed fully here.

If Maimonides was indeed not a mystic, it may reasonably be asked why he would resort to mystical terminology and symbolism. In this connection a remark by L. V. Berman in 'Maimonides, the Disciple of Alfārābī' (167 n. 44) is particularly enlightening. Berman claims that 'Maimonides' "back projection" of philosophy into Rabbinic expressions [such as the Account of the Beginning, the Account of the Chariot, the *pardes*]' must be understood in terms of his desire to trace the Jewish tradition of philosophic knowledge back to ancient or, at least, rabbinic times. By identifying philosophy with the ancient teachings of the Jews (see *Guide* i. 71, p. 175) and the secret teachings of the rabbis, he could justify both its pursuit and the necessarily private character of its study. To the extent, then, that the *merkavah* terminology and symbolism was compatible with or adaptable to his philosophy, it was desirable (in addition, it of course blended in well with the esoteric character of the *Guide*). My brother, W. Zev Harvey, has suggested to me that this explanation of Maimonides' intention in appropriating *merkavah* terminology and symbolism might well explain Maimonides' radical change in attitude towards the *Shi'ur Qomah*; see A. Altmann, 'Moses Narboni's "Epistle on *Shi'ur Qomah*" ', in his *Jewish Medieval and Renaissance Studies*, 231–2, and S. Lieberman, 'Mishnat Shir ha-Shirim', in G. Scholem (ed.), *Jewish Gnosticism, Merkabah Mysticism, and Talmudic Tradition* (New York, 1960), 124–5). According to this interpretation, Maimonides believed in his youth that he could successfully include the *Shi'ur Qomah* among the *merkavah* elements in his writings. Later he came to understand the grave and persisting dangers inherent in the gross anthropomorphism of the *Shi'ur Qomah*, and that this doctrine could not be adapted successfully to his teachings. So subversive did the *Shi'ur Qomah* emerge in Maimonides' eyes that he not only excluded it from his teachings, but even stripped it of its rabbinic authority, denied ever having

certain, however, is that the parable in iii. 51 is intended as a Chariot text; I mean specifically a parabolic explanation of the Account of the Chariot. Maimonides alludes to this with a brief citation from the account of *pardes* ('paradise', or more specifically the heavenly Garden of Eden or sphere of celestial palaces) in the Babylonian Talmud, 'Ben Zoma is still outside', as talmudical support for his description of the fourth rank of men.[65] A few lines later Maimonides writes: 'If you have achieved perfection in the natural things and have understood divine science, you have entered into the sultan's place into *the inner court*.' Maimonides here employs a Hebrew phrase *he-ḥaẓer ha-penimit* for 'the inner court'. This phrase occurs frequently in Ezekiel, but most significantly, as the attentive reader will know, in the Account of the Chariot in Ezek. 10.[66]

It thus comes as no surprise that the ultimate object of knowledge in the parable of the palace is God's governance of the beings. Maimonides explicitly writes: 'They direct all the acts of their intellect toward an examination of the beings with a view to drawing from them proof with regard to Him, so as to know His governance of them in whatever way it is possible.'[67] That this is indeed the highest knowledge possible to man is clear from the very end of the *Guide*: 'It is clear that the perfection of man that may truly be gloried in is the one acquired by him who has achieved . . . apprehension of Him, may He be exalted, and who knows His providence extending over His creatures as manifested in the act of bringing them into being and in their governance as it is.'[68] As we have seen, the act of bringing them into being is the Account of the Beginning; their governance is the Account of the Chariot.

Rabbi Akiba, the only one to enter the *pardes* and emerge unscathed, was successful, Maimonides tells us early in the *Guide*, because he did not aspire to apprehend what he was unable to apprehend.[69] Moses, who apprehended as much as humanly possible, and more than any one before him had or after him will, was informed, according to Maimonides, that God's essence cannot be grasped as it really is and that his attributes are his actions. This is the most one can

considered its authenticity, and recommended its destruction (Altmann, loc. cit.). These extreme actions were necessary, for just as rabbinic authority could give legitimacy to the teachings of philosophy, so it could speak for the corporeality of God.

[65] *Guide*, iii. 51, p. 619. On the precise meaning of this statement from *BT*, *Ḥagigah*, 15*a*, see Halperin, 'Merkabah and Ma'aseh Merkabah', 169.

[66] Ezek. 10: 3.

[67] *Guide*, iii. 51, p. 620.

[68] Ibid. iii. 54, p. 638. Cf. i. 54, p. 124.

[69] Ibid. i. 32, p. 68.

apprehend of God, and through his actions one can know how he governs beings in general and in particular.[70]

The highest knowledge possible for man is the knowledge of God's governance of the universe, that is, the secrets of the Account of the Chariot. But in Maimonides' palace parable, this knowledge is held by men of the sixth rank. What then is the extra effort they must make in order to enter into the seventh rank? Once one achieves the apprehension of God, that is, of his governance of beings, what more is there to cognize intellectually?

THE ULTIMATE END OF MAN AND SOLITUDE

The presentation of the palace parable in iii. 51 is neither the purpose nor a main theme of the chapter. It is rather a preface of sorts to the subject of the chapter and, like all good parables, a key to understanding it. The subject of the chapter is the ultimate worship of God, and the chapter's express purpose is to explain this kind of worship and to guide and direct the worthy towards the achievement of this worship, which Maimonides informs us is the 'end of man (*al-ghāya al-insāniyya*)'.[71]

Maimonides' interpretation of the palace parable leaves unstated, as we have seen, the precise distinction between the men of the sixth rank, who are, if you will, in God's habitation, and those of the seventh rank, who are in his presence. We know that those of the sixth rank must 'make another effort', and that in addition to turning to God they must renounce everything that is other than him. But it is not otherwise clear in what their difference consists. What is clear is that those of the seventh rank, and not those of the sixth rank, have attained the end of man.

There is, it thus appears, an identification between those of the seventh rank and those who achieve the ultimate worship of God. Those of the seventh rank have gone a step beyond the understanding of divine science and the ascertaining in divine matters what can possibly be ascertained. They are in the presence of God (*bayna yaday al-sulṭān*). Those who achieve the ultimate worship of God have gone a step beyond the apprehension of him. They too are described as in his presence (*bayna yadayhi*).[72]

[70] *Guide*, i. 54, pp. 123–5.
[71] Ibid. iii. 51, pp. 618, 620.
[72] Ibid. pp. 618, 623.

Maimonides, as he promises, explains the ultimate worship of God. It is 'intellectual worship (*al-'ibāda al-'aqliyya*), and it consists in nearness (*al-qurb*)[73] to God and being in His presence'. Maimonides tells us that 'this end (*al-ghāya*) can be achieved by those of the men of knowledge (*ahl al-'ilm*) who have rendered their souls worthy of it by training (*al-irtiyāḍ*) of this kind'. Maimonides' reference to a special kind of training is not ambiguous, for he has just finished advising us how to go about this training. The training is in emptying our mind of all worldly things, of everything, and then concentrating completely on what we are saying, hearing, or doing. This training when 'practiced consistently for years' enables the mind to think and reflect free of distraction. Maimonides is perfectly clear that the programme of training consists of 'acts of worship, such as reading the Torah and prayer' and the observance of the commandments with intent, and he patiently teaches us how these acts of worship and commandments can enable us, if we are worthy, to achieve the great end, the ultimate worship of God.[74]

This intellectual worship, then, is not accompanied by deeds or words.[75] It is pure contemplation. And as Maimonides has previously explained: the more one thinks of God and of being with him, the more his worship increases.[76] This worship is similar and ultimately, I believe, identical with the passionate love (*'ishq*) described in the *Guide* and the proper love (*ha-ahavah ha-re'uyah*) described in the *Mishneh Torah*, where 'no thought remains that is directed toward a thing other than the Beloved'.[77] This is the end of man.[78]

It is in this context of the discussion of the ultimate worship that Maimonides' statement on solitude is located. It is part of his aim to guide the worthy to achieving this worship. Maimonides writes:

It is clear that after apprehension, total devotion to Him and then employment of intellectual thought (*al-fikra al-'aqliyya*) in constant passionate love for him

[73] *Al-qurb* is a cognate of the Hebrew equivocal term explained in i. 18. Maimonides uses it here in the figurative sense (explained in i. 18) of 'nearness through cognitive apprehension (*idrāk 'ilmī*)' (p. 44). See further, Falaquera, *Moreh ha-Moreh*, 138, and Kaspi, *'Ammude Kesef*, 145.

[74] *Guide*, iii. 51, pp. 622–3. Cf. i. 39. p. 89. See further, E. Goldman, 'Ha-'Avodah ha-Meyuḥedet be-Massige ha-Amitot', *Bar Ilan Annual*, 6 (1968), esp. 287–93. On Maimonides' notion of training, see also *Guide*, i. 49, p. 109, and iii. 52, p. 630.

[75] See similarly *Guide*, iii. 27, p. 511; iii. 54, p. 635.

[76] Ibid. iii. 51, p. 620.

[77] See ibid. pp. 621, 627. Maimonides' discussion of *ha-ahavah ha-re'uyah* is in *Mishneh Torah*, *Hilkhot Teshuvah*, x. 3, 6.

[78] See *Guide*, iii. 51, p. 618; iii. 27, p. 511; iii. 54, p. 635.

(*fī 'ishqihi*) should be aimed at. Mostly this is achieved in solitude (*al-khalwa*) and isolation (*al-infirād*). Hence every excellent man stays frequently in isolation and does not meet anyone unless it is necessary.[79]

Maimonides' meaning here is quite clear: total devotion to God requires complete concentration and the absence of distractions; therefore, solitude is recommended. In the terminology of iii. 51, if man is to achieve his highest end, the intellectual worship and love of God, the emptying of the mind of all thoughts save that of God alone, then clearly solitude is required.[80] In this state, the bond (*al-wuṣla*), which is the intellect, is strengthened and fortified. The longer one remains in this state, the stronger the intellect will be until that individual becomes rational in actuality and attains his ultimate perfection (*al-kamāl al-akhīr*). It is absolutely fitting that Maimonides concludes iii. 51 with the following advice: 'Direct your efforts to the multiplying of those times in which you are with God or endeavoring to approach Him and to decreasing those times in which you are with other than He and in which you make no efforts to approach Him.'[81]

THE SOLUTION

The profundity of the paradox of Maimonides' life is now clear. Solitude is indispensable for his perfection. He strongly recommends that his reader pursue it and goes so far in the last chapter of the *Guide* to advise, 'Do not weary and trouble yourself for the sake of others, O you who neglect your own soul.'[82] Indeed, the characterization of the perfect man in ii. 36 is of *one who lives in solitude* (*al-mutawaḥḥid*) and does not think of the multitude except 'with a view to saving himself from harm . . . or to obtaining a needed advantage from them'.[83] This last view is in complete conformity with Maimonides' teaching that the ultimate perfection of man pertains to the individual alone and 'no one else is associated in it with [him] in any way'.[84] For Maimonides, ultimate perfection is in this respect in contrast to the perfection of the moral virtues 'which do not perfect the individual in anything, for he

[79] See *Guide*, iii. 51, p. 621.

[80] Cf. *Mishneh Torah*, *Yesode ha-Torah*, vii. 4. The exceptions are Moses and, presumably, the patriarchs (see *Guide*, iii. 51, pp. 623–4). See also *Mishneh Torah*, *Shemiṭṭah we-Yovel*, xiii. 12–13.

[81] *Guide*, iii. 51 p. 628.

[82] Ibid. iii. 54, p. 635.

[83] Ibid. ii. 36, p. 372.

[84] Ibid. iii. 54, p. 635.

only needs them and they again become useful to him in regard to someone else'.[85]

Since the ultimate perfection of man consists in neither actions nor moral qualities but only in the actuality of the intellect, and since the multitude are a manifest distraction from the achievement of this perfection, it would seem evident that they must be shunned or, in Maimonides' words, not thought of 'except with a view to saving oneself from harm . . . or to obtaining a needed advantage from them'. This view would seem to argue for the life of the solitary. But given Maimonides' understanding of the nature of man, it does not.

For Maimonides, like the Muslim *falāsifa* before him, man is a political animal. He is 'political by nature and it is his nature to live in society'.[86] Indeed, it is precisely the same two reasons that compel the perfect man in ii. 36 to think of the multitude that compel man to enter into a political association—protection from harm, and bodily advantage. Intellectual perfection can therefore not be sought in isolation. As Maimonides explains, man cannot develop his intellect 'if he is in pain or is very hungry or is thirsty or is hot or is very cold'. The welfare of the soul (*ṣalāḥ al-nafs*) depends upon the welfare of the body (*ṣalāḥ al-badan*), and the latter can only be attained through political association.[87] This teaching is perfectly clear and reflects explicit statements of Alfarabi and Avicenna that 'the isolated individual cannot achieve all the perfections by himself',[88] and that man 'cannot lead a proper life when isolated as a single individual, managing his affairs with no associates to help him satisfy his basic wants'.[89]

In short, while solitude is virtually indispensable for the achievement of ultimate perfection, it stands in the way of the attainment of man's primary perfection, the perfection of the body, which is itself a precondition of ultimate perfection. And thus, unless we are fortunate enough to live on an island like Gaunilo's 'lost island' or like the delightful uninhabited island of Ibn Ṭufayl's Ḥayy b. Yaqẓān, the desired life of solitude must be forsaken.

Our paradox, however, still remains. The solitude (*al-khalwa*) Maimonides recommends is not what his son Abraham would call 'complete external solitude', that is, the abandonment of society and

[85] Ibid.

[86] See ibid. ii. 40, p. 381, and iii. 27, p. 511. See further, Fines, 'Philosophic Sources', pp. lxxxvii–lxxxviii.

[87] *Guide*, iii. 27, pp. 510–11.

[88] Alfarabi, *Attainment of Happiness*, 60.

[89] Avicenna, *Kitāb al-Shifā'*: *Metaphysics*, x, ch. 2, trans. M. Marmura, in *MPP* 99, and id., *Kitāb al-Najāh* (Cairo, 1938), 303.

the retirement to the desert or mountains; but rather what he would call 'incomplete external solitude', that is, the solitude in houses and places of worship.[90] For Maimonides, the seeking of this solitude is not an anti-political or necessarily anti-social act, but rather the recognizing, seizing, and increasing of those times when one is alone. This is the solitude Maimonides recommends in iii. 51.

This solitude is no less important than complete solitude, and for Maimonides, as we have seen, it must be sought with no less avidity and fervour. Certain actions, however, will necessarily, although not ideally, take priority over this solitude. This is the political reality that Glaucon came to understand in Plato's account of the cave. At first he objected to the injustice of forcing the philosophers to return to the cave, 'to make them live a worse life when a better is possible for them'. But he soon came to realize that in compelling the philosophers 'to care for and guard others', the city was 'laying just injunctions on just men'.[91] This does not mean that the philosophers enjoy their role in the city; on the contrary, they despise it, but they recognize the extreme importance and necessity of their assuming these responsibilities.

Was this really Maimonides' attitude toward political activity? Some leading expositors of Maimonides' thought would disagree. L. V. Berman has argued that for Maimonides the final stage in man's perfection is the imitation of God's actions, which for man is the 'activity of founding or governing a state'. Berman further writes: 'In so far as Maimonides is concerned, action in imitation of God after intellectual perfection has been achieved is at least equal in dignity to the intellectual contemplation of the eternal verities.'[92] Pines, as we have seen, has gone a step further, asserting that this sort of political activity is for Maimonides 'the highest perfection of man'.[93] The

[90] See Abraham Maimonides, *The High Ways to Perfection*, ii. 383, 387. The same distinction is drawn by Baḥya b. Paqudah in *Duties of the Heart*, ix. 3 (ed. J. Kafiḥ (Jerusalem, 1973), 390–1; trans. M. Hyamson (repr. Jerusalem, 1970) vol. ii, 302), in his account of the first two classes of true ascetics (*ahl al-zuhd al-ṣādiq*). For Maimonides' views on the extreme form of solitude, see e.g. *Guide*, ii. 39, p. 380, and *Eight Chapters*, trans. Raymond L. Weiss and Charles E. Butterworth, in their *Ethical Writings of Maimonides* (New York, 1975), ch. 4, p. 70; but cf. ibid. 69–70, and *Mishneh Torah*, *De'ot*, vi. 1 (trans. 46–7). See further, Twersky, *Introduction to the Code*, 459–67.

[91] *Republic*, vii. 519*d*–520*e*, trans. Allan Bloom (New York, 1968), 198–9.

[92] L. V. Berman, 'The Political Interpretation of the Maxim: The Purpose of Philosophy is the Imitation of God', *Studia Islamica*, 15 (1961), 61 n. 1. See also id., 'The Ethical Views of Maimonides', this vol., ch. 1, and id., 'Maimonides, The Disciple of Alfārābī', 170–1.

[93] See n. 18. Cf. Pines's 'Foreword' to David Hartman, *Maimonides: Torah and Philosophic Quest* (Philadelphia, 1976), pp. xi–xv.

argument is thus made that for Maimonides, man's ultimate perfection is either in part or wholly, a political activity, indeed the same activity that limits man's opportunity for solitude and contemplation. For the reader who grants this argument, there is no longer a paradox. But many students of the *Guide* cannot agree.[94] For example, M. Galston has raised some very important objections to Berman's thesis, and ultimately I think her reading of the first perfection in iii. 54 that 'being a great king contributes nothing to the growth of an individual's true self' is correct.[95] Likewise, W. Z. Harvey has recently taken issue with Pines's interpretation of political activity as man's highest end and argued, in part on the basis of a principle of Maimonides' cosmology, that man's perfection consists in intellectual activity and not political activity.[96] Moreover, A. Altmann has underscored a passage in iii. 54 that argues against the active life as the ultimate perfection of man.[97] I have tried to show that for Maimonides ultimate perfection refers to the actualization of the intellect and that, as he explicitly states, 'to this ultimate perfection there do not belong either actions or moral qualities'.[98] In support of this position, two points may be emphasized. First, perfection for Maimonides pertains to the individual alone and is independent of his relations with other individuals. The only perfection that answers to this description for Maimonides is the perfection of the soul (*kamāl al-nafs*), that is, theoretical perfection. Second, the perfect man or philosopher does not and ought not want to be ruler.[99] It diverts him from the straight path to intellectual perfection, consumes his time, and may even be dangerous. Nevertheless, just as in the account of the cave, he is obligated to help. Maimonides explains this obligation explicitly in ii. 37 and illustrates it with a reference to the prophet Jeremiah.[100] This reluctance to help

[94] See Strauss's conclusion in *Persecution*, 92, cited by Berman in 'Political Interpretation', 61 n. 1. For a medieval view, see Falaquera, *Moreh ha-Moreh*, 139.

[95] M. Galston, 'Philosopher-king v. Prophet', *IOS* 8 (1978), 216–17. See *Guide*, iii. 54, p. 634.

[96] See W. Z. Harvey, 'Ben Filosofyah Medinit la-Halakhah be-Mishnat ha-Rambam', *Iyyun*, 29 (1980), 211–12. On the principle that the higher does not exist for the sake of the lower, see Alfarabi, *Al-Siyāsa al-Madaniyya*, ed. F. Najjar (Beirut, 1964), 48 ff.

[97] A. Altmann, 'Maimonides' Four Perfections', *IOS* 2 (1972), 24. Altmann's comments should be viewed in light of the objections of Galston and Harvey.

[98] See *Guide*, iii. 54, p. 635. See also in this light *Guide*, i. 2, esp. p. 24.

[99] See ibid. ii. 36, p. 372. Cf. *Mishneh Torah*, *Hilkhot Sanhedrin*, iii. 10.

[100] *Guide*, ii. 37, p. 375.

could hardly be explained if the activity of helping itself constituted the ultimate perfection and final end of man.[101]

For Maimonides, the most nearly perfect individuals are those who as a result of the capacity and training of their intellects can emerge from and return to the cave at will; or to use another allegory, can ascend to and return from the vision of the Chariot at will. For Maimonides this is further represented, as we have seen, by Jacob's ladder:

> How well put is the phrase *ascending* and *descending*, in which *ascent* comes before *descent*. For after the *ascent* and the attaining of certain rungs of the ladder that may be known comes the descent with what ever decree the prophet has been informed of—with a view to governing and teaching the people of the earth.[102]

But for Maimonides the descent is not part of the ultimate perfection of man, and that perfection is not directly dependent on whether or not anyone listens to his message.[103]

The three solutions to the paradox of Maimonides' life sketched in the second part of this paper each contain very valuable insights, but each falls short of a complete solution because each fails to appreciate the supreme importance for Maimonides of the yearning for contemplation and intellectual perfection. How then can the paradox be resolved? A. J. Heschel has suggested: 'He may have . . . come close to the state in which one talks with other people and at the same time thinks constantly of God, being in the presence of God constantly in the heart even though in the body among men.'[104] This, however, is a state Maimonides reserves for Moses and perhaps the Patriarchs, and I see no evidence that he suggested or even believed that he himself achieved such a state.[105] But Maimonides did not take us so far without pointing to the way in which men endowed with knowledge can pursue theoretical perfection, even amidst the burdens of the *bios praktikos*. Maimonides writes:

[101] Maimonides certainly did not consider his own political or court activity as part of his highest perfection. On the contrary, he considered his high position neither 'a happiness nor desired perfect good, nor little evil. . . . but the ultimate burden, labor, and toil'; see *Iggerot ha-Rambam*, ed. D. H. Baneth (Jerusalem, 1946), 93, and Baneth's comments and interpretation on pp. 92, 94.

[102] *Guide*, i. 15, p. 41.

[103] See ibid. ii. 37, p. 375, and similarly Alfarabi, *Attainment of Happiness*, 81, para. 62.

[104] Heschel, 'The Last Days of Maimonides', 290. Heschel was more assertive of this possibility in an earlier work; see his *Maimonides: Eine Biographie* (Berlin, 1935), 275. Cf. id., 'Ha-He'emin ha-Rambam' (n. 18 above), pp. 168–9.

[105] See *Guide*, iii. 51, p. 623.

When you are alone with yourself and no one else is there and while you lie awake upon your bed, you should take great care during these precious times not to set your thought to work on anything other than the intellectual worship consisting in nearness to God and being in His presence in that true reality that I have made known to you and not by way of affections of the imagination. In my opinion this end can be achieved by those of the men of knowledge who have rendered their souls worthy of it by training of this kind.[106]

The tremendous value of the commandments in this endeavour has already been indicated.

A final thought. Maimonides advises us to 'direct [our] efforts to multiplying of those times in which [we] are with God or endeavouring to approach Him', but we can only conjecture when during Maimonides' relentlessly active daily routine, particularly as described to Ibn Tibbon, he was able to find the solitude necessary for following his own advice. It will be recalled that Maimonides explained in this letter to Ibn Tibbon that he spends his days in the palace of the sultan in his capacity as court physician and his evenings taking care of the sick in his home.[107]

The most plausible surmise is that Maimonides found the desired solitude in the late hours of the night and perhaps the wee hours of the morning after his patients had left.[108] He certainly could not have had much occasion for solitude and contemplation from the time of his return from the palace to nightfall and beyond while he was treating the invariably hectic multitude of patients. Maimonides' daily activities in Fusṭāṭ during this period were doubtless well known to the Jewish community and were, we can imagine, as exhausting as he described them. But there may have been another opportunity for solitude.

[106] Ibid.

[107] Cf. this account of his daily routine with that in the letter to Joseph b. Judah (cited in Twersky, *Maimonides Reader*, 6). In a letter to R. Jonathan ha-Kohen of Lunel, written in the same year as that to Ibn Tibbon, Maimonides similarly complains of his lack of time as a result of 'those people who continually importune me (*elu ha-meẓa'arim li tamid*)'. In particular, Maimonides laments being burdened with a multitude of patients who exhaust him day and night, the inevitable concomitant of a fame that 'has spread through many lands'. See *Teshuvot ha-Rambam*, ed. J. Blau (Jerusalem, 1961), iii. 56–7; trans. Twersky, *Introduction to the Code*, 39–40. See also the fragment of Maimonides' letter translated into Hebrew in D. H. Baneth, 'Me-Ḥalifat ha-Mikhtavim shel ha-Rambam', in *Sefer Zikkaron le-Asher Gulaq u-le-Shemu'el Klein* (Jerusalem, 1942), 53 (trans. 55–6).

[108] The opinion of e.g. Suessmann Muntner. See the Introduction to his edition of Moses b. Tibbon's Hebrew translation of Maimonides' *Hanhagat ha-Beri'ut* (Jerusalem, 1963), pp. x, 9.

My conjecture is that Maimonides may have been able to find the solitude in which he could contemplate and draw near to God in the palace of the sultan amidst his daily duties. After all, while his activities in Fusṭāṭ were well known to the community, his specific duties in the palace during the course of a long day were not. In support of this conjecture is Maimonides' special relations with the two princes to whom we know he served as personal physician, al-Qāḍī al-Fāḍil and Sultan al-Afḍal.[109] Let us consider each in turn: al-Qāḍī al-Fāḍil was the chief minister of Saladin. It is known that he was a bibliophile and that he built a large and impressive royal library.[110] It is also known, and to this Maimonides bears witness,[111] that he was a patron of scholars. Al-Fāḍil had great respect for Maimonides, trust in his learning, and commissioned him to write books for him and his people. It stands to reason that al-Fāḍil would have made available to his distinguished physician and scholar the books, time, and place necessary for him to carry out his research and writings. Moreover, Maimonides himself appears to refer to such an arrangement in his *Treatise on Poisons and their Antidotes*, a work commissioned by al-Fāḍil. In dedicating this book to al-Fāḍil, 'our Master, the exalted and excellent *qāḍī*', Maimonides praises him for spending his money, *inter alia*, on 'the building of academies (*al-madāris*) . . . and thus increasing the number of men of knowledge (*ahl al-ʿilm*) and inquiry'.[112] Al-Afḍal was Saladin's son and became sultan in 1198. He also was a patron of Maimonides, respected his learning and judgement, and asked him to write books for him.[113] He is the sultan referred to in the letter to Ibn Tibbon, and he too may well have opened his library to Maimonides for study, research, and writing. Given the spirit of the time, characterized as 'a highly bookish age with its deep veneration for

[109] As for the often quoted statement of Ibn abī Uṣaybiʿa, that Maimonides was court physician of Saladin, see Bernard Lewis, 'Maimonides, Lionheart, and Saladin', *Eretz-Israel*, 7 (1964), 70–5.

[110] On al-Fāḍil see Heschel, *Maimonides*, 203–5.

[111] See e.g. Maimonides' *Treatise on Poisons and Their Antidotes*, trans. S. Muntner (Philadelphia and Montreal, 1966), 1–2.

[112] Ibid. I have modified Muntner's translation of this passage on the basis of the Judeo-Arabic Paris manuscript of the *Treatise*, reproduced in his edition. The expression *ahl al-ʿilm* ('men of knowledge') refers to worthy and learned scholars; see e.g. *Guide*, i. 51, p. 112, where it may be contrasted with the *ahl al-naẓar* ('men of speculation'; see Munk, *Guide*, i. p. 184 n. 3). In a passage from *Guide*, iii. 51, p. 623 cited above, Maimonides states that it is the *ahl al-ʿilm* who can attain the highest human perfection if they 'have rendered their souls worthy of it'. He certainly included himself among the *ahl al-ʿilm*.

[113] On al-Afḍal and Maimonides see Heschel, *Maimonides*, 261–5.

scientific attainments',[114] a time when leading physicians entered the entourages of viziers and sultans and unreservedly gave advice on a surprisingly wide range of personal and communal problems, it is not at all difficult to envisage such viziers and sultans affording a scholar such as Maimonides time alone for research and study.

I would suggest that there may even be allusion to such a scenario in the letter to Ibn Tibbon, or more specifically, the short autobiographical sketch in the letter (which unlike most of the rest of the letter is written in Hebrew),[115] which I would further suggest may be read on one level as a parable.[116] Now we know that Maimonides rarely uses parables, to such an extent that Strauss can explicitly claim that he excludes parables from the *Guide*.[117] But the *Guide* does contain a few parables, and some of these are even stated to be parables. The favourite illustration Maimonides uses in his parables is that of the sultan. Two such parables are found, in i. 46 and iii. 6, where the governance of the sultan represents the governance of God. But the most important such parable and the key parable of the *Guide* is the one in iii. 51, which we have already discussed. Here, coming to be in the palace of the sultan represents coming to be in the presence of God. In the letter to Ibn Tibbon Maimonides writes that the sultan 'dwells' in his palace in Cairo and that Maimonides 'sees' him every day. In fact, he usually spends 'most of the day in the palace of the sultan'. He 'ascends' to the palace in Cairo early in the morning and it is only after a full day that he 'returns' to his home and 'descends' from his mount to the waiting multitude. The figurative meanings of equivocal terms like 'dwells (*shokhen*)', 'sees (*ro'eh*)', 'returns (*ashuv*)', 'ascends (*'oleh*)', and 'descends (*ered*)' would surely be appreciated by a careful student of the *Guide* like Ibn Tibbon;[118] and so would the parabolic allusion to Maimonides' being in the sultan's palace.

[114] See S. D. Goitein, *A Mediterranean Society* (Berkeley—Los Angeles, 1971), ii. 241.

[115] See n. 4 above.

[116] In suggesting that the letter to Ibn Tibbon may be read on one level as a parable I should not be understood to be denying or even doubting that the letter must also be taken literally. Maimonides' daily journey to the sultan's palace in Cairo is history, and there can be no denying that court and communal responsibilities indeed consumed his time and energies.

[117] See Strauss, *Persecution*, 66–71, esp. 68, 71.

[118] For the various Hebrew versions of this section of the letter to Ibn Tibbon, see above n. 4. For the figurative meanings of the equivocal terms *shokhen*, *ro'eh*, *ashuv*, *'oleh*, and *ered*, see *Guide*, i. 25, i. 4, i. 23, i. 10, and i. 15, respectively.

4

Maimonides on the Philosophic Sciences in his Treatise on the Art of Logic

JOEL L. KRAEMER

I

MAIMONIDES' *Treatise on the Art of Logic* (*Maqāla fī Ṣināʿat al-Manṭiq*), written in his youth, may be said to be his only purely philosophic work.[1] It is certainly not a 'Jewish book' the way the *Guide of the Perplexed* is, for example. It was addressed to someone said to be 'an eminent man, one of those engaged in the sciences of the religious law and of those having clarity of style and eloquence in the Arabic language'. Maimonides does not indicate whether this person was Jewish. The 'sciences of the religious law' does not necessarily refer to the Jewish religious law.[2] The allusion to the recipient's clarity of style and eloquence in Arabic may rather suggest that he was a non-Jew, but this also is not conclusive.[3] The recipient's involvement in the sciences

[1] Israel Efros edited two fragments of the Arabic original and the Hebrew translations of Moses b. Tibbon, Aḥituv b. Isaac, and Joseph b. Joshua b. Vivas and published an English translation of the work in *Maimonides' Treatise on Logic* (New York, 1938). Mubahat Türker discovered two manuscripts of the treatise in Arabic, in Ankara and Istanbul, and published the text along with an introduction and Turkish translation: 'Al-Maḳāla fī Ṣināʿat al-Manṭiq de Mūsā ibn Maymūn (Maïmonide),' *Revue de la Faculté de Langues, d'Histoire et de Géographie de l'Université d'Ankara*, 18 (1960), 9–64; first published in the *Review of the Institute of Islamic Studies*, 3 (1959–60), 49–100 (Publications of the Faculty of Letters, Istanbul University). Efros subsequently published the entire Arabic text in Hebrew characters in *PAAJR* 34 (1966). On other earlier editions, see Efros (1938), 4 n. 2; Türker (1960), 14–15 n. 6.

[2] The Hebrew translations of Ibn Tibbon and Ibn Vivas render *al-ʿulūm al-sharʿiyya* by *ha-hakhamot ha-toriyyot*, suggesting Jewish legal sciences. Aḥituv translates more correctly *ha-ḥakhamot ha-datiyyot*, i.e. legal sciences in general.

[3] The superscription to the work (in the edition by Efros) is *bismi llāh al-raḥmān al-raḥīm* ('In the name of God, the merciful, the compassionate'), i.e. the Muslim *basmala*. Türker's edition has *bismi llāh rabb al-ʿālamīn*, an islamicized translation of 'In the name of the Lord, God of the world' (Gen. 21: 33), presumably a more accurate rendition of the original text. Maimonides began the three parts of the *Guide*, as well as his halakhic

of the religious law and his linguistic proficiency are presumably noted to explain his curiosity about logic and perhaps even to suggest a link between religious law and language, on the one side, and logic and philosophy on the other. The recipient, it is said, had asked 'a man who was studying the art of logic' to explain to him the meaning of the many terms frequently used in logic and the technical terminology used by practitioners of this art. He requested that this be done with utmost concision, as his aim was not actually to learn the art of logic but merely to understand recurrent terms as they are usually employed. The treatise, then, was not written for a philosopher, nor was it composed to clarify philosophic issues, but rather to explain the terminology used by logicians.

In the course of his résumé in the final chapter of the treatise, Maimonides moves from a treatment of logical terms to a brief survey of the philosophic sciences. He gets into this by way of defining the term *falsafa*, or 'philosophy'. The survey of the sciences presumably belongs to the category of technical terminology that the recipient of the treatise had inquired about. Maimonides alludes again to this aspect of terminological concern at the end of the treatise when he states that the terms discussed are most of those used in the art of logic, and that the treatise *also* contains some technical terms used in physics, metaphysics, and political science. He takes note of the fact that there are fourteen chapters in the treatise, in which 175 terms are discussed (i.e. 7 × 25).[4]

The brief survey of the sciences includes Maimonides' well-known 'statement on political science'. On the basis of this concise account Leo

works and his *Treatise on Resurrection*, with the quotation from Gen. 21: 33. His medical works, addressed to Muslim potentates, begin with the *basmala*. According to H. Atay, in his edition of the *Guide* in Arabic letters, based upon MS Jarullah 1279 (Ankara, 1972), the manuscript reading of the superscription in the *Guide* is *bismi llāh al-raḥmān al-raḥīm* (ibid. 7 n. 1). It is most likely that a Muslim hand substituted the Islamic invocation for the biblical verse in this case and in the *Treatise on the Art of Logic*. On the superscriptions to Maimonides' works, see also S. Lieberman's Introduction to his edition of *Hilkhot ha-Yerushalmi le-Rabbenu Mosheh ben Maimon* (New York, 1948), n. 7. See also J. L. Kraemer, '*Sharī'a* and *Nāmūs* in the Philosophy of Maimonides' (Heb.), *Te'udah*, 4 (Tel Aviv, 1986), 185–202, esp. 186.

Circumstantial evidence for the Muslim identity of the addressee may be found in the reference in ch. 4 ibid. to Abū Isḥāq al-Ṣābi', the famous secretary and one of the greatest epistolary stylists in the Arabic language. The attempt by Efros (Introd., p. 13; trans., 39 n. 5) to eliminate him by a textual emendation is, of course, superfluous. The Hebrew translations substitute Ezra the Scribe for Abū Isḥāq.

[4] Cf. e.g. also *Mishneh Torah*, *Hilkhot Ishut*, ii. 27, where a similar inventory of terms is made, it is said, for pedagogical purposes.

Strauss drew rather far-reaching conclusions concerning Maimonides' notion of political philosophy in general and his conception of the function of the Torah and religious laws in particular. Strauss contended, for example, that Maimonides' statement implies that 'the function of the Torah is emphatically political'.[5] Now had he merely inferred from Maimonides' remarks that *one* of the functions of the Torah is political, his position might be readily defended; on the other hand, it would be somewhat innocuous. The significance of Strauss's comment is underscored by the words 'the' and 'emphatically'. As Strauss's conclusion has considerable bearing upon an understanding of Maimonides' thought in general, as expounded in the *Guide* for instance, it is a good idea to examine carefully his reading of the text. Strauss expected a competent reader to do precisely this and not to adhere to any authority, even his own.

On a number of points Strauss followed in the wake of Harry A. Wolfson.[6] Both Wolfson and Strauss were considerably hampered by the circumstance that the original Arabic text of the relevant part of the treatise (ch. 14) was unavailable to them. They had to depend upon Hebrew translations, which tend to be misleading, to say the least. Wolfson occasionally offered conjectures concerning the presumed Arabic *Vorlage* of the extant Hebrew versions—a diverting but risky enterprise. Now that the actual text of chapter 14 has come to light and has been published, we are clearly on firmer ground.[7]

In this paper I intend to comment upon chapter 14 of the *Treatise on the Art of Logic* with an eye to the section on political science in particular. In order to bring out my understanding of the text clearly and unambiguously I shall offer my own translation of the chapter, although excellent translations into English by Charles E. Butterworth

[5] L. Strauss, 'Maimonides' Statement on Political Science', *PAAJR* 22 (1953), 115–30; repr. in *What Is Political Philosophy?* (Glencoe, Ill. 1959), 155–69. See also below, n. 64.

[6] H. A. Wolfson, 'The Classification of Sciences in Mediaeval Jewish Philosophy', *Hebrew Union College Jubilee Volume, 1925*, 263–315; repr. in I. Twersky and G. H. Williams (eds.), *Studies in the History of Philosophy and Religion*, i (Cambridge, Mass., 1973), 493–545; id., 'Note on Maimonides' Classification of the Sciences', *JQR* 26 (1936), 369–77; reprinted in Twersky and Williams, *Studies*, i. 551–60.

[7] See n. 1. See also Efros, 'Maimonides' *Treatise on Logic*: The New Arabic Text and its Light on the Hebrew Versions', *JQR* 53 (1963), 269–73; L. V. Berman, 'Some Remarks on the Arabic Text of Maimonides' *Treatise on the Art of Logic*', *JAOS* 88 (1968), 340–2; and 'A Reexamination of Maimonides' Statement on Political Science', *JAOS* 89 (1969), 106–11.

and Muhsin Mahdi already exist.[8] I shall take note of the dependence of the text upon Alfarabi's writings, without trying to be exhaustive, touch upon a number of exegetical conundrums, and finally turn to the implications of my reading of the text for understanding Maimonides' conception of the civil and religious law and the question of the allegedly political function of the latter.

II

Maimonides begins chapter 14 with a definition of the term *manṭiq*. The term reflects Greek *logos* and carries a similar semantic range (that is, 'speech', 'reasoned discourse', 'logic').

[1.1] The term *manṭiq*, in the usage of the ancient sages of bygone nations (*milal*), is an equivocal term having three meanings.[9] The first is the faculty specific to man by which he cognizes the intelligibles, acquires[10] the arts, and distinguishes between the bad and the good. They call this also the rational faculty.[11] The second meaning is the intelligible itself, which man has

[8] Ch. 14 has been translated in its entirety by Charles E. Butterworth, on the basis of Efros's revised edition (1966), supplemented by Türker's edition (1960); see *Ethical Writings of Maimonides*, ed. R. L. Weiss with C. E. Butterworth (New York, 1975), 158–61. The section on political science (below, 3.6.1.–4) has been translated by Muhsin Mahdi, on the basis of Türker's edition, in *Medieval Political Philosophy: A Sourcebook*, ed. Ralph Lerner and Muhsin Mahdi (Glencoe, Ill., 1963), 189–90 (hereafter *MPP*). I have used Türker's edition for my translation.

[9] The word *milal* (plural of *milla*) means also 'religious communities'. Maimonides mentions the sages of bygone nations here at the beginning of ch. 14 and again at the end; see below, 3.6.4. He alludes to the ancient Sages throughout our text, referring to them simply as 'they'. Maimonides ascribes views to the ancients even when he quotes directly from Alfarabi, as here. He presumably regarded Alfarabi's presentation, which he follows closely, as a summary of the view of the ancients.

Alfarabi quotes the ancients (*al-qudamā'*) in connection with the three meanings of the term *manṭiq* in his *Introductory Treatise on Logic*; see D. M. Dunlop, 'Al-Farabi's Introductory *Risālah* on Logic', *Islamic Quarterly*, 4 (1957), 224–35, on 227, l. 25–228, l. 1 (trans. 233). For the work, see below, n. 12.

[10] The text (61, l. 13) reads *wa-yajūz*. Berman, 'Some Remarks', 341, and Butterworth, *Ethical Writings*, 163, suggest the reading *wa-yaḥūz*, following the text in Alfarabi's 'Introductory *Risālah* on Logic', 226 l. 2 (trans. 233).

[11] The definition of *manṭiq* (logic) as distinguishing between good and bad actions is not uncommon in Arabic sources. See e.g. Yaḥyā b. 'Adī: 'an instrumental art by which one discriminates between truth and falsehood in theoretical science and between good and bad in practical science' ('On the Four Scientific Questions', trans. N. Rescher and F. Shehadi, *Journal of the History of Ideas*, 25 (1964), 574); see also Joel L. Kraemer, *Humanism in the Renaissance of Islam* (Leiden, 1986), 111 n. 22. And see F. Zimmermann,

cognized. They call this meaning also inner speech. The third meaning is the utterance in speech of those concepts that are impressed upon the soul. They call this meaning also external speech.

Maimonides depends here rather heavily upon Alfarabi's formulation in his *Introductory Treatise on Logic*.[12] In fact, the beginning of chapter 14 (1.1–1.2) may be fairly considered a restatement of Alfarabi's discourse in this treatise. Defining *manṭiq*, Alfarabi comments that the term is derived from *nuṭq*, that is, 'articulate speech'. He then goes on to observe that according to the ancients the term *manṭiq* designates three things: (*a*) the faculty by means of which man cognizes the intelligibles, by which the sciences and the arts are acquired, and by which good and bad actions are distinguished; (*b*) the intelligibles that accede to the soul of man by the understanding, which the ancients call

Al-Farabi's Commentary and Short Treatise on Aristotle's De Interpretatione (London, 1981), p. cxxiii n. 1.

According to Aristotle, cogitation (*dianoia*), or the cogitative soul (*dianoētikē psychē*), distinguishes the true from the false and good from bad; see *De Anima*, iii. 7, 431*a*14–17; *Metaphysics*, vi. 3,1027*b*25–27.

See also Maimonides' Introduction to *Avot*, or *Thāmaniyat Fuṣūl* (Eight chapters), ed. J. Kafiḥ, *Mishnah 'im Perush Rabbenu Mosheh ben Maimon*, *Seder Neziqin* (Jerusalem, 1964), 375–6; J. I. Gorfinkle, *The Eight Chapters of Maimonides on Ethics* (New York, 1966), 43 (trans.). Maimonides states there that the rational part (of the soul) is the faculty found in many by which the individual has intellectual cognition, by which the sciences are acquired, and by which he distinguishes between bad and good actions.

12 Cf. Alfarabi, *Introductory Treatise*, 227–8 (trans. 232–3). I have modified Dunlop's translation in places. Cf. the similar text in Alfarabi's *Iḥṣā' al-'Ulūm* (The enumeration of sciences), ed. Ángel Gonzales Palencia, 2nd edn. (Madrid, 1953), 35–6.

Dunlop based his edition of the *Introductory Treatise* on MS Hamidiye 812. The text, under the title *Al-Tawṭi'a fil-Manṭiq*, was also edited by M. Türker, on the basis of additional manuscripts, in *Revue . . . d'Ankara*, 16 (1958), 187–94. My references to this work are, for the sake of convenience, to Dunlop's edition and translation.

On Maimonides' use of Alfarabi's *Introductory Treatise*, see Türker's Introduction, p. 17, and Berman, 'Reexamination', 106 n. 2. Türker also mentions three other introductory works on logic utilized by Maimonides in his treatise. (Cf. also Efros, *Maimonides Treatise on Logic*, 19.) Türker notes, *inter alia*, that from the beginning of the treatise to ch. 8 Maimonides treats subjects discussed by Alfarabi in his *Kitāb al-Qiyās al-Ṣaghīr*. Other titles of the work are *Kitāb al-Mukhtaṣar al-Ṣaghīr fī Kayfiyyat al-Qiyās* and *Kitāb al-Mukhtaṣar al-Ṣaghīr fil-Manṭiq 'alā Ṭarīq al-Mutakallimīn*. Türker edited this work in *Revue . . . d'Ankara*, 16 (1958), 244–86. The basis for her edition is the manuscript in which she discovered Maimonides' *Treatise on the Art of Logic*. Ch. 8 of Maimonides' treatise, which defines the various kinds of self-evident propositions and types of syllogism, depends upon Alfarabi's *Introductory Sections* (*Fuṣūl fil-Tawṭi'a) on Logic*; see the text and translation by D. M. Dunlop, *Islamic Quarterly*, 2 (1955), 264–82, and Dunlop's comments on p. 264 and p. 275 n. 2. The text was also edited by M. Türker, *Revue . . . d'Ankara*, 16 (1958), 203–13. Another introductory work on logic by Alfarabi which Maimonides appears to have consulted is his *Tafsīr Kitāb al-Madkhal* (Commentary on the Isagoge); see the edition with introduction by 'Ammār al-Ṭālibī,

inner speech; and (*c*) the linguistic utterance of what is in the mind, which they call external speech.[13]

The first sense of *manṭiq* is, then, logic, and *qua* logic, it is an art (*ṣināʿa*). Maimonides, therefore, goes on to speak of the art of logic.

[1.2] This art, which Aristotle posited, completing its parts in eight books,[14] gives the rational faculty rules pertaining to the intelligibles, i.e. inner speech, so that it is guarded by them against error and is guided[15] toward what is correct, so as to attain certainty insofar[16] as it is in man's power to attain certainty. This art also gives rules common to all languages by which external speech is guided toward what is correct and guards it from error, so that what is uttered in speech corresponds to what is in the mind and is equivalent to it, and the utterance does not add to the concept that is in the soul nor detract from it. Because of these things that this art provides they called it the art of logic. They said that the relation of the art of logic to the intellect is as the relation of the art of grammar to language.

This section of chapter 14 also follows Alfarabi's presentation in his *Introductory Treatise on Logic*, actually continuing where the preceding text left off. Alfarabi had written that 'this art is called *manṭiq* because it gives the rules to the rational faculty for the inner speech, which is comprised of the intelligibles, and rules common to all languages for the external speech, which consists of the utterances, by which the

Kalām Abī Naṣr al-Fārābī fī Tafsīr Kitāb al-Madkhal, in *Nuṣūs Falsafiyya*, ed. ʿUthmān Amīn (Cairo, 1976), 81–97 (text 93–7).

As is well known, Maimonides recommended Alfarabi's works to Samuel b. Tibbon in his famous letter to the translator of the *Guide*, and stated that as far as books on logic are concerned one should study only Alfarabi's writings. It would not be inaccurate to view the greater part of Maimonides' *Treatise on the Art of Logic* as an elementary textbook derived in the main from Alfarabi's introductions to logic.

[13] See Zimmermann, *Alfarabi's Commentary*, p. cxxiii and n. 3 on p. cxxiv, where he discusses this passage from Alfarabi's *Introductory Treatise*. The word *nuṭq*, which I have rendered by 'speech', is translated by Zimmermann as 'articulation' and 'articulacy'. Internal *nuṭq*, i.e. thought, he says is from Greek *logos endiathetos*; and external *nuṭq*, i.e. speech, from Greek *logos prophorikos*.

[14] The *Organon* of Aristotle, in the Arabic philosophic tradition, consists of eight books: *Categories*, *On Interpretation*, *Prior Analytics*, *Posterior Analytics*, *Topics*, *Sophistical Refutations*, *Rhetoric*, *Poetics*. They are mentioned by Maimonides in ch. 10 of this treatise; see, *inter alia*, Ibrahim Madkour, *L'Organon d'Aristote dans le monde arabe*, 2nd edn. (Paris, 1969), Introd. The inclusion of the *Rhetoric* and *Poetics* in the logical canon of Aristotle was highly significant for medieval Islamic political thought. In this classification they followed the Alexandrian scheme of Ammonius and Olympiodorus; see R. Walzer, *From Greek into Arabic* (Cambridge, Mass., 1962), 133.

[15] The text (61, l. 20) reads *wa-yusaddiduhā*; read instead *wa-yusaddadu bihā*. Cf. Alfarabi's *Introductory Treatise*, 228, l. 6.

[16] Text (61, l. 20): *bi-kullihā*; read *bi-kulli mā* (with Heb. trans.). See also Butterworth, *Ethical Writings*, 163 n. 10.

rational faculty is guided in both matters toward what is correct; and it protects from error in both of them together'. The notion that logic is related to the intellect as grammar is related to logic is mentioned by Alfarabi elsewhere as well. And he explains in this vein that whereas grammar sets down rules for utterances that are specific to a particular nation and for people using the languages, logic gives rules for utterances that are common to all languages. Each language, then, has a 'particular grammar', whereas logic is understood to be a kind of 'universal grammar'.[17]

The claim that logic is related to reason, a universal possession of all mankind, as grammar is related to the language of a particular nation was also put forth by Alfarabi's contemporary, the Christian philosopher Mattā b. Yūnus, in a celebrated debate with the Muslim jurist and philologist Abū Sa'īd al-Sīrāfī that took place in the presence of the vizier Ibn al-Furāt in Baghdad in 932. The issue was argued also by Alfarabi's disciple, the Jacobite Yaḥyā b. 'Adī, and by a number of his contemporaries and pupils. The claim was thus a *cause célèbre* in tenth-century Baghdad, whence it moved to the ambience of Maimonides in twelfth-century Andalus.

The contention of the *falāsifa* that logic is a sort of universal grammar takes on further significance in light of the parallel drawn by them between the specific languages of particular nations and their specific systems of (religious) law. The specific languages and specific laws stand in counterpoise to logic, which (as stated above) is a mode of universal grammar, and to philosophy, which is a kind of universal religion. Let us recall that the recipient of the treatise was someone engaged in the legal sciences and eloquent in the Arabic language. A knowledge of logic raises him to a more universal level in the realm of speech. Philosophy, to be discussed below, raises him to a more universal level in the realm of religion.[18]

[17] Alfarabi, *Introductory Treatise*, 228 (trans. 233). For the notion that the relation of grammar to language is as the relation of logic to intellect, see 225 (trans. 230); and *Enumeration of the Sciences*, 21–3. The existence of a universal grammar expressing deep-seated regularities applying to all particular languages, is of course a corner-stone of Noam Chomsky's theory of language; see e.g. his *Aspects of the Theory of Syntax* (Cambridge, Mass., 1965), 5–7.

[18] On Alfarabi's treatment of the relation between logic and grammar and the notion of grammar: language = logic: intellect, see also Alfarabi, *Tafsīr Kitāb al-Madkhal*, 93; id., *Kitāb al-Ḥurūf*, ed. M. Mahdi (Beirut, 1969), Introd., 44–9 (text, 80, 111–12, 137, 142, 146); R. Arnaldez, 'Pensée et langage dans la philosophie de Fārābī', *SI* 45 (1977), 57–65; *Kitāb al-Alfāẓ al-Musta'mala fil-Manṭiq*, ed. M. Mahdi (Beirut, 1968), 43, 107.

On the debate between Mattā b. Yūnus and Abū Sa'īd al-Sīrāfī, see M. Mahdi,

Having discussed the various senses of the term *manṭiq*, and having discussed logic (*manṭiq*) as an art (*ṣināʿa*), Maimonides goes on to discuss the term *ṣināʿa*. The word, which often renders Greek *technē*, means 'art' but is also used for what we would call 'science', as is its Greek precursor.

[2.1] The term *ṣināʿa*, according to the ancients, is an equivocal word that they apply to every theoretical science (*ʿilm naẓarī*) as well as to productive activities. Thus they call each of the philosophic sciences a theoretical art (*ṣināʿa naẓariyya*). And they call each of [the arts of] carpentry, weaving,[19] needlework and the like a productive art (*ṣināʿa ʿamaliyya*).

Wolfson notes, in connection with our passage, that Aristotle uses the term *technē* in two general senses. In *Metaphysics*, i. 1, he uses the word *technē* for theory, or speculation (*theōria*), in contrast with experience and perception; whereas in *Nicomachean Ethics*, vi. 3, he uses *technē* in the sense of productive science (*epistēmē poiētikē*), in contrast with both theoretical science (*epistēmē theōrētikē*) and practical science (*epistēmē praktikē*). The tripartite division of the sciences into theoretical, practical, and productive, which underlies this section and the following, is based upon *Metaphysics*, vi. 1, 1025*b*25. Note that here the theoretical art, which includes the philosophic sciences, comprises both theoretical and practical philosophy.[20]

'Language and Logic in Classical Islam', in G. E. von Grunebaum (ed.), *Logic in Classical Islamic Culture* (Wiesbaden, 1970), 50–83. For Ibn ʿAdī, see G. Endress's edition of Yaḥyā b. ʿAdī's treatise *Fī Tabyīn bi-Faṣl bayn Ṣināʿatay al-Manṭiq al-Falsafī wal-Naḥw al-ʿArabī* published in *Journal for the History of Arabic Science* (Aleppo), 2 (1978), 38–50 (181–93); and for the issue in general, see his 'The Debate between Arabic Grammar and Greek Logic in Classical Islamic Thought' (Arab.), *ibid.* 1 (1977), 339–51 (English summary, 320–2). See also Zimmermann, *Al-Farabi's Commentary*, pp. xliii, cxxiii-cxxx; and Joel L. Kraemer, *Philosophy in the Renaissance of Islam* (Leiden, 1986), 143 f. Cf. Aristotle, *On Interpretation*, 16*a*4–7, which states that while spoken words are different for different peoples, the thoughts and the things of which they are resemblances are the same for all alike.

[19] The text reads (62, l. 3): *wal-ḥabbāla* (*wal-ḥibāla?*). Berman, 'Some Remarks', 341, plausibly suggests *wal-ḥiyāka*, following Aḥituv's translation. In Alfarabi's paraphrase of Aristotle's *Topics* (*Al-Jadal*), (MS Hamidiye 812, fo. 92*b*), weaving (*ḥiyāka*) is actually mentioned along with the arts of carpentry (*nijāra*), shoemaking (*sikāfa*), and *khiyāṭa* (needlework). And it is also given as an example of such arts by Alfarabi in *al-Madīna al-Fāḍila* in *Al-Farabi on the Perfect State*, ed. R. Walzer (Oxford, 1985), 266.

[20] On the senses of *technē* in Aristotle, see Wolfson, 'Classification of Sciences', 510, where this passage is treated. On the division into theoretical, practical, and productive sciences in 2.1 and 3.1, see Aristotle, *Metaphysics*, 1025*b*20 ff.; Wolfson, 493 (see also *Nicomachean Ethics*, vi. 2, 1139*a*27). And see W. Jaeger, *Aristotle: Fundamentals of the History of His Development*, trans. R. Robinson (Oxford, 1948), 374; *Al-Farabi on the Perfect State*, ed. Walzer, 407. On *ṣināʿa ʿamaliyya* in the sense of productive (*poietikē*)

Having treated *manṭiq* and *ṣināʿa*, Maimonides now turns to *falsafa*, philosophy. He had stated at the beginning of the treatise that its purpose was to explain the meanings of the numerous terms frequently employed in logic and the technical terminology used by logicians. Philosophy and its component parts presumably belong to the second category. Furthermore, Maimonides had mentioned the philosophic sciences in the preceding section on *ṣināʿa*, in view of the fact that each of the philosophic sciences is called a theoretical art. He therefore goes on to say what the philosophic sciences are. The classification of these sciences takes up the bulk of the final chapter of the treatise. In addition, Maimonides' aim, or one of his aims, was to raise the recipient (and others like him) from the level of the religious sciences and rhetoric to a basic understanding of what philosophy is.

[3.1] This term *falsafa* is also an equivocal word. [The ancients] sometimes use it for the art of demonstration and sometimes they use it for the sciences. This term applies, according to them, to two sciences. One of the two sciences they call [theoretical philosophy, and the other they call] practical philosophy.[21] They call [practical philosophy] also human philosophy, and they call it also political science. Theoretical philosophy is divided into three parts: mathematics, physics, and the divine science.

Maimonides begins this section in a novel way, that is, by saying 'This term *falsafa* . . .' instead of simply 'The term *falsafa* . . .' The referent of 'this' is evidently the adjective 'philosophic' in the previous section.

In his *Introductory Treatise on Logic*, Alfarabi states clearly that philosophic discourse is called demonstrative. He says that it strives to teach and explain the truth in matters which may afford certain knowledge about something.[22] And in the same treatise he alludes to the equation of philosophy with demonstration when he divides the syllogistic art into five parts, namely, philosophy, dialectic, sophistic, rhetoric, and poetry. Philosophy is thus mentioned in the place of the demonstrative part of the syllogistic art.[23] In the same treatise Alfarabi divides philosophy into four parts: mathematics, physics, the divine

art/science rather than practical (*praktikē*) art/science, see Wolfson, 'Classification of Sciences', 496. Cf. also Maimonides' *Eight Chapters* (ed. Kafiḥ, 376, trans. Gorfinkle, 43), where he says that some actions are practical (*ʿamalī*) and some theoretical (*naẓarī*), going on to subdivide the practical into productive (*mihnī*) and cogitative (*fikrī*).

[21] The text omits (62, ll. 5–6) the words *al-ʿilmiyya wa-yusammūna al-ʿilm al-ākhar al-falsafa*, which are added on the basis of the Hebrew translations; see Berman, 'Some Remarks', 341.

[22] *Introductory Treatise*, 226 (trans. 231).

[23] Ibid. 275 (trans. 230).

science, and political science. In connection with political science he says first that it includes the investigation of true happiness and what is thought to be happiness, and the things which cause the inhabitants of cities to attain happiness or to deviate therefrom; and he then states that this science is called human philosophy and also practical philosophy.[24] This, he says, is because (in contrast to physics) it inquires only into matters that are done by, or attained by, human will. In his *Enumeration of the Sciences*, Alfarabi subsumed jurisprudence (*fiqh*) and dialectical theology (*kalām*) under political science. Significantly, Maimonides mentions neither *fiqh* nor *kalām* when discussing political science.[25]

The division of theoretical philosophy into mathematics, physics, and the divine science, or metaphysics (*al-'ilm al-ilāhī/theologikē*) is traceable to Aristotle (for instance, *Metaphysics*, vi. 1, 1026*a*18). Aristotle applies the expression 'human philosophy' (*ta anthrōpina philosophia*), at the end of *Nicomachean Ethics* (x. 9 1181*b*15), to political science in the broad sense.[26]

Maimonides now takes up the subdivisions of theoretical and practical philosophy, beginning with theoretical philosophy, dealing first with mathematics.

[24] Ibid. 227 (trans. 232). In his *Tafsīr Kitāb al-Madkhal*, 96–7, Alfarabi briefly surveys the sciences, beginning with mathematics and going on with physics, metaphysics (the 'divine science') and politics. On theoretical and practical philosophy and their divisions according to Alfarabi, see also *Kitāb al-Tanbīh 'alā Sabīl al-Sa'āda* (Hyderabad, 1927), 20–1.

[25] The text of Alfarabi's *Enumeration of the Sciences*, ch. 5 has been edited by Muhsin Mahdi in his edition of Alfarabi's *Kitāb al-Milla wa-Nuṣūṣ Ukhrā* (Book of religion and related texts), (Beirut, 1968), 69–76. It is translated by F. N. Najjar in *MPP* 24–30, on the basis of the second edition by Osman Amine ('Uthmān Amīn), (Cairo, 1948), 102–13. See also id., 'Al-Farabi on Political Science', *The Muslim World* (1958), 94–103. And see esp. M. Mahdi, 'Science, Philosophy, and Religion in Alfarabi's Enumeration of the Sciences', in J. E. Murdoch and E. D. Sylla (eds.), *The Cultural Context of Medieval Learning* (Boston, 1973), 113–45.

As Alfarabi added the sciences of language to the classification of the sciences of the Alexandrian prolegomena to Aristotle, so he appended the Islamic topics of jurisprudence (*fiqh*) and dialectical theology (*kalām*) to political science. Maimonides, as stated, omits *fiqh* and *kalām*, as well as the sciences of language, from his summary of the sciences. We may recall that the addressee of the *Treatise on the Art of Logic* was engaged in the religious sciences and in rhetoric.

[26] On the expression 'human philosophy' and 'political science' (Maimonides), or 'human philosophy' and 'practical philosophy' (Alfarabi), see Wolfson, 'Classification of Sciences', 537. He points out that Aristotle uses 'political science' (*politikē*) in the general sense as inclusive of ethics (the science of individual conduct), politics, and economics (management of a household), and that he also uses 'the science of human nature' (*anthrōpina philosophia*) in referring to politics in the widest sense of the term, as in *Nicomachean Ethics*, x. 10, 1181*b*15.

[3.2] As for[27] mathematics (*'ilm al-ta'ālīm*), it does not investigate bodies as they are; it rather investigates concepts abstracted from their matter, even if these concepts exist only in matter. The parts of this science, which are its roots,[28] are four, namely, arithmetic, geometry, the science of the stars, I mean, astronomy, and the science of composing melodies, that is, music. [The ancients] call all these parts the propaedeutic-mathematical sciences (*al-'ulūm al-riyāḍiyya*).

Alfarabi notes the fourfold division of mathematics into arithmetic, geometry, astronomy, and music in his *Introductory Treatise*, without however specifying the objects of mathematical investigation. That these objects are numbers abstracted from bodies is stated in his *Enumeration of the Sciences*. This fourfold classification, which came to be known among the Scholastics as the quadrivium, goes back of course to Ammonius Hermiae.[29]

Maimonides, presumably following Alfarabi, having begun his survey of theoretical philosophy with mathematics, then goes on to physics and metaphysics. Aristotle had proceeded according to this order in *Metaphysics*, vi. 1, 1026*a*19, but elsewhere (*De Anima*, i. 1, 403*b*10–16) he located mathematics between physics and metaphysics. Beginning with mathematics amounts to proceeding from the lower to the higher (see *Metaphysics*, vi. 1, 1026*a*23). In addition, starting with mathematics seems to follow the order of study of the sciences.[30] In the *Guide*, Maimonides encouraged his pupil, Joseph b. Judah, to proceed in an orderly manner in scientific investigation. In the Epistle Dedicatory (pp. 3–4), he mentions that Joseph was first trained in mathematics and then in logic, at which point he wished to have explained certain notions concerning divine things (i.e. metaphysics) and the intentions of the *mutakallimūn*, the dialectical theologians, in this regard, thus skipping natural science. Maimonides encouraged him to proceed more methodically. In *Guide*, i. 34, (p. 75), Maimonides states that one who wants to attain human perfection should first train himself in logic, then in mathematics, and thereafter in the natural

[27] Maimonides begins new sections either with or without the particle *ammā* ('as for'), which need not be translated. I have preferred to translate it in order to mark the difference between sections where it is used and others where it is not.

[28] On the use of the term 'roots' (*uṣūl*) for the topics of the quadrivium by Maimonides and others, see Wolfson, 'Classification of Sciences', 530.

[29] Alfarabi *Introductory Treatise*, 227 (trans. 232); id., *Enumeration of the Sciences*, 55; Wolfson, 'Classification of Sciences', 493.

[30] See Wolfson, 'Classification of Sciences, 515–16.

sciences and in the divine science.[31] And in iii. 51, p. 619, in the well-known parable of the palace, the order in which he ranks the degrees is mathematics and logic, physics, metaphysics.

The science following mathematics, then, is physics, which Maimonides treats next.

[3.3] Physics (*al-'ilm al-ṭabī'ī*) investigates bodies that exist by nature, not by human will, such as the various species of minerals, plants, and animals. Physics investigates all of these and whatever exists in them, I mean, all their accidents, properties, and causes,[32] as well as all that in which they exist by necessity, like time, space and motion.

In his *Introductory Treatise on Logic*, Alfarabi merely states that physics comprises inquiry into bodies and all that exists in a body by nature, that is, not by human will. In his *Enumeration of the Sciences* the discussion is more extensive.[33]

Following physics is metaphysics or natural theology.

[3.4] The divine science (*al-'ilm al-ilāhī*) is divided into two parts. One of them is the investigation of every entity that is neither a body nor a force in a body. It is discourse concerning what pertains to the deity—may his name be exalted—and the angels as well, according to the opinion [of the ancients]; for they do not believe the angels to be bodies, but call them instead separate intellects, by which they mean that they are separate from matter. The second part of the divine science investigates the ultimate causes of everything that the other sciences include. And they call the divine science also metaphysics.

These are all the sciences of the ancients.[34]

In his *Introductory Treatise on Logic*, Alfarabi merely states that 'metaphysics includes investigation of what is neither a body nor a force in a body and investigation of the ultimate causes of everything

[31] References to *Guide of the Perplexed* are to the Arabic edition of S. Munk and I. Joel, *Dalālat al-Ḥā' irīn* (Jerusalem, 1930–1); and to the English translation by Shlomo Pines, *The Guide of the Perplexed* (Chicago, 1963).

[32] Text (62, l. 15); *asbāb* (ed. Efros: *asbābuhā*). Read *wa-asbābuhā*, with Hebrew trans. (Berman, 'Some Remarks', 342).

[33] Alfarabi *Introductory Treatise*, 227 (trans. 232); id., *Enumeration of the Sciences*, 76 ff.

[34] The text reads (62, l. 21): *fa-yusammūna hādhā ayḍan al-'ilm al-ilāhī mā ba'da al-ṭabī'a*, which literally means, 'and they call this also the divine science metaphysics'. Berman, 'Some Remarks', 342, suggests that we read *wa-mā ba'da al-ṭabī'a*, which would make it mean: 'and they call this also the divine science *and* metaphysics'. This is certainly an improvement but the text remains somewhat difficult; it would have been smoother had the divine science not been mentioned here at all, and had the reading been: *fa-yusammūna hādhā ayḍan 'ilm mā ba'da al-ṭabī'a*, 'and they call this also the science of metaphysics'. Accordingly, *al-'ilm al-ilāhī* may have originally been a marginal gloss (to *hādhā*) that crept into the text.

that the other sciences include'.[35] In the *Enumeration of the Sciences*, he says that metaphysics is divided into three parts: (*a*) investigation of existent beings and things that pertain to them in so far as they are existent beings; (*b*) investigation of the principles of demonstration in the specific theoretical sciences; and (*c*) investigation of existents that are neither bodies nor in bodies.[36]

Aristotle had spoken of metaphysics as (*a*) the science of what is eternal, immovable, and separable from body (*Metaphycis*, 1026*a*10–11); (*b*) as the science of being *qua* being (1026*a*31–2); and (*c*) as inclusive of the principles of mathematics, logic, and physics (983*a*24, 1005*a*20, 1005*b*5–8).

Between the theoretical and the practical sciences, Maimonides inserts the art of logic; this was treated in 1.2 (above) in general terms but here it is reconsidered with regard to its status within the system of sciences:

[3.5] As for the art of logic (*ṣināʿat al-manṭiq*), it is not included among the sciences according to (the ancients); it is rather an instrument of the sciences. They said that no orderly instruction or learning can be sound save by the art of logic. It is the instrument for all [the sciences], and the instrument for something does not belong to it.

Alfarabi writes in his *Introductory Treatise on Logic* that 'the art of logic is an instrument by which, when it is employed in the parts of philosophy, certain knowledge is obtained by all that is included in the theoretical and practical arts, and there is no way to certainty of the truth in anything the knowledge of which is sought save by the art of logic'. That logic is an instrument of the sciences and not a science in itself, or a part of philosophy, was commonplace among the *falāsifa*.[37]

[35] Alfarabi, *Introductory Treatise*, 227, ll. 17–232. The text reads: *wa-lā huwa fī jism* (so also Türker edn., 191, l. 3), that is, '[is not a body] and is not in a body'. Read perhaps *wa-lā quwwa fī jism* ('and is not a force in a body'), as in Maimonides' text. Cf., however, Alfarabi, *Enumeration of the Sciences*, 88, l. 14 (*laysat bi-ajsām wa-lā fī ajsām*).

[36] Id., *Enumeration of the Sciences*, 88; and see also id., *Fī Aghrāḍ Mā Baʿda al-Ṭabīʿa* (On the aims of metaphysics), (Hyderabad, 1930).

On the subjects treated by metaphysics, according to Aristotle, see Wolfson, 'Classification of the Sciences', 517–18; also P. Merlan, *From Platonism to Neoplatonism*, 2nd rev. edn. (The Hague, 1960), ch. 7; J. Owens, *The Doctrine of Being in the Aristotelian Metaphysics* (Toronto, 1951), 3 ff.; I. Düring, *Aristoteles: Darstellung und Interpretation seines Denkens* (Heidelberg, 1966), 594 ff. (esp. n. 46); and Kraemer, *Philosophy*, 210.

[37] Alfarabi, *Introductory Treatise*, 227 (trans. 232). Logic is thus not part of the sciences or of philosophy but rather an instrument for knowing them. The term *organon* was applied to logic by Andronicus and Alexander of Aphrodisias, and Aristotle's logical works came to be known as the *Organon* in the Renaissance; see Wolfson, 'Classification of the Sciences', 535; Zimmermann, *Al-Farabi's Commentary*, pp. xxi, cxxiii.

Having dispensed with the theoretical sciences and logic, Maimonides now turns to practical, or political, science. It is with this part of chapter 14 that I am primarily concerned.

[3.6.1] As for political science (*al-'ilm al-madanī*), it is divided into four parts: First is self-governance of the individual; second is governance of the household; third is governance of the city; and fourth is governance of the great nation (*al-umma al-kabīra*), or the nations (*al-umam*).

The four parts of political science noted here actually amount to three, namely: (*a*) ethics (the individual's self-governance); (*b*) economics (governance of the household); and (*c*) politics, including governance of the city, and governance of the great nation, or the nations. This division conforms with Aristotle's division of practical science into politics, economics, and ethics.[38] At this point, Maimonides breaks away from Alfarabi's formulations as exposited in his *Introductory Treatise on Logic* and related works, and moves on to the conceptual climate of Alfarabi's political writings.

Wolfson was of the opinion that the difference between city and great nation, or nations, is not a distinction of size (as it would indeed appear) but of kind. He claimed that the word *umma* (translated here by 'nation') should be understood to mean 'religion' or 'religious sect'. He then proposed that the fourth part of political science be translated 'the government of the great religion or of the other religions'. He identified 'the great religion' with Judaism and 'the other religions' with 'the heathen nations of antiquity'. The distinction between governance of the city and governance of the great nation, or the nations, Wolfson claimed, amounts to a difference between governance of a civil state on the one hand and of a religious state on the other.[39] Here, Wolfson ventured a guess concerning the underlying Arabic text. He suggested that the Hebrew word for 'great' in 'great nation' may mean 'excellent', reflecting Arabic *fāḍila*. Maimonides, he observed, would naturally apply this qualification to the Jews. But the

[38] Aristotle divides the practical sciences into politics, economics, and ethics in *Nicomachean Ethics*, 1142*a*9–10; see Wolfson, 'Classification of the Sciences', 493. See also ibid. 537, where Wolfson observes that Maimonides divides practical philosophy into four parts rather than three as in the Aristotelian scheme. This observation is based on his view that there is a qualitative difference between governance of the city and governance of the great nation, or the nations (p. 541). But they actually belong together, both under the heading of politics.

[39] Wolfson, 'Classification of the Sciences', 541; and 'Note on Maimonides Classification of the Sciences', Twersky and Williams, *Studies*, i. 555–6.

text actually reads *kabīra* ('great'). And it certainly would not be natural to apply this adjective to the Jews.

Wolfson's reading of the text, suggesting a distinction between the civil polity of cities and the religious polity of nations, was adopted by Leo Strauss.[40] The governance of the city, Strauss said, is assigned by Maimonides to one branch of political philosophy, and the governance of the great nation, or the nations, is assigned to another. Strauss took the argument even further: the suggestion that the pagan nations and Israel represent different forms of the religious state, as opposed to the civil state (the city), he claimed, implies that the governance of Israel, that is, the Torah, is a subject belonging to political philosophy. In fact, according to Strauss, Wolfson's suggestion implies that the governance of the great nation, which is the Torah, and the governance of the nations by the *nomoi* 'are the subjects of one and the same branch of political philosophy'. Strauss took issue with Wolfson on one point: he found no justification for identifying the great nation with Israel. He proposed instead that Maimonides meant by 'the nations' the ancient pagan nations, and that by 'the great nation' he intended not Israel exclusively but rather 'any group constituted by a universalistic religion'. But this is problematic, for if Maimonides meant any nation with a universalistic religion, why, then, did he stipulate the singular 'the great nation'? How can *the* great nation be equated with *any group* constituted by a universal religion? Strauss tried to maintain that the singular nation refers to the universalistic and exlusivist claim of each of the monotheistic religions, but this explanation is rather forced.

Maimonides' statement on the government of the city, the great nation, and the nations must be understood on the basis of passages in the political writings of Alfarabi in which the different sizes of political association, including these, are mentioned. Consideration of these texts will lead us to a proper understanding concerning the true nature of these political associations. Let us first consider a passage from Alfarabi's *Al-Siyāsa al-Madaniyya* (The political regime):

> Man belongs to the species that cannot accomplish its necessary affairs or achieve its best state except through the association (*ijtimāʿ*)[41] of many groups (*jamāʿāt*) of them in a single dwelling-place. Some human societies are large,

[40] Strauss, 'Maimonides' Statement', 120–2.

[41] Arabic *ijtimāʿ* often renders Greek *homonoia* in Graeco-Arabic translation literature, and like its Greek counterpart it means 'association', 'community', etc. See e.g. Wolfson, 'Note on Maimonides' Classification', 552. *Ijtimāʿ* may also be used to render Greek *koinōnia*; see Walzer, *Al-Farabi on the Perfect State*, 430.

others are of medium size, still others are small. The large societies consist [of a group][43] of many nations that associate and cooperate with one another; the medium ones consist of a nation; the small are the ones embraced by the city. These three are the perfect societies. Hence the city represents the first degree of perfection. Associations in villages, quarters, streets, and households, on the other hand, are the imperfect associations.[42]

In the sequel Alfarabi states that the nation is divided into cities, and that the perfect human association is divided into nations. He then goes on to stipulate how nations differ from one another by natural characteristics, language, and so on. There is no hint here of a qualitative difference between cities and nations, no suggestion that the polity of the city is civil and that of nations religious. In a parallel passage in *Ārā' Ahl al-Madīna al-Fāḍila* (The opinions of the inhabitants of the best city), Alfarabi lists the perfect and imperfect human associations or unions.[44] The adjective 'perfect' has to do with the minimal size for true human association.

There are three kinds of perfect society: great, medium, and small. The great one is the association of all the societies in the inhabitable world (*ma'mūra/oikoumenē*); the medium one the association of one nation in one part of the inhabitable world; the small one the association of the people of a city in the territory of any nation whatsoever. Imperfect are the association of people in a village, the association of people in a quarter, then the association in a street, eventually the association in a house, the house being the smallest association of all.

Alfarabi then discusses the imperfect associations, observing that the city is the minimal entity in which the supreme good and final perfection are attainable. And he continues:

The city, then, in which people aim through association at cooperating for the things by which felicity in its real and true sense can be attained, is the excellent city, and the society in which there is a cooperation to acquire felicity is the excellent society; and the nation in which all of its cities cooperate for

[42] Alfarabi, *Al-Siyāsa al-Madaniyya* (The political regime), ed. F. M. Najjar (Beirut, 1964), 69 (trans. Najjar *MPP* 32). Cf. also 79–80 (trans. 37).

[43] The words 'of a group' are added to the translation on the basis of the text, which reads *jamā'āt umam kathīra* (69, l. 18).

[44] Alfarabi, *Ārā' Ahl al-Madīna al-Fāḍila*, ed. Walzer, 228 (trans. 229). I have substituted 'association' where Walzer uses 'union' to render *ijtimā'*. In fact, Walzer translates *ijtimā'* by 'association' elsewhere; see p. 294 (where he translates *i'tilāf* as 'union'); and see Index, p. 563 (association = *koinōnia* = *ijtimā'*); and Commentary, 430.

See also Alfarabi, *Al-Madīna al-Fāḍila*, 246–7, where the excellent city, the excellent nation, and the universal state (*ma'mūra/oikoumenē*) are listed.

those things through which felicity is attained is the excellent nation. In the same way, the excellent universal state will arise only when all the nations in it co-operate for the purpose of reaching felicity.

Maimonides' classification, it will be noticed, differs from Alfarabi's in several respects. Treating the subjects of political science, Maimonides begins with the individual and then goes on to the household, the city, thereafter mentioning the great nation, or the nations. In other words, he proceeds from smaller to larger associations. Moreover, instead of 'nation', Maimonides has 'great nation', and instead of 'groups of many nations', which is the formulation in *Al-Siyāsa al-Madaniyya*, or 'the association of all the societies in the inhabited world', as Alfarabi puts it in *Al-Madīna al-Fāḍila*, Maimonides has merely 'the nations'. Now in my opinion, it is not true that Maimonides omitted 'small nation', as is sometimes claimed; for Alfarabi does not, in fact, mention small nation, and consequently it could not be omitted.[45] Nor can it be maintained that Maimonides used the expression 'great nation' in a sense that is equivalent to 'the nations' or 'many or all nations', thereby deleting 'nations' altogether. The reason why Maimonides has merely 'the nations' instead of a locution suggesting a world state (as in Alfarabi) is evidently related to his own particular Messianic vision.[46]

Maimonides' classification of political entities has its closest parallel in a passage from Alfarabi's *Kitāb al-Milla* (Book of religion), which states: 'The group is sometimes a tribe and sometimes a city or province and sometimes a mighty nation (*umma 'aẓīma*) and sometimes many nations.'[47] Note that both Maimonides' and Alfarabi's classification here proceed from smaller to larger entities, and that both present the nation as great (or mighty). The only difference between the two presentations is that in place of 'many nations' Maimonides has simply 'the nations'. The table below may illustrate the correspondence of Maimonides' text with the three passages quoted from Alfarabi.

[45] Cf. Strauss, 'Maimonides' Statement' (above, n. 5), 119; Berman, 'Reexamination' (above, n. 7), 107.

[46] See J. L. Kraemer, 'On Maimonides' Messianic Posture', in I. Twersky (ed.), *Studies in Medieval Jewish History and Literature*, ii (Cambridge, Mass., 1984), 109–42. See also n. 47.

[47] Alfarabi, *Kitāb al-Milla*, 43. Berman noted the present relevance of this passage in 'Reexamination', 108. It is possible that the vagueness of the political association expressed in Maimonides' 'the nations' stemmed from the fact that he was merely restating this text.

Alfarabi also wrote a work entitled *Fil-Ijtimā'āt al-Madaniyya* (On political associations); see Ibn abī Uṣaybi'a, '*Uyūn al-Anbā' fī Ṭabaqāt al-Aṭibbā*', ed. A. Müller (Cairo–Königsberg, 1882–4), ii.139; Walzer, *Al-Farabi on the Perfect State*, 430.

Maimonides' and Alfarabi's classifications of political entities

	Maimonides	Alfarabi		
	Logic	*Siyāsa Madaniyya*	*Madīna Fāḍila*	*Kitāb al-Milla*
Perfect				
Large	Nations	Group of many nations	All societies in inhabited world	Many nations
Medium	Great nation	Nation	Nation	Mighty nation
Small	City	City	City	City, province
Imperfect		Village	Village	Tribe
		Quarter	Quarter	
		Street	Street	
	Household	Household	Household	

As the political thought of Plato and Aristotle was circumscribed by the *polis*, we may naturally wonder on what textual basis Alfarabi arrived at the larger associations of nation (*umma/ethnos*) and especially the concept of a world state, expressed in the phrase group of many nations or all societies in the inhabited world. Wolfson traced this development to a passage in the *Politics* in which Aristotle refers to three types of association: the confederacy (*symmachia*), the nation (*ethnos*), and the city (*polis*). Alfarabi's description of the great state corresponds, according to Wolfson, to Aristotle's description of a confederacy as something that 'is naturally formed for the sake of help—*boētheias*'.[48]

Shlomo Pines has suggested that Alfarabi's classification goes back to certain remarks in Aristotle's *Politics*, i. 1.[49] Aristotle says, for instance,

[48] Aristotle, *Politics*, ii. 2, 1261*a*24–29; Wolfson, 'Note on Maimonides' Classification', 552.

[49] S. Pines, 'Aristotle's *Politics* in Arabic Philosophy', *IOS* 5 (1975), 156–9. Note that in bk. I. 1–2 Aristotle proceeds in ascending order of size from household to village to *polis* (1252*a*7); he also speaks of *polis*, family, and individual (1252*a*19), and of the *polis* and the individual (1252*a*25). He discusses household management (*oikonomia*) from i. 3 to the end of bk. i (at 1260*b*24).

On the notion of the 'world state' in Alfarabi, see e.g. M. Mahdi, 'Alfarabi', in L. Strauss and J. Cropsey (eds.), *History of Political Philosophy* (Chicago, 1963), 174. And see Walzer, *Al-Farabi on the Perfect State*, 433, which suggests that Alfarabi follows, in his idea of a world state, 'a late Greek predecessor', adding that this notion would not have been conceivable without Alexander the Great, and the Roman and Sassanian empires. See also J. L. Kraemer, 'Humanism in the Renaissance of Islam: A Preliminary Study', *JAOS* 104 (1984), 163–4.

that the *polis* is the perfect community made up of several villages (1252*b*28), and that a village is composed of several households (1252*b*15). In this context Aristotle makes a passing reference to 'nations' (in 1252*b*20), which (as Pines observes) he may have regarded as typical of non-Greeks. And he mentions the city (1252*a*5) as the supreme community that aims at the most supreme of all goods. As for a concept of a universal state, Pines notes that Alfarabi may have relied upon a paraphrase of part of the *Politics* composed in the Hellenistic or Roman period which may have been influenced by Stoic doctrine.

It is possible, in my opinion, that the classification of human associations into city (or city-state, *polis*), nation (or nation-state) and many nations is more closely related to *Politics*, iii. 14, 285*b*33 f., where Aristotle states that 'as the master's rule is a sort of monarchy in the home, so absolute monarchy is domestic mastership over a city, or over a nation or several nations'.[50] We have here sequentially the governance of the household, of the city, of the nation, or the nations, just as we find it in Alfarabi and Maimonides. It is plausible to assume that Alfarabi and (perhaps) Maimonides had access to a paraphrase of the *Politics* which, as Pines suggests, was known in Arabic guise. If this suggestion is correct, then this paraphrase included texts of Book III.

Having set forth the parts of political science, Maimonides turns first to man's self-governance, that is, ethics.

[3.6.2] As for man's self-governance (*tadbīr al-insān nafsahu*), it is his acquiring for himself virtuous moral qualities and removing from himself vile moral qualities if they come about. Moral qualities are the settled dispositions that form in the soul until they become habits, from which actions proceed.[51] The philosophers depict a moral quality as being either a virtue or a vice. They call fine moral qualities moral virtues, and they call base moral qualities moral vices. The actions proceeding from the virtuous moral qualities they call good, and the actions proceeding from the base moral qualities they call evil. And they likewise depict reasoning, which is conceiving the intelligibles, as being a virtue or a vice, so that they speak of intellectual virtues and intellectual vices.[52] The philosophers have many books on ethics. And all governance by which a man governs another they call a regime.

[50] See the edition and translation of H. Rackham (Cambridge, Mass., 1959). I have changed his 'race' (*ethnos*) to 'nation'. In addition Walzer calls attention to *Politics*, vii. 7, 1327*b*21, where Aristotle considers the Greek city-states (*poleis*) and the (non-Greek?) nations (*ethnē*) that are distributed throughout the entire inhabited world (*pasan tēn oikoumenēn*); *Al-Farabi on the Perfect State*, 431.

[51] Cf. *Nicomachean Ethics*, ii. 4, 1105*a–b*; 1106*b*22–24; ii. 8, 1108*b*11.

[52] Cf. ibid. i. 13, 1103*a*3–10; *Eight Chapters*, ed. Kafiḥ, 377 (trans. Gorfinkle, 49).

Strauss observed that one of the difficulties in Maimonides' presentation is the unusual division of political science, namely, by his assigning the study of virtues to ethics and the understanding of happiness to politics, that is, to governance of the city, the last part of practical philosophy, rather than to ethics, its first part.[53] Strauss took this unusual division to imply that ethics is the investigation of moral virtues but not an inquiry into happiness, or a human being's true end, which Maimonides places rather within politics proper (see 3.6.4 below). If so, Strauss argues, the moral virtues and their exercise are not the true end of a human being, according to Maimonides, and they can only be understood with a view to their political function. It is worth noting in this regard that Alfarabi likewise assigns the investigation of happiness to politics. Avicenna, on the other hand, who also divided practical philosophy into three parts (ethics, economics, politics), makes ethics the superior part. This is because ethics gives human beings knowledge of how their moral qualities and actions may render their life in this and the next world happy. Economics, says Avicenna, leads to happiness only in this world. And politics, he claims, is unrelated to the attainment of happiness.[54]

The significance of assigning the inquiry into happiness (*sa'āda/eudaimonia*) to politics rather than to ethics (where Aristotle had situated it) is that this final aim of human life cannot accordingly be achieved by a human being in solitude but only within the framework of a political association. However, I am not sure that Maimonides would have pressed this point or that he was entirely consistent in this respect.

Following self-governance is governance, or management, of the household, i.e. economics (*tadbīr al-manzil/oikonomia*).

[53] Strauss, 'Maimonides' Statement' (above, n. 5), 116, 127. See also Wolfson, 'Classification of the Sciences', 538.

[54] Avicenna, 'Fī Aqsām al-'Ulūm al-'Aqliyya' (On the divisions of the rational sciences), in *Tis' Rasā'il* (Cairo, 1908), 105, 107–8 (trans. M. Mahdi in *MPP* 96–7). See Miriam Galston, 'Realism and Idealism in Avicenna's Political Philosophy', *Review of Politics*, 41 (1979), 570–2, where this passage is discussed and contrasted with Maimonides' formulation. She appears to suggest that Maimonides adopted the distinction between theoretical and practical philosophy and the subdivision of practical philosophy into three parts from Avicenna, and regards Maimonides' assignment of happiness to the section on political governance as 'an unequivocal retort to Avicenna and those who would relegate political life to a peripheral role in the pursuit of the highest human good'. But Maimonides, it seems, mainly follows Alfarabi in assigning the discussion of happiness to political science proper.

[3.6.3] As for governance of the household (*tadbīr al-manzil*), it is knowing[55] how [its members] help one another and what they require[56] so that their circumstance may be well ordered as far as possible in accordance with the requisite conditions in that time and place.[57]

The final part of political science is governance of the city (or politics).

[3.6.4] As for the governance of the city (*tadbīr al-madīna*), it is a science that provides its inhabitants with knowledge of true happiness and the way of striving to attain it and with knowledge of true misery and the way of striving to guard against it; and with training of their moral qualities to abandon things that are presumed to be happiness, so that they do not relish them or avidly pursue them. It also explains to them what are presumed miseries, so that they do not suffer and dread them. It likewise prescribes for them rules of justice by means of which their associations are well ordered. The learned men of bygone nations used to posit[58] governances (*tadābīr*) and rules (*qawānīn*) in accordance with the perfection of each individual among them, by means of which their kings governed subjects. They called them *nomoi* (*nawāmīs*). The nations were governed by these *nomoi*. The philosophers have many books concerning all these things which have been translated into Arabic, and what has not been translated may even be more extensive. But in these times all of this has been dispensed with, I mean, the regimes (*al-siyāsāt*) and the *nomoi*. For people are governed[59] by the divine commands (*bil-awāmir al-ilāhiyya*).

In his *Introductory Treatise on Logic*, Alfarabi states: 'Politics includes investigation of the happiness which is in truth happiness, and of what is happiness in thought but not in truth, and of things which when they are employed in the cities their inhabitants obtain happiness thereby. It also indicates the things which when they are employed in the city their inhabitants decline from happiness.' And in his *Enumeration of the Sciences*, Alfarabi says that political science explains that some ends of actions and ways of life are true happiness, while others are presumed to be happiness.[60] In assigning the investigation of true

[55] Text (63, l. 11): *tu'allam*. Read: *yu'lam* (Berman, 'Some Remarks', 342).

[56] Text (63, l. 11): *yaqtaṣirūna*. Read: *yaqtaḍūna*.

[57] On this passage, see Wolfson, 'Classification of the Sciences', 539.

[58] Text (63, l. 18): *taṣna'u*. Read: *taḍa'u* (with Ibn Tibbon and Aḥituv). See Mahdi's translation, *MPP* 190 n. 2.

[59] Text (63, l. 22): *wa-t-d-b-r*. Berman, 'Some Remarks', 342, suggests: *wa-tadbīr*. Read perhaps: *wa-yudabbaru*.

[60] Alfarabi, *Introductory Treatise*, 227 (trans. 232); id., *Enumeration of the Sciences* (trans. Najjar, *MPP* 24). Wolfson, 'Classification of the Sciences', 540, refers to Aristotle's *Politics*, i. 1 and vii. 1, which states that the purpose of society is to attain some good, that the best government leads to the attainment of that good, and that different kinds of good exist.

and presumed happiness to politics, or the governance of the city, Maimonides thus follows Alfarabi.

III

The discussion of Maimonides' 'statement on political science' by Strauss rested, for the most part, upon his interpretation of the last paragraph. Let us see how he understood it. He translated the last sentence as follows: 'But we have no need in these times for all this, viz. for [the commands], the laws, the *nomoi*, the governance by [of] [these] human beings in divine things [for the laws and the *nomoi*; the governance of human beings is now through divine things].'[61] The brackets indicate alternative readings. Strauss acknowledges that the meaning of the statement is unclear, recalling that the Arabic original of the second half of the treatise 'is lost'. Indeed, this is a fine example of how reliance on Hebrew translations of Arabic texts wreaks havoc with our understanding. Strauss interpreted the text to be saying that 'Maimonides rejects the books of the philosophers on politics proper as useless for "us" "in these times".' But, in the first place, if we consider the true text, Maimonides never actually says that he rejects the books of the philosophers; he says, rather, that in these times the regimes and the *nomoi* may be dispensed with. Moreover, he does not say that *we* have no need in these times, and therefore Strauss cannot sustain the view that by 'we' Maimonides meant the men who speculate about principles and roots. In the original text no 'we' appears.[62] In fact, those who can dispense with all of this, namely, the regimes and the *nomoi* (not the books of the philosophers), are identified as 'people' who are said to be governed by the divine commands (not 'things', as Strauss thought on the basis of the Hebrew translations). Furthermore, there is obviously no reason to assume that by 'people' Maimonides intended Jews; indeed, the most commendable interpretation of this text is that the people who can dispense with the regimes and the *nomoi* and are governed by the divine commands 'in these times' are not Jews alone but rather monotheists, that is, Jews,

[61] Strauss, 'Maimonides' Statement', 116.

[62] Ibid. 118. The question of the identification of the 'we' here is introduced by Strauss on the basis of the Hebrew translations. The pronoun does not exist even implicitly in the Arabic text, where there is a passive verb rendered by 'has been dispensed with'. Cf. also Wolfson, 'Notes on Maimonides' Classification', 558.

Christians, and Muslims. It is consequently incorrect to infer, as Strauss does, that the philosophic books on politics (and perhaps economics) 'have been rendered superfluous by the Torah', not to mention the further inference—'This implies that the function of the Torah is emphatically political.'[63] Note that Strauss has unobtrusively substituted 'the Torah' for the 'divine things' (or rather 'divine commands'), whereas Maimonides did not imply such a restriction. Divine commands, as surprising as this may appear, would be the commands postulated in other religions as well, that is, in Christianity and Islam.

As stated above, both Wolfson and Strauss contended that the governance of the pagan nations and the governance of Israel (Wolfson), or of any group constituted by a universalistic religion (Strauss), was governance by a religious polity, in contrast to the civil polity of cities. But the real distinction in our text is between the bygone nations that were governed by *nomoi* on the one hand and people 'in these times' who are governed by divine commands on the other. There is no reason to believe that the *nomoi* of the ancient nations are religious laws; on the contrary, the clear implication is that they are not. The *nomoi* are framed in accordance with the perfection of individuals, and they differ in this respect from divine laws.[64]

As Maimonides referred to the copious books that the philosophers possess on ethics (3.6.2 above), so here he mentions that they have many books on 'all these things'. By 'all these things' he intends the *nomoi*, but he evidently means to include also other topics of politics, such as knowledge of true happiness and rules of justice. He ends his treatise with the pregnant remark that 'in these times all this has been dispensed with', clearly stating that by this he means 'the regimes and the *nomoi*'. He does not say that the *books of the philosophers* have been dispensed with, as Strauss read him, nor is it reasonable that he would have said so, as these books (e.g. Plato's *Republic* and *Laws*, as well as

[63] Strauss, ibid. 117; cf. 119 'he [Maimonides] in effect suggests that the function of revealed religion is emphatically political'.

[64] Cf. *Guide*, iii. 24, pp. 534–5, where Maimonides asserts that 'the Law does not pay attention to the isolated' and 'was not given with a view to things that are rare', but is rather 'directed only toward the things that occur in the majority of cases . . . ' The Law as a divine thing is compared with natural things in which 'the general utility' is overriding. Cf. also iii. 26 and 45; and Maimonides' *Responsa*, ed. J. Blau (Jerusalem, 1957–61; rev. edn. 1986), ii. 399. Cf. the view, put forth in Plato's *Statesman* (294*a*, 295*a*, 299*d*), that the true monarch attends to individuals and is flexible, whereas the law is inflexible and invariable, and cannot provide for individual cases. See also Kraemer, '*Sharīʿa* and *Nāmūs*', 200–1.

some version of Aristotle's *Politics*) were rather often consulted, even by people 'in these times' who are guided by divine commands. Now, the *nomoi* may really be dispensed with because people 'in these times' are governed by the divine commands; not Jews but people, and not the Torah but the divine commands.[65]

The true distinction, then, is not between the civil law of the city and the religious law of the pagan nations and of Israel or of any group constituted by a universalistic religion, but between the governance of the ancient nations and the governance of people 'in these times'. The former was by the *nomoi*, the latter by the divine commands.

As we have seen, on the mistaken assumption that philosophic books on politics have been replaced by the Torah, Strauss inferred that in Maimonides' view, 'the function of the Torah is emphatically political'. Now Strauss adds to this the observation that this interpretation is confirmed by the *Guide of the Perplexed*, in which Maimonides says (in Strauss's words) that 'the Torah gives only summary indications concerning theoretical subjects, whereas regarding the governance of the city, everything has been done to make it precise in all its details'.[66] This reading brings Maimonides perilously close to the view of Spinoza, if not right to it, namely, that the purpose of Scripture was merely to induce obedience and piety and not to teach philosophic truths.[67] But the assertion that the function of the Torah is political is based upon a shaky interpretation of the text, as we have seen.

There is, then, no ground for Strauss's inference that according to Maimonides the function of the Torah is emphatically political. On the contrary, Maimonides in fact stresses that the purpose of the divine Law is to promote sound belief and to teach correct opinions pertaining to God and the angels, and to enlighten human beings so that they may know the whole of what exists as it really is.[68] Maimonides claimed that the Torah does convey philosophic truths, for

[65] Wolfson, 'Note on Maimonides' Classification ', 559 n. 22, suggests that the phrase 'We nowadays [are not in need of all these books]', which Wolfson had taken to imply that 'the Jewish religious books have *nowadays* taken the place of the ancient heathenish books', may also include the Muslims and Christians, since they also are contrastd with the Sabeans in so far as they grant the veracity of the Jewish scriptures (*Guide*, iii. 29). And see Berman, 'Reexamination', 110, where it is clearly stated that Islam and Christianity, as well as Judaism, are intended, 'for they claim to govern men through divine commands'. If the treatise was written for a non-Jew, the general reference makes much sense.

[66] Strauss, 'Maimonides' Statement', 117.

[67] See Spinoza's *Theologico-political Treatise*, chs. 13, 14.

[68] *Guide*, ii. 40, pp. 383–4.

instance concerning God's existence and oneness. It also commands people to cultivate love and knowledge of God and of his manifestation in the world. In other words, the purpose of the divine Law is to communicate to people philosophic truths in terms they are equipped to understand, and to guide them to pursue knowledge about the nature of being. In this respect, Maimonides says, the divine Law differs from political *nomoi*. The entire purpose of a law that is nomic is aimed at social and political order and the establishment of justice, in order that what is presumed to be happiness by the chief who determined the actions of the law may be obtained.[69] The nomic law does not attend to speculative matters, or to the perfection of the rational faculty, and it is not concerned with the question of whether opinions are correct or not. The function of the nomic law, not the Torah or the divine Law, is indeed emphatically political in Maimonides' view.

IV

Strauss's interpretation of Maimonides' statement on political science has, as we have seen, implications for understanding the *Guide*. Strauss went so far as to suggest that 'Maimonides' prophetology as a whole is a branch of political science'.[70] And elsewhere he argued quite passionately that the *Guide* is not a philosophic book but rather a Jewish book.[71] What does it mean to say that the *Guide* is not a philosophic book? In Maimonides' own terms, which should determine the scope of the discussion, philosophy meant either the art of demonstration or else it meant the sciences, specifically theoretical and practical philosophy. Now, that the *Guide* is not a philosophic book in the first sense is clear. Nor is it a book whose subject is theoretical philosophy (mathematics, physics, and the divine science), although some aspects of these sciences are treated. And it would not be

[69] The expression *al-sharīʿa nāmūsiyya* (271, l. 23; trans. Pines, 384; and see n. 28 ad loc.) is somewhat strange, in view of the usual contrast understood to obtain between *sharīʿa* and *nāmūs* (see Kraemer, 'Sharīʿa and Nāmūs'). We must understand *sharīʿa* here to mean law in the general sense and not religious law. The word *nāmūsiyya* is predicative, and the phrase is best rendered, 'Know that this law is nomic.' (Cf. Pines, 'You must know that that law is a *nomos*.')

[70] Strauss, 'Maimonides' Statement', 120.

[71] See e.g. 'The Literary Character of the Guide for the Perplexed', in *Persecution and the Art of Writing* (Glencoe, Ill. 1952), 42–3; and esp. 'How to Begin to Study the Guide of the Perplexed', in *The Guide of the Perplexed*, trans. S. Pines, p. xiv.

accurate to depict the *Guide* as a book about practical philosophy, that is, political science, although, again, some facets of political science are touched upon.

The question properly framed—that is, in Maimonides' terms—is whether the *Guide* should be classified as a demonstrative, dialectical, or rhetorical work.[72] I think that the evidence is overwhelmingly in favour of the view that the *Guide* is essentially a dialectical work. This does not mean, however, that it does not contain demonstrative arguments, or for that matter even rhetorical and poetical statements. I intend to treat the question in more detail on another occasion. Suffice it for the present to say the following. The *Guide* is written in the form of an epistle for a student, thereby meeting the condition that dialectical discourse entails two interlocutors. Furthermore, it is aimed precisely at the level of the addressee, which appears to be the stage of dialectic prior to disciplined study of the demonstrative sciences. Moreover, Maimonides stresses in the *Guide* the need for dialectical arguments, and even claims that on the most exalted subjects we are bound to dialectic and can attain no more.[73]

Now the *falāsifa*, following Aristotle, regarded dialectic as the stepping stone to philosophy proper, as the servant of philosophy, and as the means for establishing its first principles. Furthermore, they regarded it as the way by which the philosopher participates in society. To be sure, they criticized the *mutakallimūn*, as did Maimonides, but this was because the *mutakallimūn*, in their opinion, did not understand the difference between demonstration and dialectic; they misused dialectic. Not only were they non-philosophers, they were not even decent dialectitions.[74]

A number of passages in Alfarabi's section on dialectic (*al-Jadal*) in his paraphrase of Aristotle's eight books on logic may help us dispel some of the fog concerning the question of the character of the *Guide*

[72] On these types of argumentation, well known from Alfarabi and the *falāsifa* in general, see *Treatise on the Art of Logic*, ch. 8.

[73] I have discussed this in 'Maimonides on Aristotle and Scientific Method', in *Moses Maimonides and his Time*, ed. E. L. Ormsby (Washington, DC, 1989), 53–88, and in 'Maimonides' Use of Aristotelian Dialectic', first given as a lecture in May 1985 at the Sixth Jerusalem Philosophical Encounter.

[74] See e.g. Averroes' Middle Commentary on the *Topics: Talkhīṣ Kitāb al-Jadal*, ed. Charles E. Butterworth and A. A. Haridi (Cairo, 1979); Butterworth, 'Averroes: Politics and Opinion', *American Political Science Review*, 66 (1971), 894–901; and his edition and translation of Averroes' *Three Short Commentaries on Aristotle's 'Topics', 'Rhetoric', and 'Poetics'* (Albany, 1977);. See also Avicenna, *Kitāb al-Shifā', al-Manṭiq, al-Jadal*, ed. I. Madkour (Cairo, 1965), 11–14.

and related questions.[75] The ultimate aim of philosophy, Alfarabi says, is supreme happiness, and the aim of dialectic is to enable a human being to attain the faculty to investigate its principles and objectives to prepare him mentally for philosophy. In sum, the aim of the art of dialectic is to serve the art of philosophy. Dialectic, then, Alfarabi says, is useful for philosophy; it is so in five ways:

1. It trains man and prepares his mind for the sciences by making him critical and objective. It is consequently impossible for man to attain philosophic truth save by the dialectical faculty.
2. It provides for the sciences their subject matter and their *quaesita*.
3. It provides the initial doubt, without which nothing can be perfectly apprehended. The setting up of contradictory statements is a necessary prerequisite for the demonstrative art, which ultimately removes initial doubt and perplexity (*ḥayra*). (*Nota bene.*)
4. Dialectic conveys accepted beliefs (*mashhūrat*, *endoxa*) to the masses, and in this way the philosopher participates with them and is protected, and his enterprise is not rejected; for the masses reject what is alien to them.
5. Only dialectic can deal with sophistry and protect philosophy from it.

A philosopher, says Alfarabi, may intend to teach the masses opinions that are true, certain, and demonstrative. But as the proofs of these statements are alien to them, he will then prefer to teach them these opinions by dialectic or rhetoric, and thereby disseminate among them necessary opinions (*ārā' ḍarūriyya*) that are beneficial to them.[76] He does this by means of political governance (*al-tadbīr al-madanī*).

The *Guide*, it may be said, is a book of political governance (just as the Torah is a book of political governance). The difference between a political book and a book of political governance is this: a book of political governance teaches true and correct opinions that are necessary for the sake of the happiness of the city, or nation, and its inhabitants; a political book merely contains laws that regulate the

[75] The following summary is based upon Alfarabi's paraphrase of Aristotle's *Topics* (*Al-Jadal*). I have used MS Hamidiye 512. The section appears on fos. 84*b* ff. In my opinion, this paraphrase is of crucial importance for understanding the purpose and character of the *Guide*. G. Vajda used this work to shed light on the quotation from Alfarabi in *Guide*, ii. 15, p. 292; see 'A Propos d'une citation non identifiée d'Al-Fārābī', *JA* 253 (1965), 43–50.

[76] Maimonides refers to opinions necessary for the sake of political welfare, such as the belief that God is angry with those who disobey him, in *Guide*, iii. 28.

social and political order. Maimonides uses political governance to impel human beings toward happiness, and this is done by teaching them the truths of the theoretical sciences according to their capacity, by means of arguments that are demonstrative, dialectical, or rhetorical. The nature of these forms of argumentation is discussed in chapter 8 of the *Treatise on the Art of Logic.* And the treatise as a whole, in particular chapter 14, which contains a classification of the sciences and Maimonides' 'statement on political science', is a stepping stone towards understanding the nature of the *Guide.*

5

Why Maimonides was not a Mutakallim

WARREN ZEV HARVEY

I

WHY was Maimonides not a *mutakallim*? At first blush, this question might seem downright simple-minded. Why was Napoleon not an Englishman? Why is a square not a triangle? Why is a horse not a camel?

Indeed, Maimonides took great pains to differentiate himself from the *mutakallimūn*, and to explain just what he had against them. Following Alfarabi, he distinguished sharply between philosophy and *kalām*. According to this distinction, a philosopher—like Alfarabi or Maimonides—is interested in the objective and open-minded pursuit of truth, while the *mutakallim* is interested in supporting religious beliefs. The *mutakallim*, Maimonides tells us, violates the rule of Themistius: instead of seeking to make his ideas conform to that which exists (*al-wujūd*), he seeks to make that which exists conform to his ideas. To put the matter simply: a philosopher seeks to subject his imagination to his intellect, while the *mutakallim* subjects his intellect to his imagination.[1] Maimonides quite plainly was a philosopher and not a *mutakallim*, for he was interested in the open-minded pursuit of truth, sought to make his ideas conform to what exists and not *vice versa*, and aimed to live by his intellect not his imagination.

Our question, therefore, might well seem simple-minded. None the less, some of the finest Maimonidean scholars have in recent years

[1] Maimonides, *Guide of the Perplexed*, trans. S. Pines (Chicago, 1963), i. 71, pp. 177–9; cf. i. 73, premiss 10, pp. 206–7. L. V. Berman has aptly remarked that the subject of pt. i of the *Guide* is 'the imagination and its perils', and that Maimonides' critique of the *Kalām* is thus to be seen as part of his treatment of this subject; L. V. Berman, 'The Structure of Maimonides' *Guide of the Perplexed*', *Proceedings of the Sixth World Congress of Jewish Studies 1973* (Jerusalem, 1977), 8–9. Regarding Alfarabi, see e.g. *Enumeration of the Sciences*, partial trans. F. M. Najjar, in *MPP* ed. R. Lerner and M. Mahdi (Glencoe, Ill., 1963), v. 27–30.

made certain statements suggesting that Maimonides was really a *mutakallim*.

The first statement I wish to mention is that of the late Professor Leo Strauss: 'the *Guide* . . . is not a philosophic book . . . but a Jewish book'.[2] Now, it is curious that this unfortunate statement should have been uttered by Strauss, whose brilliant studies have made it clear that the *Guide*, on its esoteric level, is in a fundamental way a work of political philosophy. However, to those accustomed to the esoteric manner in which Strauss wrote about what he understood to be Maimonides' esoteric doctrine, it is understandable why Strauss felt he had to make such a statement.[3] Strauss believed that Judaism and philosophy are irreconcilable, and he believed that this was also Maimonides' belief.[4] According to Strauss's esoteric interpretation of the *Guide*, Maimonides held a Jewish position in his exoteric teaching, but a philosophic position in his esoteric teaching. Strauss's simplistic statement that 'the *Guide* is not a philosophic book but a Jewish book' is evidently an example of Straussian misdirection, intended to mirror and to preserve what in his opinion was the original Maimonidean misdirection. What Strauss was esoterically implying is that the *Guide* is *exoterically* not a philosophic book but a Jewish book, although *esoterically* it is not a Jewish book but a philosophic book.[5] In stating

[2] Strauss, 'How to Begin to Study *The Guide of the Perplexed*', in Pines's trans. of *Guide*, p. xiv; cf. id., *Persecution and the Art of Writing* (Glencoe, Ill., 1952), 42–6.

[3] See Strauss, *Persecution*, 55–60. 'The position of Maimonides' interpreter is . . . to some extent identical with that of Maimonides himself. Both are confronted with a prohibition against explaining a secret teaching and with the necessity of explaining it. . . . Since the *Guide* contains an esoteric interpretation of an esoteric teaching, an adequate interpretation of the *Guide* would thus have to take the form of an esoteric interpretation of an esoteric interpretation of an esoteric teaching' (ibid. 56). Cf. my 'The Return of Maimonideanism', *Jewish Social Studies*, 42 (1980), 253–5, 265.

[4] Strauss 'How to Begin', p. xiv. His belief that Maimonides considered Judaism and philosophy irreconcilable is, in my judgement, the chief flaw in his generally perspicacious approach to the *Guide*.

[5] Typically Straussian is Strauss's argument by the process of elimination that the *Guide* is not a philosophic book. The *Guide*, he argues convincingly, is not mathematics, economics, ethics, physics, or metaphysics. What about political philosophy? 'There is practically complete agreement among the students of Maimonides that [the *Guide*] is not devoted to political science' (*Persecution*, 44). This statement is doubly suspicious! First, even *complete* agreement among students of Maimonides would not prove anything. Second, why *practically* complete? Which student of Maimonides is the exception, if not Strauss himself? That Strauss considered the *Guide* to be a work of political philosophy is evident from his *Philosophie und Gesetz* (Berlin, 1935), esp. 108–22, but it also may be gathered from several comments in his later writings: e.g. the subject of the *Guide* is 'the Torah or more precisely . . . the true science of the Torah' ('How to Begin', p. xiv; cf. *Persecution*, 41); 'the function of the Torah is emphatically

that the *Guide* is not a philosophic book but a Jewish book, Strauss was only trying to be morally decent towards Maimonides by observing his adjuration not to reveal publicly the secrets of the *Guide*.[6] Yet regardless of what Strauss's intentions were, the statement that 'the *Guide* is not a philosophic book but a Jewish book' seems to me to be true only to the extent that it is true to say that Plato's *Republic* is not a philosophic book but a Greek book, or Hobbes's *Leviathan* is not a philosophic book but a British book.

The second statement I wish to mention is also by Strauss: the *Guide* is 'an intelligent, or enlightened *Kalām*'.[7] 'The intention of the science of the *Kalām*', writes Strauss, 'is to defend the law, especially against the opinions of the philosophers.' The *Guide*, he reasons, is devoted to 'the true science of the law', which at least in part includes defending the law against the philosophers, for 'the central section of the *Guide* is . . . devoted to the defense of the principal root of the law, the belief in creation, against the contention of the philosophers that the visible world is eternal'. The *Guide* and the *Kalām*, Strauss concludes, share the same intention, and thus belong to 'the same genus'. Their specific difference, he explains, is in *method*: the *Kalām* is imaginative, 'mistaking imagination for intelligence', while the *Guide* is intelligent or enlightened, distinguishing fundamentally between intelligence and imagination. 'Maimonides insists on the necessity of starting from evident presuppositions, which are in accordance with the nature of things, while the *Kalām* . . . starts from arbitrary presuppositions, which are chosen not because they are true but because they make it easy to prove the beliefs taught by the law.'[8] After having thus described the *Guide* as 'an intelligent, or enlightened *Kalām*', Strauss suddenly remarks that his descriptions have been only 'tentative', that they are indeed 'useful . . . even indispensable, for the purpose of counteracting certain views', but that 'to arrive at a more definitive description of [the *Guide*], we have to make a fresh start'.[9] In other words, Strauss's description of the *Guide* as 'intelligent, or enlightened *Kalām*' was seen by him as serving a dialectical purpose,

political'; *What is Political Philosophy?* (Glencoe, Ill., 1959), 157; 'the governance . . . of Israel, i.e. the Torah, is a subject of political philosophy' (ibid. 160); 'the recovery of . . . what Maimonides called . . . political science or political philosophy is, to say the least, an indispensable condition for understanding his thought' (ibid. 168).

[6] *Persecution*, 55. Cf. *Guide*, i. Introd., p. 15. To the best of my knowledge, Strauss was the first scholar, medieval or modern, to opine that the very fact of the *Guide*'s being a philosophic book is part of its secret teaching.

[7] Strauss, *Persecution*, 41.

[8] Ibid. 38–41.

[9] Ibid. 41.

but not as being a definitive statement about the truth of the matter. Strauss presumably reasoned that just as Maimonides *exoterically* gave the impression of agreeing with the intention of the *Kalām* (e.g. regarding the belief in Creation), so the decent-minded historian of Maimonides should *exoterically* give the impression of classifying the *Guide* as some kind of a kalamic or super-kalamic work.

The two above mentioned exoteric statements of Strauss' have been restated and elaborated by no less than the foremost student of the *Guide* today, Shlomo Pines. That Pines could have taken Strauss's exoteric statements at their face value is remarkable, for in his magisterial study 'The Philosophic Sources of *The Guide of the Perplexed*' Pines portrayed Maimonides as a 'philosopher' and a 'philosopher-statesman',[10] and was careful to brand as 'ostensible' the view that Maimonides 'saw eye to eye' with the *mutakallimūn* on the question of the creation of the world.[11] Perhaps Pines is to be understood as meaning that the *Guide* is *ostensibly* a kalamic work, but *truly* a philosophic one. In any case, Pines has indeed written that the *Guide* is 'not a philosophic treatise',[12] and that 'according to the terms of Alfarabi's definition [accepted by Maimonides] . . . the *Guide* might be described as a *Kalām* work'.[13] Pines observes that Maimonides, like Alfarabi, 'states that the purpose of the *Kalām* is . . . to protect religion'. He observes further that to Maimonides' mind 'the doctrines of *Kalām* have no theoretical validity' in as much as 'directly or indirectly they were formulated with a view to the defense of religion, i.e., they had an ulterior, non-theoretical purpose'. Having thus duly reported Maimonides' description of the *Kalām*, he then remarks: 'In part at least this description also fits the *Guide of the Perplexed*' because 'the main purpose or one of the purposes for which the *Guide* was written was to persuade the philosophers or would-be philosophers to observe the religious law'. Pines's point is simple. The *Kalām* is defined by Alfarabi and Maimonides as apologetics for religion, but the *Guide* itself is a kind of apologetics for religion; therefore, 'the *Guide* might be described as a *Kalām* work'. Pines, however,

[10] In his trans. of *Guide*, p. cxxxiv.

[11] Ibid. pp. cxxiv–cxxv.

[12] Pines, 'Some Traits of Christian Theological Writing in Relation to Moslem *Kalām* and to Jewish Thought', *Proceedings of the Israel Academy of Sciences and Humanities*, 5 (1973), 106 n. 5. Pines writes there that 'Maimonides himself makes it clear that [the *Guide*] is not a philosophical treatise,' and refers us to *Guide*, ii. 2, p. 253 (a text cited by Strauss in *Persecution*, 44); but while that text may deny that the *Guide* is a work of physics or metaphysics, it does not deny that it is a work of political philosophy.

[13] Pines, 'Some Traits', 106.

immediately adds that according to Maimonides there is a difference between his brand of apologetics and that of the *mutakallimūn*. This difference, Pines explains, is that 'to Maimonides' mind the presuppositions of *Kalām* contradict the "nature of existence" (*ṭabīʿat al-wujūd*), while his own do not'.[14]

Pines, following the exoteric Strauss, thus argues that according to Maimonides' own definition the *Guide* is kalamic in that it is a defence of religion, and non-kalamic in that the defence is based on 'the nature of existence'. It seems to me, however, that to Maimonides' mind the question of whether or not presuppositions are based on 'the nature of existence' is not merely one among several points of dispute between the philosophers and the *mutakallimūn*, but it is *the essential point of dispute between them*. To argue on the basis of 'the nature of existence' is to argue objectively, scientifically, philosophically; to argue on any other basis is to argue tendentiously, unscientifically, unphilosophically. The difference between an argument based on the nature of what exists and an argument *not* based on the nature of what exists is the difference between an argument based on reason and one based on imagination. It is reason alone that knows what exists, while that which does not exist is simply imaginary.[15] If the thesis of the *Guide* is argued on the basis of the nature of what exists, then the *Guide* is not a kalamic but a philosophic book. If Maimonides' discussion of religion is based on the nature of what exists, then it is not *Kalām* but philosophy. Should we wish to determine whether the *Guide* is a kalamic or philosophic book, there is one question we must ask. Does Maimonides seek to make what exists conform to his ideas, or his ideas conform to what exists?

Pines has also raised some questions as to the historical accuracy of Alfarabi's and Maimonides' descriptions of the *Kalām*. On the basis of his analysis of a use of the word *mutakallimūn* in an eleventh-century historical work, Pines suggests that the early *mutakallimūn* were indeed 'political and religious propagandists, or missionaries'. He then argues that Alfarabi's critical statements about the *mutakallimūn* fairly reflect the early *Kalām*, but are not true with regard to the *Kalām* of Alfarabi's own day. Citing *mutakallimūn* like al-Jubbā'ī and his son Abū Hāshim,

[14] Ibid. 106–7. Cf. Strauss, *Persecution*, 40–1.

[15] *Guide*, i. 73, premiss 10, pp. 209–11. On reading these comments of mine, Pines reaffirmed his definition of *Kalām*. In addition, he remarked that he now casts doubt on whether Maimonides, when he wrote the *Guide*, still believed in the possibility of knowing 'the nature of existence'.

Pines argues that several *mutakallimūn* of Alfarabi's day 'appear to have had a very great interest in theory'.[16] Now, I do not doubt the historical fact that certain *mutakallimūn* of Alfarabi's or Maimonides' day were proficient in the theoretical sciences. My impression, however, is that the distinction drawn by Alfarabi and Maimonides between philosophy and *Kalām* was not primarily intended by them as historical, but rather as *conceptual*. It is a distinction between philosophy and tendentious argumentation. It is thus similar to the distinction between philosophy and sophism. To be sure, it is sometimes difficult to decide whether or not a given individual is a philosopher. It may not always be obvious that Socrates is a philosopher but Protagoras and Gorgias are sophists.[17] But what is clear, I think, is Maimonides' rule of thumb for distinguishing philosophy from *Kalām*. Is the argument based on the nature of what exists? Is it based on reason, or on some concoction of the imagination?

Strauss's exoteric statement that the *Guide* is not a philosophic book but a Jewish book has been accepted almost as a truism by Lawrence Berman.[18] Berman also has endorsed emphatically the view that the *Guide* is a kalamic work. 'In his *Guide of the Perplexed*', contends Berman, Maimonides 'appears as a theologian [= *mutakallim*] in the Alfarabian sense. . . . In his role as a theologian, Maimonides accepts the fundamental principles of a particular tradition, in this case Judaism, and uses *all means at his disposal* to defend the claim of religion to validity and, consequently, to authority.'[19] Now, a careful analysis of the arguments Berman brings to support this contention shows that he is really talking only about the exoteric level of the *Guide*, not the esoteric one. Berman, if I understand him correctly, believes that Maimonides is a philosopher who for political reasons expounded by Alfarabi has chosen to write a kalamic book. The *Guide*, as Berman would have it, is a dialectical—'one is tempted to say sophistical'—book, but it is a book by *a philosopher*, albeit a philosopher who is playing the role of a theologian. As philosopher, Maimonides sometimes esoterically addresses himself to fellow philosophers, as for example in his discussion of political *imitatio Dei* in the final chapter of

[16] Pines, 'A Note on an Early Meaning of the Term *Mutakallim*', *IOS* 1 (1971), 224–8.

[17] Cf. Strauss, *Persecution*, 42. Some years ago, I asked Pines whether Thomas Aquinas was a philosopher or a theologian (in the kalamic sense). After brief reflection, he replied: 'a theologian, because there are no loose ends'.

[18] See e.g. Berman, 'The Structure of Maimonides' *Guide*', 8, 10, 11.

[19] Id. 'Maimonides, the Disciple of Alfārābī', *IOS* 4 (1974), 163–4. Emphasis mine.

the *Guide*.[20] All this means that in Berman's view the *Guide* is kalamic (i.e. dialectical or sophistical) with regard to the vulgar reader, but philosophic with regard to the élite reader. If this is Berman's view (and, for that matter, if this is Pines's view), I have no quarrel with it.

The statements by Strauss, Pines, and Berman about the non-philosophic and kalamic (or partially kalamic) nature of the *Guide* have been cited approvingly by Joel Kraemer, who has then gone on to suggest that kalamic features are present also in Maimonides' *Mishneh Torah*. Kraemer writes: 'Indeed, wielding more sophisticated weapons, he [Maimonides] attempts to achieve the very aim of the theologians, namely, to defend religion by means of non-demonstrative arguments. . . . If we accept the thesis that the *Guide* is in a sense a *Kalām* work, it is plausible to suggest that the statement of the foundations of belief at the beginning of the *Mishneh Torah* also exhibits *Kalām* features.'[21]

The point on which I shall insist in my following remarks is that in both the *Mishneh Torah* and the *Guide*, Maimonides' true teachings are *not* kalamic. I say 'true teachings' because I recognize that some of his exoteric teachings in the *Guide* are indeed kalamic, and that some of his simplistic formulations in the *Mishneh Torah* might have been intended by him to seem kalamic to the non-philosophical reader. As far as his *true* teachings are concerned, however, both the *Guide* and the *Mishneh Torah* are free of *Kalām*, that is, they are not tendentious or sophistical.

II

Was Maimonides really interested in the objective, open-minded pursuit of truth, or was he at bottom interested in marshalling dialectical arguments for religious presuppositions? Was he a philosopher or a *mutakallim*?

Maimonides' position is stated clearly in *Guide*, ii. 23. In the course of his discussion of the touchy theological question of creation in time

[20] Ibid. 163–4, 169–71. Of Alfarabi, Berman writes: 'Alfarabi is looking at the *Kalām* from the perspective of philosophy; he himself is not a *Mutakallim*, although he could easily assume that role were it necessary' (160 n. 22). Berman, I think, would say that Maimonides, *qua* 'disciple of Alfarabi', also looked at the *Kalām* from the perspective of philosophy, but unlike Alfarabi he *did* assume the role of a *mutakallim*. I think Berman might also agree that Maimonides assumed this role only on the *exoteric* level of the *Guide*.

[21] Kraemer, 'Alfarabi's *Opinions of the Virtuous City* and Maimonides' *Foundations of the Law*', *Studia Orientalia Memoriae D. H. Baneth Dedicata* (Jerusalem, 1979), 108–10.

vs. eternity *a parte ante*, Maimonides turns to his reader and addresses him as follows: 'This comparison [between the doubts attaching to the opposing opinions] can be correctly made only by someone for whom the two opposing opinions are equal. But whoever prefers one of the two opinions because of his upbringing or for some advantage is blind to the truth [the correct opinion, *al-ṣawāb*].'[22] In other words, in examining a theoretical question, even a putatively sensitive one like that of creation in time *vs.* eternity *a parte ante*, one must strive for uncompromised objectivity; one must seek to free oneself of all preconceived opinions (e.g. notions about creation learned in religious school) and of all ulterior motives (e.g. the desire to defend one's religion). If, however, someone should examine the question of creation in time *vs.* eternity *a parte ante* with an eye to supporting creation in time, his tendentiousness will blind him to the truth. Now it is also a principle of Maimonides that only the truth (*al-ḥaqq*) pleases God, and only falsehood angers him.[23] It follows necessarily that the *mutakallim* who exerts himself to prove the creation of the world in time may imagine that he is serving God, but according to Maimonides he is in reality *angering God*! For Maimonides, therefore, the difference between the philosopher and the *mutakallim* is the difference between someone who pleases God and someone who angers him; and anger, Maimonides teaches us, is attributed to God only with regard to idolatry and unbelief (*kufr*).[24] Maimonides' critique of the *Kalām* is thus not only a philosophic critique, but also a *religious* one. The tendentiousness and sophistry of the *Kalām* are obnoxious to Maimonides' *religious* sensibility. Both as philosopher and as religionist, Maimonides rejected the *Kalām*. Surely Maimonides himself would say that he was *not* a *mutakallim* not only because he was a committed philosopher, but also—and no less—because he was a committed Jew.[25] All this coheres with Maimonides' view that the bond between man and God is *the intellect*.[26]

III

What, then, about Maimonides' own treatment of the problem of creation in time *vs.* eternity *a parte ante*? It is, after all, Maimonides'

[22] *Guide*, ii. 23 (trans. Pines, 321).
[23] Ibid. ii. 47, p. 409.
[24] Ibid. i. 36 and 54.
[25] See ibid. i. 71, pp. 175–7.
[26] Ibid. i. 1, p. 23; iii. 51, pp. 620–1; iii. 52, p. 62; cf. i. 68.

treatment of this problem which has been cited as the prime evidence for the *Guide*'s being a kalamic work. On the exoteric level, Maimonides of course argues in the *Guide* for the creation of the world in time, but it is not one of the deeper secrets of the *Guide* that Maimonides really prefers the Aristotelian notion of eternity *a parte ante* because it best conforms to *the nature of what exists*.[27] Moreover, Maimonides' position in the *Mishneh Torah* is the same as his position in the *Guide*. In both the *Mishneh Torah* and the *Guide*, knowledge of God's existence and unity is derived from knowledge of the first mover,[28] which knowledge is in turn derived from the eternal motion of the celestial sphere.[29]

Maimonides' own notion of creation is explained in *Guide*, i. 69, one of the most thoroughly philosophic chapters of the *Guide*. This chapter is exceptional in that the key word *al-bārī'* (= the Creator) appears in it four times.[30] Maimonides writes there:

> For the universe exists in virtue of the existence of *the Creator*, and the latter continuously endows it with permanence by virtue of the thing that is spoken of as overflow. . . . Accordingly if the nonexistence of *the Creator* were supposed, all that exists would likewise be nonexistent. . . . God has, therefore, with reference to the world, the status of a form with regard to a thing possessing a form, in virtue of which it is that which it is . . .
>
> Know, however, that in some people from among the *Mutakallimūn* engaged in speculation, ignorance, and presumption reached such a degree that finally they said that if the nonexistence of *the Creator* were assumed, the existence of the thing *the Creator* has brought into existence—they mean, the world—would not follow necessarily. . . . [But] as He, may He be exalted, is . . . the Form of the world . . . and as He continuously endows the latter with permanence and constant existence, it would be impossible that He who

[27] Cf. my 'A Third Approach to Maimonides' Cosmogony–Prophetology Puzzle', *HTR* 74 (1981), 287–301.

[28] Like Avicenna but unlike Averroes, Maimonides held that the first mover is not God, but created by him (*Guide* ii. 4, 258–9; *pace* Pines, 'The Philosophic Sources of the *Guide*', p. cxiv). According to the *Mishneh Torah*, the first mover = *ḥayyot ha-qodesh* (*Yesode ha-Torah*, ii. 7; iii 1).

[29] *Mishneh Torah*, *Yesode ha-Torah*, i. 5 and 7, '*Akum*, i. 3. *Guide*, ii, Introd. premiss 26; 2, p. 252. Cf. Strauss, 'Notes on Maimonides' Book of Knowledge', in *Studies in Mysticism and Religion Presented to G. G. Scholem* (Jerusalem, 1967), 263.

[30] On the key word word *al-bārī'*, see A. Nuriel, 'The Question of a Primordial or Created World in the Philosophy of Maimonides' (Heb.), *Tarbiz*, 33 (1964), 372–87 (to the 19 instances of *al-bārī'* cited by Nuriel, add *Guide*, i. 49, p. 109, and i. 68, p. 165); i. 69 is the only chapter in which this key word appears four times. There is no chapter in which it appears three times, but it appears twice in two chapters (i. 63; iii. 13). The appearance of *al-bārī'* four times in i. 69 is thus clearly meant to signal something to the attentive reader.

continuously endows with permanence should disappear and that that which is continuously endowed by Him and which has no permanence except in virtue of this endowment should remain.[31]

This Avicennizing passage is quite obviously an explication of the opening passage of the *Mishneh Torah*:

The foundation of foundations and the pillar of the sciences is to know that there is a First Existent, and He brings into existence every existing thing; and all the existing things of the heavens and the earth and what is between them do not exist except in virtue of the true reality of His existence. And if it should enter the mind that He is not existent, nothing could exist.[32]

The cryptic phrase 'He brings into existence every existing thing', which might have been construed by the reader in some kalamic sense, is unmistakably explicated in the *Guide* as univocally designating both the religious concept of *the Creator* and the philosophic concept of *the formal cause of the world*. As usual in Maimonides, the *Guide* helps us to understand the *Mishneh Torah*, and the *Mishneh Torah* helps us to understand the *Guide*. The teaching of both books is, after all, one teaching—and that teaching is *not* kalamic because Maimonides, a committed religionist and a committed philosopher, was *not* a *mutakallim*.

[31] See pp. 169–71.
[32] *Yesode ha-Torah*, i. 1–2.

6
Neoplatonic Currents in Maimonides' Thought

ALFRED L. IVRY

I

MAIMONIDES' relationship to Neoplatonic thought can be discerned through a comparison of his writings with those of his contemporaries in both the Islamic and Jewish world. This would include philosophers as well as theologians and mystics, both those who lived when and where Maimonides did, as well as those who preceded him, in Egypt and elsewhere, whose writings were current and influential in twelfth-century Egypt.

Some of this work has been charted by Shlomo Pines, most recently in an appendix to his monograph on 'Shīʿite Terms and Conceptions in Judah Halevi's *Kuzari*'.[1] Pines here draws our attention to the probable presence of some Ismāʿīlī influence on Maimonides' thought, though less than that found in Halevi. Maimonides' formulation of the doctrine of negative attributes (*Guide*, i. 59 and 60), in which the method of negation is viewed as a kind of affirmation, *ithbāt min ṭarīq al-nafy*, is located in the work of the Ismāʿīlī theologian Ḥamīd al-Dīn al-Kirmānī (died *c.*1021), *Rāḥat al-ʿAql*;[2] while Alfarabi, suspected of harbouring 'Ismāʿīlī proclivities', is apparently viewed as a possible conduit for Shīʿī influence upon Maimonides' political philosophy.

The limited number of these examples does not betoken a major influence of Ismāʿīlī doctrine upon Maimonides' thought, but does point the way to future research in this direction. As Pines says, Maimonides had 'ample opportunity' to become familiar with Ismāʿīlī theology, which was the official religion of Fāṭimid Egypt at the time of

[1] *JSAI* 2 (1980), 240–3.

[2] Ed. M. K. Hussein and M. M. Hilmy (Leiden, 1953), 51 f., as quoted by Pines, 'Shīʿite Terms', 242. The *Rāḥat al-ʿAql* is regarded by W. Ivanow as the 'most important' of al-Kirmānī's works, 'a compendium of Fatimid philosophy as it was in its prime'. (See the Foreword to Hussein and Hilmy's edn., p. xi.)

Maimonides' arrival there in 1165.[3] We may thus assume that the same sort of books which, directly or indirectly, influenced Halevi in distant Spain in the eleventh century were known to Maimonides in the heartland of Western Shīʿism in the twelfth century.

II

It would have been through these books of Shīʿī literature that Maimonides would also have been exposed to Neoplatonic literature. This dimension of Ismāʿīlī theology has been well illustrated by Pines in his monograph, and it surfaces in such themes as the emanation of universal substances and the hierarchical arrangement of all beings.[4]

Maimonides would have been familiar with these originally Neoplatonic ideas through other sources as well, and these more specifically 'philosophical', including in all probability the specific texts of Neoplatonism in their Arabic recensions. A close comparison of these texts with Maimonides' thought could do much to establish the relation between them. Therefore, I should like to take this opportunity to review some of the teachings of the major work of Neoplatonic thought, the *Enneads*, and compare them with some of the themes of Maimonides' philosophical *magnum opus*, the *Guide of the Perplexed*. The striking parallels that emerge offer persuasive evidence

[3] Pines, 'Shīʿite Terms', 240. Maimonides would have achieved familiarity with Islamic doctrines of both a theological and philosophical sort also through personal contact with the Islamic intelligentsia of his day. An example of such a meeting, in Cairo in 1191, is described by ʿAbd al-Laṭīf b. Yūsuf al-Baghdādī (*c.*1162–1231). Though this encounter took place probably after the *Guide* was finished, it represents the sort of exchange that Maimonides could have had earlier, during the formative period of composing the *Guide*. Al-Baghdādī has incorporated Neoplatonic excerpts in his own *Metaphysics* (cf. below, n. 5, pt. 3), and this is the type of literature with which Maimonides would have been familiar. For al-Baghdādī's perceptions of Maimonides and his work, see the report found in the *ʿUyūn al-Anbāʾ fī Ṭabaqāt al-Aṭibbāʾ* of Ibn abī Uṣaybiʿa, ed. A. Müller (Cairo, 1882), ii. 205, trans. S. de Sacy, *Relation de l'Égypte* (Paris, 1810), which has one interesting emendation of the manuscript tradition, presenting Maimonides' character in a more favourable light). See too the entry on al-Baghdādī by S. M. Stern, *Encyclopaedia of Islam*, 2nd edn. (Leiden, 1971), i. 74.

[4] Cf. Pines 'Shīʿite Terms', 177, 180 ff., also al-Kirmānī, *Rāḥat al-ʿAql*, ch. 4, pp. 77 ff. Among the more well known works cited by Pines which are either authored by Shīʿīs or report Shīʿī ideas are the late 10th cent. *Rasāʾil Ikhwān al-Ṣafāʾ* and the parallel text *Al-Risāla al-Jāmiʿa*, and the 12th cent. *Kitāb al-Milal wal-Niḥal* of al-Sharastānī. These are among the more popular works Maimonides may well be assumed to have read. The fact that he does not endorse books of this kind has led scholars to underestimate the degree of influence Neoplatonic thought in its various manifestations had on his philosophy.

that this text, originally in Greek, had considerable influence in its Arabic versions[5] upon Maimonides' thinking, directly as well as indirectly, and that it is a major source of Maimonides' philosophy.

How much of the *Enneads* Maimonides could have known directly, even if in paraphrastic form, is something we cannot yet say definitively. Though much of *Plotinus Arabus* has been identified, despite its Aristotelian or other cover, much more could have been current than is now extant. The 'Long Theology', or a version of it, may have been known to Maimonides, as well as what we have as the 'Theology of Aristotle'. It is advisable, therefore, to mention themes found throughout the *Enneads*, wherever they are relevant to Maimonides' writing. Thus it is worth investigating *Enneads*, i. 1–iv. 3. 17, despite the lack at present of an Arabic paraphrase or translation of this material.

III

There is much in this first half of the *Enneads* that strikes a chord audible to the reader familiar with Maimonidean writings, particularly as concerns Plotinus' remarks on causation, matter, and providence.

[5] Besides the *Theology of Aristotle* and the still unpublished, 'Long Theology'—concerning the importance of which cf. Pines, 'Shī'ite Terms', 245—the Arabic versions of the *Enneads* take a number of forms:

1. Collections attributed to a 'Greek Sage' (*Dicta Sapientis Graeci*) appear in the writings of al-Sijistānī and al-Sharastānī, as well as in two Oxford MSS of unknown authorship. F. Rosenthal edited the manuscripts that had not been published, and translated all the *Dicta*, with likely *Enneads* references, in a three-part monograph, 'Aš-Šayḫ al-Yūnānī and the Arabic Plotinus Source', *Orientalia*, 21 (1952), 461–92; 22 (1953), 370–400; 24 (1955), 42–66.

2. 'A Treatise on the Divine Science' (*Risāla fil-'Ilm al-Ilāhī, Epistola de Scientia Divina*), falsely attributed to Alfarabi, is actually a collection of *Enneads* passages. Two MSS are extant, the correct identification being first made by P. Krauss, 'Plotin chez les Arabes', *Bulletin de l'Institut d'Egypte*, 23 (1940–1), 281–9. Cf. too F. Rosenthal, 'From Arabic Books and Manuscripts V', *JAOS* 75 (1955), 19.

3. Chs. 21–4 from the *Metaphysics* of 'Abd al-Laṭīf b. Yūsuf al-Baghdādī, which quote and paraphrase the *Theology*. This work appears in the same Istanbul manuscript codex which contains the 'Treatise on the Divine Science'.

Most of the above material (in Arabic) was edited, together with the *Theology*, by 'A. Badawī, *Plotinus apud Arabes* (Cairo, 1955). Cf. too id., *La Transmission de la philosophie grecque au monde arabe* (Paris, 1968), 46–59, and see Krauss's evaluation, 'Plotin chez les Arabes', 263–95. G. Lewis, working from manuscripts, has presented the *Theology* and (1) and (2) above in English translation, correlating them with the Greek text. Cf. *Plotini Opera*, ii, ed. P. Henry and H-R. Schwyzer (Paris–Brussels, 1959), *passim*.

These themes are also touched upon in the extant Plotinian Arabic corpus, but they do not receive there the extensive treatment Plotinus gives them in the material not adapted. True, the concept of God as the first cause, for example, is mentioned already in the *Proœmium* to the *Theology*,[6] while the first few 'Sayings of the Greek Sage' describe God in the same terms.[7] The 'first agent' is said to be the final as well as formal and (remote) efficient cause of things. Though the significance of the concept of causation in connection with God is thus affirmed, the extant Arabic material does not go much beyond these basic statements.

It is in the unparaphrased first tractate of the third *Ennead* that we find causation discussed in broader terms than this. Plotinus is anxious there to establish a theory of causation which leaves room for individual responsibility. As such, he is not content with deterministic theories which describe all events as due to one kind of cause only, be it atomic materialism or divine agency of any rigorous sort. The atomic theory of causation is inadequate, in his view, to explain both the orderly nature of our world and the reality of differentiated human responses to material factors. This latter fact is testimony for Plotinus to a psychic reality which cannot be controlled or explained by physical factors only.[8] The complex nature of physical reality defies identification of a particular single cause or of a series of such causes external to a person as responsible totally for a given response.[9] The presentation of an all-pervading deterministic system is regarded as theoretically illogical, seen as entailing an all-encompassing unity of substance which is inconsistent with the supposedly separate reality of substances relating to each other as cause and effect.[10]

Plotinus is thus determined to defend our intuitive and common-sense experience of diversity and freedom here, within a causal matrix of events which he does not deny. A coalescence of external formal and material causes is accepted as determining much of what transpires, but not everything. The soul of the individual is identified as the

[6] Cf. Badawī, *Plotinus apud Arabes*, 6; and see the translation of Lewis, *Plotini Opera*, ii. 487.

[7] Cf. ibid. 185 (Lewis, 281). See too al-Baghdādī, *Metaphysics*, 200 ff.

[8] Cf. *Enn*. iii. 1. 3; Greek edn. of Henry and Schwyzer, *Plotini Opera*, i (1951); iii (1973); English translations by A. H. Armstrong, *Plotinus* (Cambridge, Mass., 1966, 1967); and see too S. MacKenna, *Plotinus: The Enneads*, 2nd edn. (London, 1956).

[9] *Enn*. iii. 1. 5.

[10] Ibid. iii. 1. 4. Plotinus makes a similar point in *Enn*. iii. 2. 9, in saying that Providence cannot be exhaustively all-inclusive, since then there would be no individual realities over which Providence could act, it being synonymous with all that is.

additional factor which is 'free', beyond the reach of cosmic cause; though not totally free, being part of the cosmic process.[11] The soul's sovereignty is a function of its asserting itself over its physical and material surroundings—and temptations, an assertion which the human soul is seen as free to make.

'Necessity' is described as the condition which obtains when the will is compromised by external circumstances and bows to them, acting as an 'unreflecting acceptance' of external stimuli.[12] When the soul is true to itself, however, to its own *logos* or principle of reason, then there is voluntary action. 'Fate' is seen as describing the effects of externally derived compulsion, while 'wisdom' that of self-expression.

Plotinus thus locates freedom from necessity in causal terms in the human soul, and presumably in its rational faculty. The addition of the human factor in the causal chain breaks what might be thought of otherwise as its predetermined nature. This predeterminism, the strongest possible sense of necessity, is however undermined also by Plotinus' conception of matter, as expressed particularly in the fourth treatise of the second *Ennead*. In *Enn.* ii. 4. 1 ff., Plotinus follows Aristotle in regarding matter as the base and recipient of forms, in itself formless and indeterminate. Going beyond Aristotle, Plotinus emphasizes this indeterminateness as the very essence of matter, its polar opposition to form. In itself, matter is viewed as a mass without magnitude, unextended yet with a 'primary aptness for extension'.[13]

True to his Platonic inspiration, Plotinus finds the archetype of this notion of matter in the heavens, in the idea of matter, considered as the undifferentiated basis which serves as the condition for differentiation. Uniform, intelligible matter is regarded as an ontological substrate in which the multiplicity and diversity of forms can 'reside'.[14] This intelligible matter thus 'houses' or 'embodies' the appearance of diversity and multiplicity, functioning as an idea like all others. Intelligible matter is thus to be found already in the Nous and Psyche of the world, though matter as such is usually considered as lower in

[11] Ibid. iii. 1. 8. Cf. *Enn.* iii. 3. 4 l. 6, in which man is described as 'no mere thing made to rigid plan; his nature contains a Principle apart and free' (following MacKenna, translating *ou gar monon ho pepoiētai estin, all'echei archēn allēn eleutheran.*

[12] Following MacKenna, *Enn.* iii. 1. 9. The soul's action in l. 7, *hoion typhlē tē phorā chrōmenē*, is rendered by Armstrong as that which 'drives on in a sort of blind rush'.

[13] Cf. *Enn.* ii. 4. 11. This view of essential matter, or rather 'first matter', as it was generally called, is widespread in the Middle Ages. Cf. H. Wolfson, *Crescas' Critique of Aristotle* (Cambridge, Mass., 1929), 582 ff.

[14] Cf. *Enn.* ii. 4.4. and 5.

the scale of values than all other 'formal', i.e. specific ideas.[15] This low estimation of matter, also a Platonic heritage, stands in marked contrast to its largely overlooked ontogenic primacy as described in the second *Ennead*. For there the entire process of emanation is viewed as the increasing emergence of the many from the One, and the basis for the differentiation of the many, and its first appearance, is ideal matter.[16] The estrangement from the One is thus facilitated by the existence of this principle of non-determination, the condition for the appearance of multiplicity, of distinct entities.

Matter is thus an entity for Plotinus, though indistinct in all but its intelligible mode, where it may be regarded as 'distinctly' indistinct. The passage from the celestial or intelligible to the corporeal realm may be viewed as one of increasing indeterminism for matter, to the degree that its status in the physical realm is regarded as bordering on that of the non-existent.[17] This corresponds to the increasingly tenuous existence of the forms as they are manifested in nature, appearing as they do here as ephemeral off-shoots of the World Soul. Yet these forms, for all their 'fallen' status, still represent Being and the Good, and 'below' them is the complete obliteration of distinct form, the absence or privation of form.[18] This is matter in its 'pure' state here, a state which never exists by itself, matter never existing without form, yet which always threatens existing forms with change and opposition.

Plotinus does not leave matter here with a totally negative image. It too has its 'redeeming' features, both in the service it renders form—providing the base for manifestations of the good to appear, however diluted—and in the necessity of its very presence. For privation and change are also part of that which exists necessarily in our sphere, even as evil is, and our sphere is still, for all its lowly status, part of an ultimately benevolent cosmic order.[19] Plotinus certainly does not

[15] Cf. e.g. *Enn*. v. 8. 7.

[16] See n. 14, above. The theory of intelligible matter here expressed, which affirms the presence and to some degree even primacy of matter in Intellect and Soul, is regarded by some scholars as not typical of Plotinus' view of matter. Cf. P. Merlan, *From Platonism to Neoplatonism* (Nijhoff, 1953), 115, as quoted by H. A. Armstrong, 'Spiritual or Intelligible Matter in Plotinus and St. Augustine', *Plotinian and Christian Studies* (London, 1979), 278. Cf., however, Armstrong's defence there of this view, within the dynamic of Plotinus' emanative system.

[17] Cf. *Enn*. ii. 4. 5; iii. 4. 1; 9. 3. See too J. Rist, 'Plotinus on Matter and Evil', *Phronesis*, 6 (1961), 155 ff.

[18] Cf. *Enn*. ii. 5. 4 f., and see i. 7. 2, 8. 5, 8. 10.

[19] Cf. Rist, 'Plotinus', 157, and see *Enn*. i. 8. 15; iii. 2. 3, 4, and 11. Cf. too *Enn*. v. 2. 1, rendered in the *Theology* as well; Badawī, *Plotinus*, 134 f., Lewis, *Plotini Opera*, 291 f.

celebrate the existence of matter or of evil and physical change, the physical world in general; but neither does he totally deny its reality. He accepts even this most base, fragile, and wayward element of being as part of the providential plan. Matter, thus, for all its features of non-existence and evil, is ultimately recognized as also participating in existence, and is thereby related to the good, even if primarily by opposition.[20]

Plotinus' acceptance of matter is not, then, an endorsement of it. It remains in his consciousness as an antithetical if complementary force to form and order. From the viewpoint of necessary causality, matter represents a further destabilizing agent, capable of reacting unpredictably to the causes which affect it. The very nature of matter should alert us to this, though Plotinus prefers to speak in terms of the 'destructive' and 'discordant' nature of corporeal beings.[21] Our physical realm of nature is seen as possessing inevitable conflict, with the beneficent influences of the heavens deflected.[22] Left to act without any hindrance, the celestial forms would endow our world with their effects necessarily. These effects, however, become tarnished and altered when encountering the matter of our world, with its recalcitrant nature.

All this prevents the 'original' plan of the celestial forces from being automatically realized, and it is only by subsuming that plan within a broader design, in which the very conflicted response of our world is affirmed as ultimately necessary and even positive to some degree, that Plotinus can rescue his notion of a cosmic providence. The generation and corruption of our world, its turmoil and change, are accordingly viewed as the most fitting and appropriate expression of its nature, complementing that which is eternal and unchanging, forming part of a cosmos which is in its totality most beautiful.[23] Causation is thus affirmed, though the idea of a predetermined specific necessary causation is in effect negated.

Man and matter thus provide the counter-forces to a strict determinism in Plotinus' scheme, man seen as capable of countering

[20] Cf. *Enn.* i. 8. 6; ii. 4. 13 and 16. At the end of the sayings attributed to the Greek Sage in the Oxford MS Or. Marsh 539, ed. and trans. F. Rosenthal (above, n. 5) in *Orientalia*, 22 (1953), 382 (and cf. Badawī, *Plotinus apud Arabes*, 194), evil is described as 'the good in the last things which have not attained anything from the First Good'.

[21] Cf. *Enn.* iii. 2. 2.

[22] Ibid. iii. 2. 4. Cf. too the MS referred to above, n. 20, as presented by Rosenthal in *Orientalia*, 21 (1952), 490 (Badawī, *Plotinus*, 189).

[23] Cf. *Enn.* iii. 2. 3.

external natural causes with actions based on his own reason and volition. Man is thus depicted as a free agent, or a potentially free agent, responsible in good part for his own actions and destiny.[24] The evil which is a natural part of our existence is avoidable to some extent, with man held responsible for his own misfortunes. The 'necessity' for evil here is seen as a general condition of being human, part of the nature of our physical selves, but a nature which the given individual can resist.[25] His life is not externally determined beyond the degree to which he is subject to the broad sweep of forces which surround him. Even where a person is caught up in forces beyond his control, when he is the innocent victim of natural or man-made evils, his fate is not regarded as predetermined.[26] The general outline of man's destiny is known in advance, even as the existence of evil in general may be taken for granted; but within this general perspective the individual can yet make the most of the good available to him, just as in the perspective of the universe as a whole, the good is dominant and ultimately victorious.

As is known, all the Arabic Plotinian material published to date derives from the fourth, fifth, and sixth *Enneads*. It thus deals with the emanative process at all levels of being, particularly in the celestial realm. The relation of the universal Intelligence and Soul to each other, to individual souls and to the 'One' is explored at some length, and in general the Arabic material may be seen as a good if abridged paraphrase of the Greek. Like its source, the Arabic material does not clarify issues which Plotinus left unanswered, as the question of whether our individual forms exist as such in the heavens, or whether the heavenly bodies perceive objects in our world as they are.[27]

A clear picture does emerge, however, of some of the more striking aspects of Plotinus' metaphysics—striking in themselves and for the

[24] Cf. *Enn.* iii. 2. 7 and 9. Al-Baghdādī says (*Metaphysics*, 226) that both man and animals are characterized by having will and choice (*al-irādah* and *al-ikhtiyār*).

[25] *Enn.* iii. 2. 10.

[26] The suffering of the righteous is, moreover, not regarded as an indictment of Providence, for Plotinus believes in a transmigration of souls in which this suffering is compensated and the good triumphs. Cf. *Enn.*, iii. 2. 13. Transmigration is also adduced by the Greek Sage as a punishment for wicked souls (Bodleian MS Ouseley 95, published by Rosenthal in *Orientalia*, 24 (1955), 45 (cf. above, n. 5).

[27] Regarding the existence of ideal archetypes of particular beings, cf. *Enn.* v. 7. 1–3 and v. 9. 10; and compare the latter with the *Epistola De Scientia Divina* (henceforth *Epistola*), ed. Badawī, 169 (trans. Lewis, 419). As for the celestial substances knowing terrestrial objects individually, cf. *Enn.* iv. 4. 1 (*Theology*, ed. Badawī, 32; Lewis, 67) and *Enn.* iv. 4. 9 with *Enn.* iv. 4. 25 f.

influence they had, in all probability, upon Maimonides' thought. Thus the Arabic Plotinian corpus emphasizes the unique nature of the One, regarded as the Creator and cause of all else.[28] Its transcendent nature makes all attribution meaningless,[29] though besides the designation of 'cause' and 'Creator' or 'Originator', the One is seen also as the 'Good',[30] with justice and righteousness singled out as rooted in its being.[31] The world in all its diversity is regarded as emanating from this First Cause, which for all its absolute unity is yet considered responsible, in some mysterious fashion, for all the forms which then appear.

Whether this responsibility is always direct or, as seems more likely, mostly indirect, is not completely clear in our sources,[32] an ambivalence which undermines a literal understanding of Plotinus' insistence that the One knows all that comes to be. This knowledge in any case is depicted as transcending all that we normally understand by that term. It is a creative activity as well as a cognitive one, for all that the One is prior also to thought and knowledge. The knowledge of the One is thus a knowing that is beyond knowledge of any discursive or reflective kind; it is an immediate, intuitive sort of comprehension–creation.[33]

Though ostensibly unique to the One, this non-analytic form of cognition, or a kindred sort, is found again at the hypostatic level of being, particularly at the stage of universal Intelligence, or Mind.[34] The unified nature of this first emanated being requires that it knows without discrete divisions in its being, 'without reasoning (*qiyās*) or

[28] Cf. e.g. the Procemium to the *Theology*, ed. Badawī, 7 (Lewis, 487), and 134 (Lewis, 291; *Enn.* v. 2. 1); *Dicta Sapientis Graeci* (henceforth *Dicta*), ed. Badawī, 186 (Lewis, 474; *Enn.* vi. 9. 6).

[29] Cf. *Dicta*, ibid. See too the *Dicta* found in the writings of al-Sijistānī and al-Sharastānī, as brought by Lewis, 481 (*Enn.* vi. 7. 32); *Epistola*, Badawī, 175 f. (Lewis, 323; *Enn.* v. 3. 13), Badawī, 178 (Lewis, 333; *Enn.* v. 4. 1). See too al-Baghdādī, *Metaphysics*, 202.

[30] The 'Pure One' (*al-wāḥid al-maḥḍ*, called by Lewis the 'Real One') is 'The True Pure Good', *al-khayr al-maḥḍ al-ḥaqq*, as expressed in the *Dicta* (above, n. 28); cf. too the *Epistola*, Badawī, 181 f. (Lewis, 355; *Enn.* v. 5. 10, 13).

[31] Cf. *Theology*, Badawī, 129 (Lewis, 285; *Enn.* v. 1. 11). The terms for justice and righteousness, or 'the good', *to dikaion* and *to kalon* in the Greek, are rendered as *al-'adl* and *al-ṣalāḥ*.

[32] Contrast *Theology*, Badawī, 134 (Lewis, 291; *Enn.* v. 2. 1) and ibid. 147 (Lewis, 453; *Enn.* vi. 7. 8), with ibid. 50 (Lewis, 205; *Enn.* iv. 7. 8) and *Dicta*, ed. Lewis, 281 (*Enn.* v. 1. 8).

[33] Cf. *Theology*, Badawī, 118 f. (Lewis, 407; *Enn.* v. 8. 12); *Epistola*, Badawī, 174 f. (Lewis, 321; *Enn.* v. 3. 12); *Dicta*, Rosenthal, *Orientalia*, 22 (see above, n. 5), 399 f., Lewis, p. 485; al-Baghdādī, *Metaphysics*, ed. Badawī, 227.

[34] Cf. *Epistola*, Badawī, 180 (Lewis, 345; *Enn.* v. 5. 2, 3).

proof (*burhān*)'. So too must Soul know Mind, even as must man, when he aspires to understand this highest of emanated beings.[35] It is only at the 'lower' stages of knowledge, concerning issues of a mundane and physical sort, that the analytic and discursive intellect is used, and that speech is required. The soul which has recourse to 'reason' and 'thought' is the soul still essentially involved with its body and with practical, corporeal concerns, for which it requires semantically intelligible expressions.[36]

Plotinus, then, posits a form of human knowledge similar to the divine which is greater than the discursive and rational, apprehending the truth of its object in an instantaneous and totally unified manner. This knowledge beyond knowledge is regarded as the acme of human achievement, and fulfils the natural longing in man's soul to return to the source of his intelligible being.[37] The human soul is thus understood as originating in and returning to the World Soul, even as the latter derives from Mind, and it from the One. Each 'lower' level of being is located in the 'higher', even as physical nature is rooted in the celestial sphere of the intelligible forms.[38] Though Plotinus would not accept it, one almost could extend his analogy and say with the medievals that the world as a whole is 'located' in God, in that he may be regarded as the 'place' of the world, its sustaining and maintaining force.[39]

The relation of God to the world is thus construed along non-spatial as well as non-temporal lines, in as it were a time beyond time,[40] a

[35] Cf. *Dicta*, Lewis, 37; and see Enn. iv. 3. 18; *Theology*, Badawī, 22 (Lewis, 225; *Enn.* iv. 8. 1).

[36] Cf. *Dicta*, loc. cit. in n. 35.

[37] Cf. *Epistola*, Badawī, 181 (Lewis, 355; *Enn.* v. 5. 10); *Theology*, Badawī, 102 (Lewis, 75; *Enn.* iv. 4. 5).

[38] Cf. *Theology*, Badawī, 42 (Lewis, 43; *Enn.* iv. 3. 20); *Epistola*, Badawī, 181 (Lewis, 353; *Enn.* v. 5. 9); and al-Baghdādī's *Metaphysics*, Badawī, 201 f.

[39] The utter transcendence of the One for Plotinus precludes his use of this metaphor; cf. *Epistola* extract mentioned in n. 38. Aquinas' use of this imagery in *Summa Theologiae*, i. 8. 1, 2 is mentioned by J. Deck, *Nature, Contemplation and the One* (Toronto, 1967), 78. Cf. too *Guide of the Perplexed*, i. 8; and see Efodi's comment in *Sefer Moreh Nevukhim*, ed. I. Goldman (Warsaw, 1892; repr. New York, 1946), 25*a* (Subsequent Heb. citations are to this edn.) Maimonides gives a similar exegesis to the term 'life' in i. 69, 90*a* and i. 72, 103*b* of the *Guide*. (Pagination following the Arabic, *Dalālat al-Ḥā'irīn*, ed. S. Munk, rev. I. Joel (Jerusalem, 1929).) References to this edition are to be found in the inner margins of S. Pines, *The Guide of the Perplexed* (Chicago, 1963).

[40] The One is beyond both finite and 'eternal' time, beyond the temporal (and spatial) dimensions of the physical and celestial spheres. Cf. e.g. the *Theology*, Badawī, 6 (Lewis, 487); Badawī, 29 f. (Lewis, 63; *Enn.* iv. 4.1); Badawī, 130 (Lewis, 287; *Enn.* v. 1. 11); al-Baghdādī, *Metaphysics*, Badawī, 225.

place beyond place; even as his knowledge of the world is, as we have remarked, a knowledge beyond knowledge. The emanation of the major hypostatic substances is intelligible to us, consequently, only in the dimmest of ways, and we must abandon our normal methods of knowing to apprehend it even somewhat. The mystery of God's being and of the world's origins and foundations remains essentially that in Neoplatonism—a mystery. Put another way, that which is known in this doctrine is 'known' most strangely.

Plotinus finds the strange nature of this divine kind of knowledge best expressed by the term 'ignorance', which is, as the *Theology* says, 'an ignorance more sublime than any cognition'.[41] This 'ignorance' is the ignorance of multiplicity, of discrete existence and all that it entails as we know it, knowledge of the sort which man is to attempt to flee already in this life.[42] It is the unity of knowledge and of being which attracts both the individual and universal soul, which yearn to unite and conjoin with their source.[43] The 'knowledge' had in this conjunction is unique, in that it is the epistemic equivalent of the ontic identification of knower and known, i.e. of subject and object, such that there is no longer any difference between them, and thus no distinguishing characteristic. The All in this manner approaches the One, even as it was originally within it, and known to it as such.

'Love', that is, intellectual love, is the term which Plotinus uses for this primary state of being.[44] This love is depicted as both a unifying force and as the very constituent of the intelligible world. That world is 'pure love', love supreme; whereas in our corporeal world it must compete with matter and its concomitants. Man's use of his capacity for intellectual love thus elevates him beyond the physical sphere, and unites him with the eternal spiritual forms. It is clear that this kind of love goes beyond that of the intellect only, though as 'intellectual' eternal love it does not dispense with intellect entirely. We have here a supposedly higher level of intelligence, non-discursive and bordering on the non-descriptive.

As in the first half of the *Enneads*, Plotinus similarly here acknowledges the presence of 'forces of variance and antagonism' in our world. The source of the antagonism of terrestial bodies is located

[41] Cf. *Theology*, Badawī 37: *dhālika al-jahl ashrafu min kull ma'rifa* (Lewis, 71 f., *Enn.* iv. 4. 4).

[42] Cf. *Enn.* iv. 3. 32, iv. 4. 1; *Theology*, Badawī, 29 (Lewis, 63).

[43] *Theology*, Badawī, 34 f. (Lewis, 69 f.; *Enn.* iv. 4. 2).

[44] Cf. *Theology*, Badawī, 99 (Lewis, 473): love, *philia*, is translated *maḥabba* (cf. *Enn.* vi. 7. 14).

in their irregular motions, that is, in the very variety and diversity of their activities.[45] These divisive forces, it is acknowledged, sometimes overpower the unifying force of love, a conflict which is presented as a fact of nature.[46] The more noble and ontically superior forces are thus bested by their inferiors here, which is again not seen as a basic contradiction in the system. Our world is presented as an arena of natural conflict, and this is not considered to be an indictment of the Good. For Plotinus, the proliferation of the many from the One and the corporealization of the intelligible makes diversity and conflict inevitable. Yet this does not indicate impotence in the One, for all is a natural outflowing of his being and will. The totality is, again, regarded as perfect and beautiful,[47] so that the antagonism and friction of bodies here is seen *sub species aeternitatis*, as part of the ideal whole.

In the extant Arabic material, we again find that God and the hypostases are not considered responsible for the evils which befall man, since their knowledge is generally not regarded as concerned with particular and discrete physical events. Physical nature thus has a real role to play in Plotinus' scheme, negative in the short run, positive in the long. Though the material is not perfectly consistent, the picture that emerges here is the familiar one of forces emanating upon the corporeal world and becoming altered in diverse and unpredictable ways both by the matter which receives the forms and by the reaction which a given person chooses to make.[48] The matter is responsible because of the natural limits upon it, in that it cannot fully reflect the nature of the forms it receives and thus alters them. Similarly, man's intellect is imperfect and thus at times misinformed. We do not all or always reach conjunction with the supernal intelligences, even as they do not affect an individual conjunction with us automatically. Indeed, they do not know us personally, and do not, on their own, determine our future.[49] Though Plotinus, or rather the 'Greek Sage', refers to nature as the realm of pure necessity and the intelligible world as inclining to that of freedom, it would seem neither description is fully adequate, and that indeed the opposite is closer to the truth.[50]

[45] Cf. *Dicta*, Badawī, 189 (Lewis, 476); and see above, n. 22.

[46] See n. 44 above.

[47] Cf. *Theology*, Badawī, 152 (Lewis, 459; *Enn.* vi. 7. 11); and see n. 44 above.

[48] Cf. *Dicta*, Lewis, 255 (*Enn.* iv. 9. 2); *Theology*, Badawī, 75 (Lewis, 135 f.; *Enn.* iv. 4. 39); Badawī, 131; Lewis, 287 (*Enn.* v. 1. 12).

[49] Cf. e.g. the strong remarks of Plotinus in *Enn.* iv. 4. 31, which express an attitude not contradicted by such passages as *Enn.* iv. 3. 24.

[50] Cf. *Dicta*, Lewis, 241 (*Enn.* iv. 8. 5). Complete freedom is there regarded as the property of an agent who sometimes acts and sometimes does not act. Cf., however, *Theology*, Badawī, 75 (Lewis, 135; *Enn.* iv. 4. 39).

IV

The Plotinian material highlighted in the above has hopefully convinced the reader of the *Guide* of its relevance to Maimonides' thought. That much of Maimonides' presentation depends ultimately on this source seems clear. Thus Maimonides' adoption of the mechanism of emanation is central to his explanation of the processes of creation and revelation, even as his adoption of the Plotinian view of the One as beyond attribution is crucial to his concept of God.[51] Maimonides' view of the relation between the upper and lower worlds, with the limited liability of the former for the latter, also indicates Plotinian influences. For both authors, God is not to be held responsible for an individual's specific fate, a product for both of the despised vagaries of matter and of man's own free will. Providence is similarly considered in general terms primarily, as part of the causal explanation of things.[52] The goal of man's existence is to achieve, in equal measure, a level of apprehension which sees the divine unity in all things, and an identification with it.

Each of these themes is presented discreetly in the *Guide*, and requires an elaboration which I have essayed elsewhere.[53] Some of this is well known, and has given rise to the label of 'Neoplatonized Aristotelianism' as a description of Maimonides' philosophy. This mixture of doctrines is generally taken as a harmonious synthesis of originally competing views, obscuring the fundamental differences in both approaches. Though Maimonides' God is strictly neither Plotinian or Aristotelian, he is closer to Plotinus than to Aristotle in that he is the knowing source of all that is, and not just a self-knower and cause of the movement of the outermost sphere. He actually resembles the Plotinian World Mind more than the absolutely transcendent One, in that he is said to possess all forms, though as a unity. Yet Maimonides' view of God has much in common with that of

[51] Regarding emanation, cf. esp. *Guide*, i. 58, 69, and ii. 12. In the first part of the *Guide*, in particular, Maimonides is determined to deny any meaningful direct predication of the deity; and see *Guide*, i. 51 ff.

[52] For providence, cf. *Guide*, iii. 17–21; and see the appendix for my readings of key passages which highlight Maimonides' position as being of an impersonal kind. Cf. too Maimonides' remarks emphasizing man's freedom and real choice, *Guide*, iii. 20, 51; and his comments on matter, *Guide*, iii. 8, 9, 16.

[53] See my 'Providence, Divine Omniscience and Possibility: The Case of Maimonides', in T. Rudavsky (ed.), *Divine Omniscience and Omnipotence in Medieval Philosophy* (Dordrecht–Boston, 1985), 143–59.

Plotinus. For both, the deity is a One beyond all knowing, every essential description of which regarded as equal to every other, all standing ultimately for the concept of a Being from whom all else derives. Much of the *Guide* is an exercise in negating the appropriateness of attributions *per se* to the deity, since predication of any sort other than tautologous is considered as introducing plurality into the divine unity.[54] While the variations on this approach of negating attributes may well have reached Maimonides from some contemporary source, such as al-Kirmānī,[55] the basic approach is Plotinian, and would have been familiar to Maimonides from the Arabic Plotinian corpus. Moreover, Plotinus' inconsistency in choosing certain terms as appropriate for God, notwithstanding the strictures against attribution, would also have served Maimonides well as a precedent. Maimonides is fully aware that these terms are not meant to be taken literally, that they are either indirect and rather convoluted ways of almost saying something intelligible about God's essence,[56] or they are terms which are used in completely *sui generis* ways, and thus are essentially incomprehensible to us. It is in this latter category that Maimonides uses terms like Divine Will, Wisdom, and Goodness.

Maimonides is very explicit about the correct use of 'will' as a divine attribute, when used of God in an essential sense.[57] He discusses this apropos of advancing arguments for the possibility of creation from nothing in ii. 18 of the *Guide*. The Divine Will, it emerges, is one for which there is no real parallel or model, however much Maimonides tries to find analogies in the will and activities of the intelligences of the spheres, and particularly in the Active Intellect. Only the Divine Will is totally uncaused, with no real constraints or necessary relationships. This will does not act essentially for the sake of something else, it does not essentially respond to anything, it does not want anything—God

[54] See n. 51; also 29. Cf. also *Enn*. vi. 7. 17; vi. 7. 38; vi. 8. 8, 8. 10, 8. 11, and 8. 20; and see Deck, *Nature, Contemplation, and the One*, 11; Armstrong, 'Negative Theology', 176–89; and H. Wolfson, 'Maimonides on Negative Attributes', in I. Twersky and G. H. Williams (eds.), *Studies in the History of Philosophy and Religion* (Cambridge, Mass., 1977), ii. 195–230.

[55] Cf. n. 2; see too al-Baghdādī's *Metaphysics*, Badawī, 218: 'The Creator, Praised be He, is apprehended only by denying that to which an indication [i.e. assertion] refers, and by negating that which is negated by the indication' (*wa-lā yudraku subḥānuhū ilā bi-nafy mā yaqa'u 'alayhi al-ishāra wa-salbi ma suliba 'anhu al-ishāra*).

[56] Such even are the attributes of action and the 'negative' attributes, for which cf. *Guide*, i. 58.

[57] Cf. the equivocal uses of 'will' in the *Guide*, as discussed by A. Nuriel, 'The Divine Will in the *Moreh Nevukhim*' (Heb.), *Tarbiẓ*, 39 (1969), 39–61.

not wanting for anything. Where it does act 'for the sake' of the world, it does so out of its own internal motivation, desiring innately that optimal existence prevail in all species. The will of God is thus totally free, it would seem, to act and not to act, or as Maimonides says, 'to will and not to will'.[58]

This view of the Divine Will is strikingly like the concept of Divine Freedom which Plotinus, or rather the Greek Sage, has described, as given in one of his statements concerning individual souls and their relation to nature on the one hand and to the celestial sphere on the other.[59] 'When the soul is intellectual, it performs its function necessarily and freely, or freely and necessarily; it cannot perform a function that is purely necessary, because that belongs to the realm of nature, nor a function that is free, because that is proper to the agent who sometimes acts and sometimes does not act.'

This, however, is not as clear a demarcation between freedom and necessity as may at first appear, for as the text continues, 'And this is not complete freedom of action, because the completely free agent does not exist unless his action exists; indeed, his existence is the same as the existence of his action. This is the complete freedom of action, which resembles necessity in its functioning, without belonging to the realm of necessity.'

In this cryptic manner, the arabicized Plotinus expresses the complete identification of the being of the 'completely free agent', that is, God, with his action. It is only as an active being that the deity really exists. He is never without action of one sort or another, never not fully actual. Indeed, he cannot but be fully actualized, given his perfection. It is thus that the action of the One is an essential condition of his being, and is in fact identical with it. To act, for the One, is to be. This dynamic core of being serves as the basis for all other, specific actions. These latter are expressions, in whatever state of realization or non-realization they are found, of the basic presence of an active and fully self-realized One. That is, both the action and the non-action of a specific act are the results of an active agent. He is free, as his wisdom dictates, to act or not to act in a specific way in a given 'moment'; but he has to act one way or the other, his being demands action, it is action.

[58] See my 'Maimonides on Possibility', in J. Reinharz *et al.* (eds.), *Mystics, Philosophers and Politicians* (Durham, 1982), 81 f.

[59] Cf. *Dicta*, i. 84 (Lewis, 241).

It is in this sense that 'the complete freedom of action . . . resembles necessity'; on the other hand, it does not 'belong' to the realm of necessity, as Plotinus says, presumably because there is no external constraint on the divine action, which performs rather of its own volition. The action of the One is thus its very essence, 'free' and yet 'resembling necessity'.

For Maimonides, the will of God is similarly free, constrained by nothing but itself, with which it is identical. The deity does not, therefore, exist without its will functioning. This functioning, however, having no external constraints, can be in either of two ways, or rather, as Maimonides says, in both ways, willing and not willing. 'To will and not to will' is one and the same activity for God, and does not express any essential change in his being. What appears as a change of will is not that, not only because, as Maimonides says, the model of change invoked does not apply; but also not that because the very essence of the Divine Will is change, in the most comprehensive sense of the term, that which represents energy and action *per se.*

The 'change' which we perceive in God's will is nevertheless real in so far as it affects our world, the radically changed status of which Maimonides feels justified in calling 'creation'. Following the Plotinian model hitherto adduced, we should say that for Maimonides this creation is one expression of the total Divine Will, a partial manifestation of that eternally dynamic activity which both 'creates' and does not create, which encompasses both together in a mode of being foreign to our experience.

Maimonides says that God created the world after, as it were, not creating it,[60] that is, He acted first in one way, and then in another, though both are expressions of the same action, called 'will'. However, the forms of the world may be said to have subsisted from all eternity in God's mind, and at one point they became involved with matter in the way we recognize. Before that, though, the forms subsisted in themselves, as thought by God eternally. This change in their physical

[60] Cf. *Guide*, ii. 13. More exactly, Maimonides says that 'God brought everything [in the world] into existence after absolute pure privation (*allāhu awjadahū ba'da al-'adam al-maḥḍ al-muṭlaq*)'. This privation, however pure, is not synonymous with absolute non-being, in my opinion. Taking it as such has led most critics who wish to see Maimonides as a consistent philosopher to doubt his ostensible endorsement of this view as his true position. Cf. W. Z. Harvey's summary of recent attempts to analyse Maimonides' view of Creation, 'A Third Approach to Maimonides' Cosmogony–Prophetology Puzzle', *HTR* 74/3 (1981), 287–301.

status, which does not affect their essential natures, is called 'creation'.[61]

This picture is complicated by Maimonides' assertion that God's action does not change and that he has no new knowledge.[62] From this we must infer that he has from all eternity related to the forms in what appears to us as contrary modes. He has, as it were, always created and not created the world, there is no before and after sequence in his knowledge, even as there is no separate mode of being in which one form is distinguished from another. His knowledge is unitary; 'He knows with one single knowledge the many and numerous things.'[63] There are, then, 'many and numerous things' known to God, but known in a unique way. His knowledge encompasses all that may possibly exist, and encompasses all the possible forms of a given existence, such that whatever possibility comes into actual existence was already known to God. He knows the forms of everything, then, in all their possible multiplicity, 'before' they come into existence in a specific manner.

This description of God's action, will, and knowledge makes sense only on the Neoplatonic model of a multi-tiered ontology, at the top level of which, the World Mind, subsist as a unity all the forms which subsequently become individualized. This individualization of forms can be detected on the second level of being, that of World Soul, though the forms are found there as pure ideas, divorced from space and time. It is only at the 'lowest' level of being, that of Nature, that time and place become completely specific and linked to the physical. For Neoplatonic thought, this is only one level of being.

With this Plotinian conceptualization in mind, we can appreciate the fact that Maimonides' created world is an act of the creative will at that 'level' of the divine action in which discrete actions can be identified and distinct entities take shape. On the Plotinian scale, this would be between the level of World Soul and Nature. Maimonides, however, eschewing the Plotinian hypostatic model, has God's will acting on all levels of being 'indiscriminately', without formalized gradations of being. This cannot erase the impression, however, of a primary and unified state of real being, and of a derivative and partial state of existing 'natural' beings. The former state resembles more the realm

[61] My interpretation of Maimonides' view of matter, privation and creation is given in 'Maimonides on Creation', in D. Novak and N. Samuelson (eds.), *Creation and the End of Days* (Lanham, 1986), 185–213.

[62] Cf. *Guide*, i. 60, p. 76*a*; iii. 20.

[63] Ibid. iii. 20, p. 41*a*.

of necessity, the latter that of freedom. That is, it is necessary that the One relate to that which it eternally knows, but it does not relate only in one particular way. The One is free, as it were, to act or not to act upon its knowledge, causing certain ideas to be realized on earth at certain times and not at others. In relation to the physical universe, therefore, God is free to act and not to act, to create and not to create.

The 'true' freedom, however, is necessity, or resembles necessity, as the Greek Sage has said. The reason for this is twofold. Firstly, because the One relates to being most fully and purely in the realm of necessarily subsisting forms, that realm in which it is 'free' to be itself alone, the totality and unity of these forms; and secondly, because the freedom of the One to will or not to will a certain form into physical existence is determined by the nature of God's goodness, which necessarily wants that whatever may exist will exist. This, because physical existence, however problematic, is regarded as a virtue, a further manifestation of God's benevolent presence.[64]

The One, however, relates only indirectly to the realm of time and place, since his knowledge and actions are eternal. That which occurs here is thus removed from him and mediated through other eternal forces, specifically the intelligences of the spheres, and particularly the Active Intellect.[65] The individual occurrences of particular forms within a physical frame thus stem from God originally, but they are known to him only in a general way, as members of a given species. His responsibility for what occurs here is, accordingly, indirect and remote.

God's freedom for Maimonides is thus in one sense very circumscribed, and may best be expressed in the relation he has to possible forms. These forms exist as possibilities, that is they subsist, in God's mind, and as real beings there. God 'thinks' them into existence from 'subsistence' at some point, after having always only thought them before that.[66] In this new stage, God moves them along from the purely celestial and formal to the terrestial and material plane. These possible beings are possible because God has caused them to be such.[67] Their possible existence is not thus a function purely of logical possibility, but of God's willingness to create certain beings. This divine will is controlled by, or is an expression of, God's

[64] Cf. *Guide*, iii. 10, p. 17*a*.

[65] Ibid. ii. 4, p. 14*a*; ii. 12, p. 25*b*.

[66] Cf. *Guide*, i. 60, p. 76*a*; iii. 20.

[67] Cf. *Guide*, ii. Introd., Principle 19, and ii. 1, p. 9*a* (articulated in terms of the actualization of potential being). Saying that possible beings are caused does not exclude the intrinsically possible nature of these forms, or the fact that they become necessary once acted upon by God.

goodness, so that he wills only the best of possibilities, others do not even exist before him. God does not weigh diverse possibilities to choose the best. He thinks, a priori, only the best, as determined by his wisdom.[68] This wisdom, and goodness, determine that all possible beings will be realized eventually on earth, that all will 'exist', sooner or later.

Ideal beings cannot subsist without eventually existing, for in Maimonides' eyes such a restricted sphere of being is imperfect, running counter to God's will. It is a mystery to us why God should want it thus. His unity and purity of presence is not particularly strengthened by the process of emanation and existence–creation. It is here that the notion of Divine Grace, *ḥesed*, may play a role in Maimonides' thought, in addition to Will and Wisdom. Alternatively, one may also conceive of emanation from the perspective of final causality, the existence here of possible beings representing the fulfilment of their purpose, as willed by God.

In positing a value to earthly existence, Maimonides would seem to be expressing an Aristotelian bias. Yet the Plotinian world view also saw the realm of nature as a necessary stage in the unfolding of being, the point from which the return to conjunction with the forms begins. This conjunction aims at more than an understanding of the forms, it aims beyond them to conjunction with the giver of the forms himself, or to a stage as near that as can be attained.

Knowledge of the One is itself quite impossible for man, since the One contains beings in a mode totally beyond our temporal–spatial experience. Indeed, the One itself, as a union of the many in which the multiplicity is totally absorbed by the unity, is totally unrecognizable. That which we may know of the One is beyond our descriptive powers to explain. Our knowledge thus appears incoherent, a form of ignorance. Following in the footsteps of Plotinus and others, Maimonides in effect says that our ignorance of God is a form of knowledge,[69] beyond knowledge as it is normally understood. For while knowledge is of the discrete and the discernible, 'ignorance' is of the unified and the indiscernible. This kind of knowledgeable ignorance is also called 'devotion' and 'love',[70] terms which, for all their affective colouration, also entail intellection, but intellection of a special kind, that which goes beyond cognition as it is normally

[68] Ibid. iii. 25, p. 56*a*.

[69] Cf. above, p. 125 and notes there; and see *Guide*, i. 59.

[70] Ibid. iii. 51, p. 124*b*. 'Devotion' is *'ibāda/'avodah*, 'love' *mahabba/ahavah*.

understood, and which identifies with its object as a lover does with his beloved.

It is this kind of knowledge to which Maimonides refers in the closing chapters of the *Guide*, this kind of insight which alone can clarify for the initiated the necessary relation between the theoretical and the practical spheres. Awareness of the interrelation of all seemingly separate events and objects gives the illuminant an apprehension of the validity of particular actions and commandments, elevates them above the merely utilitarian, and places them within the context of perfection and beauty. The divine commandments and religious law are revealed to this person in their fullest dimension, as necessary expressions of God's loving-kindness, judgement, and righteousness.[71] The claims for the superiority and absolute validity of Mosaic law which Maimonides has made previously are validated only now,[72] with the apprehension of their necessary connections in the metaphysical realm. These connections work a metamorphosis upon the specific and practical actions prescribed, and reveal their essential connection to the universal and theoretical realm of being, a realm which is ultimately 'part' of the divine. It is thus that 'assimilation' to God's ways, to his actions, is the highest form of conjunction with the divine, for it is an identification with the totality of being, through an endorsement of the seemingly particular.

The necessity of the relation between the particular and the universal is not, as we have noted, one which can be explained in conventional analytic terms. Appreciation of it is granted only to the person who goes beyond the normal modes of cognition, one who 'sees' the essential unity in the apparent diversity, the necessary in the seeming unnecessary. This person 'knows' directly, without requiring speech or the constructs of the imagination to formulate his thoughts. Indeed, the individual events and objects to which speech and the imagination are tied, as too the senses, are but impediments to the true devotee's intellect. It soars beyond such discrete 'facts' towards an understanding of their essential nature, which is their participation in the unity of being, their being part of the One.

For Maimonides, it is Moses who had this experience in its most complete form, he alone whom God addressed 'face to face', directly, without the intermediary and impediment of imagination or that speech which reflects the activity of our sensory and imaginative

[71] Rendered as *ḥesed, mishpaṭ*, and *ẓedakah*, respectively. Cf. *Guide*, iii. 53, 54.
[72] Ibid. ii. 39.

faculties. The discrete concepts which form the basis of language were not required for Moses, who comprehended God fully, beyond such partial—and hence misleading—expressions.

This interpretation of Maimonides' view of Mosaic prophecy follows from Maimonides' detailed exposition of it in both his *Commentary on the Mishnah* and in the *Mishneh Torah*,[73] to which he refers in the *Guide*, ii. 35. The very term 'prophet', Maimonides there says, refers to Moses and other prophets amphibolously, that is, it is applicable only in non-essential ways. The giving of the Torah in the form we have it must be reckoned as foremost among these 'accidental' features of Mosaic prophecy. This, because the Torah as we have it is an imaginative, narrative work, full of parables and 'riddles', in anthropomorphic language which constantly requires interpretation. As such, the Torah is a standard, if archetypical, example of prophecy, not at all unique in form or style. As such, though, it does not support Maimonides' claims for it, it is not the unique document which Mosaic prophecy should be. The conclusion to which we are forced is that Maimonides believes the Torah as we have it is the result of Moses' religious imagination, his interpretation of the purely intellectual experience which he underwent but could not describe in its own terms, it being indescribable in the 'language of man'.[74] It is this indescribable experience, however, which directs Moses' imagination to choose that discourse which is most appropriate and 'true' to it. The discourse in itself cannot do more than persuade one of its efficacy; the appropriateness of its symbols and the utility of its laws are matters for which no decisive proofs can be offered. The 'proof' for the veracity of Scripture and for Mosaic prophecy lies outside of the text and tale as told.[75]

Part of the paradoxical nature of Mosaic prophecy as understood by Maimonides is evident in his treatment of the Gathering at Mt. Sinai, the very centerpiece of biblical revelation. In *Guide*, ii. 33, Maimonides

[73] Cf. the *Commentary on the Mishnah*, *Sanhedrin* x (*Pereq Ḥeleq*), Seventh Principle of Faith; *Mishneh Torah*, *Yesode ha-Torah*, vii. 6.

[74] Cf. also K. Bland, 'Moses and the Law According to Maimonides', in Reinharz *et al.*, *Mystics, Philosophers and Politicians*, 61 f.; see too A. Reines, 'Maimonides' Concept of Mosaic Prophecy', *HUCA* 40–1 (1969–70), 388 ff. As the reader may well infer, I do not, however, concur in Reines's remarks (340 n. 47) concerning Maimonides' relationship towards his predecessors.

[75] The limitations of normative philosophical proofs in Maimonides' assertions are discussed in my 'Revelation, Reason and Authority in Maimonides' Guide of the Perplexed', in N. Samuelson (ed.), *Studies in Jewish Philosophy* (Lanham, 1987), 326–42.

offers various interpretations of the divine Voice which was heard at that time, and distinguishes it from the words supposedly uttered by that Voice. The people as a whole hear the Voice, and understand it either not at all or just partially. It is only Moses who fully understands the Voice, and he alone who is able to decipher it in terms of words and letters, intelligible and communicable language. Moses, in other words, is the only one to whom the 'meaning' of revelation is entirely clear, both in its most exalted and transcendent moment, and in its 'commonplace' expression and adaptation.

It would appear that the Voice heard at Sinai is not exceptional for Maimonides, when and as it is broken down into ordinary speech. The first two commandments as we have them are considered demonstrable, 'knowable by human speculation alone', while the remaining commandments are considered conventional and traditional opinions.[76] As such, though, the last eight commandments would certainly have been known to the Israelites as much if not more than the first two commandments, which require some philosophical sophistication. The Ten Commandments in their present form thus add nothing new to human knowledge, and are in themselves no guarantee of divine authorship. It is the revelation itself, the mysterious phenomenon of a Voice which is 'seen' (Exod. 20: 15), which supplies this authority. It is this which justifies belief in the sacred nature of otherwise conventional and rational propositions. These propositions are rooted in a reality which is beyond language and normal comprehension in itself, a reality which is barely apprehended by most people, and which must be interpreted radically to be understood at all.

The radical nature of this linguistic and phenomenological transformation is brought home to the reader of the *Guide* with the realization that none of the interpretations of the Gathering at Mt. Sinai which Maimonides has offered is free of imaginative (and thus deceptive) language. That is, none of the interpretations Maimonides offers escapes the 'language of man', and thus none expresses the truth fully. This is evident from Maimonides' summary statement concerning biblical anthropomorphisms in *Guide*, i. 46, in which speech as well as actions are understood to be imaginative representations of the emanative process, not literally speech or action.

[76] The logical status of these utterances is discussed by Maimonides in ch. 8 of his *Treatise on Logic*. Cf. I. Efros's trans. (New York, 1938), 47 and *passim*, supplemented by the complete Judaeo-Arabic edition, 'Maimonides' Arabic Treatise on Logic', *PAAJR* 34 (1966), 21 ff.

Thus, God does not speak, as he does not see or hear, in the literal, actual sense of the term, having neither voice, eyes, nor ears. There was, then, no Voice at Sinai, and no words issued from God's mouth to Moses' ears. Much of Maimonides' distinction between the Divine Voice and words thus threatens to collapse, with the realization that neither occurred as described.

Maimonides has anticipated this, and declares in *Guide*, i. 46 that all prophetic visions of the Divine are really of forms created by God. The events described in prophecy thus have an objective correlate, though not the one first supposed. Accordingly, says Maimonides at *Guide*, ii. 33, the voice of the Lord heard at Sinai was really a 'created voice', with all the effects previously described. This interpretation would seem to save the 'objectivity' of the event itself, as well as of Maimonides' interpretation of it, but for his insistence that Moses' prophecy was from God himself, unmediated by any other form or substance. The created forms in which miracles appear, if taken literally, are just the sort of imaginative construct, however 'real', which Moses, on Maimonides' own reading, did not require. Belief in a 'created voice' at Sinai thus reduces Moses' prophecy to that of other prophets, his perceptions differing from theirs in degree but not in kind.

Maimonides' interpretation of the revelation at Sinai thus has multiple layers of meaning, the truth hiding behind various levels of reality. As in classical Neoplatonic thought, diverse phenomena give way to substances that are more comprehensive, though less understood, and these in turn point to higher realities and to the One who is above all else and responsible for it. The literal as well as the interpretative symbols used are all of only partial efficacy, and we are left without any real understanding of how God communicated his will to man.

The overriding purpose of these biblical representations, Maimonides says in i. 46, is to establish belief in God's essence, that of a living being who is both aware of itself and of others, and who is ultimately responsible for all others. This responsibility is seen as executed through the process of emanation, as we have said, and it is here too that the Neoplatonic element is dominant, albeit in principle more than in detail. The essential truth of the Gathering at Sinai is that God exists and that his will is emanated upon the world in the forms we recognize. It is Moses' skill to translate these universal insights into particular commandments and to present them in a figurative and symbolic manner. For Maimonides, Moses can only point the way towards that ultimate experience of standing in the presence of the Divine, called more prosaically 'conjunction' or 'knowledge' of God. Mosaic language thus reveals something of the unity of divine being, even while concealing it. The concealing is necessary, an inevitable result of the use of the 'language of man'. The enlightened philosopher can, however, decode this language, as Maimonides does throughout the *Guide*, and get a glimpse of that reality which Moses fully experienced. That glimpse is something which only the person experiencing it can appreciate; it cannot be communicated to another in normal language without again betraying its insight.

The philosophy Maimonides is advocating is something which he knows could not be 'proved' logically.[77] It is not built upon discrete premisses and conclusions which follow necessarily from them, and it does not refer to a physical reality with which we are familiar normally, one to which we can point and which we can dissect. It is in this respect the very opposite of that physical world to which Maimonides as a scientist-physician and philosopher was attracted. It is no wonder that he was uncomfortable with endorsing this world view, and that he refers to it as sparingly as possible. Yet it is this Neoplatonic background which serves as the ultimate prop in his defences against both the *mutakallimūn* and the philosophers, that is, the Aristotelians.

The notion of a realm of being totally beyond that familiar to us, of ideas which exist there in ways incomprehensible to us, as part of a divine unity, from which our world derives through a process of selective emanation, can alone save Maimonides 'philosophically' in his advocacy of the doctrine of creation, will, providence, and knowledge. It also provides the only philosophical justification for his specific claims on behalf of Mosaic prophecy and Jewish law. The irony is that the 'philosophical' aspect of these doctrines is one which is rational only in terms of philosophical Realism, and not at all in those epistemological and 'empirical' terms to which Maimonides was most attracted. It is not the least of the paradoxes of the *Guide*, therefore, that Maimonides' underlying philosophical base is one he was loath to acknowledge. Or should we say that this is one of the better-kept secrets of the *Guide*, the adoption of Neoplatonic doctrines and perspectives while arguing for and against Aristotelian positions. Could it not be that in this secretive dissembling of his that Maimonides is reflecting in part the widespread practice, in important

[77] See n. 75.

matters of faith, of Shīʿī Islam? For this and other reasons adduced at the beginning of this article, the composition of the *Guide* in Egypt is probably of more than accidental significance.

APPENDIX

The following translations of key passages pertaining to Maimonides' treatment of Divine Providence and Omniscience are offered as tenable alternatives to existing translations, identified as follows:

P S. Pines, *The Guide of the Perplexed* (Chicago, 1963).
M S. Munk, *Le Guide des égarés* (Paris, 1860 repr. 1959), iii.
F M. Friedländer, *The Guide for the Perplexed*, 2nd edn. (New York, 1904, Dover reprint).

The Arabic original on which my translation is based is found in S. Munk, *Dalālat al-Ḥā'irīn* (*DH*), rev. edn. (Jerusalem, 1929). The medieval Hebrew translation of Samuel b. Tibbon (*T*) was also consulted: *S. Moreh Nevukhim*, ed. I. Goldman (Warsaw, 1892, repr. 1946).

The passages below represent an apparent affirmation of individual providence, in the literal sense of the term. That this is not necessarily so may be deduced both from the discreet language of the texts, and from Maimonides' entire discussion of the topic. A full analysis is found in my 'Divine Omniscience and Possibility' (see n. 53).

iii. 17; *DH* 340. 15. (cf. *P* 471, *M* 129, *F* 286, *T* 25^{v}.)

I believe that divine providence refers to individuals of the human species only in this lower, sublunar world. All the circumstances of individuals of this species only, and the good and evil which occurs to them, follow that which is deserved.[78]

Guide, iii. 17. *DH* 340. 27 (*P* 472, *F* 287, *M* 130, *T* 25^{v})

The species with which that intellectual emanation is conjoined . . . is the one which divine providence accompanies, and all of its actions [those of the species, i.e. of its members] are evaluated by way of reward and punishment . . .[79] It is not, in our opinion, by chance that those people entered that boat, and that others sat in the house [the roof of which collapsed], but it occurred by divine

[78] *DH*: *tābiʿ l-istiḥqāq*. *T*: *nimshakh aḥar ha-din*, literally, 'follow the law', conveying the more stringent aspect of *al-istiḥqāq*, which can be translated also as 'that which is necessary'.

[79] *DH*: *Wa-quddirat afʿāluhu kulluhā*. *P* reads the verb with others, in the active voice, 'divine providence, which appraises all its actions from the point of view of reward and punishment'.

will, in accordance with that which is deserved in his judgements,[80] the canon of which our intellects cannot comprehend.

Guide, iii. 20. *DH* 347. 24 (*P* 480, *M* 147, *T* 29)

Similarly, we say that he has known, and known perpetually, all these newly produced things before they were generated. In no way, therefore, is his knowledge newly acquired. For in knowing that someone is now non-existent, that he will be brought into existence at some time,[81] and remain in existence for some such duration, then becoming non-existent, then, whenever[82] that individual like him of whom there had been previous knowledge[83] comes into existence, there will be no additional knowledge nor shall anything new have occurred that was not known to him. On the contrary, something occurred which was always known as going to occur in the way it exists.[84]

Guide, iii. 20. *DH* 349. 16 (*P* 483, *M* 152 *F* 294 *T* 30ᵛ)

Fifthly, [God's knowledge differs from ours] in accordance with the view of the law, in that his knowledge—may He be exalted—will not save one of the two possibilities,[85] even though He successfully knows the end result of one of them.[86]

Guide, iii. 21. *DH* 351. 3 (*P* 485 *M* 157)

These things follow his prior knowledge, which establishes them as they are: either as a separate existence [i.e. an intelligence of a sphere], or as an individual existence having a permanent matter [i.e. the sphere], or as an existence having a matter that undergoes individual changes, following[87] an order that neither decomposes nor changes.

[80] *DH: Bi-ḥasbi al-istiḥqāq fī aḥkāmihi. P*: 'in accordance with the deserts of those people as determined in His judgements'.

[81] *DH*: *fulān . . . al-waqt al-fulānī. P*: 'a certain man . . . a certain time'. *M*: *tel . . . telle époque.*

[82] *DH*: *idhan. P*: 'when', M: *lorsque.*

[83] *DH*: *wujida dhālika al-shakhṣ kamā taqaddama al-'ilmu bihi. P*: 'that individual comes into existence as He had known beforehand'.

[84] *DH*: *sa-yuḥdithu 'alā mā wujida 'alayhi. P*: 'would be produced in the way it came into existence'.

[85] *DH*: *la yukhalliṣu 'ilmuhu. T*: *la tevarer yedi'ato. M*: *la prescience divine n'opte pas pour l'un des deux cas possibles. P*: 'God's knowledge . . . does not bring about the actualization of one of the two possibilities.'

[86] *DH*: *wa-in kāna qad 'alima ta'ālā māla aḥadahumā 'alā al-taḥṣīl. P*: 'knows perfectly how one of them will come about'.

[87] *DH*: *tābi' li-niẓām. P*: 'but follows'. *M*: *mais qui (dans leur ensemble) suivent.*

7

Maimonides' Quest beyond Philosophy and Prophecy

ITHAMAR GRUENWALD*

I

It has occasionally been noticed that certain elements in the writings of Maimonides may be interpreted as testifying to the presence of a mystical thread artfully woven into the philosophical texture of his writings.[1] It is particularly in Maimonides' version of the (Alfarabian) theory of the elevation of the human, passive intellect to a state of utmost closeness to, or even unification with, the celestial Active Intellect that some resemblance to a mystical experience can be discerned. We shall see below what this 'unification' with the Active Intellect actually entails, and whether this state can justifiably be called

* I wish to express my gratitude to Joel Kraemer, Michael Schwarz, and Isadore Twersky for reading earlier versions of this paper. Its quality owes much to their erudition, critical observation, and attentiveness; its shortcomings, however, rest on my shoulders only.

[1] See A. Altmann, 'Das Verhältnis Maimunis zur jüdischen Mystik', *MGWJ* 30 (1936), 305–30; Eng. trans. in A. Jospe (ed.), *Studies in Jewish Thought* (Detroit, 1981), 200–19. J. Guttmann, however, is more hesitant in his assessment of Maimonides' affiliation to Jewish mysticism. In *Philosophies of Judaism* (New York, 1964), 156, Guttmann realizes the inner problems in the mystical aspects of Maimonides' metaphysics. However, in his discussion of the religious motifs in Maimonides' philosophy, Guttmann admits that there are indeed mystical points of thinking and expression in Maimonides. See J. Guttmann, *Religion and Knowledge* (Heb.), (Jerusalem, 1955), 90. See further, I. Efros, 'Some Aspects of Yehudah Halevi's Mysticism', in *PAAJR* 11 (1941), 27–41, which discusses some general aspects of the relationship between mysticism and philosophy in medieval Islamic and Jewish Philosophy. The attempt made by I. Weinstock, *Studies in Jewish Philosophy and Mysticism* (Heb.), (Jerusalem, 1969), 107 ff., to read mystical elements, and particularly kabbalistic notions, into Maimonides' philosophy, has been rightly rejected by A. Goldreich in *Kiryat Sefer*, 47 (1972), 206–9. See also the valuable article by J. Sermoneta, 'Yehuda and Immanuel Haromi: Rationalism Culminating in Mystic Faith', in M. Hallamish and M. Schwarcz (eds.), *Revelation, Faith, Reason* (Heb.), (Ramat Gan, 1976), 54 ff.

'mystical'. Some scholars have gone so far as to seriously consider the possibility that Maimonides actually had a prophetic experience of mystical quality.[2] Although it appears rather doubtful that Maimonides would actually have claimed prophetic inspiration for himself—since he argued that the hardships suffered by the Jewish people in exile deprived them of the positive mood that psychologically preconditions prophetic inspiration[3]—there remains the likelihood that Maimonides followed the path that was believed to take the true philosopher to the above-mentioned (mystical or quasi-mystical) unification with the Active Intellect.[4]

There are good reasons for believing that Maimonides was familiar with some of the mystical writings of the *merkavah* mystics, which (among other things) state clearly that the technique which led to heavenly ascent and related experiences had proved efficacious even in the diaspora.[5] In any event, it is noteworthy that Maimonides refers to the philosophical deliberations of metaphysics by the term *ma'aseh merkavah*, which in rabbinic circles signified mystical speculation.[6]

To my mind, the fact that Maimonides understands the term *ma'aseh merkavah* to mean the highest branch of philosophic speculation is more telling than is sometimes understood. It indicates that Maimonides saw in metaphysics an intellectual activity that was shared not only by the best philosophers of the Greek and Islamic traditions, but also by many of the Jewish prophets and by some of the Sages of the Mishnah and Talmud as well. Thus, cross-references could be drawn between the spiritual contents of philosophy and prophecy. The question that must be posed, however, is whether the relationship between philosophy and prophecy is symmetrical, or whether one of these two modes of cognition is prior to the other. More interesting even, from this point

[2] See e.g. the discussion of A. Heschel, 'Did Maimonides Believe that He Was Worthy of Propehcy' (Heb.), in *Louis Ginzberg Jubilee Volume* (New York, 1946), 159–88. See also sources cited in n. 16 below.

[3] See Maimonides, *The Guide of the Perplexed*, ii. 32. English quotations are from S. Pines's translation (Chicago, 1963).

[4] This kind of mystical unity with the Active Intellect is aptly referred to by P. Merlan, *Monopsychism, Mysticism, Metaconsciousness*, 2nd edn. (The Hague, 1969), 2, 17–25, as 'mysticism of reason' or 'rationalistic mysticism'.

[5] For a discussion of the relevant passages in the Hekhalot literature see I. Gruenwald, *Apocalyptic and Merkavah Mysticism* (Leiden–Cologne, 1980), 172, 189. For Maimonides' acquaintance with the changing attitude towards the mystical lore of the *merkavah* tradition (including the *shi'ur qomah*), see S. Lieberman's comments in G. Scholem, *Jewish Gnosticism, Merkabah Mysticism and Talmudic Tradition*, 2nd edn. (New York, 1965), 124.

[6] See M. Maimonides, *Mishneh Torah, Yesode ha-Torah*, ii. 11–12; iv. 13.

of view, is the question of whether Maimonides considered the issue of the relationship between philosophy and prophecy to be a trap best avoided, and that he consequently attempted to find a way beyond these two modes of cognition. It is to this last possibility that we shall address ourselves.

I have referred above to the notion that the human mind may achieve a state of perfection, whereby it is conceived as being, so to speak, united with the Active Intellect. The state of unification between the human intellect and the Active Intellect was known by a variety of Arabic and Latin terms.[7] It is rewarding to follow Maimonides' view of the process by which that union is effected. Essentially, Maimonides presents it in three complementary stages:

1. Any act of true prophetic and philosophic intellection is brought about with the active help and participation of the divine overflow (*Guide*, ii. 12, 37).

2. The highest stage of intellection is achieved when the human mind is transformed and reaches a status identical to the principal qualities of the Active Intellect, that is, when the cognizing subject, the cognized object, and the means of cognition are no longer separate (i. 68).

3. Once that state of perfect intellection is achieved by the human mind, the divine overflow reaches out to it so as to create a bond or unity, the duration of which is dependent upon the human intellect. In one's lifetime that bond is only temporary, since the needs of the body distract the mind from enjoying a permanent state of union, while in its posthumous condition the mind is likely to enjoy that union permanently (iii. 51, 52).

Whenever that union or bond occurs, it signifies the highest intellectual achievement the human mind may desire. Although Maimonides does not explicitly say so, this union may be viewed as typical of a mystical bond. And if we bear in mind that Maimonides conceives the ideal achievement of a human being to be the knowledge of God as an act of love, and that he calls the most advanced branch of philosophy *ma'aseh merkavah* (that is, the doctrine of the divine chariot as perceived in a mystical experience that usually entailed a heavenly ascension), then it is possible to see in that union of the divine and human elements an experience that embodies the

[7] See Merlan, *Monopsychism*, 18–19, 28–9.

neo-Platonic (or neo-Aristotelian) concept of the soul's ascent to its celestial origin.[8]

We must nevertheless be careful not to view Maimonides' conception of a unification between the passive human intellect with the divine Active intellect as a mystical experience in the full sense of the term. The Active Intellect, the qualities of which are shared by the passive intellect in its highest stage of achievement, is not identical with God; it is only an intermediary being, a major 'angelic' agent through which God operates in the lower forms of existence and in which this unification is accomplished.[9] The Active Intellect functions mainly as one of the channels through which the divine overflow, emanating like a spring of water from God, is distributed in the lower worlds. Yet, it is noteworthy that this unification between the human and divine intellects is occasionally referred to by Maimonides in eschatological terms. Maimonides understands the Hebrew term *ha-'olam ha-ba'*, that is, the World to Come, as implying that state in which the cognizing subject, the cognized object, and the means of cognition become one. In other words, the Hebrew term signifies that state in which the human, acquired intellect becomes like the Active Intellect.[10] Yet, it should once again be noted that Maimonides does not, *expressis verbis*, incorporate into his writings the notions found in Alfarabi, Ibn Bājja, and Ibn Rushd concerning a complete unity (*ittiḥād* or *ittiṣāl*). The word used by Maimonides in this connection is *waṣla* (iii. 51, 52), which literally means 'bond', and is so translated by Pines.

In any event, Maimonides views the concept of *'olam ha-ba'* as designating a qualitative, not a temporal (posthumous) state of intellectual existence. In fact, one may reach the status of *'olam ha-ba'* in one's lifetime! While in life that status is interrupted by daily activities and by the attention given to the needs of the body, after one's death the state may become permanent. In the Messianic days, however, the conditions of life will hopefully be so favourable that many people will be given the opportunity to share in this state, whereas during the present time of Exile only a very limited number of people, if anyone at all, enjoy that blessed condition. This is

[8] See A. Altmann, 'The Ladder of Ascension', in *Studies in Mysticism and Religion Presented to G. G. Scholem* (Jerusalem, 1967), 1 ff. For a close analysis of this Neoplatonic concept, see Merlan, *Monopsychism*, 1 ff.

[9] See further H. A. Davidson, 'Alfarabi and Avicenna on the Active Intellect', *Viator*, 3 (1972), 109–78.

[10] See Maimonides *Commentary on the Mishnah*, *Pereq Ḥeleq*, Introd. In some respects this idea is based upon Aristotle, *Metaphysics*, bk. viii.

Maimonides' central contribution to our understanding of the term, as expounded in his Introduction to *Pereq Ḥeleq*.

The picture that one gains here can also be viewed from a different angle. The absolute transcendence of God, which is so relentlessly stressed in all Maimonides' writings, is somehow mitigated by the concept of the divine overflow acting through the agency of the Active Intellect. God is conceived as acting upon the intellects of selected and gifted persons, prophets, and philosophers by means of this divine overflow. So also does divine providence operate. This is the quintessence of Maimonides' religious philosophy, or the point at which the contours between religion and philosophy fade away. What we encounter here is the watershed between two conflicting attitudes. On the one hand, there is the idea of God's absolute and incomprehensible transcendence, according to which he is beyond the direct and positive cognition of man. On the other hand, we have the idea of the divine overflow which emanates from God through the Active Intellect and which under certain, though rare, conditions reaches out to man, who in turn finds in it a stimulant and means of being elevated to that selfsame Active Intellect. We may see the Active Intellect as the meeting place of the emanating divine overflow with the human intellect. Thus, the rigid type of transcendentalism as professed by Maimonides is to some extent successfully mitigated or circumvented.

If this observation is correct, then we may here locate the point at which occurs a significant break with the uncompromising type of philosophic rationalism that is so often attributed to Maimonides. In fact, only thanks to that break can Maimonides be considered at all a religious philosopher. Since absolute transcendentalism is, at best, synonymous with deism, it does not leave much room for a personal type of religion. Yet, it should be noticed that the position which the Active Intellect occupies in Maimonides' philosophy verges precariously close to the doctrine of intermediaries. If what a man can conceive of God is restricted to the Active Intellect, it clearly serves as a substitute or, at most, as an intermediary. Thus, the notion that man's intellectual and religious goal is achieved in a state resembling a unification with that Intellect is equivalent to the idea of a union with a divine hypostasis. If this is really so, then what we encounter in this doctrine is a rather disturbing parallel to mystical Christology.[11] Maimonides was certainly not aware of this.

[11] For the mystical aspects of (Pauline) Christology see A. Schweitzer, *The Mysticism of Paul the Apostle* (London, 1956).

However, of greater concern in this context is the fact that two apparently conflicting strains of thought may be perceived in Maimonides. As we have seen, rational transcendentalism characterizes Maimonides' doctrine of God along with a theory of the divine overflow. Although we may consider this divine overflow to be a process of automatic, natural emanation, Maimonides believed that God was able to prevent this overflow from adventing to people who have prophetic aspirations.[12] Maimonides' philosophy thus permits the coexistence of two conflicting elements: transcendentalism along with divine emanationalism. This is not the only case in which Maimonides appears to maintain a self-contradictory position. In his Introduction to the *Guide* he lists several types of seemingly self-contradictory statements that authors (e.g. Maimonides himself) deliberately introduce into their works.[13] He even tries to account for this procedure by giving methodological and pedagogical reasons. Yet the problem seems to be far more complex, and is not restricted to apparently self-contradictory statements and arguments. What concerns us here are those problems involving contradictions between whole lines of thought in Maimonides' writings that cannot be resolved by mere harmonization. We shall presently discuss at some length such a case. Unless these self-contradictions are logically resolved, Maimonides' philosophical integrity may be called into question. Great minds, however, do not always satisfy the expectations of the critical scholar. One may find in their writings points at which one direction that has been followed consistently is somehow abruptly abandoned for the sake of a completely new, sometimes even opposite, direction.

The multiplicity of directions does not necessarily indicate philosophical dereliction. It may rather indicate a rich, impressive landscape. Although we may not ignore Maimonides' forewarnings in his Introduction to the *Guide* concerning the presence of deliberate, subtle self-contradictions, and although systematic thinkers generally strive to avoid ambiguities, it is nevertheless true that a great mind is bound to surmount its own paradoxical, even polarized, attitudes.

One need not be an expert to discern the systole and diastole of Maimonides' philosophical rhythm. Although a decision is highly desirable as to where Maimonides' allegiance lies, it is nevertheless not a simple task. When the alternative presented by Maimonides is

[12] See A. Altmann, 'Maimonides and Thomas Aquinas: Natural or Divine Prophecy?' *AJS Review*, 3 (1978), esp. 8.

[13] See L. Strauss, *Persecution and the Art of Writing* (Glencoe, Ill., 1952).

between two possibilities, a scholar may find his job comparatively easy—whether he subscribes to an esoteric reading of Maimonides or not. However, there are cases (and I shall immediately turn to one such example) in which Maimonides appears to contradict himself on more than one plane. In this event, the task put before the scholar is much more complicated, and there seems to be no convenient way out of the confusion.

In point of fact, more than a few of Maimonides' 'self-contradictions' may be more adequately conceived in terms of an interplay between a multiplicity of dialectical attitudes. At stake in these cases are not either–or alternatives, but complex philosophic attitudes characterized by their internal and multilayered logical difficulties.[14]

Maimonides' theory of prophecy may, in my view, be regarded as the coping-stone of his entire philosophic enterprise. Yet it constitutes a typical example of the cohabitation and interplay of a multiplicity of dialectical attitudes. In fact, prophecy is only one of the wheels that sets Maimonides' philosophy in motion. Its partner is the doctrine of temporal creation,[15] and both wheels are connected by an axis that hinges on the notion of miracles. Discovering that Maimonides contradicts himself at certain points in his doctrine of prophecy soon leads to the realization that he does so on a number of levels. So it is by no means simple to discern what his true intention was in each of the controversial issues involved in his discussion of the subject. In such a case, I believe, unveiling the allegedly esoteric layer of Maimonides' thought can hardly save us from ambiguities or render better service than timid harmonizations. Admittedly, if we take the statements which Maimonides makes in the Introduction to the *Guide* at their face value, then we must look for one kind of truth, which has to be discovered by a scrupulous reading of the rather controversial series of utterances. However, it is readily evident to the unbiased student that matters are not always as clearly and unambiguously delineated as one may wish. Loose ends and question marks characterize the outcome of some of the central philosophical deliberations in the *Guide*, and attempts at levelling down the difficulties prove tantalizing.

[14] For a similar position, taken however with regard to Maimonides' concept of prayer, see M. M. Fox in G. H. Cohen (ed.), *Ha-Tefillah ha-Yehudit* (Jerusalem, 1978), 142–67.

[15] For phrasing of the doctrine with emphasis on the concept 'in time', see H. Davidson, 'Maimonides' Secret Position on Creation', in I. Twersky (ed.), *Studies in Medieval Jewish History and Literature* (Cambridge, Mass., 1979), 16–40.

II

Maimonides' theory of prophecy is in all likelihood the most dramatic phase of his entire philosophic activity. It is the platform upon which the great dispute between philosophy and the Law—the latter being the most positive product of prophecy—takes place. Maimonides' theory of prophecy includes not only a discussion of the nature of prophecy as such, but also a thorough analysis of prophecy as a mode of cognition equal in its intellectual efficacy to that of philosophy. In other words, the entire drama of Maimonides' intellectual enterprise unfolds in his discussion of prophecy. It is also the point at which Maimonides comes closest to defining his own spiritual identity.[16] Maimonides considers philosophy and prophecy as means of attaining the highest truth, which is in his own terms the 'acquisition of the rational virtues . . . which teach true opinions concerning the divine things'.[17] Although philosophy and prophecy appear, on the surface, to be two rival modes of cognition, Maimonides makes great efforts to expose the philosophic dimensions of the latter. Thus, in the last chapter of the *Guide*, Maimonides clearly phrases the ultimate goal of man in terms that equally apply to philosophy and to prophecy:

> The prophets too have explained to us and interpreted to us the self-same notions—just as philosophers have interpreted them—clearly stating to us that neither the perfection of possession nor the perfection of health nor the perfection of moral habits is the perfection of which one should be proud or that one should desire; the perfection of which one should be proud and that one should desire is knowledge of Him, may He be exalted, which is the true science.[18]

In his book on the halakhic and philosophic aspects of Maimonides' thought, Twersky repeatedly stresses what he so aptly calls 'the Archimedean point of Maimonideanism'.[19] Twersky points out that

[16] Some of the scholarly works which have been consulted on the Maimonidean theory of prophecy are: F. Rahman, *Prophecy in Islam* (London, 1958); A. J. Reines, *Maimonides and Abrabanel on Prophecy (Cincinnati, 1970);* id., *'Maimonides' Concept of Mosaic Prophecy', HUCA* 40–1 (1969–70), 325–61; J. Levinger, 'The Prophecy of Moses according to Maimonides' (Heb.), *Papers of the Fourth World Congress of Jewish Studies* (Jerusalem, 1968), ii. 335–9.

[17] *Guide*, iii. 54, p. 635. Cf. also iii. 27, pp. 510–12.

[18] Ibid. iii. 54, p. 636.

[19] I. Twersky, *Introduction to the Code of Maimonides* (New Haven, 1980), 358.

Maimonides was 'constantly aware of the abiding need to demonstrate with great deliberation and emphasis the inseparability and complementarity of the two apparently discordant but harmonious disciplines', namely, the Law and philosophy.[20] Law, according to Maimonides, is the apex of prophetic activity, and Twersky correctly underscores the 'ongoing reciprocity between normative action and philosophical reflection'[21] which feeds the dynamics of Maimonides' thought. Twersky also rightly observes that 'Maimonides had a master plan from the very beginning to achieve his overarching objective: to bring Law and philosophy, two apparently incongruous attitudes of mind, two jealous rivals, into fruitful harmony'.[22] In short, the interaction between philosophy and Law is the point at which the philosophic, exegetical, educational, and halakhic deliberations in Maimonides' writings meet.

However, this harmonistic structure in which Aristotelian philosophy and Mosaic law are presented as co-existing in a state of edifying complementarity—nay, even integration—is not as peaceful as may appear. Beyond the spirited effort to harmonize the cognitive contents of philosophy and prophecy, one may detect a disturbing tension that cannot be ignored if we carefully observe the interplay of elements within this structure. In fact, certain cracks may be discerned in the seemingly idyllic coexistence between philosophy and prophecy envisaged by some students of Maimonides. J. Guttmann is one of the few scholars who have noticed that there is no perfect congruence between philosophy and prophecy in Maimonides' thought.[23] Guttmann correctly demonstrates that the Maimonidean theory of prophecy entails a two-pointed critique of Aristotelian philosophy which results, in this case, in an uncompromising break with it, with all the consequences that such a rupture entails. Guttmann's remarks to this effect are rather brief and may thus be overlooked by his readers; but as they seem to me to be of utmost importance for understanding and evaluating correctly the nature and scope of Maimonides' obligation towards Aristotelian philosophy, it seems proper to enlarge upon them here.

It has already been noticed that it is no mere accident that Maimonides links his discussion of prophecy to that of the creation of the world. The reason for his doing so Maimonides makes clear when he argues that 'with the belief in the creation of the world in time, all

[20] Ibid. 359. [21] Ibid. 360. [22] Ibid. 369.
[23] Guttmann, *Philosophies of Judaism*, 172–3.

miracles become possible and the Law becomes possible'.[24] Prophecy, too, entails a clearly miraculous element: 'For we believe that it may happen that one who is fit for prophecy and prepared for it should not become a prophet, namely, on account of the divine will. To my mind this is like all miracles and takes the same course as they.'[25] If the belief in the creation of the world in time—as opposed to the Aristotelian concept of the eternal existence of the world—makes the belief in miracles possible, then it logically follows that prophecy, which has an element of the miraculous in it, in that God may deprive people who have reached the point of being worthy of it from becoming prophets, becomes possible too. *Mutatis mutandis*, the connection between Maimonides' concept of temporal creation and his theory of prophecy can be stated also in the following manner. In both cases Maimonides departs from the groundwork of Aristotelian philosophy. In the case of the doctrine of temporal creation, Maimonides maintains a view that is critical of Aristotelian physics and metaphysics alike. Consequently, the belief in miracles, which now becomes possible, sustaining Maimonides' theory of prophecy, is tagged on to that criticism of Aristotelianism and to some extent reinforces it. Moreover, the Maimonidean theory of prophecy as it stands by itself entails a substantial break with Aristotelianism. We shall now turn to see how this is accomplished.

It has been observed that as a matter of epistemological principle in Maimonidean thinking, all forms of knowledge that a human being is likely to acquire are subject to the rational capacity of the human mind.[26] No act of intellection is conceivable beyond the rational faculty of man. In fact, Maimonides goes to great lengths to show the limits of the human mind in its quest for knowledge. In other words, according to a conventional view of the Middle Ages, which Maimonides shares, no human being is likely to break through the rational modes of cognition as shaped by philosophic, or scientific, speculation. Briefly stated, 'there are therefore things regarding which it has become clear to man that it is impossible to apprehend them'.[27] Both philosophy and the Law agree on that matter too: 'Do not think that what we have said with regard to the insufficiency of the human intellect and its having a

[24] *Guide*, ii. 25, p. 329.

[25] Ibid. ii. 32, p. 361.

[26] For the following discussion, see particularly S. Pines, 'The Limitations of Human Knowledge according to al-Fārābī, ibn Bājja and Maimonides', in Twersky, *Studies in Medieval Jewish History and Literature*, 82–102.

[27] *Guide*, i. 31, p. 64.

limit at which it stops is a statement made in order to conform to Law. For it is something that has already been said and freely grasped by the philosophers without their having concern for a particular doctrine or opinion.'[28] Maimonides stresses this fact regarding 'the intellects of human beings [which] have a limit at which they stop' for two principal reasons. First, he wants to discourage people from venturing into subjects which they are not capable of grasping; second, he strives to drive home the idea that the essence of God's being can be grasped only indirectly, through contemplation of created things and by means of negative attributes. *Prima facie*, prophecy, which enjoys perfect congruence with philosophy, is no exception to the rule.

However, matters are not left at this simple level. At one point, after defining the nature of prophecy, Maimonides makes the following observation: 'This [prophecy] is the highest degree of man and the ultimate term of perfection that can exist for his species.'[29] This, together with another statement made at a later stage of his discussion of prophecy, to the effect 'that the true prophets indubitably grasp speculative matters; by means of his speculation alone, man is unable to grasp the causes from which what a prophet has come to know necessarily follows',[30] may be interpreted as expressing the view that prophecy is the highest achievement of the human mind, even higher than philosophy. Particularly noteworthy is the second statement, to the effect that prophets seem to enjoy a certain degree of priority over other people, including philosophers, in their ability to grasp basic metaphysical principles from which one can draw all kinds of philosophical conclusions.[31] In other words, prophecy can facilitate a degree or quality of knowledge unattainable when philosophical, that is, rational, means of speculation are employed. Yet, the question arises whether this quality of knowledge really transcends the epistemological reach of philosophy, or whether with the help of prophetic inspiration one is able to grasp more readily speculative premisses which philosophers take a longer time to apprehend. The answer seems simple: in matters of divination, that is, foreseeing future events, the faculty of divination helps the prophets to attain and 'give information regarding future events in the shortest time'.[32] This sounds

[28] Ibid. i. 31, p. 67. [29] Ibid. ii. 36, p. 369. [30] Ibid. ii. 38, p. 377.

[31] Pines also, in 'Limitations', p. 90, remarks: 'Maimonides' Introduction thus appears to indicate that only prophets . . . can cognize incorporeal entities. This seems to mean that the cognition that can be achieved by the prophets is different in kind from that of all other men (including the philosophers) and may be beyond their ken.'

[32] *Guide*, ii. 38, p. 377.

like a quantitative difference, yet the sentence quoted above regarding comprehension of speculative matters by prophets unmistakably refers to a qualitative difference between prophets and philosophers, in that the former enjoy primacy over the latter.

Thus, in discussing Maimonides' theory of prophecy, particularly in relation to the compatibility of philosophy and prophecy as modes of cognition, one should keep an eye on the two conflicting tendencies that coexist in the master's thought. On the one hand, we find the tendency to treat both philosophy and the Law, which is the major product of prophecy, as equals, with neither enjoying precedence over the other. On the other hand, certain utterances and lines of thought in his writings quite clearly point to the fact that Maimonides, after all, considered the prophets to be more capable of attaining the ultimate truth than the philosophers.[33]

III

In his discussion of the resemblance between prophets and philosophers, Maimonides underscores two points: (*a*) both prophets and philosophers come under the spell of the intellectual overflow that emanates from God and passes through the Active Intellect. (*b*) Whereas in the case of the prophets one finds that the intellectual overflow first operates upon the rational faculty and then upon the imaginative faculty, in the case of the philosophers, only the rational faculty is put into action.[34] It is noteworthy that Maimonides thinks that philosophers also come under the spell of this divine overflow. This fact can only be interpreted as indicating Maimonides' desire to bring prophets and philosophers as close together as possible. However, the fact that the imaginative faculty of the philosophers remains unmotivated by the divine overflow deprives them of the ability to divine the future and to realize the truth in plastic clarity, if this can be considered a real deprivation in the framework of Maimonidean thinking. The prophets, on the other hand, whose imaginative faculty is highly developed, have dream-visions in which angels, who according to the Maimonidean interpretation are the intellects of the heavenly spheres, present them with all kinds of

[33] Some scholars would have even claimed that Maimonides postulated an undeniable primacy of philosophers over prophets. See my discussion below.

[34] Both points are discussed in *Guide*, ii. 37, p. 374.

information put in the enigmatic language of symbols and metaphors. Since imagination is commonly considered to be inferior to the rational faculty, its presence in the case of the prophets is not necessarily to be interpreted as a great advantage, particularly when the prophetic type of truth comes in metaphorical images. Thus, the primacy of the prophets may easily be interpreted as a disadvantage, placing the prophets on account of their peculiar technique and way of expression in an inferior position to that occupied by the philosophers. If we are still in doubt what Maimonides really thought of the imaginative faculty of the prophets, then a close look at the characteristics of Moses' prophecy can enlighten us. In the case of Moses, who experienced the highest degree of prophecy, Maimonides claims that 'the imaginative faculty did not enter into his prophecy . . . as the intellect overflowed toward him without its intermediation'.[35] But we must equally bear in mind that in speaking of the imaginative faculty of the philosophers, Maimonides claims that 'the rational faculty . . . does not overflow at all toward the imaginative faculty—either because of the scantiness of what overflows or because of some deficiency existing in the imaginative faculty in its natural disposition, a disposition that makes it impossible for it to receive the overflow of the intellect'.[36] In other words, Moses resembles, at least formally, the philosophers whose imaginative faculty remains unaffected by the divine overflow. The imaginative faculty is innate and, contrary to the rational faculty, cannot be developed by study or practice. In its operation on the human mind, it is complemented by two other faculties: courage and divination.[37] Thus, on the one hand, we find that prophets possess qualities which philosophers lack; on the other hand, Moses, the father of all prophets, resembles the philosophers in that his imaginative faculty is not affected by the divine overflow. This almost amounts to a contradiction in terms, though it may be resolved quite easily. One may argue that the philosophers were not affected in their imaginative faculty because there was a deficiency in either themselves or in the overflow, while the perfection of Moses' mind was so total that there was no need to assist his process of (prophetic) intellection with the imaginative faculty operative in the case of all the other prophets.

In other words, the whole question of the relationship between prophecy and philosophy may be said to depend upon how one

[35] Ibid. ii. 36, p. 373.
[36] Ibid. ii. 37, p. 374.
[37] Ibid. ii. 38, p. 378.

assesses the functioning of the imaginative faculty in each case. Here the substantial difference between prophets and philosophers, or men of speculative science, may be pinpointed. Does the inclusion of the imaginative faculty detract from or add to the process of cognition? As it appears, Maimonides' view is that the inclusion of the imaginative faculty in the cognitive process is vital to any act of reasoning that entails divination or a very clear comprehension of ideas. However, in the process of 'knowing things that are real in their existence',[38] only the functioning of the rational faculty is required. We may at this point conclude that the prophets do indeed enjoy a certain degree of priority over philosophers, and that this priority is primarily limited to the faculty of divination by which the prophets are commonly characterized. But in matters that pertain to the apprehension of 'things that are real in their existence', it seems correct to conclude that in principle no essential difference exists between the prophets and philosophers. But we may not overlook Maimonides' explicit statement that only prophets can grasp certain speculative matters that other people, philosophers included, find difficult or even impossible to grasp.

Thus the question arises again: what, after all, did Maimonides mean when he said that prophets grasped certain premisses that lay beyond the apprehension of philosophers? The language used by Maimonides in this connection clearly does not limit the issue to acts of divination. We are thus forced to conclude that there is a lack of congruity in what Maimonides' arguments achieve at this point. One may well argue that every case of lack of congruity or even self-contradiction in Maimonides may be resolved by saying that the contrasting statements are aimed at different types of addressees. Indeed, it has become accepted to think that Maimonides addressed different classes or levels of people.[39] Thus everyone is entitled to find in Maimonides concepts that suit his training and intellectual accomplishments. Although some passages in the *Guide* are conducive to such an interpretation, it seems that his having left quite a number of crucial issues in a seemingly unresolved formulation must be interpreted differently. I suggest that contradictory formulations emerge because in the master's mind certain issues can properly be handled only when examined from more than one point of view.

In trying to account for Maimonides' differing positions we should not resort to apologetic harmonization, nor should we press too hard to

[38] Both points are discussed in *Guide*, ii. 38, p. 377.

[39] Thus, for instance, Strauss, *Persecution*, 53 ff.

unearth 'either—or' solutions which restrict the area of dialectical implications. The special interest of the *Guide* lies in the fact that at some points the book may sound equally true on different planes of philosophical and theological exposition. This is not a naïve simplification or an easy way out of a complicated philosophical problem. The ultimate question regarding Maimonides' philosophical thought is whether there is more than one set of tracks that lead to the top of the mountain. Understandably, scholars are inclined to opt for the existence of only one track. Ideally, sincerity and systematic thinking reap a single truth. Ambiguity is not expected of a proficient philosopher such as Maimonides. However, if the choice is between a philosophical cul-de-sac to which two contradictory lines of thought lead and the coexistence of two dialectically related positions, I prefer the latter. Since in several cases, the one under discussion being a prominent example, Maimonides' deliberations move in circular forms, we do more justice to the master's thought if we adopt such an attitude rather than an esoteric mode of reading Maimonides or artificial harmonization. Although it is typical of 'the medieval mind' to strive to ascertain monolithic truth, faced with the validity of revelation and the demonstrative necessity of philosophical rationalism we should allow Maimonides greater philosophical or dialectical flexibility than is usually granted him—particularly by those of us who hunt for the esoteric truth in his writings.

The dilemma with which we are faced may also be phrased in different terms: did Maimonides conceive of prophecy as a natural phenomenon or a supernatural one? There are good reasons for subscribing to the view that he held prophecy to be a natural phenomenon. The divine overflow that emanated from God and passed through the Active Intellect was an automatic process that did not depend upon divine intervention. However, according to Maimonides, philosophical premisses of a naturalistic order did not sufficiently account for the nature of prophecy. A miraculous element had to be introduced into the notion—a divine overflow. God could interfere with the emanation and prevent the potential prophet from reaching it. In other words, even in that automatic natural process, God had a free hand to veto its operations. Yet, when we subscribe to the view that prophecy is basically a natural phenomenon, the conclusion may easily be reached that ultimately prophecy is not a superior mode of cognition *vis-à-vis* philosophical intellection. In both cases, in prophecy and philosophy, the individuals involved are under the influence of the (automatic) divine overflow. Where, then, do we find the ultimate proof for the primacy of prophecy?

It has variously been noticed that the prophecy of Moses serves as this kind of proof. Moses embodies the highest degree of prophecy. All the scriptural prophets, with the exception of Moses, achieved one or another of the eleven degrees of prophecy. Moses alone reached a twelfth degree. That degree is classified as *sui generis*, and almost everyone of its features differs from the corresponding ones present in the prophets of the first eleven degrees. Technically speaking, Moses' mature prophecy is characterized by the following qualities:

1. The divine overflow that advened to Moses reached only his intellectual, but not his imaginative, faculty.
2. No angels were involved in his prophecy.
3. Moses was able to prophesy even in his waking hours, and to perceive God speaking to him, as it were.
4. He was in complete control of his senses at the time of his prophecy.
5. Moses' prophecy is not disguised in parables and metaphors.
6. Moses was able to prophesy whenever he wished, though extreme anguish affected his ability to prophesy, as it did all the other prophets.

The unique nature of Moses' prophecy needs no further comment. Its ontological significance lies in the direction in which it points. Moses' prophecy, which in Maimonides' view shares the name of prophecy only amphibolously, makes it evident that whatever we may think about the relationship between prophecy and philosophy, there is one element in the area of prophecy that unequivocally points beyond the cognitive framework of prophecy itself. Thus, we may say, Moses' superprophecy unequivocally epitomizes Maimonides' quest beyond prophecy. And if there really are realms in which prophecy transcends the realms of philosophy, then Moses' prophecy transcends ordinary prophecy—to say nothing of philosophy. Yet, and here we find ourselves in a vicious circle, in one major respect Moses resembles the philosopher: the divine overflow did not touch his faculty of imagination. Thus Moses at his best is but an *alter philosophus*. What, then, are the other prophets? And if Moses is but a philosopher, what is the real point of the Law? What is its major objective? If its main objective is to prepare the way for spiritual, moral, and political perfections that are the preconditions of philosophy, may we say that 'superprophecy' is mainly subservient to philosophy? These are difficulties that cannot be resolved as satisfactorily as we may wish. In the face of all this, the theory of the coexistence of a multiplicity of dialectically related positions in Maimonides' thinking finds substantial support.

EPILOGUE

Writing this paper, I became convinced that one cannot do full justice to Maimonides' thinking, even to one clearly defined segment of it, within the compass of a relatively short space. Maimonides' thought has to be viewed in its totality, even when the light is made to fall upon one part of it. The comprehensiveness of his great mind deserves the dimensions of a book, not the framework of an article. Only then can full justice be done to the complexity of his philosophy.

8
The True Perplexity: *The* Guide of the Perplexed
Part II, Chapter 24

TZVI LANGERMANN

THE incompatibility of the models used by professional astronomers with the basic tenets of the Aristotelian world-view is the issue discussed by Maimonides in ii. 24 of the *Guide of the Perplexed*.[1] On the one hand, the epicycles and eccentrics employed by astronomers seem to violate the principle that the motion of the heavenly bodies be uniform, circular, and about a fixed centre. On the other hand, the results achieved through the use of these very devices are startlingly precise. This, Maimonides says, is the 'true perplexity'.

In this paper I wish to look at three aspects of this 'true perplexity'. Both philosophers and astronomers had expressed themselves on this problem, so I shall first sketch Maimonides' place among these thinkers. My second and main concern will be a comparison of the views expressed in the *Guide* with the rules laid down in the third chapter of the 'Laws Concerning the Basic Principles of the Torah', which forms the first section of the *Mishneh Torah*. I shall be particularly concerned with two questions: did Maimonides consider the true configuration of the heavens to be inscrutable? and can a close reading of both texts offer any clues about this true configuration? Finally, I shall mention the views of some of Maimonides' followers on these questions.

I

The mathematical models presented by Ptolemy in his *Almagest* and the three-dimensional explanations proffered in his *Planetary Hypotheses*

[1] All quotations and page numbers come from the translation of the *Guide of the Perplexed* by Shlomo Pines (Chicago, 1963).

were criticized by medieval scientists and philosophers for having violated principles of Aristotelian natural philosophy.[2] A number of prominent Spanish scholars, whose objections went hand in hand with the interest in that country in reaffirming the true Aristotelian doctrines, participated in this criticism. Ibn Bājja, perhaps the founder of this trend, is known from Maimonides' remarks in *Guide*, ii. 24, to have written on this problem. The astronomer al-Biṭrūjī, who himself developed an alternative system, albeit an unsatisfactory one, informs us that Ibn Ṭufayl, the next great Spanish philosopher, also took an active interest in this issue.[3] Several detailed discourses of Ibn Rushd, the greatest representative of the Spanish school and Maimonides' contemporary, exist on this problem.[4]

Maimonides tells us in the context of another astronomical discussion (ii. 9) that he read texts under the guidance of some pupils of Ibn Bājja. This fact and the space given to Ibn Bājja's views at the beginning of ii. 24 demonstrate Maimonides' connection to this Spanish school.[5] However, the subsequent discussion in ii. 24 shows that Maimonides' investigations went beyond what we know to have been the range of issues discussed by the Spanish school. For example, by simply computing the planetary eccentricities in terms of terrestrial radii on the basis of the values found in al-Qabīṣī's *Epistle Concerning*

[2] Pines deals briefly with this issue in his 'Translator's Introduction' to the *Guide*, pp. lxiii, lxxi–lxxii, cix–cxi. Cf. also L. Gautier, 'Une réforme du système astronomique de Ptoleomée tentée par les philosophes arabes du XIIe siècle', *Journal asiatique* (1909), pt. ii. 483–510; Juan Vernet, 'L'Astronomie dans l'Islam occidental', *Archives internationales d'histoire des sciences*, 16 (1963), 225–40, esp. 235–7; and A. I. Sabra, 'The Scientific Enterprise', in Bernard Lewis (ed.), *The World of Islam* (London, 1976), 181–200, esp. 191–2. The most recent treatment of this problem is Bernard R. Goldstein, 'The Status of Models in Ancient and Medieval Astronomy', *Centaurus*, 24 (1980), 132–47.

[3] Regarding Ibn Ṭufayl, see B. R. Goldstein, *Al-Biṭrūjī: On the Principles of Astronomy*, 2 vols. (New Haven, 1971), i. 61.

[4] The only study to date on Ibn Rushd's role in this problem (apart from brief discussions in the literature cited in n. 2) is F. Carmody, 'The Planetary Theory of Ibn Rushd', *Osiris*, 10 (1952), 556–86. Carmody does not make use of Averroes' summary of the Almagest, which survives only in Hebrew but in many copies (cf. M. Steinschneider, *Die hebraeischen Übersetzungen der Mittelalters und die Juden als Dolmetscher* (Berlin, 1893), 546–9), nor the astronomical material found in the treatises on Aristotle's *De Caelo* and *Metaphysica* included in *Rasā'il Ibn Rushd* (Hyderabad, 1948). See also n. 47 below.

[5] Note also Maimonides' high regard for the Spanish astronomer Jābir b. Aflaḥ, mentioned in *Guide*, ii. 9. In fact, Maimonides edited Jābir's astronomical treatise, as we are informed by Ibn al-Qifṭī, *Ta'rīkh al-Ḥukamā'*, ed. J. Lippert (Leipzig, 1903), 319. However, Jābir's criticisms of Ptolemy focused on various technical matters and not on the problem of epicycles and eccentrics. Cf. R. P. Lorch, 'The Astronomy of Jābir ibn Aflaḥ', *Centaurus*, 19 (1975), 85–107.

the Distances, Maimonides noticed that the centres of the eccentric orbs of most of the planets lie between the spheres of other planets (e.g. the centre of Jupiter's eccentric lies between Venus and Mercury, etc.), and he was thus able to raise a strong objection of his own to the Ptolemaic configuration.[6] Maimonides also brings in the necessity of positing intervening spheres, the existence of which only raises further problems regarding the location of their centres and their own proper motion. Maimonides has learned of these spheres from a treatise by the Harranian Thābit b. Qurra.

The philosophically weak points of the accepted astronomical models came under attack in Egypt as well as in Spain. In fact, the most comprehensive and biting attack on the Ptolemaic system known to us is Ibn al-Haytham's *Doubts on Ptolemy*.[7] Ibn al-Haytham's doubts led him to brand the configuration presented in the *Almagest* as unequivocally false (*bāṭila*).[8] Ibn al-Haytham's arguments include very detailed analysis demonstrating how such Ptolemaic constructions as the equant and the lunar *prosneusis*[9] violate the principles of natural philosophy and, in general, that the planetary motions are governed in the Ptolemaic system by imaginary points rather than by real bodies. Yet it seems significant that Ibn al-Haytham does not, for example, reject epicycles *per se*; he proves the impossibility of the Ptolemaic features by working out in step-by-step fashion the consequences of, say, the moon's epicycle moving exactly as Ptolemy prescribes.[10] If indeed the epicycle by itself is a gross violation of the principles of natural philosophy, why should Ibn al-Haytham go to all that bother? We have recently discovered that Maimonides was familiar with at least one of Ibn al-Haytham's mathematical treatises.[11] Nevertheless, neither Ibn al-Haytham nor the *Doubts* are mentioned anywhere in the

[6] B. R. Goldstein, review of Fuat Sezgin, *Geschichte der arabischen Schriftums*, vi, *Astronomie*, in *Isis*, 71 (1980), 341–2, at 342.

[7] Ibn al-Haytham, *Al-Shukūk 'alā Baṭlamyūs*, ed. A. I. Sabra and N. Shehaby (Cairo, 1971). Cf. also S. Pines, 'Ibn al-Haytham's Critique of Ptolemy', *Proceedings of the Tenth International Congress of the History of Science in Ithaca 1962* (Paris, 1964), 547–55. On Ibn al-Haytham, who did most of his work in Egypt, see A. I. Sabra, 'Ibn al-Haytham', *Dictionary of Scientific Biography* (New York, 1972), vi. 189–210.

[8] Ibn al-Haytham, *Al-Shukūk*, 34.

[9] On the technical features and terminology of Ptolemaic astronomy see O. Pedersen, *A Survey of the Almagest* (Odense, 1974) and O. Neugebauer, *A History of Ancient Mathematical Astronomy* (Berlin–Heidelberg–New York, 1975).

[10] Ibn al-Haytham, *Al-Shukūk*, 15–20.

[11] T. Langermann, 'The Mathematical Writings of Maimonides', *JQR* 75 (1984), 57–65.

Guide, and there is no evidence to show that Maimonides knew of that work.

II

Maimonides ends his criticism of contemporary astronomical models with several observations. First, he notes that

> all this does not affect the astronomer. For his purpose is not to tell us in which way the spheres truly are, but to posit an astronomical system in which it would be possible for the motions to be circular and uniform and to correspond to what is apprehended through sight, regardless of whether or not things are thus in fact.[12]

Maimonides then makes a few remarks which strongly hint that the true state of affairs in the heavens is indeed beyond the power of human comprehension: 'to fatigue the minds with notions that cannot be grasped by them and for the grasp of which they have no instrument, is a defect in one's inborn disposition or some sort of temptation. Let us then stop at a point which is within our capacity.'[13]

In sharp contrast to the doubts expressed in *Guide* ii. 24, both concerning the details of the Ptolemaic system and, in general, our ability to understand the configuration of the heavens, stand the descriptions found in the third chapter of the 'Laws Concerning the Basic Principles of the Torah'.[14] In the first five *halakhot* of this chapter, Maimonides does not limit himself to the facts that the orbs (*galgalim*)[15] are 'pure and transparent like glass and crystal',[16] and that

[12] *Guide*, 326.

[13] Ibid. 327.

[14] The astronomical material found in another part of the *Mishneh Torah*, 'Sanctification of the New Moon' (published in the translation of Solomon Gandz, New Haven, 1956) appertains strictly to the computational side of astronomy, and hence Maimonides' adherence therein to the Ptolemaic model cannot figure in the present discussion. For, as Maimonides explains in *Guide*, ii. 24, p. 326, the discussion of the physical shape of the universe does not affect the working astronomer in his daily practice. See the English translation of the 'Laws Concerning the Basic Principles of the Torah' by Moses Hyamson, *Mishneh Torah: The Book of Knowledge* (Jerusalem, 1962), 34*a*–46*a*. However, the translation of the passages quoted in the following discussion are my own; I shall explain in the footnotes any significant points on which I disagree with Hyamsons's choice of words.

[15] I consistently translate *galgal* as 'orb', a technical term of medieval astronomy; the Arabic equivalent is *falak*. Similarly, I render *kadur* as 'sphere', a term common to astronomy and geometry; the Arabic equivalent is *kura*.

[16] The Hebrew is *sapir*, which Hyamson translates as 'sapphire'. Maimonides states clearly that the heavens are transparent. It is true that sapphire is 'often used in a general

the planetary orbs are arranged 'like the layers of an onion'. In the fourth *halakhah* he specifically refers to epicycles, which he calls 'small orbs':

All these orbs which encompass the earth are round like a sphere and the earth is suspended in the middle. Some of the stars have small orbs which are fixed inside of them, and those orbs do not encompass the earth. Rather, a small orb which does not encompass [the earth] is fixed in the large, encompassing orb.

It is clear that in this *halakhah* specifically, and in the chapter in general, Maimonides is speaking not of the computational models, which are much more complicated, but of the physical configuration of the heavens.

In the next *halakhah*, Maimonides reveals more details: there are eighteen 'encompassing orbs' and eight small, non-encompassing orbs. This is a very acceptable count, both for epicyclic and non-epicyclic orbs, according to Ptolemaic theory.[17] Furthermore, in the

sense so as to include all corundum of gem quality regardless of colour. Hence clear and colourless corundum is known as white sapphire or 'leucosapphire'. Such stones have occasionally been cut as lenses for microscopes, being recommended for such use by their high refractivity, weak dispersion and great hardness' (F. W. Rudler, 'Sapphire', *Encyclopaedia Britannica*, 11th edn., xxiv (Cambridge, 1911), 202). However, it seems to me that in current usage, sapphire refers to a coloured stone. Sa'adya Gaon translates the biblical *sapir* (Exod. 28: 18) as *mahā*, synonymous with *ballūr* and meaning a transparent stone or crystal. Cf. J. Kafiḥ, *Perushe Rabbenu Sa'adya Gaon 'al ha-Torah* (Jerusalem, 1963), 73, and Ibn Manẓūr, *Lisān al-'Arab*, xv (Beirut, 1956), 299. I feel that Maimonides uses *sapir* in accordance with the translation of Sa'adya; so also Shemuel ha-Nagid, 'heavens as clear (*tehorim*) as *sapirim*' (Y. Cana'ani, *Oẓar Lashon ha-'Ivrit*, xii (Jerusalem, 1972), *s.v.* sapir). Abraham b. Ezra (commentary to Exod. 28: 9) disagrees with Sa'adya, claiming that *sapir* is a red stone.

[17] The commentator (ad loc. cit. in the various printings of the *Mishneh Torah* with commentaries) writes: 'This is their reckoning. The moon has three orbs and these are their names: *al-jawzahar* (node) and *al-mā'il* (inclined) and *khārij al-markaz* (eccentric). Mercury also has three orbs and they are *al-mumaththal* (parecliptic) and *al-mudīr* (turning) and *khārij al-markaz*. This makes six. Each of the five remaining planets has two orbs, *mumaththal* and *khārij al-markaz*. This makes sixteen. The eighth orb, in which are the remaining, fixed stars, and the ninth orb. This makes eighteen.' Note that the commentator gives the names in Arabic.

The eight epicycles are: two apiece for Mercury and Venus (the extra epicycle is needed to help account for the planet's latitude), and one each for the moon, Mars, Jupiter, and Saturn. Note the commentator's remark: 'The later astronomers say that the sun has no *falak tadwīr* (epicyclic orb).' Note in particular that eccentric orbs *are* included in this list. It would seem, however, that Maimonides wishes to exclude eccentrics, since he says, 'the earth is suspended in the middle (*emẓa'*)'; compare his unequivocal statement elsewhere in the *Mishneh Torah* that the planetary deferents encompass the world, but the earth is not at their centre (*emẓa'*) 'Sanctification', xi. 13; p. 45 in Gandz's translation; note that here eccentrics are allowed, since computations only

same *halakhah*, Maimonides states that we can infer the 'way of encompassing' of the orbs, that is, whether they encompass or, as in the case of epicycles, do not encompass, the earth from the proper motions of the stars, their latitudinal crossings, and their apogees and perigees.

And from the motion of the stars and the knowledge of the measure of their revolution in each day and each hour, and their passage from south to north and from north to south, and from their height above the earth and their nearness, the number of all these orbs, the form of their motion, and their way of encompassing, is known.[18]

Though the remarks found in the *Guide* may reflect Maimonides' most mature ponderings on this subject, it seems to me to be beyond any doubt that at the time he wrote the *Mishneh Torah*, Maimonides was well aware of the problematic state of contemporary astronomy. For example, in his famous letter to the rabbis of southern France, Maimonides remarks that in his youth he read all there was to be found on the subject of astrology,[19] and it is, of course, impossible (at least for the serious medieval scholar) to become expert in astrology without a thorough knowledge of astronomical theory. Indeed, it seems very reasonable to presume that Maimonides learned of the criticisms voiced by Spanish scholars while still in his native country.[20]

Now there is no question that Maimonides, in the *Mishneh Torah*, does claim that certain matters lie beyond human understanding when he feels compelled to do so. Thus Maimonides concludes his discussion of fate and free will in the fifth chapter of the *Hilkhot Teshuva* (Laws of repentance) with the statement that man can never understand the meaning of 'God's knowledge'.[21] The particular issue discussed in that chapter, it seems to me, is of far more importance than the description of the details of the heavens. If Maimonides is

are involved; cf. xi. 17 (Gandz, 46) and also n. 14 below). We shall return to this point at the end of sec. ii; see also n. 37.

[18] Hyamson's translation of *neṭṭiyah* as declination is unacceptable; the reference is to the latitudinal crossings of the ecliptic, not of the equator.

[19] A. Marx, 'The Correspondence between the Rabbis of Southern France and Maimonides about Astrology', *HUCA* 3 (1926), 359–70, esp. 318, 351.

[20] This is my impression, based upon Maimonides' remarks in *Guide*, ii. 9, concerning his personal contacts with Andalusians involved with astronomical problems.

[21] This proclamation of inscrutability exposed Maimonides to a strong attack on the part of Rabad ('Laws of Repentance', loc. cit.). Cf. also I. Twersky, *Rabad of Posquières* (Cambridge, Mass., 1962), 280–1.

willing there to stop the discussion by pleading that man can never know these things, there seems no reason not to do so in the chapter which we are now examining.

In this connection it would be illuminating to look at an interesting passage from Maimonides' *Commentary to the Mishnah* (*'Eruvim*, i. 5). At issue is the irrationality of π. Maimonides writes: 'You ought to know that the ratio of the diameter of the circle to its circumference is unknown, nor will it ever be possible to express it precisely. This is not due to any shortcoming of knowledge on our part, as the ignorant think. Rather, this matter is unknown due to its nature, and its discovery will never be attained.'[22] In my opinion, Maimonides' jibe here at 'the ignorant' may be aimed at those who are less than circumspect in listing all sorts of wonders which are claimed to be beyond human comprehension. In the case of π, we are dealing with a particular mathematical property. Human understanding, Maimonides would claim, certainly has its limits, but these should be investigated more rigorously. The notion of inscrutability has its precise place and ought not be invoked indiscriminately.[23]

It seems clear to me, then, that Maimonides does regard the true configuration of the heavens as something humanly attainable. He may have had tactical reasons in the *Guide* for making the situation appear to be hopeless, as Pines once suggested: 'The contradiction between astronomy and physics served his purpose. It proves according to him, the limitations of human knowledge: man is unable to give a satisfactory scientific account of the world of the spheres.'[24]

It was in fact true that at the time of Maimonides no one had offered

[22] See the edition and Heb. translation by Rabbi J. Kafiḥ (Jerusalem, 1963), ii. 98.

[23] By way of example only I shall cite Abraham b. Ezra's short commentary to Exod. 23: 20 (ed. A. Weiser, Jerusalem, 1976, ii. 305). Ibn Ezra lists here quite a number of phenomena whose inscrutability is strongly implied and sometimes explicitly stated. Among these are some matters of astronomy which agree with Maimonides' observations in *Guide*, ii. 19—in Ibn Ezra's words, 'why one place on the orb is full of stars and another is not, some are big and some are small, some are white [and some] red, and all [of this] in one orb'. Yet alongside this Ibn Ezra lists the known irrationality of the square root of two, and the differences of opinion regarding this. I do not mean to imply that Maimonides' criticism is aimed at Ibn Ezra. (In fact, I find these two thinkers quite close on some basic issues concerning what may be called the Jewish attitude towards science, and I hope to develop this in some future paper.) I am sure that it would not prove difficult to find quite a few examples of wholesale invocation of human inscrutability among Maimonides' contemporaries, both Muslim and Jewish.

[24] S. Pines, 'Maimonides', *Dictionary of Scientific Biography*, ix (New York, 1974), 27–32, at 30. See, however, my remarks towards the end of n. 25.

an acceptable solution. Nevertheless, I regard Maimonides' remarks at the end of ii. 24—'It is possible that someone else may find a demonstration by means of which the true reality of what is obscure for me will become clear for him'[25]—not as rhetoric, but as a statement that the problem of the true configuration of the heavens, however difficult, may after all admit of a solution. Hence, on this particular point, there need not be any contradiction between the *Guide* and the *Mishneh Torah*.

A very interesting approach to the problem of the scrutability of the heavens was taken by the anonymous commentator to the 'Basic Principles', someone who was rather knowledgeable in the field of astronomy.[26] Commenting on the beginning of the third *halakhah*, 'None of the orbs is either light or heavy', he writes:

> It is clear from the words of the philosophers that the matter (*golem*) of the heavens is not like the matter of the four elements nor what is composed from them. The true nature of the matter of the heavens was not known to them. Therefore it is said of them that they are not light and not heavy and [have] no taste nor smell, because all these accidents are below the orb of the moon, and of that whose essence is not known, the nature is not known either.[27]

[25] In a discussion of the incompatibility of the Ptolemaic system with Aristotelian physics published some 20 years ago, Pines wrote: 'It can even be maintained that the thoroughly skeptical position was, for the reasons he [Maimonides] gave, the only consistent and logical one. Yet it seems to me that such agnosticism would stultify all that Maimonides set out to accomplish in the *Guide*, and would also be quite irreconcilable with his general views, expressed in quite different contexts, on man's highest destination and man's knowledge'. ('Translator's Introduction', *Guide*, p. cxi). Pines has since moved away from this view and now emphasizes the limitations which the *Guide* places on the capacity of the human mind to understand celestial affairs. Cf. 'The Limitations of Human Knowledge according to al-Fārābī, ibn Bājja, and Maimonides', in I. Twersky (ed.), *Studies in Medieval Jewish History and Literature* (Cambridge, Mass.–London, 1979), 82–109, esp. on 93: 'in contradistinction to that theory [or Ibn Bājja], Maimonides is of the opinion that no scientific certainty can be achieved with regard to objects that are outside the sublunar world'.

[26] Cf. n. 14. It is significant that in his commentary to the fifth *halakhah*, 'Greek scholars wrote many books . . .' he writes: 'This science is the science of astronomy (*tekhunah*) and in Arabic it is called *'ilm al-hay'ah*.' *'Ilm al-hay'ah* is used for astronomy in general, but it also is the specific connotation of that branch of astronomy which deals with the configuration of the heavens. Cf. David Pingree, "Ilm al-Hay'ah', *Encyclopaedia of Islam*, 2nd edn., iii (Leiden, 1971), 1135–8. Maimonides continues at the end of the fifth *halakhah*: 'this is the science of the computation of seasons and signs [*tequfot u-mazalot*, a phrase commonly used to denote astronomy].' In this context, 'computation' must refer to the calculations which demonstrate (in the medieval view) the planetary distances, the existence and sizes of the epicycles, etc.

[27] Jonathan b. Joseph of Ruzhany, in his own commentary to this *halakhah* (*Yeshu'ah be-Yisrael* (Frankfurt, 1720), repr. in vol. i of *Po'al ha-Shem* (Bnei Brak, 1969), 2),

In other words, Maimonides' conclusion—'All that Aristotle says about that which is beneath the sphere of the moon is in accordance with reasoning . . . However, regarding all that is in the heavens, man grasps but a small measure of what is mathematical'[28]—refers to our inability to understand the nature of the 'fifth element' of which the heavens are formed, and not to any inability to comprehend the three-dimensional layout of the celestial spheres.

Close inspection of *Guide*, ii. 19 will bolster this claim. Here Maimonides distinguishes between two unsolved features of the heavens: there is no clear relationship between the velocities of the spheres, the direction of their motions, the number of spheres assigned to each star, and their ordering; and it can be shown—either on the basis of different transparencies (Alfarabi) or on the principles of motion and rest (Maimonides himself)—that the matters and forms of stars and spheres differ from one another.[29] Now the first feature is patently a problem in astronomy—and here I include the issue of the physical configuration—and in this connection I have found no unambiguous statement that the matter is inscrutable. Maimonides' comment is: 'Now if Aristotle had been able—as he thought—to give us the cause for the differences between the motions of the spheres so that these should be in accordance with the order of the positions of the spheres with regard to one another, this would have been extraordinary.'[30] However, regarding the second feature (called by Maimonides 'the existence of the stars'), Maimonides is explicit: 'no one would be able to find a cause particularizing it other than the purpose of one who purposes'.[31]

In sum, Maimonides' general purpose in raising doubts about our understanding of the celestial regions is clearly aimed at attacking the underpinnings of the doctrine of the eternity of the world. However, it seems to me that in the context of these arguments, Maimonides takes

correctly points out that the remarks of the anonymous commentator are motivated by *Guide*, ii. 24. To my knowledge, the only other writer to refer to the two seemingly contradictory texts is the great modern historian of astronomy, Otto Neugebauer, in 'The Astronomy of Maimonides and its Sources', *HUCA* 22 (1949), 322–63, esp. 336. After discussing the objections raised in the *Guide*, Neugebauer states without further comment: 'No such doubts are voiced in the Mishneh Torah (completed 1147). The Ptolemaic arrangements of the planets is accepted without restriction.'

[28] *Guide*, 326. This remark, in my view, does not imply that man's ability is limited to the computation of the planetary motions since, as I maintain, the 'Basic Principles' clearly presents a physical description. As I commented in n. 26, the physical descriptions also are inferred from mathematical data.

[29] Ibid. 308–9. [30] Ibid. 309. [31] Ibid.

care to distinguish between those aspects of the problem which indeed do not admit of solution—these belong ultimately to the realm of metaphysics—and those which, however elusive they may seem at present, may someday yield their secrets to human inquiry. This second class, I contend, includes the physical configuration of the heavens.

This view notwithstanding, there remains the need to square some of the details of the presentation of the *Mishneh Torah* with the specific criticisms found in the *Guide*. My claim is as follows. When writing the *Mishneh Torah*, Maimonides knew of the difficulties elaborated in the *Guide*. There was no known solution to these problems, and (I emphasize) Maimonides did not intend to offer any new cosmology in the *Mishneh Torah*. However, basing himself upon the minimal demands of the principles of natural science on the one hand, and the irrefutable evidence of mathematical astronomy on the other, Maimonides was confident enough of the general scheme of any correct cosmology to offer the descriptions found in the 'Basic Principles'.

A careful reading of *Guide*, ii. 24 reveals that Maimonides may not have rejected epicycles out of hand. The first objection to epicycles, that the epicycle 'rolls and changes its place completely',[32] applies only if the revolution of the epicycle takes place about a centre other than the centre of the orb which carries the epicycle (known also as the deferent)—in other words, if eccentricity of some sort (including an equant or rotating deferent centre, one must assume) is posited as well. If the epicycle revolves about the centre of the deferent, no such rolling would occur.

There then follow two objections aimed specifically at the epicycles, but these, I emphasize, are brought in the name of Ibn Bājja. These objections are: (*a*) the motion of the epicycle belongs to none of the three allowable categories of motion—namely, towards, away from, and about the centre of the world; (*b*) the motion of the epicycle is not about 'some immobile thing'.

The remaining objections apply to eccentricity, and here, interestingly enough, Maimonides takes credit himself for pointing out the impossibilities: 'It was by me that attention was drawn to this point.'[33] These difficulties concern the location of the eccentres, which, as we noted earlier, was indeed an original observation of Maimonides, and

[32] *Guide*, 323.
[33] Ibid.

the difficulty connected with the treatise of Thābit, also noted above.[34]

Now we note that in the *Mishneh Torah* epicycles are mentioned, but eccentricity not. How then, however, would Maimonides deal with the objections to epicycles brought in the name of Ibn Bājja? It is a fact that the epicycle has at least two motions. Its revolution about its own centre is the cause for criticisms such as those of Ibn Bājja. However, the epicycle as a whole also moves around the fixed earth with a motion which, if we assume no eccentricity, should raise no difficulties. In short, the fact that the epicycle is fixed within an orb which has a perfectly legitimate motion of its own about the earth mitigates to a large degree the objectionable features of the epicycle's motion about its own centre, if it does not completely remove those objections.

Profiat Duran, relying upon Levi b. Gerson, understands the discussion in the *Guide* along these lines, and this without any reference to the *Mishneh Torah*. In his commentary to *Guide*, ii. 24, we read:

> . . . but rather he wishes to explain that it is impossible to do without an immobile body about which it shall move, even if the body moves on a thousand bodies, since it is necessary that the lowest of them be immobile. As proof [we note] that a man moves on a ship, and it moves, but since the water is immobile, it is correct to say that the man is moving on an immobile thing, namely the water. So explained Rabbi Levi of blessed memory; even though the epicycle moves on the orb while it [the orb] is in motion, since the great orb moves about a fixed thing, the epicycle moves about an immobile thing.[35]

In answer to Maimonides' question, 'Furthermore, how can one conceive the retrogradation of a star, together with its other motions, without assuming the existence of an epicycle?'[36], we can now simply say that one does use epicycles. If eccentricity is eliminated, and if we accept Levi b. Gerson's view that what counts is that ultimately, whatever other motions it may have, the epicycle does move about an immobile centre, we are not troubled by Maimonides' second question, viz. 'How can one imagine a rolling motion in the heavens or a motion about a centre which is not immobile?'[37] We thus arrive at an

[34] That the objection based upon the treatise of Thābit is aimed at eccentrics we learn from Maimonides' introductory statement (*Guide*, 324): 'in all cases in which one of the two spheres is inside the other and adheres to it on every side, while the centers of the two are different'. Epicycles do not fulfil the first of the two conditions.

[35] Efodi on *Guide*, loc. cit. (Heb.). See the Hebrew edition of the *Guide* with commentaries (New York, 1946), 50.

[36] *Guide*, 326.

[37] Ibid.

essential difference between Maimonides and the Spanish school.[38] Ibn Rushd, for instance, does not limit his concern to the elimination of the difficulties of the Ptolemaic system. He is rather interested in restoring Aristotle's own model, which, in his incomplete understanding,[39] was comprised of concentric earth-centred spheres whose poles do not all lie on the same line. As a result of the combined motions of these spheres, a spiral (*lawlabī*) motion ensues which, it is hoped, will account for the observed motion of the star or planet.[40] Maimonides, on the other hand, is not necessarily interested in rediscovering, as it were, the Aristotelian cosmology, for as he says several times in the *Guide*, astronomy in the time of Aristotle was relatively underdeveloped.[41] Maimonides' attitude thus seems to be closer to that of Ibn al-Haytham, in that he hopes that some configuration, not necessarily that of Aristotle, will be found that can satisfy the constraints of natural philosophy.

A significant difficulty with the explanations which I suggest is the fact that in the *Mishneh Torah*, as noted above, Maimonides gives a specific number for the epicycles and 'encompassing orbs', as if he knows more than just the type of configuration found in the true cosmology. Though eccentric orbs are not specifically mentioned, Maimonides' count of the 'encompassing orbs' fits a scheme which allows eccentrics; and indeed, eccentric orbs do encompass the earth. Though it appears that the phrase in the fourth *halakhah*, 'the earth is

[38] The essential difference between Maimonides and Ibn Rushd was noted by Pines in his *Dictionary of Scientific Biography* article (n. 24 above) and in his 'Translator's Introduction', p. cx.

[39] It is highly doubtful that any medieval astronomer understood just how the homocentric model of Eudoxus accepted (with modifications) by Aristotle really worked. It was only in the 19th cent. that the Italian astronomer G. Schiaperelli worked out Eudoxus' system, showing that this arrangement is an ingenious way of producing the type of curve desired, but simply cannot be made to fit the observational data in most cases. Cf. Neugebauer, *History of Ancient Mathematical Astronomy* (see n. 9 above), ii. 677–83. Goldstein observes (*Al-Biṭrūjī*, vol. i, p. ix) that al-Biṭrūjī, far from reviving Eudoxus' models, 'does not even draw attention to the relevant passages in Aristotle's works'. Ibn Rushd, however, does refer to these passages, in his Great Commentary to Aristotle's *Metaphysica* (*Tafsīr Mā ba'da aṭ-Ṭabī'a*), ed. M. Bouyges, vol. iii (Beirut, 1948), 1657 ff.).

[40] Carmody, 'Ibn Rushd', 570–2. Carmody suggests (571 n. 24) that the *Kitāb al-Iqtiṣāṣ* 'perhaps' refers to the commentary of Theon of Alexandria of the *Almagest*. In fact, this is the Arabic title of Ptolemy's own *Planetary Hypotheses*. Cf. Sezgin, *Geschichte der arabischen Schriftums*, vi. 94–5.

[41] *Guide*, ii. 24, p. 326: 'For in his [Aristotle's] time mathematics had not been brought to perfection.' *Guide*, ii. 19, p. 308: 'However, as I have let you know, the science of astronomy was not in his [Aristotle's] time what it is today.'

suspended in the middle', excludes eccentricity, there may be some ambiguity as to whether the intention is that the earth is at the centre of *all* the orbs, or perhaps just at the centre of the universe. In any event, eliminating eccentrics would leave a serious gap in astronomical theory.[42] We can only suggest that this state of affairs reflects the dilemma with which Maimonides was faced. He openly proclaims the existence of epicycles, since, as we have seen, the philosophical problems entailed by these devices are not insurmountable. However, the epicycles were placed by astronomers in eccentric orbits, and on this point Maimonides is less open; he does not mention eccentrics, but he may not necessarily exclude them either.

III

The question of the scrutability of the heavens and the challenge of finding the true configuration generated a great deal of interest among Maimonides' successors. For example, Solomon Corcos, in an unpublished commentary to Book II, chapter 9 of Isaac Israeli's *Yesod 'Olam*, where an alternate configuration of the heavens is the topic of a short discussion,[43] wrote as follows: 'One should really be surprised at this author [i.e. Isaac Israeli]. How did he include it all in one chapter? It requires a large book all to itself in order to understand the profundity of the issue.'[44]

Some scholars attempted new cosmologies of their own. These have for the most part not been subjected to modern analyses. We would like now to sketch the views of some of these thinkers.[45]

Joseph Albo took the remarks of the *Guide* to imply that the principles of the astronomer and those of the natural philosopher are irreconcilable.[46] In Book IV, chapter 2 of his *'Iqqarim*, their difference

[42] See n. 17 above. I cannot help wondering whether Maimonides may have had in mind a system wherein epicycles are embedded in concentric spheres whose axes are inclined to the axis of daily rotation. This is sheer speculation, and I do not know if, theoretically, such a system could overcome the difficulties cited in n. 34.

[43] Al-Biṭrūjī is not mentioned by name, but it seems likely that he is the astronomer whose views are discussed. See Goldstein, *Al-Biṭrūjī*, i. 43.

[44] The manuscript I consulted was Munich 261, fo. 19*a*. I wish to thank the Institute of Microfilmed Hebrew Manuscripts in Jerusalem for their co-operation.

[45] On Jewish reaction to the alternative models of al-Biṭrūjī, see Goldstein, *Al-Biṭrūjī*, i. 40–4.

[46] Albo refers specifically to *Guide*, ii. 24, in connection with Maimonides' observation that the centres of the eccentric orbs lie above the orb of the moon. To this

of opinion is developed into a paradigm for the sort of disagreement which because it depends ultimately on opposing basic assumptions cannot be decided by reason alone. In the following chapter, Albo explicitly states: 'the human mind is not adequate to know this, any more than it is able to explain the causes of the heavenly motions without doing violence to the theories of physics'.[47] In his next sentence he goes even further, claiming that even some terrestrial phenomena are beyond the comprehension of the human intellect.

Levi b. Gerson took a very different position. The investigation of the heavenly phenomena demands both the mathematical expertise of the astronomer and the mastery of physics which belongs to the natural philosopher. Levi states that both of these will be utilized in his own astronomical treatise; in that same treatise, models alternative to those of Ptolemy are discussed, and complicated models of Levi's own invention are proposed. Levi would thus not seem to hold that the nature of the heavens is inscrutable.[48]

The approach taken by Profiat Duran in his *Ḥeshev ha-Efod*[49] looks to be in line with the views expressed in his commentary to the *Guide*. In chapter 3 Duran demonstrates the necessity of positing either epicycles or eccentres. At the end of this chapter he opts for the epicyclic model for the sun, against accepted practice from Ptolemy onwards.

> Even though all the masters of astronomy have chosen the eccentric model (*tekhunah*) for the sun over the epicyclic model, due to its simplicity, I, in this treatise, choose the epicyclic model for the sun so that the models of the sun and the moon shall be the same, and you will not be confused by an eccentricity for the sun, nor for the moon, since the epicyclic model is easier and simpler for the moon, and there is no place in it [the lunar model] for eccentricity—this is true for the times of conjunction and opposition, i.e. the *molad*, with which the intention and fulfilment [of this treatise lie].[50]

are added, in this chapter and the next, difficulties associated with epicycles and other astronomical matters not discussed in the *Guide*. See Joseph Albo, *Sefer ha-'Iqqarim* (Book of principles), ed. and trans. I. Husik (Philadelphia, 1930), iv. 17–18.

[47] Ibid.

[48] The astronomical work of Levi b. Gerson has been the subject of intensive and fruitful research by B. R. Goldstein; see his *The Astronomical Tables of Levi ben Gerson*, Transactions of the Connecticut Academy of Arts and Sciences, xlv (Hamden, Conn., 1974), and the literature cited therein. The first chapter of Levi's *Astronomy* (actually pt. i, bk. 5 of his *Wars of the Lord*) was translated by Goldstein in 'The Status of Models', (see n. 2 above), 145–7.

[49] I consulted MS Parma 800 (2776), fos. 101–33.

[50] Ibid. fo. 103*b*. Maimonides (*Guide*, ii. 11, pp. 273–4) is aware that the eccentric

Duran is apparently reviving the simple lunar model of Hipparchus, which may be satisfactory for the syzygies but is not so for other points of the lunar orbit. We recall that when calculations alone are involved, as in the present case, Maimonides himself has no objections to all the complications of the complete Ptolemaic lunar model. It would be foolish to say anything more on the subject until this interesting treatise has been thoroughly studied.

Joseph Naḥmias is the author of a book known in English as *Light of the World*,[51] an original attempt at an astronomical system based upon correct principles. A thorough study of this treatise is perhaps the chief desideratum for the history of Jewish astronomy. We must therefore limit ourselves again to some preliminary observations made on the basis of the author's introduction. Naḥmias sees astronomy as being forced to accept one of two unsavoury devices in order to account for the planetary motions: epicycles and eccentres, or 'contrary motion', that is, circular motion in opposite directions. Epicycles and eccentres are rejected out of hand, and Naḥmias will do the best he can (philosophically and mathematically) with the principle of contrary motion. We observe that the latter does not figure among the objections raised by Maimonides in *Guide*, ii. 24, and in the 'Basic Principles', iii. 2, it is explicitly stated that some of the orbs turn from west to east and some from east to west. Contrary motion does figure prominently in the objections of the Spanish school.[52]

In the course of his introduction, Naḥmias expresses astonishment at Maimonides' remarks in *Guide*, ii. 24, on the impossibility of explaining the planetary motion without recourse to epicycles or eccentres. Naḥmias credits al-Biṭrūjī with reviving the investigation of the true principles, something which stands to al-Biṭrūjī's credit despite the technical shortcomings of his work.

model was chosen for the sun for reasons of economy, and Duran must have known this too. In the light of Duran's remarks on the *Guide*, I suggest that physical–philosophical motivations lay behind Duran's choice of the epicyclic model, in addition to the proclaimed simplicity of the system.

[51] The treatise was written in Arabic (*Nūr al-'Ālam*) and rendered into Hebrew by an unknown translator. I consulted the Hebrew version, Bodley 2778. Cf. Steinschneider, *Hebraeischen Übersetzungen*, 597–8.

[52] Carmody, 'Ibn Rushd', 562. However, in his commentary to the *Metaphysica* (cited in n. 39), 1673–5, Ibn Rushd appears willing to accept some type of contrary motion, spurred, in part, by contemporary ideas on the trepidation of the equinoxes. There is need for a thorough study of the views of Ibn Rushd on matters astronomical. See also Goldstein, *Al-Biṭrūjī*, i. 67.

CONCLUSION

Maimonides, like many of his contemporaries, was concerned with the philosophical weaknesses of the Ptolemaic system; in this he was influenced by the Spanish school of criticism, but differed considerably from it. Though it may seem from *Guide*, ii. 24 that epicycles and eccentrics are unacceptable, and that in fact the true configuration of the heavens is beyond human comprehension, a careful reading of that chapter in conjunction with the relevant portion of the *Mishneh Torah* suggests that Maimonides did indeed have some idea of what the true configuration would be, and that in this configuration epicycles are allowed. The problems raised in *Guide*, ii. 24, were a matter of continued interest among Maimonides' successors and evoked quite different responses.

9

Maimonides on Religious Language

ARTHUR HYMAN*

MOSES Maimonides maintained a lively interest in questions of language, particularly language concerning God, throughout his life. In his very first work, the *Treatise on the Art of Logic*,[1] he discusses language in its relation to logic; in his two major legal works, the *Commentary on the Mishnah*[2] and his great code, *Mishneh Torah*,[3] both of which are addressed to a general, non-philosophic audience, he stresses that anthropomorphic and anthropopathic terms applied to God cannot be taken literally; and in his philosophic *Guide of the Perplexed*[4] he devotes most of the first part of the work to a more rigorous, philosophic discussion of divine attributes and names.

Maimonides' concern with religious language is part of his overall philosophic programme in which the correct understanding of language applied to God is one of the central themes. Not only is it obligatory for the intellectual élite to have a philosophically correct understanding of divine attributes, but even the unsophisticated masses must be taught that anthropomorphic and anthropopathic terms applied to God cannot be taken in their literal meaning. Maimonides expresses this view when he writes in *Guide of the Perplexed*, i. 35:

* Research for this paper was done under a Category A Fellowship from the National Endowment for the Humanities, which I held during the academic year 1980–1. I gratefully acknowledge this support.

[1] *Treatise on the Art of Logic*, ch. 13; Arab. ed. I. Efros, *PAAJR* 34 (1966); Heb. and Eng. ed. and trans. I. Efros, *PAAJR* (1938).

[2] *Commentary on the Mishnah*, *Sanhedrin*, *Introduction to Pereq Ḥeleq*, 13 principles; pinciples 2 and 3, Arab., ed. J. Kafiḥ (Jerusalem, 1964), 211; Heb., ed. S. Rabinowitz, *Haqdamot le-Ferush ha-Mishnah* (Jerusalem, 1961), 137–8; Eng. in I. Twersky, *A Maimonides Reader* (New York, 1972), 417–18.

[3] *Mishneh Torah*, *Yesode ha-Torah*, i. 7–12; ii. 4, 6; *Teshuvah*, viii. 2–5; ed. and trans. M. Hyamson (Jerusalem, 1962).

[4] *Guide of the Perplexed*, Arab. ed. I. Joel (Jerusalem, 1929); Heb. ed. S. Even Shemu'el (Jerusalem, 1981); Eng. trans. S. Pines (Chicago, 1967).

> The negation of the doctrine of the corporeality of God and the denial of His having a likeness to created things and of His being subject to affections are matters that ought to be made clear and explained to everyone according to his capacity and ought to be inculcated in virtue of traditional authority upon children, women, stupid ones, and those of a defective natural disposition, just as they adopt the notion that God is one, that He is eternal, and that none but He should be worshipped.[5]

As reason for his opinion he states in the continuation of this passage that 'there is no profession of [the] unity [of God] unless the doctrine of God's corporeality is denied'. Maimonides' interest in religious language, especially in divine attributes, is thus primarily determined by a concern for safeguarding the absolute unity of God, and it is this concern which influences much of what he has to say.

In demanding so stringently the enlightenment of the masses, Maimonides takes issue with the divergent position of his contemporary, Averroes, who, in his *Decisive Treatise*, stated that the masses must be left to their literal understanding of anthropomorphic and anthropopathic terms applied to God. More than that, Averroes maintained that Islamic law prohibits their enlightenment. 'As for the man who expresses these allegories [of the Koran] to unqualified persons,' writes Averroes, 'he is an unbeliever on account of his summoning people to unbelief.'[6] I have tried to explain in my essay 'Maimonides' Thirteen Principles'[7] why Maimonides should be so insistent that even

[5] While in the present passage Maimonides maintains that the masses must be taught not only that anthropomorphic but also anthropopathic terms cannot be applied literally to God, he is more lenient with respect to anthropopathic terms in a political context. Thus he states in *Guide*, iii. 28 that to instill obedience to the commandments of the Torah, the masses may believe that God gets angry at those who disobey him. Cf. *Guide*, i. 55.

My present purpose is to show how Maimonides' theory of divine attributes is based on the proposition that they cannot ascribe multiplicity to God. However, at times his arguments are based on the proposition that there cannot be any likeness between God and creatures. Summarizing his views, he states in *Guide*, i. 55: 'The basis of the matter is that anything that leads to one of the following four kinds of attribution ought of necessity to be negated in reference to Him [God] by means of clear demonstration; namely, (1) anything that leads to attributing to Him corporeality, or (2) that leads to attributing to Him affection and change, or (3) that leads to attributing to Him, for example, a statement that He has not something in actuality, or (4) that leads to attributing to Him a likeness to a thing among His creatures' (Arab., pp. 87–8; Heb., p. 110; Eng., pp. 128–9).

[6] *Decisive Treatise Determining the Nature of the Connection between Religion and Philosophy*, Arab., ed. G. Hourani (Leiden, 1959), 22; Eng., trans. G. Hourani (London, 1961), 66.

[7] A. Altmann (ed.), *Jewish Medieval and Renaissance Studies* (Cambridge, Mass., 1967), 119–45.

the masses must receive a measure of enlightenment concerning correct language about God, and it is not within the confines of this paper to restate my arguments here.

To present Maimonides' views on religious language, we must undertake a threefold task: we shall first examine a passage from the *Treatise on the Art of Logic* in which Maimonides analyses the various ways in which terms may signify; we shall then discuss how he uses the distinctions of the *Treatise* in the *Guide* to show that anthropomorphic and anthropopathic terms occurring in Scripture must be taken in a spiritual sense; and, finally, we shall consider the reasons which brought him to his position that accidental attributes predicated of God must be interpreted as attributes of action, and essential attributes as negations or negations of privations.[8] By way of conclusion we shall discuss how Maimonides' account of divine attributes influenced his attitude towards prayer.

I

Maimonides, as he tells his reader, wrote the *Treatise on the Art of Logic* at the request of someone who was versed in the juridical sciences and the clarity and eloquence of the Arabic language and desired to gain some familiarity with basic logical terms. As Mubahat Türker, the editor of the full Arabic text of the *Treatise* has pointed out,[9] Maimonides drew upon four Alfarabian *opuscula* for his exposition. While the *Treatise* is thus a rather conventional summary of the logic of the day, it is of help in clarifying certain passages of the *Guide*.

Of special interest for our investigation is a section of chapter 13 of the *Treatise* in which Maimonides discusses the three basic significations that 'words' or 'terms' may have. Terms, he holds, may be distinct (*mutabayyina*), synonymous (*murādifa*), or equivocal (*mushtiraka*).[10] When different words have different meanings—water, fire, tree, for example—they are distinct. Here Maimonides simply points out that individuals, species, and genera are each called by their own terms. When different words have the same meaning—for

[8] For the distinction between these two terms, see below, pp. 187–90.

[9] See M. Türker, 'Musa b. Maymun'un Makāla fi Ṣinā'at al-Manṭiḳ'i', *Publications of the Faculty of Letters, Istanbul University, Review of the Institute of Islamic Studies*, 3/1–2 (1956–60), 58–9 n. 17; also A. Hyman, 'The Liberal Arts and Jewish Philosophy', in *Arts libéraux et philosophie au moyen âge* (Montreal–Paris, 1969), 101–2.

[10] See *Maimonides' Treatise on Logic*, ed. and trans. I. Efros (New York, 1938), 59. This classification applies to 'all languages'.

example, Arabic *al-jamal* and *al-ba'īr*, both of which mean 'camel', or the Hebrew *adam*, *ish*, and *enosh*, all of which mean 'man', they are synonymous. When the same word has several meanings it is 'equivocal'. Since the notion of 'distinct' terms is rather trivial, and since terms applied to God and creatures can hardly by synonymous, only equivocal terms need to be considered here.

For Maimonides, the term 'equivocal' has two senses: generic and specific. In its generic sense, the term has the meaning that has already been mentioned, namely, it refers to any term that has different meanings in different contexts. In this sense it refers to any non-univocal or oblique use, the conditions of which are that the same term should appear in two or more propositions and that there should be some similarity and some difference in its varying uses.

Having defined the term 'equivocal' in its generic sense, Maimonides proceeds to divide it into six species. That this division is not exhaustive becomes clear from a comparison with a parallel passage in Averroes' *Epitome of the Categories* in which the Muslim philosopher presents a longer list of 'specific' equivocal terms.[11] The six kinds that Maimonides lists are: (*a*) completely equivocal terms (*al-mushtiraka al-maḥḍat al-ishtirāk*), (*b*) univocal terms (*al-mutawāṭi'a*), (*c*) amphibolous terms (*al-mushakkika*), (*d*) terms used in general and in particular (*mā yuqāl bi-'umūm wa-khuṣūṣ*), (*e*) metaphorical terms (*al-musta'āra*), and (*f*) extended terms (*al-manqūla*).[12] If one examines Maimonides' sixfold division and compares it with the relevant passages in the *Guide*, one finds that three of the specific kinds of 'equivocal' predications are useful for interpreting anthropomorphic and anthropopathic terms applied to God, while three are not. Univocal terms, such as the term 'animal' applied to man, horse, scorpion, and fish, are inapplicable to God since they refer to a common genus or difference; but God and his creatures do not share a common genus or difference. Similarly, terms used in general and particular, examples of which are the Arabic *kawkab* and the Hebrew *kokhav*, which in their general sense refer to any star and in their particular sense to Mercury, cannot be applied to God, since they refer to a genus and one of its species; but God and his creatures cannot have that relation. Finally,

[11] Heb., *Kol Meleket Higgayon* (Riva di Trento, 1560), 2ʳ–3ʳ; Latin, *Aristotelis Opera cum Averrois Commentariis* (Venice, 1562–74), i. 2*b*, 36ʳ–37ʳ; repr. Frankfurt, 1962. For a shorter list, see al-Ghazālī, *Maqāṣid al-Falāsifa*, ed. S. Dunya (Cairo, 1961), 42–3. Cf. S. Rosenberg, 'Signification of Names in Medieval Jewish Logic' (Heb.), *Iyyun*, 27 (1976–7), 105–44.

[12] See Efros, *Maimonides' on Logic*, 59.

extended terms, such as the Arabic word *ṣalāt* and the Hebrew word *tefillah*, which at first referred to any request and afterwards to prayer, a specific request, are inapplicable to God since these terms are related as a species to one of its members; but God and his creatures cannot have this relation.

This brings us to the three specific 'equivocal' terms that can be applied to God. The first of these are completely equivocal terms, an example of which is '*ayin*, which in both Arabic and Hebrew refers to the eye as well as to the fountain. Completely equivocal terms have only a name in common and they are the most likely candidates for the interpretation of attributes applied to God. It should be noted, however, that while such terms have nothing in common but the name, each of these terms has it own definition or description.[13] Then there are amphibolous terms, such as the term 'man' applied to Zayd, the corpse of a man and the picture of a man, which have in common the appearance or the shape of a human being, but this common factor is an accidental property and hence does not constitute their essence. Finally, there are metaphorical terms, such as the Arabic *al-asad* and the Hebrew *aryeh*, whose first meaning refers to the lion but is then transferred to the description of a courageous man. In this case the term has a fixed usage in its original meaning and is then transferred to another object in which it does not have a permanent meaning. As with amphibolous terms, the common factor in metaphorical terms is not the essences of the things compared but some accidental property. It should be stressed that while in the exegetical context Maimonides concedes that anthropomorphic and anthropopathic attributes applied to God may be understood as amphibolous and metaphorical terms, he excludes these uses from his philosophic account.[14]

II

In his *Guide of the Perplexed*, Maimonides discusses language about God in two contexts: one exegetical (*Guide*, i. 1–49), the other

[13] Cf. Aristotle, *Categories*, 1, 1*a*, 1–6: 'Things are said to be named "equivocally" when, though they have a common name, the definition corresponding with the name differs for each. Thus, a real man and a figure in a picture can both lay claim to the name "animal"; yet these are equivocally so named, for, though they have a common name, the definition corresponding with the name differs for each. For should anyone define in what sense each is an animal, his definition in one case will be appropriate to that case only.'

[14] See *Guide*, i. 56.

philosophical (*Guide*, i. 50–70). Maimonides' great concern with the correct understanding of scriptural terms applied to God emerges from the very beginning of the *Guide* when, in the Introduction,[15] he writes: 'The first purpose of this Treatise [the *Guide*] is to explain the meanings of certain terms occurring in the books of prophecy.' And using the enumeration of the *Treatise on the Art of Logic*, he goes on to state: 'some of these terms are "equivocal" (*mushtarika*), . . . others are "metaphorical" (*musta'āra*), . . . and others are "amphibolous" (*mushakkika*)'.[16] In each of these cases the ignorant masses take the term in an inappropriate sense, and Maimonides undertakes to correct their mistakes by providing the right interpretation.

In devoting most of the first forty-nine chapters of the *Guide* to matters of exegesis,[17] Maimonides addresses not only the philosophic audience for which the *Guide* was primarily intended, but also the masses, the beginners in speculation, and those rabbinic scholars who were only engaged in the legalistic study of the Torah.[18] Pursuing his programme of the philosophic enlightenment of these, Maimonides shows these non-philosophers that the mere comparison of scriptural texts reveals that the same term may have different meanings, so that anthropomorphic and anthropopathic terms applied to God, interpreted correctly, can be seen to have a figurative sense. In taking this stance, Maimonides does not speak primarily as a philosopher, but he places himself, as Leo Strauss has noted,[19] in the line of traditional biblical exegetes who attempted to discover the meaning of the text through careful philological and contextual analysis.

While the details of Maimonides' method and its backgrounds still require monographic exploration, some of its principles are clear enough. There are, Maimonides notes, scriptural terms, which, never denoting a corporeal quality, are most appropriately applied to God; and there are others which, always denoting a corporeal quality, can

[15] Arab., p. 2; Heb., p. 4; Eng., p. 5.

[16] Ibid.

[17] Concerning the non-exegetical chapter, Maimonides writes: 'We shall include in this Treatise some chapters in which there will be no mention of an equivocal term. Such a chapter will be preparatory for another, or it will hint at one of the meanings of an equivocal term that I might not mention explicitly in that place, or it will explain one of the parables or hint at the fact that a certain story is a parable' *Guide* i. Introd. (Arab., p. 6; Heb., p. 9; Eng., p. 10). Leo Strauss points out in his 'How to Begin to Study *The Guide of the Perplexed*', in *Guide of the Perplexed*, trans. Pines, pp. xxiv–xxv, that 30 of the first 49 chapters are lexicographic.

[18] *Guide*, i. Introd. (Arab., p. 2; Heb., p. 4; Eng., 5). Cf. Strauss, 'How to Begin', pp. xv ff.

[19] See Strauss, 'How to Begin', p. xxiii.

never be applied to him. An example of the former is provided in *Guide*, i. 1, by the verse 'Let us make man in our image (*be-ẓalmenu*) and likeness (*bi-demutenu*)' (Gen. 1: 26). There were some, Maimonides comments, who inferred from this verse that God must have a body, since this could be the only likeness between man and God. On the contrary, Maimonides interprets, the term *ẓelem* never refers to the appearance or shape of anything, but only to its natural form or essence. There is a Hebrew term, *to'ar*, which exclusively refers to the shape or the appearance of something, but this term is never applied to God. Similarly, in *Guide*, i. 3, he points out that the term 'shape' (*tavnit*), which can only have a corporeal meaning, is never applied to God, while a similar term 'figure' (*temunah*), which has several meanings, is applied to him. Still further, he states in *Guide*, i. 26,[20] Scripture describes God only by means of attributes considered perfections by the masses; never by means of attributes considered by them deficiencies or privations, such as eating, drinking, sleeping, or being ill. The very terminology of Scripture, then, shows a sensitivity to nuances of language by never applying inappropriate language to God.

But since 'the Torah speaks in the language of the sons of men', not in the language of philosophers, it cannot avoid language that is anthropomorphic and anthropopathic in its literal sense. The exegetical comparison of texts reveals that such language is 'equivocal', and that it can be interpreted to yield non-anthropomorphic and non-anthropopathic meanings. Keeping in mind the distinctions of the *Treatise on the Art of Logic*, Maimonides shows that such terms may be predicated according to complete equivocation, amphibolously, or metaphorically.

To illustrate Maimonides' thesis, let us turn to two examples: one of completely equivocal, the other of amphibolous predication. Maimonides provides an example of the former in *Guide*, i. 13, where he discusses the term 'standing' (*'amidah*). In one of its senses this term refers to a bodily posture, in another it signifies 'to abstain' or 'to desist', and in a third it points to something stable or endurable. The first meaning is illustrated by the verse 'when he [Joseph] stood before Pharaoh' (Gen. 41: 46), the second by the verse 'and she [Leah] left off bearing' (Gen. 29: 35), and the third by the verse 'that they [the deeds of purchase] may stand many days' (Jer. 32: 14). Turning to the verse

[20] See also *Guide*, i. 46, 47.

'His [God's] righteousness standeth ('*omedet*) forever' (Ps. 111: 3), Maimonides argues that whenever the term 'standing' is predicated of God, it can only have the third sense, in this case, 'His [God's] righteousness if permanent and enduring'.

An example of amphibolous predication is provided in *Guide*, i. 4, where Maimonides discusses three terms for 'seeing'—*ra'oh*, *habbiṭ*, and *ḥazoh*. In their primary meaning, all these terms refer to sensory apprehension, that is, seeing by means of the eye; but this meaning is transferred to intellectual apprehension. An example of the first meaning is provided by Gen. 29: 2: 'and he [Jacob] saw, and behold a well in the field' (Eccles. 1: 16); 'yea my heart has seen much wisdom and knowledge' is an example of the second. Whenever the term 'seeing' is applied to 'seeing God', as in Kgs. 22: 19, 'I saw the Lord', it can only refer to intellectual apprehension.

From what has been said so far, it follows that scriptural terms signify completely equivocally, amphibolously, or metaphorically, and that the exegetical application of these distinctions yields a non-anthropomorphic and non-anthropopathic sense for anthropomorphic and anthropopathic terms predicated of God.

III

While the exegetical approach might be adequate for the enlightenment of the masses, and while it may have a preparatory function for philosophers, the problem of divine attributes is more complex. Maimonides devotes *Guide*, i. 50–70 to the discussion of its philosophic aspects. But in this section he is not concerned with establishing by means of arguments which attributes may be predicated of God, but rather with giving a philosophically adequate account of those which in fact occur in Scripture.[21]

By way of preliminary observation it should be noted that, absolutely speaking, Maimonides takes a rather dim view of the ability of human language to convey significant truths about God and he prefers silent

[21] In *Guide*, ii. 1, Maimonides offers demonstrative arguments that God exists, is one, and is incorporeal. By contrast Aquinas, in *Summa Theologiae*, i, qq. 2–26, *passim*, presents arguments for a whole series of attributes that can be predicated of God.

For a discussion of the content and structure of this section of the *Guide*, see E. Schweid, *Ṭa'am we-Haqqashah* (Ramat Gan, 1970), 105–48.

contemplation to speaking about him. He expresses this opinion when, discussing divine attributes in *Guide*, i. 57, he writes:

These subtle notions [divine attributes] that very clearly elude the minds cannot be considered through the instrumentality of the customary words, which are the greatest among the causes leading unto error. For the bounds of expression in all languages are very narrow indeed, so that we cannot represent this notion to ourselves except through a certain looseness of expression.[22]

Even more explicitly he writes in *Guide*, i. 59:

The most apt phrase concerning this subject is the dictum occurring in the Psalms (65: 2) 'Silence is praise to Thee', which interpreted signifies: silence with regard to You is praise . . . Accordingly, silence and limiting oneself to the apprehensions of the intellects are more appropriate—just as the perfect ones have enjoined us when they say (Ps. 4: 5): 'Commune with your own heart upon your bed, and be still, Selah'.[23]

While the silent contemplation of God thus seems to be Maimonides' ideal goal, it is a fact that Scripture describes God in human language and that men pray to him and speak about him. Maimonides still has to describe how human language functions correctly concerning God.

It has already been seen that as a first step towards the correct understanding of language about God, scriptural terms ascribing to God corporeality, affects, or likeness to creatures must be shown to be figurative through interpretation of the biblical texts.[24] But to be philosophically correct, propositions about God must meet two further conditions: (*a*) they must signify literally[25] and in accordance with the customary usages of human language; and (*b*) since God is one, attributes forming predicates of these propositions must not introduce any multiplicity into him.

That God is 'one' was axiomatic for Maimonides the believing Jew and competent philosopher. But what does the proposition 'God is one' mean? In its obvious sense it seems to signify that God is unique, and this is the sense in which the masses understand it. But for philosophers this meaning is not enough, for something can be unique and yet be composite. If, then, God is one, he must be not only unique, but also simple or non-composite. That God lacks any physical

[22] Arab., p. 90; Heb., p. 113; Eng., 132–33.
[23] Arab., p. 95; Heb., p. 119; Eng., 139–40.
[24] See above, pp. 179–82 and n. 5.
[25] The attributes predicated of God and human beings cannot signify metaphorically or amphibolously, but only according to complete equivocation.

composition is evident from his incorporeality, but beyond that he must also lack any kind of ontological composition.[26] It is the latter proposition that is central to Maimonides' philosophic account of divine attributes.

Before proceeding to the next step in Maimonides' exposition, we must turn briefly to some points of logic and ontology. Logic, for Maimonides, was subject–predicate logic, that is, it dealt with propositions of the form '*S* is *P*'.[27] That in all propositions of this kind the predicate is linguistically distinct from the subject is clear enough, but is it also ontologically distinct? The answer to this question depends on one's conception of the metaphysical status of attributes that form the predicates of propositions.

Attributes that form the predicates of propositions are of two kinds: essential and accidental.[28] Essential attributes are those the denial of which entails the denial of the existence of their subject. For example, if in the proposition 'Socrates is living', the predicate 'living' is denied, the existence of Socrates is denied thereby. Accidental attributes, on the other hand, are those the denial of which does not entail the denial of the existence of their subject. If, for example, in the proposition 'this table is brown', the predicate 'brown' is denied, the existence of the table is not denied thereby. For it may be the case that the table is brown at the present time, but it remains the same table even if it is painted green at some future time.

That accidental attributes introduce ontological multiplicity into the subject of which they are predicated was generally admitted by medieval philosophers, but they differed concerning essential attributes. There were those who maintained—Averroes among the Muslims and

[26] *Guide*, i. 51: 'For there is no oneness at all except in believing that there is one simple essence in which there is no complexity or multiplication of notions, but one notion only; so that from whatever angle you regard it and from whatever point of view you consider it, you will find that it is one, not divided in any way and by any cause into two notions; and you will not find therein any multiplicity either in the thing as it is outside of the mind or as it is in the mind' (Arab., p. 76; Heb., p. 96; Eng., p. 113). Also, *Guide*, i. 52: 'He [God], may He be exalted, is one in all respects; no multiplicity should be posited in Him' (Arab., p. 80; Heb., p. 101; Eng., p. 119).

[27] *Treatise on the Art of Logic*, chs. 1–2.

[28] Of this general classification, Maimonides speaks of 'essential attributes' (*al-ṣifāt al-dhātiyya/ha-to'arim ha-'aẓmiyyim*)—denying that they can be predicated affirmatively of God—but he does not speak of 'accidental attributes'. Instead, he speaks of 'attributes of actions' (*ṣifāt al-af'āl* [*fi'liyya*], *to'are ha-pe'ulot* [*pe'ilut*]), sometimes of 'attributes' (*ṣifāt/to'arim*), and in *Guide*, i. 54 he identifies such attributes with the biblical term *derakhim* and the rabbinic term *middot*. His reason seems to be that Scripture only uses those accidental attributes that can be understood as 'attributes of action'.

Gersonides among the Jews—that essential attributes are explicative, that is, they explain the meaning of the subject, so that they do not introduce any ontological multiplicity. According to this view, essential attributes can be predicated affirmatively of God, though it must still be shown how they differ in their application to God and creatures.[29] Others—Avicenna among the Muslims and Maimonides among the Jews—held that essential attributes, no less than accidental ones, are expansive, that is, they add information about the subject, so that they introduce ontological multiplicity. Hence, they cannot be applied to God with any positive signification. Agreeing with Avicenna, Maimonides writes in *Guide*, i. 57: 'It is known that existence (*al-wujūd*) [and one may add, any other essential attribute] is an accident attaching to what exists. For this reason it is something (*ma'nā*) that is superadded to the quiddity (*māhiyya*) of what exists.'[30] Having affirmed then that neither accidental nor essential attributes can be predicated affirmatively of God, Maimonides must show that propositions about God containing affirmative attributes as their predicates must be interpreted as propositions that say something significant and correct about him, yet do so without applying attributes that signify affirmatively.

For the case of accidental attributes predicated of God, Maimonides holds that they must be understood as attributes of action.[31] In the case of human beings, such attributes must meet two conditions: someone possessing them must (*a*) have certain dispositions, either habits or affects,[32] and (*b*) perform or be able to perform habitually actions of a certain kind. Since dispositions introduce ontological multiplicity into

[29] Gersonides, for example, maintains that essential attributes are predicated of God and human beings according to priority and posteriority, a kind of amphibolous predication. See *Wars of the Lord*, iii. 3 (Heb. edn. Leipzig, 1866, pp. 132–7); Eng. *Gersonides on God's Knowledge*, trans. and com. N. Samuelson (Toronto, 1977), 182–224.

[30] See A. Altmann, 'Essence and Existence in Maimonides', *Studies in Religious Philosophy and Mysticism* (Ithaca, NY, 1969), 108–27.

[31] For the logic of attributes of action, see H. A. Wolfson, 'The Aristotelian Predicables and Maimonides' Division of Attributes', in I. Twersky and G. H. Williams (eds.), *Studies in the History of Philosophy and Religion*, ii (Cambridge, Mass., 1977), 161–94, esp. 187–94.

[32] Maimonides' terminology is not very precise. For the case of human beings, he sometimes describes these attributes as dispositions (*hay'āt/tekhunot*), sometimes as habits (*malakāt/kinyanim*), and sometimes as affects (*infi'āl/hipa'alut*). Other terms used by him are moral qualities (*akhlāq/middot*) and dispositions of the soul (*hay'āt nafsāniyya/tekhunot nafshiyyot*). On balance, one gains the impression that 'disposition' is a generic term whose species are habits and affects. In *Guide*, i. 52 his examples are habits (see below, n. 35); in *Guide*, i. 54 they are affects.

the subject to which they belong,[33] they cannot be predicated of God. It only remains that accidental attributes in his case must be understood as referring to his actions. While the knowledge of actions is more limited than knowledge of dispositions and actions together, it has the advantage, in the case of God, that it does not impose any multiplicity.

Maimonides' position rests on two principles: (*a*) the relation of cause and effect can exist without there being a likeness between the two,[34] and (*b*) knowledge of the effect can provide some knowledge of the cause without providing any knowledge of the essential nature of the cause or any of its properties. Let us illustrate by means of an example.[35] Suppose that (*a*) a being *X* exists in an otherwise empty room; (*b*) wood, nails, and other materials are introduced into the room; (*c*) nothing miraculous happens in the room; and (*d*) after some time a finished table is handed out of the room. From these conditions we can infer that *X* has the ability to make a table, though we do not gain any knowledge of what kind of being *X* is or of any property that enables *X* to make a table. Expressing this point, Maimonides writes in *Guide*, i. 52:

> I do not intend to signify by the words, His action, the habitus of an art[36] that belongs to him who is described . . . But I intend to signify by the words, his action, the action that he who is described has performed . . . Now this kind of attribute is remote from the essence of the thing of which it is predicated. For this reason it is permitted that this kind should be predicated of God.[37]

Having shown that accidental attributes predicated of God must be interpreted as attributes of action, Maimonides might have gone on to affirm that essential attributes should be understood as attributes of action as well. However, he never seems to have considered this

[33] A second reason is that dispositions imply change in that to which they belong. God cannot be subject to change.

[34] In the *Guide*, Maimonides considers two kinds of causality: that in which there is a likeness between the cause and the effects, and that in which there is no likeness between the two. The former is divisible into a cause that produces one effect—for example, the motion of the hand which produces motion in the stick it moves; and a cause that produces many effects, such as the heat of fire which bleaches and blackens, burns and cooks, makes hard and melts (see ibid. i. 53). God, who is a cause of the second kind, produces many effects and is unlike any of the effects he produces.

[35] This example is based on *Guide*, i. 52, where in speaking of habits productive of certain actions, Maimonides uses the examples of carpenter, smith, builder, and weaver. For examples of effects, see ibid. i. 54.

[36] *Malakat al-ṣināʿa/qinyan ha-melakha.*

[37] Arab., p. 80; Heb., p. 101; Eng., pp. 118–19.

possibility.[38] (Aquinas in *Summa Theologiae*, i. qu. 13, a. 2 cites such an opinion in the name of Alain of Lille.)[39] Similarly, he might have held that essential attributes can be understood as amphibolous or metaphorical terms, but this possibility is rejected by him as well. For, as has been seen, such terms introduce multiplicity into God and, in addition, they require that there is some likeness between God and creatures.[40] It only remains that such terms are predicated of God and creatures according to complete equivocation, and that they signify by way of negation or negation of privation. In *Guide*, i. 58 Maimonides lists eight essential attributes together with their negated privations; these are: (*a*) existing–not-existing, (*b*) living–not dead, (*c*) incorporeal,[41] (*d*) eternal–not caused, (*e*) powerful–not powerless, (*f*) knowing–not ignorant or inattentive, (*g*) willing–not negligent, and (*h*) one–not many.

When Maimonides[42] describes in general fashion how essential attributes predicated of God are to be understood, he maintains that they must be understood as negations.[43] But, speaking more technically,

[38] To Maimonides it seems self-evident that there is a difference between essential attributes and dispositions. Essential attributes describe what something is, not what it does. He writes in *Guide*, i. 58: 'It has thus become clear to you that every attribute that we predicate of Him [God] is an attribute of action or if the attribute is intended for the apprehension of His essence and not of His action, it signifies the negation of the attribute in question' (Arab., p. 93; Heb., p. 116; Eng., p. 136).

[39] See *Basic Writings of Saint Thomas Aquinas*, ed. A. C. Pegis (New York, 1945), i. 114 n. 9. For a discussion of Aquinas' account of divine attributes, see J. F. Wippel, 'Quidditative Knowledge of God according to Thomas Aquinas', in L. P. Gerson (ed.), *Graceful Reason: Essays in Ancient and Medieval Philosophy Presented to Joseph Owens* (Toronto, 1983), 273–99 and refs.

[40] *Guide*, i. 56: 'Do not deem that they [the essential attributes] are used amphibolously. For when terms are used amphibolously they are predicated of two things between which there is a likeness in respect to some notion . . . Would that I knew accordingly whence the likeness could come so that the divine and the human attributes could be comprised in the same definition and be used in a univocal sense' (Arab., p. 89; Heb., p. 112; Eng., p. 131).

This argument, in fact, would be Maimonides' reply to philosophers such as Gersonides and Aquinas who hold that essential attributes are to be predicated of God affirmatively and that they can be understood as amphibolous or analogical terms.

[41] In Maimonides' list, this term does not have an opposite. H. A. Wolfson, 'Maimonides on Negative Attributes', *Studies in the History of Philosophy and Religion*, ii. 205, bottom, suggests that 'God is pure form' would be a proposition containing such an opposite. Maimonides does not list it because it is not in common usage. This interpretation seems to me rather forced, as my interpretation on p. 188 below tries to show.

[42] The discussion that follows is based on Wolfson's 'Maimonides on Negative Attributes'.

[43] *Salb/shelilah*.

he states in *Guide*, i. 58 that they must be understood as 'negations of privations'.[44] Since, however, privations are of different kinds, he indicates the kind of privation he has in mind by adding: 'one sometimes denies with reference to a thing something that cannot fittingly exist in it. Thus we say of a wall that it is not endowed with sight [not seeing].'[45]

In using the example of the wall that cannot see,[46] Maimonides alludes to a distinction between two kinds of privations: (*a*) the absence of some property (or habit) that can naturally be there, and (*b*) the absence of some property (or habit) that cannot naturally be there. An example of the former is provided in the proposition 'the man is blind'; an example of the latter 'the wall is not seeing'. In the case of the man, an ability is lacking that men ordinarily possess; while in the case of the wall, the property being negated is one that walls can never possess. Privations of the second kind exclude the subject of which they are predicated from a certain class of beings or properties. Since God can never have any properties (or habits) that are affirmatively predicated of him, the privation that is negated of him must be of the second kind. Thus, when the proposition 'God is wise' is understood as 'God is not ignorant', it is meant to exclude God from the class of ignorant beings.

One further distinction remains to be made. Linguistically, privative attributes predicated of God are of two kinds: (*a*) those which are negated of God, such as 'ignorant' in the proposition 'God is not ignorant', and (*b*) those which are affirmed of God, as 'not corporeal (incorporeal)' in the proposition 'God is not corporeal (incorporeal)'.[47] Since propositions of the latter kind in their literal signification serve to exclude God from certain classes of properties, Maimonides does not devote a special discussion to them. It is only for the first kind that Maimonides has to show that they are to be understood in the same manner. It is probably because the two kinds of privative attributes signify in the same fashion that Maimonides finds it possible to include 'incorporeal' in his list of eight essential attributes.

[44] *Salb 'admihā/shelilat he'adero.*

[45] Arab., p. 93; Heb., p. 116; Eng., p. 136.

[46] For greater clarity, I have simplified the terminology applying to the two kinds of privation. The distinction beween them goes back to Aristotle, who calls the first kind 'privation' (*sterēsis*), the second 'negation' (*apophasis*). Alexander of Aphrodisias provided the example of the wall that is not seeing. In Maimonides' terminology the first kind of privation is called *'adm* (*he'ader*); the second, *salb* (*shelilah*). Noted that the negation mentioned in this context differs from that in the phrase 'negation of privation'. See Wolfson, 'Maimonides on Negative Attributes', 207–13.

[47] To describe propositions of this form, Wolfson uses the term 'affirmation of privation'; see 'Maimonides on Negative Attributes', 213–16.

The distinction that was insignificant for Maimonides became crucial for Aquinas,[48] for when Aquinas speaks of divine attributes that are to be understood as negation, he only admits private attributes of the second kind. Essential attributes, by contrast, cannot simply be understood as negations; they must signify positively in some way. For Aquinas they signify according to analogy.

But does negative language about God provide any knowledge of him? Maimonides concedes that affirmative attributes provide a more adequate account of the essence and attributes of an object; but as the following example illustrates, negative attributes provide some knowledge as well (*Guide*, i. 60). Suppose someone knows that a ship exists, but does not know the object to which the term applies. Let us now imagine that someone knows that a ship is not an accident, another that it is not a mineral, a third that it is not a plant, and so forth; as the negations are multiplied, one comes closer and closer to knowing what a ship is, though the ship is never known in positive fashion. 'It is clear', writes Maimonides, 'that the last individual [in the example] has nearly achieved, by means of these negative attributes, the representation of the ship as it is.'[49] From all this it follows that we can say something significant about God's essential attributes without assigning to them affirmative signification.[50]

One question remains. If essential attributes are understood as negations, would it not be sufficient to affirm generally that God is unlike any of his creatures? In that case, however, it would follow that 'Moses our Master and Solomon [the wisest of men] did not apprehend anything different from what a single individual from among the pupils apprehends' (*Guide*, i. 59).[51] This, however, is not so.

[48] *Summa Theologiae*, i, qu. 13, a. 2. See H. A. Wolfson, 'St Thomas on Divine Attributes', in *Studies in the History of Philosophy and Religion*, ii. 497–524, esp. 497–502, 514–24.

[49] Arab., p. 98; Heb., p. 122; Eng., p. 143.

[50] This point may be further illustrated by the following example. Suppose it has been demonstrated that God is incorporeal. This does not provide any positive knowledge about God's essence or his attributes. However, should someone claim that some corporeal being (e.g. the sun or the moon) is God, knowledge that God is excluded from the class of corporeal beings allows us to counter this claim.

Maimonides' position was criticized even by medieval philosophers, for example Gersonides and Aquinas (see above, nn. 29, 48). For a recent discussion of whether the interpretation of divine attributes as negations provides any significant knowledge about God, see the exchange between G. Englebretsen, 'The Logic of Negative Theology', *The New Scholasticism*, 47 (1973), 228–32, and J. A. Buijs, 'Comments on Maimonides' Negative Theology', ibid. 49 (1975), 87–93.

[51] Arab., pp. 93–4; Heb., p. 117; Eng., pp. 137–8.

For just as each additional affirmative attribute increases the knowledge of that which is described, so each additional negation 'particularizes'[52] God more and more. Moreover, it is not enough to simply deny certain attributes of God; a philosopher must know by apodictic proof why a given attribute is to be denied. The acquisition of this knowledge requires time and training, as Maimonides explains when he writes in *Guide*, i. 59:

> A man sometimes labours for many years in order to understand some science . . . so that he should have certainty with regard to this science, whereas the only conclusion from this science in its entirety consists in our negating with reference to God some notion of which it has been learned by means of a demonstration that it can not possibly be applied to God.[53]

While the terms discussed so far are attributes predicated of God, there is one name, namely the tetragrammaton, which signifies his essence. Perhaps indicating the notion of necessary existence, this name has no association with any terms applied to creatures. 'This name', writes Maimonides in *Guide*, i. 61, 'gives a clear and unequivocal indication of God's essence.'[54]

It may finally be asked: what are the implications of Maimonides' rigorous conception of language concerning God for its religious use? Is it not the case that the believer who reads Scripture and prays means something more in saying that God is one and living than that he is not many and not dead? Would one not expect that language about God signifies positively in some way? Ever the purist, Maimonides would reply that positive predication introduces multiplicity into God and for that reason must be avoided at any cost. It is better to say little about God and say it correctly than to say much and mislead. How consequent he was becomes apparent in *Guide*, i. 59 when he inveighs against 'poets and preachers' who increase language about God, and when he approvingly cites the story of Rabbi Ḥaninah (*Berakhot*, 33*b*) who chided someone who, in the '*amidah*, added to the traditionally sanctioned phrase 'God the great, valiant, and terrible' the words 'the mighty, the strong, the tremendous'. The story of Rabbi Ḥaninah was also in Maimonides' mind when in *Mishneh Torah*, *Hilkhot Tefillah*, ix, 7 (see commentaries ad loc.) he writes that in one's devotion

[52] *Tukhaṣṣiṣ/yityaḥed*.

[53] Arab., p. 94; Heb., p. 118; Eng., p. 138.

[54] Arab., p. 100; Heb., p. 125; Eng., p. 147. Maimonides' theory of how proper names signify remains to be worked out.

one should not multiply the attributes of God saying God the great, the valiant, the terrible, the strong, the mighty, the powerful, since it is not in man's power to exhaust His praises. One should only recite the attributes used by Moses, peace upon him, that is, God the great, the valiant, the terrible.

This passage from *Mishneh Torah* provides one more example of the confluence of Maimonides' philosophic and halakhic views.[55]

[55] Cf. I. Twersky, 'Some Non-halakhic Aspects of the Mishneh Torah', in Altmann *Jewish Medieval and Renaissance Studies*, 95–118; id., *Introduction to the Code of Maimonides (Mishneh Torah)*, (New Haven–London, 1980), 356–514, *passim*.

PART II

JEWISH LAW

10

Maimonides' Guide of the Perplexed *on Forbidden Food in the light of his own Medical Opinion*

JACOB LEVINGER

IN the *Guide of the Perplexed*, iii. 48, Maimonides says:

> I say, then, that to eat any of the various kinds of food that the Law has forbidden us is blameworthy. Among all those forbidden to us, only pork and fat may be imagined not to be harmful. But this is not so, for pork is more humid than is proper and contains much superfluous matter. The major reason why the Law abhors it is its being very dirty and feeding on dirty things. You know to what extent the Law insists upon the need to remove filth out of sight, even in the field and in a military camp, and all the more within cities. Now if swine were used for food, market-places and even houses would have been dirtier than latrines, as may be seen at present in the country of the Franks [i.e. of Western Europeans]. You know the dictum [of the Sages], may their memory be blessed: 'The mouth of a swine is like walking excrement.' The fat of the intestines, too, makes us full, spoils the digestion, and produces cold and thick blood. It is more suitable to burn it. Blood, on the one hand and carcasses of beasts that have died, on the other, are also difficult to digest and constitute a harmful nourishment. It is well known that a beast that is *ṭerefah* [i.e. an animal is diseased or wounded] is close to being a carcass. . . . As for the prohibition against eating meat [boiled] in milk, it is in my opinion not improbable that—in addition to this being undoubtedly very gross food and very filling—idolatry had something to do with it. Perhaps such food was eaten at one of the ceremonies of their cult or at one of their festivals. . . . In my opinion this is the most probable view regarding the reason for this prohibition, but I have not seen this set down in any of the book of the Sabians that I have read.[1]

If we sum up the reasons given here for the prohibitions concerning food, concentrating on the medical arguments for forbidding various kinds of food, we find the following:

[1] Trans. S. Pines (Chicago, 1963), 598–9; ed. S. Munk (Paris, 1856), iii. 110–11; Arabic edn. with Hebrew trans. by J. Kafiḥ (Jerusalem, 1972), 652–3.

1. All forbidden food is harmful nourishment. It appears that this rule is meant to apply mainly to the animals forbidden by the Torah in Lev. 11: 1–28 and in Deut. 1: 3–20; that is, quadrupeds which either do not chew the cud or are not cloven-footed, fish which lack either fins or scales, certain kinds of birds named in Lev. 11: 13–15 and in Deut. 14: 12–18, as well as all other aquatic and terrestrial animals, except the four kinds of locust mentioned in Lev. 11: 22. Among the forbidden animals the Torah mentions explicitly are the camel (Lev. 11: 4, Deut. 14: 7), the hare (Lev. 11: 6, Deut. 14: 7) and the pig (Lev. 11: 7, Deut. 14: 3). Among the quadrupeds that may be eaten (Deut. 14: 4–5) the ox, the lamb, and the kid are mentioned by name. (Probably adult domestic ruminants with cloven hoofs are also meant.) So are a few wild animals, including the gazelle.

2. Among all the foods forbidden by the Torah, only with regard to the pig and fat is there room for any doubt that they are harmful from the medical viewpoint. But the truth of the matter, according to the author, is that the pig too is unhealthy on account of its excessive 'humidity' and the large quantity of refuse and superfluous matter which it contains, referring apparently to its excessive fat. To this Maimonides adds another reason, which from what he says is the main cause for the prohibition on eating swine, namely that pig-breeding too is unhygienic, but I do not relate to this in the present article. With regard to fat the author argues that it is truly harmful since it 'makes us full, spoils the digestion and produces cold and thick blood'.

3. Blood and the carcasses of beasts that have died a natural death are also forbidden by the Torah; the latter only in Deut. 14: 21, as is well known. These too are forbidden, according to Maimonides, because they are harmful nourishment, being hard to digest. Because of the prohibition on eating carcasses of beasts that have died a natural death, or perhaps on account of the medical grounds given for this prohibition, the *ṭerefah* is also forbidden (see Exod. 22: 30). An unqualified *ṭerefah* is an animal which is going to die of itself because of an injury or a severe disease, according to the explanation in the Talmud, which is apparently considered by Maimonides as being the simple meaning of the scriptural text.[2]

[2] See *Ḥullin*, 42*a* ff. And cf. Maimonides, *Mishneh Torah*, *Hilkhot Ma'akhalot Assurot*, iv. 6–9; *The Code of Maimonides*, bk. v, *The Book of Holiness*, trans. L. T. Rabinowitz and P. Grossman (New Haven–London, 1965), 170–2; *Hilkhot Sheḥiṭah*, v–x (Eng., 283–312). Thus the *ṭerefah* is, in the words of the Talmud (*Ḥullin*, loc. cit.) 'the beginning of a carcass' (or: 'close to being a carcass', in Pines's translation of the *Guide*).

4. The prohibition of the Torah against cooking 'a kid in the milk of its mother' (Exod. 23: 19, 34: 26; Deut. 16: 31) is explained in the Talmud as a prohibition against either cooking or eating meat with milk in any form whatsoever (see *Ḥullin*, 115*b*). This explanation too appears to be taken by Maimonides to be the simple sense of the verse; for, as he says in *Guide*, iii. 41, he deals in these chapters only with reasons for the 'verses', not with reasons for the talmudic laws. Now, the 'strong reason' Maimonides puts forward for this prohibition is that it was apparently an ancient pagan custom to cook meat in milk. And yet, in addition to this main reason, he suggests a medical consideration as well: 'in addition to this being very gross food and very filling'. It is the medical reason given here as if by the way which concerns us in the present paper.

The question is, do these medical arguments really represent Maimonides' medical opinion? Or are they merely given in order to make the prohibitions more palatable to the common people? For was not Maimonides, the physician, a loyal disciple of Galen? And how could Galen's medical opinion conform so closely with the commandments of Judaism? Now this question has a far-reaching consequence: perhaps all the reasons Maimonides gives for the commandments in the *Guide*, iii. 25–49 are nothing but a glorious apologetic attempt to provide a rational explanation for the commandments, whereas his true belief is that the commandments are divine decrees without reason, as he suggests elsewhere.[3]

I find four arguments for doubting the sincerity of the medical reason Maimonides puts forward in the passage from the *Guide* quoted above:

1. At the end of his *Regimen of Health* he recommends three kinds of game; namely, gazelles (*al-ghuzlān*), the hare or rabbit (*al-arnāb*), and the onager or wild ass (*ḥimār al-waḥsh*).[4] Now, as we have seen, gazelles are permitted food, but the hare is forbidden. The wild ass also seems

[3] See esp. *Guide*, iii. 52, and Maimonides' *Commentary on the Mishnah*, *Berakhot*, v. 3; *Mishneh Torah*, *Hilkhot Tefillah*, ix. 7, and *Hilkhot Teshuvah*, iii. 4; I. Twersky, *A Maimonides Reader* (New York, 1972), 76–7, 92; cf. my paper in the *Jubilee Volume for the Tenth Anniversary of Bar Ilan University* (Heb.) (Ramat Gan, 1967), 299 ff.

[4] In the Arabic original *Fī Tadbīr al-Ṣiḥḥa*, ed. H. Kroner (Leiden, 1925) (offprint from *Janus*, vol. 27–9), 55; Heb. trans. by S. Muntner, *Hanhagat ha-Beri'ut* (Jerusalem, 1957), 84–5; Eng.: 'Moses Maimonides' Two Treatises on the Regimen of Health', eds. A. Bar-Sela, H. E. Hoff, and E. Faris, in *Transactions of the American Philosophical Society*, n.s. 54 (1964), pt. 4. p. 31.

to be prohibited food, since it is not a ruminant and does not have cloven hooves as required by the Torah (Lev. 11: 3, Deut. 14: 6).

2. We have seen, as is well known, that Jews are forbidden to eat the flesh of swine. And yet precisely concerning this animal Maimonides says in his *Fuṣūl Mūsā* on the authority of Galen:[5] 'The best livestock meat is that of the pig. Then comes the meat of the kid, then the meat of calves. The meat of sheep is humid, viscid, and glutinous. As for the meat of other livestock, I instruct those who care about the good condition of the chymes to avoid eating it.'[6] Thus, according to Maimonides, on the authority of Galen, pork is the meat most recommended of all livestock. (This expression is obviously intended to exclude birds, fish, and creeping creatures which lay eggs.)[7] Maimonides says this without any reservation on his part, while elsewhere in this book he states his objections to Galen's statements wherever he differs with them. Rabbi Joseph Kafiḥ has expressed his astonishment at this in his notes to *Guide*, iii. 48.[8]

3. It is indeed quite probable that blood is difficult to digest. But why a carcass (*nevelah*)? For on the face of it, a *nevelah* is like any other meat, the only difference being that the animal was not ritually slaughtered. Nowadays we might disapprove of the meat of an animal that has died as a result of some illness because of the microbes it contains, but what medical fault could Maimonides (in whose days microbes were unknown) find with an animal that had died of natural causes, on the grounds that it is difficult to digest?

4. It is true that Maimonides' explanation of the prohibition of 'meat with milk', namely, that 'idolatry had something to do with it', is convincing, and we have become acquainted with such a custom in the course of the present century.[9] But the medical reason he gives, that meat with milk is 'very gross food and very filling', appears strange. For

[5] MS Oxford (Neubauer) 2133, fo. 84r col. 1; cf. the Hebrew version *Pirqe Mosheh* (Vilna, 1888), 82, col. 1; and *Pirqe Mosheh bi-Refu'ah*, ed. S. Muntner (Jerusalem, 1959), 230, treatise xx, para. 19; Eng. *The Medical Aphorism of Moses Maimonides*, eds. F. Rosner and S. Muntner (New York, 1970–1), ii. treatise xx.

[6] In most translations from the Arabic (but for the quotation from the *Guide* at the beginning of the present paper) I was assisted by my colleague Michael Schwarz, to whom I wish to express my gratitude.

[7] In classifying animals, the Arab physicians seem to have followed Aristotle's *Historia Animalium*; see *Hist. An.* bk. 6, ch. 18 (571*b*).

[8] *Guide*, ed. Kafiḥ, bilingual edn., 652 n. 6. Kafiḥ regards this as a quotation from Hippocrates rather than Galen, but this makes no essential difference.

[9] See H. L. Ginsberg, *Kitve Ugarit* (Jerusalem, 1936), 79, l. 14. Ginsberg's reading of the Ugaritic text has been questioned recently, but here is not the place to go into this.

we have no knowledge that the ancients were disturbed by this, and indeed there is a widespread Arab custom to this day to cook the meat of sheep and goats in milk, and this is not considered injurious to health.

Thorough investigation has convinced me that these four objections do not hold water. On the contrary, what Maimonides says in the *Guide* seems to agree fully with the opinions he expresses in the rest of his works, and especially in his medical writings.

The first difficulty encountered in comparing his statements with *The Regimen of Health* is not a real problem. Careful reading of this and the preceding passage reveals that Maimonides does not recommend the meat of these animals as *food*, but rather as *remedies*. This important distinction was made by Abū Marwān b. Zuhr, one of Maimonides' teachers of medicine. Maimonides carfully made this distinction everywhere.[10] He says concerning the hare in *The Regimen of Health* that 'it has uses verified by experience'. He then enumerates the illnesses which the meat of the hare prevents. He does the same with regard to the wild ass (loc. cit). He discusses the medical benefit of the hare and the wild ass in *Pirqe Mosheh* as well—not in Treatise XX, which is devoted to food, but in Treatise XXII dealing with remedies.[11] It is true that he does not say explicitly in the *The Regimen of Health* that the meat of gazelles is recommended as medicine only. In *Pirqe Mosheh*, too, he mentions them not in Treatises XXI–XXII among the remedies, but in Treatise XX as food. But he says there that their meat has the power to strengthen the soul.[12] Apart from this, it is not religiously forbidden food, as we have seen. The fact that hares and even gazelles are recommended not as food but only as remedies is also explicitly stated in the Hebrew version of Maimonides' *Treatise on Asthma*.[13] The same is also clearly implied in the discussion of wild

[10] Thus, for instance, treatise xx of *Pirqe Mosheh* is devoted to food, while treatises xxi and xxii deal with two kinds of medicine (or remedies).

[11] Arab., fo. 96^{r-r}; Heb., ed. Muntner, 273; Eng. (Rosner) treatise xxii. Here, too, he discusses the hare and the wild ass in close juxtaposition.

[12] Arab. fo. 87^{r}. col. 2. In the Muntner Heb. edn. 239. para. 70; Eng. (Rosner), treatise xx.

[13] Heb. ed. Muntner (Jerusalem, 1940), 73, later included in Maimonides *Ketavim Refu'iyyim*, ed. Muntner, iv (Jerusalem, 1965), 78, para. 7: 'Know that the meat of gazelles, deer and hares is good and commendable for this illness. Yet though they heal they are not useful [as nourishment?]'; cf. in English, *Treatise on Asthma*, ed. S. Muntner (Philadelphia–Montreal, 1963), 14 n. 7. Unfortunately, the Jewish National Library has no photocopy of an Arabic manuscript of the *Treatise on Asthma* that includes the pages

animals in general in *Pirqe Mosheh*.[14]

Similarly, from the passage of *Pirqe Mosheh* quoted above it appears that apart from the animals enumerated therein the meat of no other livestock should be eaten. Further—while the last chapter of *The Regimen of Health* is devoted to 'notes useful in general and in particular for healthy and sick people',[15] the first chapter deals with 'the *regimen* of health in general with regard to all men'.[16] In the first chapter, Maimonides does not recommend the consumption of the meat of any 'livestock with the exception of sheep and goats'.[17]

The second difficulty concerning Maimonides' opinion with regard to the unhealthy nature of forbidden foods is not insoluble either. Indeed, in the well-known Hebrew edition of *Pirqe Mosheh* (Vilna, 1888) there appears only the above-mentioned passage which, on Galen's recommendation, commends pork as the best among the meats of quadrupeds. But in the Arabic original of this work,[18] and likewise in Muntner's new Hebrew edition,[19] he mentions after several chapters: 'food which is dissolved with difficulty, that is, food made up of things gross and viscid, such as pork and refined bread, even when not [consumed] almost habitually, but if he goes on consuming this food, he will quickly acquire the illness of repletion'.[20]

Moreover, in the Arabic original and in the new Hebrew translation we find at the beginning of the twenty-fifth treatise of *Pirqe Mosheh* a

on which this sentence appears, nor could I find these pages in the Arabic original in any other library. (This apology applies also to the rest of the quotations from the *Treatise on Asthma* in this article. I have not been able to find any of them in Arabic sources.)

[14] Arab., fo. 84ʳ, col. 2; Heb., ed. Muntner, 230, para. 23; Eng. (Rosner), treatise xx.

[15] Kroner, *Fī-Tadbīr*, 19; Heb., ed. Muntner, 28; Eng., trans. Bar-Sela *et al.* (above, n. 4), 27 ff.

[16] Ibid. Eng., Bar-Sela *et al.*, 16 ff.

[17] Kroner, *Fī Tadbīr*, 23 (in two places); Heb., ed. Muntner, 34, 36; Eng., Bar-Sela *et al.*, 18 (in two places). In the Heb. version, ed. Muntner, 36, as well as in the first Hebrew edition, *Kerem Ḥemed*, iii (1838), 12, and in an older English version, *The Preservation of Youth*, trans. H. L. Gordon (New York, 1958), 30, bulls and steers are mentioned as well. Muntner adds 'castrated', the source of which I do not know; cf. also Bar-Sela *et al.*, n. 37. If indeed the Hebrew version is correct, this recommendation neatly fits the one quoted from Galen in *Pirqe Mosheh*, only that the author here avoided mentioning the pig, which he does not consider to be commendable (see below) and which, furthermore, is forbidden to the Muslims.

[18] MS Oxford (Neubauer) 2113, fo. 86ʳ.

[19] (Jerusalem, 1959), 237, para. 62.

[20] Apparently, repletion of the body with food and tempers to such a degree that no room for the inhaled air is left. Cf. *Teshuvat ha-Rambam bi-She'elat ha-Keẓ ha-Kaẓuv la-Ḥayyim*, ed. M. Schwarz (Tel Aviv, 1979), 19, 21, 28–9 = *Maimonides über die Lebensdauer*, ed. G. Weil (Basel, 1953), 13, 17, 18, 43, 51 n. 24. See also Ibn Sīnā, *Qānūn* (Bulaq, 1877), i. 120.

list of over forty contradictions the author came across in Galen's works. In the ninth contradiction enumerated in the Arabic original[21] (the eighth according to the new Hebrew edition[22]) we read as follows: 'In his treatise on the good and objectionable humour he preferred pork to any praiseworthy food, after which comes the meat of kids and then that of sheep.' Now, as the editor of the Hebrew edition has already pointed out, this statement is defective and must be taken together with the passage I quoted on p. 198.[23] That is to say, in his treatise on the good and objectionable humours, Galen praises pork beyond any other meat, while elsewhere he counts pork among the foods that make men ill. This is obviously a contradiction. If the suggested complementarity is correct, what Maimonides says here fits in well with what he says in the *Guide of the Perplexed* about pork. This also answers Kafiḥ's query as to why Maimonides does not take exception to Galen's words (see above, p. 198). The answer is that Maimonides' objection is implied in the very fact that he points to the contradiction in Galen's own statement.

Thus according to Galen's statement quoted in *Pirqe Mosheh* as well as according to Maimonides' *Regimen of Health*, it appears that only those livestock allowed by the Torah should be eaten, i.e. sheep and goats; and according to the quotation from *Pirqe Mosheh*, as well as according to the Hebrew version of *The Regimen of Health*, cattle too.[24] Similarly, we find in Ibn Rushd's discussion of hygiene that among all livestock he commends only calves, young sheep, and kids.[25]

Among the other kinds of meat and fish which Maimonides recommends as healthful in the first chapter of *The Regimen of Health*, no sign is to be found of anything contradicting his statements in the *Guide of the Perplexed*. Among birds he recommends chickens (*al-dajāj*), and doves (*al-ḥamām*) and, according to the Hebrew version, turtle-doves (*tor*) as well.[26] All these birds were accepted in Jewish law as permitted food. Apart from these he recommends *durrāj*, *ṭayhūj*, and *ḥajal*.[27] *Ḥajal* is explicitly mentioned in Maimonides' *Commentary on*

[21] MS Oxford 2113, fo. 110ʳ, col. 1.

[22] *Pirqe Mosheh* (Jerusalem, 1959), 328, para. 9.

[23] Ibid. n. 64.

[24] See n. 17.

[25] Averroes, *The Preservation of Health*, Heb. version published as appendix to S. Muntner's edition of Maimonides' *Regimen Sanitatis* (Jerusalem, 1959), 163–80, at 169.

[26] *Fī Tadbīr*, ed. Kroner, 23; Heb. (Muntner), 34; Eng. (Bar-Sela *et al.*), 18.

[27] Loc. cit. compare the Arabic original of *Pirqe Mosheh* in the above mentioned Oxford MS. fo. 86ʳ, cols. 1–2, where the birds are mentioned, including turtledoves

the Mishnah as a translation of *qore'*.[28] From this text of the Mishnah it is clear that a kosher bird is meant.[29] The zoological identification of the *durrāj* and *ṭayhūj* to which Maimonides refers is difficult indeed, nor do we have his word that these birds are kosher.

Durrāj has been variously identified as hazel hen (*Haselhuhn*, *tetrastes bonasia*),[30] as francolin (*francolinus francolinus*),[31] and (apparently) as partridge (*perdix perdix*).[32] It seems to me that these birds have never been identified with one of the forbidden birds, although we miss a positive tradition declaring the hazel hen and the francolin to be kosher.[33]

Maimonides seems to include the *ṭayhūj* among the birds of the mountains (*al-'aṣafīr al-jabaliyya*).[34] His translators identified it variously with the partridge (*perdix perdix*),[35] with various birds

(*ḥamām*). (In Muntner's Heb. edn. of the *Regimen*, 34, and in *Pirqe Mosheh*, 236, 58, various terms in European languages have been quoted to identify these birds but they confound the issue.)

[28] *Ḥullin*, ii. 2; Maimonides, *Commentary on the Mishnah*, ed. Kafiḥ, Arab. and Heb., *Seder Qodashim* (Jerusalem, 1967), 226.

[29] It is indeed possible that neither the Arabic *ḥajal* nor the Hebrew *qore'* signify one special kind only. Cf. Kafiḥ's n. 7 ad. loc. and I. M. Levinger, *Mazon Kasher min ha-Ḥay* (Modern kosher food production from animal sources), (Jerusalem, 1978), 55–8.

[30] Thus Kroner, as it appears from the German translation published with his edition of the *Regimen of Health*, 206, as well as from his *Zur Terminologie der arabischen Medizin* (Berlin, 1921), 42 (*Haselhuhn*).

[31] So it seems, from J. O. Leibowitz and S. Marcus, *Moses Maimonides on the Causes of Symptoms* (Berkeley, Calif., 1974), 117. Cf. the term *durrāj* in the Arabic text of the *Book of Causes*, 179; also Bar-Sela *et al.*, 19.

[32] Thus according to M. Steinschneider's German translation of '*Poisons and Antidotes*': Moses Maimonides, *Gifte und ihre Heilungen* (Berlin, 1873), 85. In the Arabic original of this work (MS Oxford (Neubauer) 1270/5, fo. 56^r) *ḥajal*, *durrāj*, and *ṭayhūj* are mentioned. Steinschneider translates these *Rebhühner und Auerhahn*. It appears that he translated both *ḥajal* and *durrāj* as *Rebhühner*, and *ṭayhūj* as '*Auerhahn*' (*capercaillie*, wood grouse). But *Rebhuhn* signifies the partridge; it is *not* a homonym, or a generic name covering several species.

[33] Talmudic law lays down that only those birds which tradition holds to be kosher are to be eaten (*Ḥullin*, 63*b* ll. 9–5 from the bottom, where further references are given). Hence even birds which have never been identified as forbidden are not eaten unless reliable tradition permits it. But the fact that Jews are thus prevented from eating most birds is not relevant to Maimonides' assertion that whatever the Torah has forbidden is unhealthy food. Only if one of the birds which he recommends as food were identified with one of the forbidden birds would this contradict his assertion in the *Guide*. For the permissibility of eating the partridge, see Levinger, *Mazon Kasher*, 57.

[34] Thus I take him to mean in the Arabic original version of *Pirqe Mosheh* in a passage lacking in the Hebrew version. See MS Oxford (Neubauer) 2113, fo. 86^r col. 2. I must confess that I do not see how Maimonides could recommend in Egypt a bird 'of the mountains'. But this is what he seems to mean, and the matter deserves further study.

[35] Thus Kroner; see the sources mentioned in n. 30 above.

belonging to the family of grouses (*tetraonidae*),[36] and more specifically with the *capercaillie* (wood grouse, *Auerhahn*, *tetrao urogallus*).[37] Among these birds with which the *ṭayhūj* has been identified, only the *capercaillie* (wood grouse) has been mentioned in various Jewish sources as non-kosher, and even explicitly identified with the *dukhifat*, which the Pentateuch (Lev. 11: 19, Deut. 14: 18) speaks of as one of the forbidden birds.[38] Nevertheless, I have found no basis for the identification of the *ṭayhūj* with the *capercaillie* (wood grouse). Neither did I find any reason whatever to suppose that Maimonides would have to accept the identification of the *capercaillie* with the *dukhifat*.[39]

Maimonides does not recommend the consumption of fish. But in the first chapter of his *Regimen of Health*, at the end of his discussions of the kinds of animal food which he recommends, he adds there are 'fish that are small of body . . . sweet of taste, from the seas or running waters', which are not bad food. As an example of these kinds of fish he mentions a fish called *būrī* or *al-rāy*.[40] Now, I can hardly accept the identification by Dozy and Kroner of *rāy* with salmon,[41] for salmon are not small fish but rather large ones, some of them up to a metre long. More convincing is the identification (by Bar Sela, Hoff, and Faris) of *rāy* with pilchard, that is *sardina pilchardus*, or the family of sardines (*clapridae*) in general.[42]

[36] So it appears from Leibowitz–Marcus, *Moses Maimonides*, where the Arabic *ṭayhūj* (p. 179) is translated by the English 'grouse' (p. 117). Cf. H. Heinzel *et al.*, *The Birds of Britain and Europe*, 2nd edn. (London, 1966), 102–5.

[37] So, apparently, Steinschneider; and see above, n. 32.

[38] See Levinger, *Mazon Kasher*, 56–7.

[39] See Hametargem (who translates the old-French terms in Rashi's commentary into German) on Rashi, *Ḥullin*, 63*a*, the passage commencing *shehodo kafut* (where Rashi's old-French term for *dukhifat* is rendered *Auerhahn*). Moreover, according to what I have been told by an expert on talmudic zoology, Professor J. Feliks of Bar-Ilan University, the description of the *dukhifat* in the Talmud (*Ḥullin*, 63*a*) does not permit the identification with the *capercaillie* (wood grouse). Rashi himself did not offer such an identification—it is the invention of 'Hametargem'. Moreover, even if we were to suppose that Maimonides recommended to the sultan of Egypt birds which did not exist in Egypt, it is very unlikely that Maimonides was acquainted with the *capercaillie* (wood grouse), a bird whose habitat is quite distant from anywhere he ever stayed. See H. Heinzel *et al.*, 38.

[40] *Fī Tadbīr*, ed. Kroner, 24; Heb., ed. Muntner, 38, Bar-Sela *et al.* 19 ('mullet or pilchard').

[41] R. Dozy, *Supplément aux dictionnaires arabes*, 3rd edn. (Leiden–Paris, 1967), i. 497, col. 2, last seven lines (*saumon*); *Fī Tadbīr*, ed. Kroner, 20, as well as in Kroner's dictionary of medical terminology (above, n. 30) 43 (*Lachs*).

[42] *Fī Tadbīr*, ed. Bar-Sela *et al.*, 19.

In contradiction with *rāy*, the identity of which is uncertain, *būrī* is nowadays commonly known as the name for the flathead grey mullet (*mugil cephalus*).[43] Hence, it is very likely that Kroner, as well as Bar Sela *et al.* are right in identifying Maimonides' *būrī* with *Meeräsche* and 'mullet' respectively, i.e. with fish of the family *mugilidae* which live in sea water as well as in rivers.[44] It is possible that the term refers to the family as a whole or to one of its species. Perhaps Maimonides means the small golden-grey mullet (*mugil auratus*), a most tasty fish.[45]

Be that as it may, grey mullets, salmon, and sardines, having fins and scales, are all kosher. Only in one place does Maimonides recommend forbidden aquatic animals (and even terrestrial animals) not only as remedies but also as food, but only for patients who require the remedies they contain.[46]

Furthermore, what Maimonides says in the *Guide* about the harm caused by fat agrees with the opinion he expresses in several places in his medical works. In his *Treatise on Asthma* he discusses the harm that fat causes to 'all people'.[47] The harm brought about by fat is also mentioned, on the authority of Galen, in *Pirqe Mosheh*.[48] In the first chapter of the *Regimen of Health* he says, in total agreement with what he says in the *Guide*: 'al-shuḥūm kulluhā radī'a tushbi' wa-tutkhim wa-tusqiṭ shahwat al-ṭa'ām wa-tūlid khilṭan balghamiyyan.'[49] ('Fat is all bad; it satiates, corrupts the digestion, suppresses the appetite and generates phlegmy humour.')[50] It is clear that 'phlegmy humour' here

[43] See L. Fishelson (ed.), *Plants and Animals of the Land of Israel*, iv (Heb.), (Tel Aviv, 1983), 53–4.

[44] See above, nn. 41–2.

[45] See Fishelson, 54. Compare also the description of fish in Maimonides, *Treatise on Asthma* (Jerusalem, 1940), 72 (Heb.) *Ketavim Refu'iyyim*, iv (Jerusalem, 1965), 77, paras. 4–5 (Eng., *Treatise on Asthma*, ed. S. Muntner (Philadelphia, 1963), 13). This also fits the *mugilidae*. It is difficult to decide whether *būrī* and *rāy* are synonyms or different species of the same family. It appears that *rāy* signifies fish from the same family as *būrī*, for Maimonides speaks of one fish called by these two names. This also disproves Kroner's identification of *būrī* as grey mullet and *rāy* as salmon. It also disproves the identification by Bar-Sela *et al.* of *būrī* as mullet and *rāy* as pilchard.

[46] See Maimonides, *Poisons and Antidotes*, ch. 6. See esp. the Arabic original, MS Oxford (Neubauer) 1270/5, fo. 56r; and S. Muntner's Heb. edn. (Jerusalem, 1942), 134.

[47] Heb. edn. (Jerusalem, 1940), 73 = *Ketavim Refu'iyyim*, iv (Jerusalem, 1965), 77, para. 6. (Eng. *Treatise on Asthma*, (1963), 14, item 6, second para.)

[48] Arab.: MS Oxford (Neubauer) 2113 fo. 86r, col. 2; Heb. ed. Muntner (1959), 237–8, para. 65; Eng. (Rosner), treatise xx.

[49] Kroner, 23; cf. Heb. ed. Muntner, *Hanhagat ha-Beri'ut* (Jerusalem, 1957), 36.

[50] Bar-Sela *et al.*, 19, col. 1.

is the same as the 'white blood' mentioned in the *Guide*; for according to medieval medicine, phlegma is the cold component in the blood.[51]

I have not found an explicit statement in Maimonides' medical works to the effect that eating a carcass is harmful since it is 'digested with difficulty'. Nevertheless, Maimonides' opinion in the *Guide* that a carcass, i.e. the meat of an animal that died naturally, is more slowly digested than that of a slaughtered or killed animal, is apparently expressed in Maimonides' *Commentary on the Mishnah*. Reference to this has already been made by Kafiḥ.[52] In *Oholot*, xi. 7, the *Mishnah* says: 'If a dog ate of the flesh of a corpse and [the dog] died and lies across the threshold . . . how long should [the impure food] have remained in its intestines [so that it no longer communicates impurity]? Three days and three nights.'[53] Maimonides expresses astonishment at the statement that the dog digests so slowly, and then explains, 'la'alla dhālika fī laḥm al-mayyit khāṣṣatan wa-hādhā lā yustab'ad.' ('Perhaps this concerns specifically the flesh of a dead person. This is not unlikely.')[54] I do not understand this explanation unless we take it to mean that perhaps this is possible in the case of the flesh of one who died, as distinct from the flesh of a human being or an animal that has been killed, either by the dog or by another agent.[55]

I assume that medieval physicians were led to the conclusion that a carcass is digested slowly by their experience, which showed that the meat of a carcass is usually not as fresh as the meat of an animal slaughtered for food, and also less hygienic because of the diseases with which it is infected. The intestinal diseases caused by the consumption of such a carcass were apparently understood to be the

[51] See on this also *Pirqe Mosheh*, treatise ii, on humours. Arab. MS Oxford 2113 fos. 9ʳ–11ʳ; Heb. Muntner, 32–5. English (Rosner), treatise ii.

[52] In his Arabic and Hebrew edn. of the *Guide* (Jerusalem, 1972), iii. 652 n. 12.

[53] Cf. *The Mishnah*, trans. H. Danby (Oxford, 1950), 666; *Mishnayot*, trans. P. Blackman, 2nd rev. edn. (New York, 1964), vi. 256.

[54] *Mishnah with the Commentary of Moses ben Maimon*, Arab. edn. and Heb. trans. J. Kafiḥ, *Seder Ṭohorot* (Jerusalem, 1968), 298.

[55] From a purely linguistic standpoint, one could, on the fact of it, take the expression 'specifically the flesh of a dead person' to mean the flesh of a corpse as distinct from that bitten off a living human being or animal. But I see no point in distinguishing between a corpse killed by a dog (or by anything else), the flesh of which the dog has eaten, and the flesh of a live animal of whose flesh the dog has eaten without killing it. Compare also *Mishneh Torah*, *Hilkhot Ṭum'at ha-Met*, xx. 4: 'How long does the uncleanness within their bowels continue to convey uncleanness *after they die*? In the case of a dog three whole days . . .' (H. Danby, *The Code of Maimonides. Book Ten: The Book of Cleanness* (New Haven, 1954), 74).

result of slow digestion. In *The Regimen of Health*, Maimonides in fact speaks clearly of the harm caused by eating meat that is not fresh.[56]

Maimonides' statement that 'meat with milk' is 'very filling'[57] also need not cause astonishment, for in the *The Regimen of Health* he says,[58] 'kull mā yu'mal min al-laban aw yukhlaṭ bihi radī' jiddan . . . wa-kadhālika mā ṭubikha min al-laban wa-mā yuṭbakh bihī radī' jiddan' ('All that is made from milk or mixed with it, is very bad . . . similarly, all that is cooked from milk or cooked in it are bad foods.')[59]

It stands to reason that milk cooked with meat, or meat cooked in milk, is no exception to this rule. Given this statement of Maimonides in *The Regimen of Health*, we are now able to understand more correctly what he says about 'meat with milk' in the *Guide*. Meat with milk is very gross food that causes much repletion, like any cooked milk. But the special interdiction of 'meat with milk' is explained by an assumed pagan custom. This custom is in his words 'the most probable view, in my opinion, regarding the reason for this prohibition'. This refers to 'meat with milk' only, not to anything else boiled in milk, which is also 'very gross and filling' food.

To sum up, all Maimonides' works, and especially his medical works, lead us to the clear conclusion that in the *Guide of the Perplexed* he indeed expressed his expert opinion as a physician regarding the unhealthy quality of prohibited food, at least as concerns consumption by healthy persons.[60]

Nevertheless, I must add that although Maimonides' medical diet agrees with the dietary prohibitions explicit in the Torah, it does not necessarily agree with talmudic law and rulings. For according to talmudic law it is not only forbiden to eat the flesh of animals prohibited in Torah, but also to drink their milk.[61] According to the Arabic original of the *Regimen of Health*, however, it appears that he recommends the milk of camels.[62] Although in the printed Hebrew version of R. Moses b. Tibbon it says 'the milk of the cow' (*ḥalev ha-*

[56] Kroner, *Fī Tadbīr*, 54 (Heb., ed. Muntner, 81; Eng., ed. Bar-Sela *et al.*, 31, col. 1.

[57] Cf. n. 20, above.

[58] Kroner, 24; cf. Heb., ed. Muntner, 37.

[59] Bar-Sela *et al.*, 19, col. 1.

[60] In the *Guide of the Perplexed*, Maimonides deals only with animal food, not with forbidden vegetables. These are not mentioned in the chapter under discussion. Thus we are not bound to examine whether the reasons given for the prohibitions of vegetables agree with his medical opinion.

[61] According to the *Mishneh*, *Talmud Bavli*, 5*b*, where further references are given.

[62] Kroner, *Fī-Tadbīr*, 24: *laban al-nūq*, i.e. the milk of she-camels; Bar-Sela *et al.*, 19, col. 1, 'the milk of the she-camel'.

parah), instead of 'the milk of she-camels',[63] it seems clear that the Arabic version is correct; for in *Pirqe Mosheh* he quotes Galen to the effect that the milk of camels is 'the most humid [= watery] milk' (*arṭab al-albān*), as opposed to cows' milk, which is 'the most viscous' (*aghlaẓ al-albān*).[64] He also mentions two paragraphs earlier the milk of camels and of asses as that in which 'watery humidity' (*al-ruṭūba al-mā'iyya*) preponderates.[65] And according to what is said it appears that the less viscous, the better. This is also confirmed by the contradiction which he discusses in the twenty-fifth treatise of the work; namely, that in one place Galen declares the milk of asses to be the best, while in another he says that the milk of camels is better; cows' milk is not considered at all.[66] Thus, it seems likely that according to the quotations from Galen, as well as according to Maimonides himself, camel's milk is considered more 'humid' and less 'viscous' and therefore preferable—perhaps even considerably so—to the grosser cows' milk.[67] However, I see no incongruity with what Maimonides says in the *Guide*, for there his only purpose was to explain the reasons for the biblical texts and not the reasons for the halakhic rulings. I have already referred to this and discussed it elsewhere.[68] The prohibition on drinking the milk of animals whose flesh is forbidden is certainly not explicit in the Torah, and there is no real basis for reading it into the text.

Finally, I should like to discuss a contradiction in this chapter of the *Guide* which appears acute indeed in the light of the medical texts I have discussed. At the beginning of the chapter, in the passage with which I began the present paper, Maimonides says that all the things

[63] The first Hebrew edition in *Kerem Ḥemed*, iii (1838) 13; and in Muntner's edn., 37. This version seems to recur in all the Hebrew and all the Latin manuscripts used by Bar-Sela *et al.*; see 19 n. 41 of their English translation.

[64] Arab. MS Oxford (Neubauer) 2113 fo. 85ʳ, col. 2; cf. Heb., ed. Muntner, 233, para. 43, English (Rosner), treatise xx.

[65] Arab., MS, fo. 85ʳ, col. 1; Heb., ed. Muntner, 232, para. 41; English (Rosner), treatise xx.

[66] Arab., MS 2113 fo. 110ʳ, col. 1; Heb., ed. Muntner, 329, para. 10; English (Rosner), treatise xxv. (In the Hebrew, Galen's contradictions are enumerated in an order different from the Arabic.)

[67] He does not recommend cows' milk at all, even as medicine. Cf. esp. *Pirke Mosheh*, Arab. MS Oxford (Neubauer) 2113, fo. 89ʳ, col. 1; Heb., ed. Muntner, 244, para. 11, where for some reason the praise of pigs' milk has been omitted. It seems that Maimonides recommended cows' milk only to Jews, who were forbidden to drink the milk of camels, asses, and pigs. See S. D. Goitein, 'An Autograph Letter of Maimonides' (Heb.), *Tarbiẓ*, 32 (1963), 188.

[68] *Tarbiẓ*, 37 (1968), 282–93, and Uriel Simon (ed.), *Ha-Mikra' we-Anaḥnu* (The Bible and us), (Ramat Gan 1979), 120–32.

forbidden in the Torah are unanimously considered bad, save two: the swine and fat. But further on in the chapter he says 'wa-afḍal al-luḥūm huwa alladhī ubīḥa lanā akluhū wa-hādhā mā lā yajhaluhū ṭabīb,'[69] which reads in Pines's translation: 'the most excellent kinds of meat [are] those that are permitted to us. *No physician is ignorant of this.*'[70] Even though fat is not one of the 'kinds of meat' strictly speaking, Maimonides has said at the beginning of the chapter that there are also doubts as to whether pork is bad. The doubts are certainly held by physicians. If we take into account what Maimonides says on the authority of Galen, i.e. that pork is the best among the meats of livestock, this means, in any case, that Maimonides knew that Galen, his principal teacher in medicine, had arrived at the conclusion in one instance, that the pig was the best among livestock. Thus with regard to this point, he was certainly not justified in claiming 'the best kinds of meat [are] those which are permitted to us' as a matter which no physician can ever doubt.

It seems to me that Maimonides means to point out that even those who consider pork better than the meat of other livestock do not consider it the most recommended meat. Everybody agrees that the meat most recommended is that of tender birds, such as certain kinds of pigeons, chickens, the *ḥajal*, the *ṭayhūj*, and the *durrāj*. As we have seen, Maimonides considers none of these as prohibited birds. And according to what he says in *The Regimen of Health*, the meat of birds is lighter than that of quadrupeds, and therefore more quickly digested;[71] and it is clearly suggested that it is also healthier.[72] Indeed, it appears that Maimonides considered this point—namely, that the flesh of birds is 'the best meat', better than the meat of all livestock—to be something no physician doubted, even those uncertain whether pork was unhealthy or not.

[69] Ed. Munk, fos. 111*b*–12*a*; ed. Kafiḥ, p. 653.

[70] (Chicago, 1963), 599.

[71] Kroner, *Fī Tadbīr*, 23; Heb., ed. Muntner, 36; Eng., Bar-Sela, *et al.* 19, col. 1 (see also loc. cit. 18, col. 2).

[72] Compare to this *Mishneh Torah*, *Hilkhot De'ot*, iv. 4; *The Book on Asthma*, ed. Muntner, 72 (= *Ketavim Refu'iyyim*, iv. 77, para. 4); *Treatise on Asthma*, ed. Muntner (Philadelphia–Montreal, 1963), 13; and *The Book of Causes*, ed. Leibowitz–Marcus), 178–9 (Arab.), and 118–19 (Eng.); Bar-Sela *et al.*, 37, col. 1.

11

Holy War in Maimonidean Law

GERALD J. BLIDSTEIN

I

MAIMONIDES' discussion of the justification and function of war moves on a number of distinct planes which do not easily lend themselves to harmonistic synthesis. I do not refer primarily to contradictions between specific texts but rather to disparate conceptual models, each sustaining a network of exemplars. These models do not arrange themselves conveniently along the axis of legalistic as against philosophic writings; the legal texts themselves provide expression to the full range of paradigms, though the *Guide* maintains a more consistently single-minded position. My present purpose is to sort out these models and to describe the immanent coherence of each as well as the interface of contact and conflict between them.

The explicit question put for each model is: why and when is war commanded, allowed, or disapproved? The basic issue underlying my discussion is: what is the weight of ideological factors in the answers that are given? I shall not attempt, in the brief compass of this presentation, to place this issue in its historical and cultural context. Our topic obviously deserves treatment from a comparative perspective, but a survey of the sources themselves takes pride of place, even as it invites cross-cultural examination. I shall also be able to raise the issue of Maimonides' relation to his talmudic sources only as it contributes to my argument as a whole. Similarly with medieval traditions that offer alternatives to the Maimonidean posture: these will be noted only when they are of methodological value, so as to allow us to gauge the quality of the Maimonidean contribution.

II

Maimonides provides for universal holy war and constructs its ideological basis. Holy war, moreover, is the only justified war. We have, then, a two-pronged thrust.

Maimonides writes:

> Moses bequeathed the Torah and the commandments to Israel alone . . . and to those of the other nations who wish to convert to Judaism. But no coercion to accept the Torah and the Commandments is practiced on those who are unwilling to do so. Moreover, Moses was commanded by God to compel all people to accept the Commandments enjoined upon Noahides. Anyone who does not accept them, is to be put to death.[1]

As argued by Heinemann in his study of the Almohade impact on Maimonides, we learn here of a duty placed upon the Jewish people to achieve universal adherence to Noahide laws, among which the ban on idolatry is likely most crucial.[2] Significantly, such universal adherence may be won by compulsion. Maimonides reads his talmudic sources expansively on this point, for while these admit of sanctions against the violator of a Noahide law, they do not demand formal commitment to that regimen ('to accept the commandments'), nor punish those who refuse to make this commitment, nor make the Jewish people responsible for obtaining this commitment.[3] Consistently, then, Maimonides claims in another context that the Jewish people, rather than the Noahide himself, is responsible for the judicial apparatus which enforces Noahide law.[4] Universal adherence to Noahide law is clearly a task for the people of Israel, as even the formal commitment to that law is phrased as a conversion supervised by Jews who 'accept'

[1] *Hilkhot Melakhim*, viii. 10 (trans. M. Herschmann, *The Code of Maimonides: The Book of Judges* (New Haven, 1949), 230. (All translations from *Hilkhot Melakhim* follow Herschmann, with necessary revisions.) See also *Hilkhot Milah*, i. 6; *Malakhim*, viii. 9; n. 17 below.

[2] I. Heinemann, 'Maimuni und die arabischen Einheitslehrer', *MGWJ* 79 (1935), 133 ff. See also S. Schwarzfuchs, 'Les Lois royales de Maimonide', *REJ* 3 (1951–2) 72, 75–6. For Noahide law, see *Encyclopedia Judaica*, xii. 1189–91. Maimonides' stress on idolatry is apparent in *Hilkhot Issure Bi'ah*, xiv. 7; *Malakhim*, viii. 9.

[3] R. Joseh Karo refers us to *Sanhedrin*, 57*a*, but R. Menahem Krakowski, *Avodat ha-Melekh* to *Hilkhot 'Avodah Zarah*, x. 6 has, among others, noted that this talmudic source cannot, if read strictly, fully support the entire Maimonidean edifice.

[4] *Melakhim*, x. 11. Cf. ix. 14, and the dissenting view of Naḥmanides, *Commentary* to Gen. 34: 13.

the Noahide.[5] Compulsion is a legitimate, indeed mandated, instrument in achieving this goal.

Furthermore, Maimonides makes the ideological element a crucial component of war. Both the 'commanded war' and the 'permitted war' (more about these later) are joined only after the non-Israelite has rejected a call to accept Noahide law along with other, political, conditions. Even the peoples of Canaan and the Amalekites are invited to renounce idolatry and remain in the Land; there is no absolute imperative to destroy or expel them. Similar conditions must be allowed any nation with whom Israel wishes to wage war.[6] Moreover, Maimonides simply does not describe the option of war against peoples who are already Noahides and need not be 'converted' (though this remains a logical possibility), and at least one twentieth-century commentator assumes such war to be disallowed.[7] Collating all these materials, R. Abraham Abusch of Frankfurt inferred that Maimonides had massively enlarged the scope of imperative holy war.[8]

This tendency to reject any war lacking ideological motive is in fact quite explicit elsewhere. Linking the discussion of the general powers of the king with the rules for his waging of war, Maimonides writes that the king's 'sole aim and thought should be to uplift the true religion, to fill the world with righteousness, to break the arm of the wicked, and to fight the battles of the Lord'.[9] Each of these phrases obviously merits close study, as does the timbre and sequence of the whole. Our immediate concern, though, is with the last phrase: 'to fight the battles of the Lord'. This is apparently not to be taken in its biblical sense alone (as battles fought by the people of the Lord); rather these are

[5] Maimonides consistently claims that Jewry (?) 'accepts' (*leqabbel*) this gentile; this usage, which so far as I know is not talmudic, is probably symptomatic of his understanding of the topic as a whole: it is *conversion*. The acceptance of the Noahide functions to allow him to reside in the Holy Land (the specific meaning of the term *ger toshav*, for Maimonides) and imposes upon the Jewish community responsibility for his welfare. See e.g. *'Avodah Zarah*, x. 6; *Issure Bi'ah*, xiv. 7–8; *Melakhim*, x. 12. Maimonides doubtless noted that the *baraita* describes the gentile's commitment to the standards of *ger toshav* as being made 'before three fellows' (in *'Avodah Zarah*, 64*b*) though he omits this detail in his Code.

[6] *Melakhim*, vi. 1–4. For contemporary disagreement, see Rabad (R. Abraham b. David), ad loc. and the citations of *Leḥem Mishneh*. Attempts to produce a systematic view of Rabad ought not to overlook his comment to *Hilkhot Milah*, i. 6 (which moved R. Me'ir Simḥah, *Or Same'aḥ*, ad loc., to emendation!).

[7] R. Abraham Karelitz, *Ḥazon Ish* to *Melakhim*, vi. 4.

[8] *Hagahot 'Emek ha-Melekh* to *Melakhim*, viii. 10. R. Abraham Abusch flourished in the 18th cent., and is most famous for his role in the Cleves divorce.

[9] *Melakhim*, iv. 10.

battles fought *for the Lord*. The Israelite must 'know that he is fighting for the oneness of the Lord', and should do battle with the 'intention of sanctifying the Name'. Such a warrior is 'assured that no harm will befall him and no evil will overtake him. He will build for himself a lasting house in Israel . . . and will gain life in the world to come.' This promise—whose parallel is more easily found, incidentally, in the literature of crusade and *jihād* than unearthed in the Talmud—is derived by Maimonides from Sam. 25: 28–9, where Abigail told David that since he fights 'the battles of the Lord', his soul would be 'bound in the bundle of life'.[10] For Maimonides, then, the 'battles of the Lord' means wars possessing religious significance, and this is how he doubtless uses the phrase. Similar statements as to the true goal of war are made in fleshing out the priestly invocation before battle; the priest is to encourage the warriors by reminding them that they are fighting for the victory of their ideals, both religious and social.[11]

Finally, an instance taken from the *Guide*, Maimonides urges the cleanliness and purity of the military camp because it is 'like a sanctuary of the Lord and not like the camps of the gentiles designed only to do wrong and to harm the others and to rob them of their property. On the contrary, our purpose is to make people apt to obey God and to introduce order into their circumstances.'[12] The ideological–ethical motive of Israel's wars is contrasted clearly with the wars of plunder and conquest that Maimonides saw waged in his environment, much as his assertion that sages and prophets of Israel do not long for the Messiah so that they might 'exercise dominion over the world, or . . . eat and drink and rejoice'[13] sets the spirituality of Jewish ambition in implied contrast with the gentile quest for power and sensualism. It is in this perspective, too, that the Canaanite wars are seen in both the *Guide* and *Book of Commandments*—they are wars against idolatry (a position which dovetails neatly with the conditional nature of even these wars which Maimonides claims in *Mishneh Torah*). Indeed, the *Guide* speaks of the war against idolatry and idolators as a universal imperative and barely notes its territorial aspect.[14]

[10] *Melakhim*, vii. 15.

[11] *Sefer ha-Mizwot*, positive command no. 191; negative command no. 58.

[12] *Guide*, iii. 41.

[13] *Melakhim*, xii. 4.

[14] *Guide*, i. 36, 54; iii. 37, 41, 51; *Sefer ha-Mizwot*, positive commands 187–8, 191; negative commands 48–51. The role of the war on Amalek remains to be clarified: is it purely of nationalistic significance? The ethical balance to Canaanite idolatry? At any rate, this war, too, is made conditional in the *Code* (see n. 6 above).

Certainly, Maimonides codifies the regulation of booty and legitimates plunder. But this is a far cry from accepting the phenomenon as a satisfactory reason for going to war in the first place. Maimonides does expect that Israel's liberation and reconstitution will be achieved in part through war, much as he includes war to defend the physical integrity of the nation in 'commanded war'. Such defensive action is to be expected, and hardly challenges the thesis developed thus far: that holy war is the only aggressive war that ought be fought, and that the people of Israel are obliged to wage this kind of war so as to spread the monotheistic faith and its social concomitants.

III

This insistence on the universality and exclusivity of holy war is at variance with the normative structure which Maimonides accepted from the Talmud. We have already had opportunity to note Maimonides' blanket division of all war into 'commanded' and 'permitted', and it would seem that both categories fly in the face of the concept of holy war. The classic definition (placed immediately after the charge to the king to fight only the 'battles of the Lord'!) reads:

> The king fights, firstly, only commanded war. What is commanded war? This is the war against the seven nations of Canaan, war against the Amalekites, and war to deliver Israel from the enemy attacker. Thereafter, he may engage in permitted war, that is, a war against neighbouring nations to extend the borders of Israel and to enhance his greatness and prestige.[15]

Commanded war does not include wars fought to spread Noahide law (nor is this goal even allowed in the rubric of permitted war), which is not mentioned at all here. The commanded wars of the normative structure are firmly defined, rather, by the history of the people and the goals of national territorial existence. Permitted war (and the term *reshut* sometimes acquires probative status with medieval legists) especially compromises the characteristics at the heart of holy war doctrine; wars may be fought that are not imperative divine commands, with material goals rather than religious or ethical aims as their purpose. All in all, the tension between the holy war rhetoric and its use in rationalizing Torah commands, on the one hand, and the normative structures embodied in commanded war and permitted war,

[15] *Melakhim*, v. 1.

on the other hand, is quite apparent; here—rather than in the problematics of the quest for the sources of Maimonidean doctrine—is the major issue raised by Maimonides on war. May we say—especially with regard to the rather open-ended permitted war—that Maimonides remains the faithful codifier of talmudic law even as he hints at his preference for a more ideologically unsullied platform? That the exclusivity of 'holy war' is Maimonides' *aggadah*, ever to be compromised, as *aggadah* always is, by norms that not only forbid but also permit?

Yet it is also the case, apparently, that Maimonides insists on the normative contours of 'permitted' war and moulds these with some ideal purpose in mind. He carefully delineates the scope of the 'permitted' so as to exclude wars fought for personal or even momentary gain; only national goals (the fortunes of the king are of course closely tied to those of the state) are allowed. And the physical well-being of the state is clearly instrumental for Maimonides: maximally, the material success of Israel's king redounds to the glory of its Lord (a consideration elsewhere allowed Messianic significance, despite its religious crudity);[16] and minimally, aggressive conquest may be the only alternative to subjugation, which for Maimonides limits severely the spiritual achievement of society. Let us recall that Maimonides in his famous letter to the community of Marseilles urged not only military competence but also the 'conquest of [foreign] lands'[17] as factors in national survival, and other indications of this pragmatic temper are to be found. Would all this allow even 'permitted war' to enter the family of holy war, as a poor relation at least? Perhaps, but this elastic concept would then have been stretched beyond usefulness.

IV

There is yet another way into our topic. Another tier of Maimonides legal thought parallels in itself the two tiers already discussed and embodies, perhaps fuses, the very tensions we have described—it may even provide the skeleton around which they are constructed. I refer to

[16] *Melakhim*, xi. 4, in uncensored versions. Amazingly, the Yale Judaica edition was translated from the heavily censored modern text and omits central passages.

[17] *Kovez Teshuvot Ha-Rambam: Ha-Rambam we-Iggerotaw*, ed. A. Lichtenberg (Leipzig, 1819), pt. ii, 25*b*.

Maimonides' law on idolatry, or more precisely to the law governing the relationship to idolators and their cult. The substance of these norms, as well as their shadings and nuances, parallels, I propose, the Maimonidean doctrine of war. This is not a very surprising idea. Given that the basic antagonist of Maimonidean holy war is idolatry, it is reasonable to find some congruence between his treatment of the two topics. Now, a survey of the materials on idolatry indicates that the monotheistic community is charged with the ultimate universal triumph of its belief, a triumph based in part on the use of physical force. Yet this martial and compulsory aspect of the imperative is graded and proportioned—compromised, if you will—by the normative tradition itself.

We have, to begin with, the uncompromising Maimonidean doctrine forbidding the making of peace with any idolatrous people, thus conceding its right to exist as such—a betrayal of the universal imperative of monotheism: 'they are to abandon their cult or be killed'.[18] (This topic, incidentally, achieves literary and conceptual prominence in the Code beyond its talmudic significance and closer to both biblical and contemporary Muslim ideology; Maimonides uses it as the organizing principle of the tenth chapter of his Laws of Idolatry.) Consequently, the Jew is forbidden to save the life of an idolator. Yet this state of universal antagonism is not a state of constant—even if undeclared—war. For if one may not save the idolator's life, one is also forbidden to kill him 'since he is not at war with us'. This distinction rests on more than prudence alone; it affirms that the existence of the idolatrous in the world is not an immediate call to battle.[19] The Jew (here, of course, the focus is on the individual and not on the community) is not expected to challenge physically or to attempt to destroy the idolator. This doctrine governs the relationship of Jews to a world outside the orbit of Jewish control (or the imperative of Jewish control); it is this world in which treaties of peace may or may not be signed, and in which the Jew ought to relent in the pursuit of his idolatrous neighbour.

[18] *'Avodah Zarah*, x. 1, in uncensored versions. In censored editions, the text relates to the Canaanites alone. It would be interesting to trace Maimonidean treatment of biblical norms relating to the Canaanites: where is the norm read literally, and where is it generalized so as to include all idolators or even all gentiles? Obviously, the talmudic backgrounds would play a central role here.

[19] Ibid. This distinction holds even if—as read by R. Moses of Trani, *Kiryat Sefer* (New York, 1953) and R. Abraham de Buton, *Leḥem Mishneh* (New York, 1957)—this release is a function of Jewish powerlessness and is included in x. 6, a point to which I return at length later.

This policy is not to be applied, Maimonides insists, to the Land of Israel in periods of ideal political conditions: then the Land is to be flushed clean of idolators; they may not even pass through temporarily as visitors or merchants (a rejection of the Islamic *amān* compromise?). Maimonides must therefore allow that the peaceful coexistence with idolators, indeed the concern for their well-being as elements of the 'ways of peace', is a pragmatic concession to diaspora powerlessness and does not characterize the ideal, which demands the destruction of the idolators in the Land rather than his cultivation.[20] Even the individual Jew is expected to do his share, it would seem. An analogous situation is created by the rulings on idolatrous artefacts, which the Jew is unconditionally obliged to destroy in his land. No such obligation exists, however, *vis-à-vis* cults found outside the Land (nor are the people of Israel required to conquer such territories so as to purify them), despite the mandate of universal monotheism.[21]

V

Maimonides on war dovetails, in important respects, with Maimonides on idolatry. In both instances, the universal monotheistic thrust is choreographed by the criteria of Jewish nationhood and its concomitants. Physical aggression against idolators is demanded only within the Jewish national territory, where monotheism is to be established quickly and unambiguously. It may be said that a monotheistic territory is a basic condition for the meaningful existence of Jewish national life; thus, the *Book of Commandments* explains the elimination of the Canaanites as functioning to remove a necessarily corruptive element from the Land. Or, to sharpen the point, the territorial imperative of the Jewish people may itself be a function of the requirement that a monotheistic beach-head be brought into being. This is, of course, the upshot of the normative structures of commanded and permitted wars

[20] *'Avodah Zarah*, x. 5–6. See Rabad, who insists that these norms apply only to Canaanites (and not to idolators in general) and who claims that the ban on even temporary passage is not talmudic. On *amān*, see J. Hatschek, *Der Musta'amin* (Berlin, 1920). For a defence of Maimonides in internal terms, see R. Menaḥem of Helmo, *Morkevet ha-Mishneh* (Jerusalem, 1974), ad loc. (I. ii. 31–2). Maimonides' limiting, pragmatic approach to the 'ways of peace' clashes, of course, with his own presentation of the norms in question as a principled act of *imitatio dei* in *Melakhim*, x. 12; and *Hilkhot Ḥannukah*, iv. 14.

[21] *'Avodah Zarah*, vi. 1.

as well: war is commanded only within the bounds of Jewish national existence (where it may indeed have as its goal the elimination of the idolatrous), and it is permitted only in areas of extended national concern. Universal 'holy war' is not the approved instrument to achieve universal monotheism. Commanded war may, in the final analysis, serve ideological goals and be motivated for Maimonides by ideological strivings, but there is no allowing it (or permitted war) to absorb wars fought for purely religious goals, i.e. the imposition of Noahide law.

The evidence for universal holy war can, in large measure, be accommodated within this scheme, though I think that the tension between holy war and permitted war remains. The rhetoric of holy war is meant to inform the Jew of the proper motive (Maimonides will even use the term *kawwanah*)[22] of his waging of war and to purify his intent. It is to be applied, though, within the normative structure, which in fact delineates when wars are to be fought. Normative wars are to be fought as holy wars—*that* is the basic point, not that holy wars may be fought beyond the bounds of the normative. Texts which speak of the imposition of Noahide law by force are probably to be seen in a more restrictive mode. Our opening citation, for example, ought then to be read as a generalization of the previous section, which specified that captives are to be allowed the choice between Noahide law and death; compulsion is thus applied against those already in Jewish control by virtue of a normative war—it is not a rationale for going to war in the first place. That discussion in fact concluded with the statement: 'for any idolator who has not accepted Noahide law is to be put to death if he is under our control', and we should probably go no further.[23] Even a ban on war against nations who are Noahides does not mean that war otherwise has the spread of Noahide law as its motive; rather, it means that the Jew is bound to the Noahide by bonds of care that preclude waging war against him.[24] It remains true, of course, that Maimonides sees the imposition of Noahide law in broad and aggressive terms, that it is a significant aspect of Jewish policy towards conquered peoples.[25]

[22] *Melakhim*, vii. 15.

[23] The passage had already been read in this manner by R. Moses of Trani, who lived in the 16th cent.; *Kiryat Sefer*, ad loc.

[24] Cf. n. 7.

[25] Even so, Maimonides may make exceptions: see *Issure Bi'ah*, xiv. 9, where he implies that a purchased slave who refuses to abandon his pagan ways is to be resold to a non-Jewish owner rather than be killed, though he is clearly in Jewish control.

But this is not yet the same thing as providing a rationale for war.[26]

These implications of the normative structure are congruent with other, broader, considerations. The career of monotheism, we know from other Maimonidean passages, is to be a gradual process.[27] In these terms, compulsion is neither warranted nor likely to achieve the ultimate goal. But compulsion can eliminate idolatry—and this is immediately required so as to provide a physical homeland in which the Lord alone will be worshipped. Here both immediacy and total success are necessary. But the achievement of universal, world-wide monotheism may well be left to other organs of the monotheistic community and to other processes in history. Compulsion, moreover, can eliminate idolators, making of them law-abiding Noahides. Yet the Noahide is not expected to worship God in any positive sense, and this—a mankind united in the worship of God—is the goal which Maimonides portrays: the Messiah 'will prepare the whole world to serve the Lord with one accord, as it is written "For then will I turn to the peoples a pure language, that they may all call upon the name of the Lord to serve Him with one consent" (Zeph. 3: 9).'[28] This universal positive recognition of God and his worship—a state of spiritual being far beyond the modest and negative structure of Noahism—is probably the domain of the Abrahamic teaching model, as developed elsewhere in the Maimonidean corpus. Certainly, Maimonides makes it very clear that this positive state is not related to compulsion or force: no one is to be compelled to adopt Judaism, a point on which Maimonides is more insistent than are some other medieval figures;[29] and the service of God—even if not identical with Judaism *per se*—is probably beyond the realm of compulsion as well. Thus, the universal vision of Maimonides is nowhere related organically to holy war. Maimonides does require the universal imposition of Noahide law in areas under Jewish control, but this is most likely the outer limit of compulsion, reflecting Jewish

[26] This holds true, as well, for *'Avodah Zarah*, x. 1, 6. Even if x. 6 applies to x. 1, the state of *yad yisra'el taqifa 'al ummot ha-'olam* refers to Jewish control and not to a general imperative to wage war.

[27] See A. Funkenstein, 'Maimonides: Political Theory and Realistic Messianism', *Miscellanea Mediaevalia*, 2 (1977), 81–103.

[28] *Melakhim*, xi. 4. I now believe, in contrast to the statement above, that Maimonides expects the Noahide to engage in the positive worship of God in the Messianic age. See my comment in *Ziyyon*, 51 (1986), 160 n. 26.

[29] See *Issure Bi'ah*, xiv. 9, and *Maggid Mishneh*, ad loc. (op. cit. xiii. 12); *Melakhim*, viii. 5, 7, and Rashi, *Qiddushin*, 22*a*, s.v. *liqquḥin*; Rashi, *Yevamot*, 47*b*, s.v. *kofah*. On the

responsibility for what *can* be achieved by compulsion, on the one hand, and the creation of circumstances in which true monotheism can develop, on the other hand.[30] The thrust to achieve such control, though, is not fuelled by universal religious motives; nor, of course, can they provide a pious and incontestable cover for political ambitions. War must be justified, rather, by the fundamentally political and national considerations recognized by the normative structures, even if these, in turn, are understood as religiously significant in greater or smaller measure.

APPENDIX

It may well be the case that the *Book of Commandments* presents a different regimen of the laws for war than does the Code, a possibility which has been raised by R. Ḥayyim Heller.[31]

The Code, we recall, provided that (*a*) all war, including that with the Canaanites and Amalekites, must be preceded by a call for peace, which if accepted would allow the original inhabitants of the land to remain; and that (*b*) the call for peace includes a demand that the opponent accept Noahide law as well as other conditions. Both these provisions do not appear in the *Book of Commandments*. There, the call for peace appears only in the context of 'permitted war', but not in relation to the war for possession of the Land of Canaan—the Canaanites, then, are unconditionally to be driven out or destroyed. Moreover, the demand that the antagonist in 'permitted war' accept Noahide law is also lacking as part of the 'call for peace', though this goal may be assumed by other norms.[32] From a purely descriptive point of view, Maimonides of the *Book of Commandments* seems quite close to other medieval legists in his delineation of the norms of war, both commanded and permitted. Yet we ought also to recall (even if we reject the more radical solution suggested by Heller) that Maimonides of the *Book of Commandments* firmly posits the ideological character of the war against the Canaanites, which is urged as necessary in the elimination of the seduction of idolatry from the

whole, of course, all agree that conversion is rigorously voluntary; the above represent marginal situations.

[30] We ought to recall that the acceptance of Noahide law is strongly related to the status of *ger toshav*, which permits residence in the Holy Land (see above, n. 5). Moreover, all areas conquered according to the prescribed sequence of 'permitted war' achieve the status (for most matters) of Holy Land (*Melakhim*, v. 1, 6). It would, however, be unwarranted to read this religious motive into the first aim of 'permitted war', i.e. 'to extend the boundary of Israel'.

[31] *Sefer ha-Mizwot la-Rambam*, ed Ḥayyim Heller (New York, 1946), positive commands, 187, 190, and n. 11 on p. 82.

[32] See above, n. 30.

Land. This ideological rationale, of course, is not Maimonidean in origin—it is unmistakably biblical, as is seen by rereading Deut. 7: 1–5, and especially Deut. 20: 16–18: 'you shall not let a soul remain alive . . . lest they lead you into doing all the abhorrent things that they have done for their gods'; similarly Exod. 23: 32–3: 'You shall make no covenant with them and their gods. They shall not remain in your land, lest they cause you to sin against me, for you will serve their gods.'[33]

[33] It is instructive to project these Maimonidean and halakhic norms upon the grid provided by J. T. Johnson in his suggestive *Ideology, Reason and the Limitation of War* (Princeton, 1975). The Maimonidean halakhic norms (especially those explored in the second part of my paper) disclose the possibility of a 'commanded' war which is nonetheless not ideological in motive. Johnson's demonstration of the heavy Maimonidean influence on certain Puritan theorists (pp. 129–31) assumes that the ideologically grounded 'holy war' is a necessary concomitant of the 'commanded war', which we have seen is not the case, as the halakhic 'commanded war' does not include wars fought for religious purposes. Further comparison of the norms presented in my paper and the structure elaborated by Johnson would take us too far afield. It is unclear whether Maimonides included conquest of the land in the rubric of 'commanded wars' as regards the biblical conquest alone or for the remainder of Jewish history. The basic points in my essay remain unchanged even if one reads Maimonides restrictively. See *Melakhim*, v. 1.

12

'To the Utmost Human Capacity': Maimonides on the Days of the Messiah

AVIEZER RAVITZKY

MAIMONIDES *Mishneh Torah*, which is essentially a halakhic work, opens and concludes with a discussion of matters pertaining to doctrines and beliefs: it begins with metaphysics and physics, and concludes with a discussion of Messianism. In both places one perceives the outstanding independence and creative power of the author, who does not hesitate to decide unequivocally on matters of views, beliefs, and fundamental concepts, defining, delimiting, and drawing precise distinctions not only in the realm of Jewish law but also in the theoretical realm ranging from theology to eschatology. Just as Maimonides' philosophic positions left their distinctive mark upon the opening chapters of his halakhic work (*Yesode ha-Torah*, i–iv), so did they leave their imprint upon its final chapters, the laws of Messiah (*Melakhim*, xi–xii). Maimonides' political philosophy and anthropology direct his *positive* Messianic models: the political realization of the Torah within Israel and the intellectual actualization of the spiritual power within the human species. His ontology and theology, on the other hand, dictate his *negative* emphases—the restrictions and limitations imposed upon Messianism: the rejection of cosmic, apocalyptic redemption, and the setting of Messianic hope within the domain of human existence. While his Messianism is dictated not by his mind but by his faith, it is essentially his mind that directs, defines, and limits the object of his faith.

In this paper, I intend to propose certain patterns for understanding the reasoning of Maimonides in his depiction of Messianic days, to establish its normative significance, and to examine the relationship established in his teaching among the three different dimensions of redemption—individual, national, and universal. The discussion will also clarify some aspects of the differing opinions among Maimonidean scholars on this subject.

The analysis will take into account the relevant passages scattered among Maimonides' various writings, but will give primary weight to the clear, well-structured, and detailed presentation found at the end of *Hilkhot Melakhim* (Laws of kings) in the light of the *Guide of the Perplexed*.[1]

I

According to *The Guide of the Perplexed*, the ideal human society is one which is directed both toward the personal security and physical well-being of men—'the welfare of the states of people in their relations with one another'—and their spiritual and intellectual perfection—'the soundness of their beliefs and the giving of correct opinions'. However, in the various chapters of this work, two distinct models, two separate levels of the ideal human society, emerge.

One model is explicitly political. It is concerned with the ideal state founded by the true prophet and with the perfection of its inhabitants. It posits the proper social order as a substratum and preparation for spiritual elevation, the physical well-being of people functioning as a precondition of their spiritual perfection. It does not presume to uproot human evil or the destructive forces operating within society, but to tame them and to negate their forces by means of an appropriate political and educational framework. Here, as in the Platonic political doctrine, a rational social order is a guarantor of the improvement of individuals.[2] This state—the political realization of the Torah—is

[1] See *Mishneh Torah*, *Teshuvah*, viii. 7; ix. 2; *Megillah*, ii. 18; *Parah Adumah*, iii. 4; *Ma'aseh ha-Qorbanot*, ii. 14; *Melakhim*, iv. 8, 11–12 (cf. *Shemittah we-Yovel*, xii. 16); *Commentary on the Mishnah*, *Sanh*. i. 3; *'Eduyot*, viii. 7; *Introduction to Pereq Ḥeleq*, trans. A. Wolf, *Judaism*, 15 (1966), 95–101, 211–16, 337–42. repr. in I. Twersky (ed.), *A Maimonides Reader* (New York–Philadelphia, 1972), 401–23; *Epistle to Yemen*, trans. Boaz Cohen, in *Iggeret Teman*, ed. A. Halkin (New York, 1952), *passim*; and Twersky, *Maimonides Reader*, 437–62. (Cf. his comments concerning the Messiah of Yemen in his Epistle to the Sages of Provence, *Qovez Teshuvot ha-Rambam we-Iggerotaw* (Leipzig, 1849), ii. 26*b*); *Ma'amar Teḥiyat ha-Metim*, ed. J. Finkel, *PAAJR* 11 (1939), 20–4; *Iggeret ha-Shemad*, in *Iggerot ha-Rambam*, ed. Rabinowitz (Jerusalem, 1960), 66–7; *Guide of the Perplexed*, ii. 29; i. 36; iii. 11 (other relevant passages will be cited below).

[2] On Maimonides' political philosophy and its relationship to the Platonic tradition, see S. Pines, 'The Philosophic Sources of *The Guide of the Perplexed*', in his translation of the *Guide* (Chicago, 1963), pp. lxxxvi ff.; L. V. Berman, 'The Political Interpretation of the Maxim: The Purpose of Philosophy is the Imitation of God', *SI* 15 (1961), 53–61;

directed towards the improvement of a given society within which the masses and outstanding individuals continue to live together: the proper social and political circumstances contribute to the elevation of both. Moreover, the dramatic cessation of these conditions, by the loss of political independence and the exile of Israel, which necessarily damaged its spiritual independence as well, was also the immediate cause of the loss of the visionary power of the prophets, the peak of the human species:

This is indubitably the essential and proximate cause of the fact that prophecy was taken away during the time of the Exile . . . being a thrall slave in bondage to the ignorant who commit great sins . . . For the instrument—the spiritual faculty for attaining prophecy—has ceased to function. This also will be the cause for prophecy being restored to us in the days of the Messiah.[3]

Just as in the life of the individual the welfare of the body enhances that of the soul, so in the life of society, social-political perfection enhances intellectual perfection:

The law as a whole aims at two things: the welfare of the soul and the welfare of the body . . . as between these two aims . . . the second aim—I mean the welfare of the body—is prior in nature and time. The latter aim consists in the governance of the city and the well-being of the states of all its people, according to their capacity. This second aim is the more certain one . . . for the first aim can only be achieved after achieving this second one. . . . The Law of Moses our Master has come to bring us both perfections. I mean the welfare of the states of people in their relations with one another . . . I mean also the soundness of the beliefs and the giving of correct opinions through which ultimate perfection is achieved. (*Guide*, iii. 27)

H. Davidson, 'Maimonides' *Shemonah Peraqim* and Al-Fārābī's *Fuṣūl al-Madanī*', *PAAJR* 31 (1963), 47 ff.; L. V. Berman, 'Maimonides, the Disciple of Alfārābī', *IOS* 4 (1974), 170 ff.

Recently, Pines has expressed the view that Maimonides saw practical political perfection as the highest possible human achievement, denying the possibility of attaining intellectual perfection. See his article, 'The Limitations of Human Knowledge According to Al-Fārābī, ibn Bājja and Maimonides', in I. Twersky (ed.), *Studies in Medieval Jewish History and Literature* (Cambridge, Mass., 1979), 89–109. This interpretation itself calls for critical study. In any event, Maimonides' doctrine of Messianism is characterized by the positing of both political and apolitical models (see below). The latter model is dependent upon intellectual perfection, if only as an infinite goal.

[3] *Guide*, ii. 36. All English quotations are taken from the translation by S. Pines, *The Guide of the Perplexed* (Chicago, 1963). Cf. *Yesode ha-Torah*, vii. 4, and I. Twersky, '*Sefer Mishneh Torah la-Rambam: Magamato we-Tafqido*', *Proceedings of the Israel Academy of Sciences and Humanities*, 5 (1976), 11–13.

Therefore I say that the Law, although it is not natural, enters into what is natural. It is a part of the wisdom of the deity with regard to the permanence of this species of which He has willed the existence, that He put it into its nature that individuals belonging to it should have the faculty of ruling. Among them there is the one to whom the regime mentioned has been revealed by prophecy directly . . . If you find a Law, all of whose ordinances are due to attention being paid . . . to the soundness of the circumstances pertaining to the body and also to the soundness of belief . . . you must know that this guidance comes from Him, may He be exalted, and that this Law is divine. (*Guide*, ii. 40)

The second model would appear to reverse these elements: physical security is no longer presented as a precondition for the perfection of the soul but as its necessary consequence and accompaniment. The ideal society is thus made contingent upon the spiritual level of the individual.[4] The apprehension of intelligibles, 'knowledge of God', removes man's awareness completely from his attachment to illusory goods and imagined interests, and completely eliminates the irrational factors which arouse mutual conflicts and violence between individuals and social groupings. Intellectual perfection is the guarantor of peace and security.[5] In contrast to the previous model, which could be characterized as a political and 'realistic' one, this latter may be described as apolitical and Utopian: it strives for the universal

[4] On the relationship between social philosophy and the Torah see, most recently, W. Harvey, 'Ben Filosofiyah Medinit la-Halakhah be-Mishnat ha-Rambam', *'Iyyun*, 29 (1980), 198–212; M. Galston, 'The Purpose of the Law according to Maimonides', *JQR* 69 (1978), 27–51. On this problem, see the full-length discussion in D. Hartman, *Maimonides: Torah and Philosophical Quest* (Philadelphia, 1976).

[5] The relationship between the two societal patterns—the one making personal perfection dependent upon political order, and the other reversing the order, making social perfection dependent upon spiritual perfection—finds an interesting parallel in Maimonides' teaching about the life of the individual and its purpose. Initially, ethical activity is presented as a preparatory stage for the attainment of intellectual perfection—i.e. knowledge of God. However, in a next stage they are reversed, and the attainment of truth enables the spiritual leader, the prophet, to infuse loving-kindness, righteousness, and judgement into society (*Guide*, iii. 54), somewhat like the Platonic philosopher returning to the cave. On the one hand, ethical activity in the realm of good and evil is viewed as a preparatory stage for intellectual perfection and involvement in the realm of truth. On the other hand, the highest intellectual level, knowledge of God, leads one to imitation of the ways of God, and to influence governance and existence into reality (beyond the realm of good and evil and the struggle of the impulses). See E. Goldman, 'Ha-'Avodah ha-Meyuḥedet be-Masige ha-Amitot', *Sefer ha-Shanah shel Universitat Bar-Ilan*, 6 (1968), 287–313; A. Altmann, 'Maimonides' Four Perfections', *IOS* 2 (1972), 23–4; Berman, 'Political Interpretation'. For other approaches to the relationship between the intellectual and the moral domains in Maimonides' thought, see M. Fox, 'Maimonides and Aquinas on Natural Law', *Dine Israel*, 3 (1972), pp. v–xxxvi; S. S. Schwarzschild, 'Moral Radicalism and "Middlingness" in the Ethics of Maimonides', *Studies in Medieval Culture*, 11 (1978), 65–94.

perfection of the human race, all of whose members shall attain knowledge of God, and envisages an idealized hypothetical society, composed entirely of a spiritual élite. 'Then', beyond the process of partial perfection of human beings, man is destined to return to his original essence, to that which he was meant to be, had not sin intervened, 'when man was in his most perfect and excellent state, in accordance with his inborn disposition and possessed of his intellectual cognition, because of which it is said of him, "Thou hast made him but little lower than *Elohim*".'[6] This promise is not concerned with appropriate political models but with the final perfection of humanity, in which 'enmity and hatred are removed', as an immediate consequence of the spiritual and intellectual perfection of the individuals. In truth, it represents the priority of intellect in the human species—practical perfection is dependent upon theoretical perfection:

> For when only the desires are followed . . . cares and sorrows multiply; mutual envy, hatred and strife aiming at taking away what the other has, multiply. (*Guide*, iii. 33)

> For through cognition of the truth, enmity and hatred are removed, and the inflicting of harm by people on one another is abolished. It holds out this promise, saying: 'And the wolf shall dwell with the lamb, and the leopard shall lie down with the kid,' and so on . . . Then it gives the reason for this, saying that the cause of the abolition of these enmities, these discords, and these tyrannies, will be the knowledge that men will then have concerning the true reality of the deity. For it says, 'They shall not hurt nor destroy in all My holy mountain: for the earth shall be full of knowledge of the Lord, as the waters cover the sea.' Know this. (*Guide*, iii. 11)[7]

The Messianic goals presented in the *Mishneh Torah* combine these two models, linking them in both chronological and causal order. The national hope for the redemption of Israel is interpreted in accord once

[6] *Guide*, i. 2.

[7] It is interesting to note that R. Joseph b. Kaspi, who took care to expunge all Utopian elements from his hopes of the future, even 'interpreted' this prophetic promise and its use in the *Guide* in terms of the past. Thus, the prophecy, 'The wolf shall lie down with the lamb', had been fulfilled 'in the days of Hezekiah, whether in regard to the people of Israel among themselves, or in regard to the other nations, particularly the Assyrians, who honored them'! See *Maskiyyot Kesef* on *Guide*, iii. 11 (Frankfurt, 1848; also printed in *Sheloshah Qadmone Mefarshe ha-Moreh* (Vienna, 1853)). Elsewhere, Ibn Kaspi criticized those *Guide* commentators who found references to the Third Temple in various verses. See *Tam ha-Kesef*, ed. J. Last (London, 1917), (photo edn. in *Kitve R. Yosef Ibn Kaspi*: *Shonot* (Jerusalem, 1970), 41–4). Cf. S. Pines, 'Histabrut Tequmatah me-Ḥadash shel Medinah Yehudit le-fi Yosef Ibn Kaspi ule-fi Spinoza', *Ben Maḥshevet Yisra'el le-Maḥshevet ha-'Amim* (Jerusalem, 1977), 285, 296.

with the logic of the former, while the universalist hope for the final redemption is cast in light of the latter.

On one level, the only distinction between the present world and Messianic times is the political and religious restoration of the Jewish people, the political realization of the Torah. The people of Israel, who at the present time are subject to the domination of the nations, and whose Torah is preserved among them as individuals only, are seeking their political renewal in their land and the return of the Torah to public life. These goals are completely subjected to the patterns of regular historical processes, including a military struggle without and political coercion within. They correspond to the realistic model mentioned above, in as much as they posit the creation of appropriate political conditions ('the days of Messiah—when sovereignty shall revert to Israel') as the basis for spiritual ascent—'that they might have relief from the wicked tyranny that does not permit them properly to occupy themselves with the study of the Torah and the observance of the commandments, that they might have ease and devote themselves to getting wisdom' (*Hilkhot Teshuvah* (Laws of repentance), ix. 2).[8] Indeed, in this portrayal of the government of the King Messiah, the 'welfare of the body' and 'welfare of the soul' are interrelated; political and military activity on the one hand, and spiritual and religious activity on the other: kingship and prophecy in one package. Moreover, even the explicitly religious dimension of the King Messiah's public leadership is portrayed along these two lines: in the political context of the *Hilkhot Melakhim*—an image of a king who utilizes his power of political coercion and makes the law of Torah the law of the state: 'He *prevails* upon Israel to walk in the way of the Torah and to repair its breaches' (*Melakhim*, xi. 4); in the educational context of the *Hilkhot Teshuvah*—an image of a prophetic teacher who functions through the authority of his personal excellence: 'He will *teach* the whole of the Jewish people and instruct them in the way of God' (*Teshuva*, ix. 2).[9] The very ideas which appear in his philosophical work within a theoretical conceptual framework are pictured in the halakhic work in concrete dress; the double intent of the Torah is depicted in terms of

[8] *Teshuvah*, ix. 2. The English translations of passages from the *Mishneh Torah* are taken, with slight amendation, from: bks. i–ii, *Mishneh Torah*, trans. Moses Hyamson (Jerusalem, 1962); bks. iii–xiv, *The Code of Maimonides*, Yale Judaica Series (New Haven, 1949).

[9] The Torah as a cause for the welfare of the body lends itself to political coercion, but as a cause for the welfare of the soul it may not be imposed by coercion.

the living, historical images of the Davidic dynasty; the hope for the future is derived from an idealization of the past:

The King Messiah will arise and restore the kingdom of David to its former state and original sovereignty. He will rebuild the sanctuary and gather the dispersed of Israel. All the ancient laws will be reinstituted in his days . . . If there arise a king from the house of David who meditates on the Torah, occupies himself with the commandments as did his ancestor David, observes the precepts prescribed in the written and the Oral Law, prevails upon Israel to walk in the way of the Torah and to repair its breaches, and fights the battles of the Lord, it may be assumed that he is the Messiah. If he does these things and succeeds, vanquishes all the nations around, rebuilds the sanctuary on its site, and gathers the dispersed of Israel, then he is beyond all doubt the Messiah. (*Melakhim*, xi. 1, 4)[10]

Because the king who will arise from the seed of David will possess more wisdom than Solomon and will be a great prophet, approaching Moses, our teacher; He will teach the whole of the Jewish people and instruct them in the way of God . . . The Messianic era will be realized in this world, which will continue in its normal course, except that independent sovereignty will be restored to Israel. (*Teshuvah*, ix. 2)

Compare to this the Introduction to *Pereq Ḥeleq*:

The 'days of the Messiah' refers to a time in which sovereignty will revert to Israel and the Jewish people will return to the Land of Israel . . . The great benefits which will occur in those days include our release from oppression by other kingdoms, which prevents us from fulfilling all the commandments—a widespread increase of wisdom . . . because then the righteous will be gathered together in fellowship, and because goodness and wisdom will prevail. They desired it also because of the righteousness and abundant justice of the messianic king, because of the salutary influence of his unprecedented wisdom, and because of his nearness to God . . . They also anticipate the performance of all of the commandments of the Torah of Moses our Teacher, with neither inertia on the one hand nor compulsion on the other.[11]

On the second level, Messianic concern is shifted from the perfection of Israel to that of the nations of the world, and from there to the final, universal redemption of the human race. Israel, believers and children of believers, who are subjugated by the nations, expect

[10] The quotations from *Hilkhot Melakhim* here and below are corrected according to the 1509 Constantinople edition, which was not subject to Christian censorship (cf. edn. of Mossad ha-Rav Kook, Jerusalem, 1967).

[11] The English translation of the *Introduction to Ḥeleq* is taken from the translation by Arnold J. Wolf, cited in n. 1 above.

political liberation first; the nations of the world, 'whose fathers inherited falsehood', but even today enjoy political independence ('regimens of *nomoi*', as distinct from 'regimens of the divine Law'),[12] do not require a political change, but rather a change in their religious cognition, in their faith: 'But when the true King Messiah will appear and succeed, be exalted and lifted up, they will forthwith recant and realize that they have inherited naught but lies from their fathers, that their prophets and forebears led them astray . . . and they shall all return to the true faith.'[13] Alongside his underlining of this radical transformation, Maimonides took care to note the place of this Messianic goal, too, within the ongoing causal process and within the present historical reality: the final turning of the nations of the world to monotheism was preceded and anticipated by the preparatory historical processes of the gradual spread of Christianity and Islam within idolatrous humanity. By its nature, this was coupled with the widespread recognition of ideas and concepts borrowed from the true faith and its commandments.[14] These concepts, despite being distorted and removed from their original context, will serve as a foundation for

[12] *Guide*, ii. 40.

[13] Cf. the description of Abraham's activities in '*Avodat Kokhavim*, i. 3: 'He realized that men everywhere were in error . . . He then began to proclaim to the whole world with great power . . . He would instruct each one according to his capacity till he had brought him to the way of truth.' Cf. also A. Funkenstein, 'Maimonides: Political Theory and Realistic Messianism', *Miscellanea Medieavalia* (Berlin–New York, 1977), 97–101; I. Twersky, *Introduction to the Code of Maimonides* (New Haven–London, 1980), 451.

In my opinion, one should distinguish between the historical return to the monotheistic religion, as in ancient times (see n. 16 below), and the final destiny, beyond the current state of history: 'The one preoccupation of the whole world will be to know the Lord' (*Melakhim*, xii. 5; see below).

[14] 'All these matters relating to Jesus of Nazareth and the Ishmaelite [Muhammad] who came after him, only served . . . to prepare the whole world to worship God with one accord . . . Thus the Messianic hope, the Torah, and the commandments have become familiar topics—topics of conversation [among the inhabitants] of the far isles and many peoples, uncircumcised of heart and flesh. They are discussing these matters and commandments of the Torah. Some say, "These commandments were true, but have lost their validity and are no longer binding"; other declare that they had an esoteric meaning and were not intended to be taken literally; that the Messiah has already come and revealed their occult significance' (from the uncensored version of *Melakhim*, xi. 4, in Twersky, *Maimonides Reader*, 226–7). Cf. H. H. Ben-Sasson, 'Yiḥud 'Am Yisra' el le-Da'at Bene ha-Me'ah ha-Shetem 'Esreh', *Peraqim*, 2 (1971), 181–3; Funkenstein, 'Political Theory and Realistic Messianism'.

In my opinion, one need not forcibly reconcile statements made in *Hilkhot Melakhim* with those in *Iggeret Teman*; see n. 56 below. See Halkin, *Iggeret Teman*, Introd., p. 14.

the final, future transformation.[15] Moreover, the future universal spread of monotheism is perceived as a return to an ancient, ideal state in the history of humanity, before its gradual degeneration into idolatry during the first biblical generations.[16] Thus, even on this level, the hope for the future corresponds to an idealized image of the past. In any event, even though not departing from the causal, historical process, both these transformations, in Israel and within the nations, are nevertheless intended to lead beyond the present dimension of human history towards its final spiritual and social perfection: beyond

[15] Cf. Judah Halevi, *Kuzari*, iv. 23. See the explanation of R. Isaac Abrabanel, *Yeshu'ot Meshiḥo* (Königsberg, 1861), (photo edn. Jerusalem, 1967), in which Jesus, Bar Kokhba (!), Muḥammad, and various false messiahs who rose within the Jewish people are all grouped together:

> The disciples of Jesus arose and elevated his name and announced that he was the Messiah whom the prophets had anticipated, and in those days their faith spread throughout most of the world. At about the same time, in Betar, Ben Kozba arose, at the end of the fourth millennium, and declared himself the Messiah. After them came Muḥammad, the prophet of the Ishmaelites, who said that God had annointed him as ruler and commander of the nations, and most of the nations followed him. In our Exile, also, many people arose who declared themselves messiahs . . . This thing was caused by God, that people throughout the world should know about the King Messiah who is to come, and that their mouths and hearts be filled with him, even if with false and distorted knowledge, in order that when the time comes, and in the radiance of his light all the inhabitants of the earth and all those who dwell there shall know that their ancestors inherited falsehood in this matter, and that our Messiah, for whom we have hoped all these years, is the one of whom God has spoken . . . At the end of his work, *Mishneh Torah*, the great rabbi wrote that these imaginary messiahs only came into the world to pave the way for the King Messiah.

Abrabanel followed Maimonides, but he was not prepared to grant to the false religions the stature of disseminators of the faith in God's unity. They prepared the path by spreading the *Messianic*, rather than the *monotheistic* idea. On the other hand, Abraham Farissol, also influenced in this matter by Maimonides, went further than Abrabanel in affirming their positive influence: 'After his [Jesus'] coming, and the spread of his opinions, they [the gentiles] were redeemed and purified of the contamination of idolatry, they gathered together by him and his disciples and his apostles to believe, in some manner, in the unity of the first cause.' See H. H. Ben-Sasson, 'Ha-Yehudim mul ha-Reformazyah', *Proceedings of the Israel Academy of Sciences and Humanities*, 4 (1970), 63 n. 10. Maimonides' position is also reflected in Naḥmanides' sermon, 'Torat Ha-Shem Temimah', *Kitve ha-Ramban*, ed. H. Chavel (Jerusalem, 1967), 144. Cf. D. Rapel, 'Ha-Ramban 'al ha-Galut weha-Ge'ulah', *Ge'ulah u-Medinah* (Jerusalem, 1979), 108–9. On other effects of Maimonides' above-mentioned statement, see Ben-Sasson, 'Yiḥud 'Am Yisrael', 182.

[16] See '*Avodat Kokhavim*, i. 1–2: 'In the days of Enosh, the people fell into gross error . . . as follows: "Since God", they said, "created these stars and spheres . . . they deserve to be praised and glorified, and honor should be rendered them" . . . their purpose, according to their perverse notions, being to obtain the Creator's favor.' What started as a cognitive error led to a mistaken cult and ended in heresy and worship of wood and stones in the literal sense.

the political and national domain, above the destructive forces existing in contemporary society, and beyond the boundaries separating the masses from excellent individuals. The process itself is a 'realistic' one, while its completion is Utopian. Just as the national Messianic goal is parallel to one model in the *Guide of the Perplexed*, the realization of the Torah in an ideal political situation, so is the universal Messianic goal parallel to the second model in the *Guide*, the acquisition of the divine intelligibles and the final perfection of society. In this plane, the parallelism is reflected even in details:

In that era, there will be neither famine nor war, neither jealousy nor strife. Blessings will be abundant, comforts within the reach of all. The one preoccupation of the whole world will be to know the Lord. Hence they will be very wise, they will know the things that are now concealed and will attain an understanding of the Creator to the utmost human capacity, as it is written, 'For the earth shall be full of the knowledge of the Lord, as the waters cover the sea'. (*Melakhim*, xii. 5)[17]

Compare this to the additional explanation found in the *Ma'amar Teḥiyat ha-Metim* (Treatise on resurrection):

'They shall not hurt nor destroy in all My holy mountain; for the earth shall be full of the knowledge of the Lord, as the waters cover the sea.' The reason for their neither robbing nor injuring has been given in their knowledge of God.[18]

Does this portrait of the final fulfilment of history deny future man the freedom of choice? Does it testify to a substantial change in human nature, or in the nature of the earth? Is this to be read only as a pathetic conclusion to the *Mishneh Torah*, breaking out of the constraint placed upon the Messianic images by philosophical and halakhic considerations? The parallel appearance of this pattern within the body of Maimonides' philosophic work would not suggest this. Moreover, it seems that the key to understanding the conclusion of the *Mishneh Torah* is to be found precisely in Maimonides' allegorical interpretation of the story of the Garden of Eden in the opening chapters of the *Guide*. According to this interpretation, Adam, who was created in the image of God, is the archetype of perfect intellectual attainment, whose mind is

[17] Efodi's commentary on *Guide*, iii. 11 appears to hint at a parallel between it and the end of *Mishneh Torah*: 'There will be among them neither conflict nor dispute nor jealousy nor strife [phrases used to describe the Messianic era in Mishneh Torah] and they shall all have one perfect faith—all this shall come about in the future in the days of the Messiah.'

[18] Cf. his *Commentary on the Mishnah*, '*Eduyot*, viii. 7.

completely involved in the realm of the intelligibles, beyond the realm of good and evil, and beyond the struggle against the impulses. Intellectual apprehension has no relation to the 'desires of the imagination'. Within its realm they are meaningless and do not need to be overcome. This is the original, true level of man, represented in a typological manner[19] by the image of one who was not born and had no need to perfect himself gradually and to actualize his intellectual power ('the intellect was called Adam'—Samuel b. Ẓarẓa).[20] Sin does not commence with the choice of evil but with the directing of the consciousness away from the pure rational plane to that of 'pleasures and imaginings', to the struggle of the impulses, to the realm of 'moral conventions'. The punishment for this is inherent in the sin itself: the loss of the original human stature and the sentence of expulsion and eternal wandering between the intellective image of God and the inferior levels of existence and consciousness. The story of the Garden of Eden thus deals with the permanent tension between man as he ought to be—'Thou hast made him but little lower than *Elohim*'—and his actual history. The commentators of the *Guide* stressed that we are dealing here with an archetype of the human species ('Adam, while he was a specific individual, was also a species unto himself . . . for the human race came into existence through one man'—Isaac Abrabanel),[21] and with the perpetual struggle of Man ('Adam–Man mentioned there is not one single individual, but the collective man'—Joseph b. Kaspi;[22] 'Everything that happened to the first man is the account of the history of man'—Shem Ṭov b. Joseph).[23] Some of the commentators also hinted at a symbolic meaning of the term 'Garden of Eden', in the sense of a supreme intellective excellence from which Adam found himself expelled.[24]

[19] *Guide*, i. 1–2. Cf. ibid., i. 14; ii. 30; *Mishneh Torah*, *Teshuva*, v. 1; *Shemonah Peraqim*, ch. 8. Cf. S. Klein-Braslavy, *Perush ha-Rambam le-Sippur Beri'at ha-'Olam* (Jerusalem, 1978), 200–17; W. Z. Harvey, 'Ha-Rambam u-Spinoza 'al Yedi'at Ṭov wa-Ra'', *Iyyun*, 28 (1979), 167–85; L. V. Berman, 'Maimonides on the Fall of Man', *AJS Review*, 5 (1980), 1–15; A. Ravitzky, 'Samuel Ibn Tibbon and the Esoteric Character of the *Guide of the Perplexed*', *AJS Review*, 6 (1981), 94 ff. See also Klein-Braslavy, 'On Maimonides' Interpretation of the Garden of Eden Story', paper presented at the Maimonides Conference at Tel Aviv University, 1982.

[20] Samuel b. Ẓarẓa, *Mikhlal Yofi*, MS Munich 64, fo. 229*a*. These remarks are directed towards Samuel b. Tibbon.

[21] Commentary to the *Guide*, i. 14.

[22] *Maskiyyot Kesef*, on *Guide*, i. 2.

[23] Commentary to *Guide*, ad loc. Cf. his commentary to *Guide*, i. 14: 'Everything that happened to Adam will happen also to his descendants', and Ephodi ad loc.: 'Everything that happened to Adam will happen to every man many times in our days.'

[24] See the commentaries of Efodi and Shem Ṭov to *Guide*, i. 8.

Now, we find that the opening of human history is united with its final perfection. The universal redemption of the human race—the supreme apprehension of intelligibles; a life lived above jealousy and strife; 'comforts within reach of all'—refers in fact to man's return to his original stature,[25] represented by the human archetype—'He who was in his most perfect and excellent state with his inborn disposition and possessed of his intellectual cognition . . . He had no faculty that was engaged in any way in the consideration of generally accepted things, and he did not apprehend them . . . He had been given license to eat good things and to enjoy ease and tranquillity.'[26] That which is today granted only to unusual individuals, to the select minority of a spiritual élite, is restored in the Messianic vision to the lot of universal man. Indeed, an individual may and ought to strive to attain his own spiritual perfection, even in his present, concrete existence, even within the Exile of Israel and in a human society from which war, jealousy, and strife have not been removed.[27] In fact, there is no difference between this world and the times of the Messiah in terms of a transformation of the nature of the individual, his destiny, or the content of his intellectual grasp. Even in the future, 'They will attain an understanding of their Creator according to the utmost human capacity (*kefi koaḥ ha-adam*)'[28] i.e. without transcending human

[25] The correction discussed here, which concerns the eradication of evil done by man (see below) should not be identified with the Messianic correction described in the Midrash: 'Even though things were created in their fullness, after Adam sinned they were spoiled, and they shall never again return to their earlier perfection until the son of Perez [i.e. Messiah] shall come' (*Bereshit Rabbah*, xii. 5). This is the correction of cosmic reality. The theme appears in more exaggerated terms in the Kabbalah; see G. Scholem, 'The Messianic Idea in Kabbalism', in *The Messianic Idea in Judaism* (New York, 1971), 40 ff.

[26] *Guide*, i. 2.

[27] 'Our Teacher . . . [Maimonides] divided his book into . . . 177 chapters, their sign [i.e. by *gematria*] being *Gan 'Eden* [the Garden of Eden]', Abrabanel, *Ma'amar Qaẓar be-Ve'ur Sod ha-Moreh*, printed in standard editions of the *Guide*.

[28] Cf. *Teshuva*, x. 6: 'A person ought therefore to devote himself to the understanding and comprehension of those sciences and studies which will inform him concerning his Master, as far as it lies in human capacity (*kefi koaḥ she-yesh ba-adam*) to understand and comprehend'; ibid. v. 5; vi. 5; viii. 7; *Tefillah*, ix. 7. Cf. *Guide*, i. 5: 'the desire and endeavor to acquire and achieve true beliefs to the extent to which this is in the power of man (*ḥasab maqdirat al-insān*)'; *Iggeret Teman*: 'attainment of the intelligibles as they are in themselves, to the extent of the power of man (*bi-ḥasab ṭāqat al-insān*)'. Maimonides used this expression in the context of the limits of human apprehension and man's attempts at its actualization. Below, this term will be used in a borrowed sense, beyond the question of the power of apprehension, in the following ways: the full potential of man as realized in Messianic times; the limitations of his power and nature, which will not be transcended in the Messianic era; and the place of human activity in Maimonides' Messianic conception.

limitations. However, the hope of redemption points towards the universal actualization of man as he was meant and ought to be, according to the original archetype.

Is this destiny historical or metahistorical? Is this a description of the future or a normative directive—a statement about the ultimate human good and final goal? How remote is this view from the concept of final perfection of man, as an infinite goal? One must clearly distinguish between two expulsions, two exiles from which Messianic redemption is promised: the Exile of Israel, and the exile of man. The first exile: the Jewish people is expelled from its ideal state, from the political realization of the Torah upon its own land. This exile is historical, and its full correction is also historical and realistic. The second exile: man finds himself expelled from the Garden of Eden, from the full realization of the image of God in the apprehension of intelligibles, above desires and jealousies. This exile is ahistorical, its full, final, universal, correction lying beyond the present historical human existence, while its personal realization is commanded to every individual in each generation, at every time and every place, beyond the limitations of current history. The first goal (the national) goes back to Sinai, while the other (the universal) goes back to the account of the creation, to the Garden of Eden. There are, indeed, causal and historical relationships between the fulfilment of one and the fulfilment of the other (a relationship which passes via the religious correction of the nations), but the final perfection transcends the present historical dimensions.

In light of the above, it would seem that the distinction between restorative Messianic doctrines and Utopian ones, between the expectation of a renewal and reconstruction of the past in its lost stature, on the one hand, and the hope for an as yet unknown new reality, on the other, is not an unambiguous criterion for the characterization of Maimonides' Messianic doctrine.[29]

Scholem distinguished between restorative and Utopian motifs in Messianism, characterizing Maimonides' Messianic doctrine as a clearly defined restorative one: 'The rational tendencies in Judaism pushed the restorative factor in Messianism decidedly into the foreground. With the influential formulation of this tendency by Maimonides restoration becomes the focus of Messianism. By

[29] See G. Scholem, 'Towards an Understanding of the Messianic Idea in Judaism', in *The Messianic Idea in Judaism* (New York, 1971), 3, 24–32.

contrast, the Utopian element quite peculiarly recedes and is only maintained at a bare minimum.'[30]

Some interesting remarks related to this question appear in R. Isaac Abrabanel's *Yeshu'ot Meshiḥo*. The author ascribes to the *amora* Samuel (in his saying 'There is no distinction between this world and the days of Messiah but the subjugation to the nations'—*Berakhot*, 34*b*) a sharp distinction between the restorative aims of Messianism ('the days of Messiah') and the Utopian aims ('the world of resurrection'—*'olam ha-teḥiya*), classifying the various components of Messianism under these two categories, 'even though these goals are mixed with one another in the prophecies'. However, some of the goals found in the *Mishneh Torah* are classified here among the restorative factors and others among the Utopian ones:

> Samuel, in his wisdom, anticipated two time periods in the future, [one] the days of Messiah, the time when the exiles shall be ingathered and leave the domination of other nations . . . Samuel thought that the character of this time would be like that of the days of old, of Moses and of David and of his son Solomon . . . that the blessing of the land and its excellence would be renewed as it was in ancient days . . . for the peak of the blessing and consolation will be that their success be renewed as of old . . . So the spirit of wisdom and understanding shall rest upon him as it did upon Solomon, the spirit of counsel and strength as it did upon David, the spirit of knowledge and fear of God, as it did upon Hezekiah . . . for he [Samuel] compared the future to the past . . . the peak of the goodness and success of the future will be that everything will return as it was in the early days, which were better than these . . . and in all this nothing shall be changed from what it was . . .
>
> However, he also anticipated a second time period, which will came about after the coming of the Messiah . . . the world of resurrection renewal . . . which the prophets anticipated in their prophecies . . . whether in the holiness of the people and the piety of its individuals . . . the diffusion of wisdom and knowledge throughout the world, as Isaiah said, 'the world shall be filled with knowledge of the Lord' . . . and they also envisaged universal peace in all corners of the world . . . and that the nations accept the faith in God . . . that the dead shall be resurrected . . . and that the evil impulse, and wars and strife shall cease.

Among the final goals, the author included significant departures from the order of nature, on which point he criticized Maimonides' words. One ought to add that below, he discusses at considerable

[30] Critical comments on this interpretation are to be found in Funkenstein, 'Political Theory and Realistic Messianism', 86, and Twersky (*Introduction*, 476).

length the eternity of the Torah and the impossibility of any change in the Law (the context of the entire treatise is one of response to Christian polemics). Thus, *Utopia* exists in conjunction with *restoration*, and even with the '*conservative* forces . . . directed towards the preservation of that which exists and which, in the historical environment of Judaism, was always in danger . . . They have established themselves most effectively in the world of *Halakha*.'[31]

The living awareness of this author, who was among those expelled from Spain, is able to reconcile and harmonize different forces.[32]

One must distinguish between the symbolic dimension and the real, between that which is potential and that which is actual. From the *symbolic* point of view there is nothing here but restoration, the renewal of the golden age both of the people and of mankind on several different levels. The national redemption will restore the Davidic dynasty upon its throne; the religious correction of the nations will restore ancient biblical generations before man descended into idolatry; and finally, the universal spread of the intellectual knowledge of God will restore Adam, the universal man, before the sin. In this borrowed sense, not only is the redemption of the people, but also the redemption of man, suitable for being considered a restoration. However, from an *actual*, historical viewpoint, a different conclusion is called for: the redemption depends upon an as yet unknown perfection, upon a realization of models that have never yet been fulfilled. The Messianic vision returns upon history and renews it as it *ought* to have been: from David and Solomon to the destiny of Abraham—'father of a multitude of nations'[33]—and back to earliest biblical generations and to Adam himself. This is a 'return' and 'restoration' in the sense that it does not anticipate a new world, a new man, a new Torah, or a new consciousness, but is directed towards that which was inherent from the beginning in this given Torah and

[31] Scholem, 'Towards an Understanding', 3.

[32] For later sources which distinguish between two periods of redemption in Samuel's approach, see M. M. Kasher, *Ha-Tequfah ha-Gedolah* (Jerusalem, 1969), 300.

[33] See *Mishneh Torah*, *Bikkurim*, iv. 3: 'A proselyte must bring first-fruits and recite the confession, since Abraham was told, "The father of a multitude of nations have I made thee", implying that he is the father of everyone who enters under the wings of the Presence.' Maimonides ruled here in accordance with R. Judah, following the Palestinian Talmud (*Talmud Yerushalmi*) and against the Mishnah. Compare *'Avodat Kokhavim*, i. 3; *Shemittah we-Yovel*, xiii. 13; Maimonides' Letter to Obadiah the Proselyte, *Teshuvot ha-Rambam*, ed. J. Blau (Jerusalem, 1965), 293; *Sefer ha-Mizwot*, positive commandment 207.

this given man; according to man's potential, not according to his actuality. The ideal picture of the past bears normative meaning for actual reality: just as the pattern of final universal redemption teaches the primacy of intellect in human species, so does the pattern of national redemption teach the primacy of law in Israel and, in the final analysis, in every society. This is the essential significance of the emphasis placed upon the restorative element in national redemption: 'The King Messiah will arise and restore the kingdom of David to its former state and original sovereignty. He will rebuild the sanctuary and gather the dispersed of Israel. *All the ancient laws will be reinstituted in his days* . . . in accordance with the commandments set forth in the Law' (*Melakhim*, xi. 1).

II

In the previous chapter, I presented the positive patterns propounded by Maimonides for the redemption of the people and of mankind, stressing the parallels between his halakhic and his philosophic works. However, the Messianic era is not only a matter for theoretical models, but also for practical halakhic instruction. The laws of the Messiah found in the *Mishneh Torah* are also intended to place in the hands of the Jewish people and its Sages a critical tool for evaluating concrete Messianic phenomena, i.e. clear-cut criteria and guide-lines for judging and reacting, in present and future. The very establishment of such guide-lines, which define and characterize when a given candidate is 'assumed to be the Messiah' and 'beyond all doubt the Messiah' (see the above quotation), and what is the right attitude towards frustrated Messianic hopes, reflects much innovation and daring. Just as, in Jewish sources, prophecy had long been subject to halakhic categories by which its validity and truth are tested,[34] so would the Messianic hope henceforth be defined within the rubric of fixed halakhic norms. Just as the primacy of Sinai over redemption, of the Torah over the Messiah, is manifested in the *material* aspect, in which Messianism is made contingent upon the fulfilment of the Torah[35] (whether as to the task of the King Messiah or as to his personal image—'who meditates on the Torah and occupies himself with the commandments as did his ancestor David'), so is it manifested in the

[34] See E. E. Urbach, 'Halakhah u-Nevu'ah', *Tarbiz*, 18 (1947), 1–27, esp. 20.
[35] See below with regard to the warnings against antinomian Messianism.

formal aspect, in the very subjection of eschatology to the set, fixed norms of a halakhic work. The norm does not exempt any historical reality from its judgement and instruction, not even a Messianic one.[36]

The normative significance of the discussion in *Hilkhot Melakhim* is clearly indicated by the fact that, together with his formulation of distinct criteria determining the patterns of Messianism in Israel, Maimonides took an agnostic view towards the specific meaning of biblical and midrashic Messianic promises, and restricted, in principle, the presumption of clear knowledge of the days to come: 'No one is in a position to know the details of this and similar things until they have come to pass . . . All similar expressions used in connection with the Messianic age are metaphorical. In the days of King Messiah the full meaning of these metaphors and their allusions will become clear to all' (*Melakhim*, xii. 2, 1). Maimonides constantly took pains to remove the focus of religious attention from Messianic speculation, from detailed *midrashim* of redemption, and from exaggerations of the imagination: 'Neither the exact sequence of those events nor the details thereof constitute religious dogmas. No one should ever occupy himself with the legendary themes or spend much time on midrashic statements bearing on this and like subjects. He should not deem them of prime importance, since they lead neither to the fear of God nor to the love of Him . . . One should wait [for his coming] and accept in principle this article of faith' (*ibid.* Compare with this *Ma'amar Teḥiyat ha-Metim*: 'None of these things are foundations of the Torah, so one needn't be particular as to what people believe about them'). These comments were not directed to the principle of Messiah itself,[37] but to the temptation to place the focus of religious

[36] There are also direct halakhic implications to the limits and stipulations governing the recognition of a given individual as the Messiah: 'King Messiah . . . will purify the descendants of Levi, declaring, "This one, of good birth, is a priest; this one, of good birth, is a Levite." Those who are not of good birth will be demoted to the rank of [lay] Israelites' (*Melakhim*, xii. 3).

[37] In his various articles, Yeshayahu Leibowitz hints that the meaning of Maimonides' statement, 'He should not deem them of prime importance (*'iqqar*)', reveals his attitude towards 'the messianic idea and the vision of messianic redemption itself', and the true significance of his positing of Messianism as a principle or dogma (*'iqqar*) of faith. (See 'Ha-Ge'ulah ha-Meshiḥit be-Mishnato shel ha-Rambam', in his *Emunah, Historiyah wa-'Arakhim* (Jerusalem, 1982), 299; 'Ha-Ge'ulah we-Aḥarit ha-Yamin eẓel Abrabanel', ibid. 108). However, this should be questioned in light of the context in *Melakhim*, which does not relate to the Messianic principle *per se*, but to various details within the portrayal of redemption. Comparison with *Ma'amar Teḥiyat ha-Metim* (see above) also makes this view unlikely, as there the point under discussion is also not 'the messianic idea itself', but the meaning of specific biblical verses anticipating changes in biological nature,

consciousness upon the specific images of redemption, a tendency which is liable to distract man away from his concrete religious obligations in this world. Thus, while in the realm of normative halakhic definitions Maimonides knows the nature of Messianic times *ad initiatem*, and portrays one who is 'beyond any doubt the Messiah' in a specific way, in non-halakhic areas this knowledge is only possible *post factum*, and the certainty is retroactive. Maimonides knows clearly the definition and task of the King Messiah and the exact criteria for evaluating his activity. This knowledge is certain, and is in no way subject to any possible historical, factual refutation, for it is this very knowledge which defines and conditions the Messianic process itself; whoever does not act within its terms, or is not successful in achieving its aims, is retroactively denied his presumption of Messianic status: 'He [R. Akiba] affirmed that the latter [Ben Kozba] was King Messiah . . . until Ben Kozba was slain in iniquities, whence it became known that he was not [the Messiah]' (*Melakhim*, xi.3). In this sense, with the establishment of distinct halakhic definitions of Messianism, the claim that in Messianic times the people of Israel would merit political and religious renewal became tautological: Messiah is Messiah (thus, the informative content of this statement became limited to the very promise that someone will appear, in the future, who meets these requirements). On the other hand, Maimonides does not know for certain what the Messianic era will hold in store, nor the detailed unfolding of the historical events, nor how its more distant results will come about. Thus, the immediate informational value of the *midrashim* of redemption is emptied: the future alone will constitute the exclusive, authentic interpretation of their meaning. As the process under discussion here is a historical rather than a cosmic one, we are in the realm of the contingent and the possible rather than that of the necessary. Imagination may presume to determine the possible, before it has been realized in actuality; reason judges in light of the actual reality, and 'no one is in a position to know . . . until they have come to pass'; the halakhic statement guides and directs reality and provides a yardstick for its evaluation.

about which Maimonides says: 'All these things are not fundamentals of the Torah *(qawā'id sharī'a)* and one needn't be particular how they are believed.' The Arabic term *qawā'id*, translated in the Introduction to *Pereq Ḥeleq* as *'iqqarim* (principles), is translated here as *pinnot* (cornerstones); Kafiḥ translates it as *yesodot* (foundations). On the status of the principles in Maimonides' various writings see A. Hyman, 'Maimonides' Thirteen Principles', in A. Altmann (ed.), *Jewish Medieval and Renaissance Studies* (Cambridge, Mass., 1967), 111 ff.

In light of what has been said, it is clear that one ought not to equate Maimonides' agnostic approach towards detailed Messianic descriptions with a lack of a normative Messianic doctrine.[38] The absence of a positive doctrine is not the appropriate guaranty against the danger of concrete Messianic tensions. On the contrary, without clear distinctions and criteria every exciting manifestation and every creation of the imagination may merit the name Messiah. It should be emphasized that halakhic guidance in this matter is not relevant for the future only: it touches the immediate, real life of the people today, with their pains and hopes, including the Messianic tensions and wakenings breaking out within it. Thus, it is not surprising that especially the longing for *national* redemption, which directly presses and excites, should be the one to be defined in a clear, normative form (see below). The proper defence against the possible dangers of concrete Messianic tensions is not the obfuscation of the nature of redemption, but its subjection to stipulations and guide-lines stressing the continuation of present natural and historical forces even in Messianic times: the expectation of redemption does not rely upon miracles, does not exempt itself from customary historical forces, and in its fulfilment will not liberate man from religious and political responsibility; moreover, it never assumes, in advance, the certainty of its future success.[39] Even Ben Kozba,

[38] For a different view, see Funkenstein, 'Political Theory and Realistic Messianism', 83–4; cf. J. Sarachek, *The Doctrine of the Messiah in Medieval Jewish Literature* (New York, 1932), 128 ff.

An interesting echo of Maimonides' statement that 'no one is in a position to know the details of this and similar things until they have come to pass', and their being essentially metaphors and figures of speech, is found in the words of his critic, R. Meir Abulafia: 'As for these things, we do not know the details of how they shall be until they shall have come to pass, and He who knows how they truly are shall show them "plainly and not in riddles"' *Yad Ramah* (Warsaw, 1898) on *Sanhedrin*, 98*b*. See Kasher, *Ha-Tequfah ha-Gedolah*, 323.

[39] See D. Hartman, 'Maimonides' Approach to Messianism and its Contemporary Implications', *Da'at*, 2–3 (1978–9), 5–33. I accept his main argument and conclusions; however, Hartman concentrated upon the first (political–historical) model, while to my mind more weight should have been given also to the second model, that of the final perfection of man, as I have noted above. Thus, one ought not to include all of Maimonides' Messianic goals under the rubric of 'uncertainty' and 'partial solutions'. There is no contradiction between 'bearing human responsibility' (Hartman, 6, 'Maimonidean "Halakhic Hope"') and the expectation of the 'future resolution to all human problems' ('radical hope'). Maimonides' Messianic vision stipulates a complete solution, albeit in the sense of an infinite goal. However, this solution too is of a normative character, to the utmost of human capacity. On the question of doubt, uncertainty and hope in Maimonides' Messianic thought, see Y. Aviad (Wolffsberg), *Hirhurim be-Philosofiyah shel ha-Historiyah* (Jerusalem, 1958), 175.

whom Rabbi Akiba and 'all[40] the wise men of his generation' imagined to be the King Messiah, was ultimately slain 'in iniquity'; even if the criteria for one 'assumed to be the Messiah' are fulfilled, future events are still liable to frustrate. The emphasis upon the inherent uncertainty within the historical process serves as a protection against any Messianic adventurism. However, this uncertainty is not directed towards the definition of national redemption, which is clearly known, but only against the certainty of their near fulfilment in any given historical situation. The principle limitation which Maimonides imposed upon predicting the future—the emphasis upon the factor of contingency in history—is not directed only towards a remote Messianic destiny, but also towards the interpretation and evaluation of current reality: there is no Messiah but he who is judged so retrospectively.

In this way, the discussion of the Messianic era is able to fulfil a double function, to seize both horns of the dilemma.

On the one hand, Maimonides knew well the possible dangers inherent in the Messianic expectation, and its contradictory manifestations reflecting the internal tension contained within the very idea of redemption. In epistles sent by him in response to acute crises in various Jewish communities, he warned both against the dangers of active Messianic pretension, as well as against the opposite danger—excessive passivity in light of Messianic hopes. The first warning was primarily expressed in the *Iggeret Teman* (Epistle to Yemen). In the conclusion of the epistle, a list of Messianic crises and the harm done by them to the Jewish people is enumerated, while in the body of the epistle the author does not hesitate to utilize any possible argument to protect a Jewish community from an illusion which begins with the disturbance of the routines of normal existence and the patterns of religious life, and ends in disaster and catastrophe:

> We do not escape this continued maltreatment which well nigh crushes us . . . If, therefore, we start trouble and claim power from them absurdly and preposterously we certainly give ourselves up to destruction . . . pretenders and simulators will appear in great numbers . . . but they will not be able to make good their claim. They will perish with many of their partisans.[41]

The second warning is formulated in *Iggeret ha-Shemad*. The author warns against excessive passivity, relying upon an anticipation of

[40] See below on the nature of this generalization in Maimonides' works.
[41] Twersky, *Maimonides Reader*, 457.

imminent redemption. He attacks an attitude which avoids necessary action in response to acute distress, which 'liberates' man from personal responsibility in light of the hope of near Messianic coming.

> In times of persecution (*shemad*), one should leave those places and go someplace where he may observe his religion and continue his occupation with Torah . . . But those who deceive themselves and say that they will remain where they are until the coming of King Messiah, when they shall go up to Jerusalem: I do not know how they shall be excused from this persecution, for they sin and cause others to sin . . . For there is no set time for the coming of the Messiah, to which one may hold fast and say 'He is near' or 'He is far'.[42]

In the same context, he also noted the possible dangers of belittling the meaning of everyday religious 'routine' as a direct consequence of Messianic tension:

> The obligation to perform the commandments is not contingent upon the coming of the Messiah, for we are required to be occupied with the Torah and the commandments and to attempt to complete their performance. After we have done that which is incumbent upon us, if God will grant us or our grandchildren to see the Messiah, then good; if not, we have lost nothing, for we have done that which is required of us.[43]

His warnings were stated from different perspectives, depending upon the context and nature of the immediate crisis. This same careful approach also left its mark upon the *Mishneh Torah*. But in that work, whose words are written for posterity and not for the immediate needs of contemporary communities, it is reflected in the stress on the ongoing character of natural order and its permanence even in Messianic times, emphasizing the contingent factor within historical processes and negating any certain guarantees of Messianic success in advance of the fact. Maimonides also took care in his halakhic work to warn against possible Messianic antinomian tendencies.[44] As in the case of a prophetic claim, so in the case of a Messianic claim any

[42] *Iggerot ha-Rambam*, 66–7. Compare *Epistle to Yemen*, 449. On other contexts of the question of active and passive Messianism, see G. D. Cohen, 'Messianic Postures of Ashkenazim and Sephardim', *The Leo Baeck Memorial Lectures*, ix (1967), 3–42 (on Maimonides, see pp. 26, 38–9).

[43] *Iggerot ha-Rambam*, 66–7. See also Leibowitz, *Emunah, Historiyah wa-'Arakhim*, 90.

[44] See W. D. Davis, *Torah in the Messianic Age and/or the Age to Come* (Philadelphia, 1962), esp. 33–50; E. E. Urbach, *The Sages, Their Concepts and Beliefs*, 2 vols. (Jerusalem, 1975), i. 293 ff. Many rabbinic texts dealing with this subject are discussed by Abrabanel, *Yeshu'ot Meshiḥo*, 67*b*–73*b*.

abrogation of the Law is, by definition, a refutation of the message, its truth and validity, beginning with he who 'imagined that he was the Messiah . . . and caused Israel to be destroyed by the sword . . . and was instrumental in changing the Torah [i.e. Jesus]',[45] and ending with every Messianic pretender, past and future, who does not follow the Law in all its details. Maimonides also drew a sharp line against any antinomian tendency by underscoring the unique character of Mosaic prophecy, which transcends the prophecy of the Messiah.[46] Thus, any possibility of revelation equal or superior to the Torah of Moses is nullified, whether in the past (Christianity, Islam, etc.) or the future. The very norm for evaluating and judging the historical process is not subjugated to the review of any historical phenomenon, either in present or Messianic times.

On the other hand, Maimonides taught Israel and its Sages the faith and aspiration for the political realization of the Torah in their land, for the turning of the nations of the world to monotheism, and for the final, universal perfection of man—that is, Messianic redemption. Within the limitations of his normative definitions and restrictions, Messianic belief was placed among the fundamental principles of faith, as opposed to the view of many other Jewish scholars. Were his only interest the negation of historical Messianic tensions, he could have

[45] *Melakhim*, xi. 4. Translation of the uncensored text taken from Twersky, *Maimonides Reader*, 226–7. See there: 'Some say, "Those commandments were true, but have lost their validity and are no longer binding"; others declare that they had an esoteric meaning and were not intended to be taken literally; that the Messiah has already come and revealed their occult significance.' Cf. 'Whoever adds aught to it, or takes away aught from it, or misinterprets it, and strips the commandments of their literal sense is an impostor, a wicked man, and a heretic' (xi. 3).

[46] 'Because the king who will arise from the seed of David . . . will be a great prophet, approaching Moses our Teacher' (*Teshuvah*, ix. 2); 'The Messiah will be a very great prophet, greater than all the prophets except for Moses our Teacher . . . his excellence will be greater than that of all the prophets, excepting that of Moses . . .' (*Iggeret Teman*). Cf. *Guide*, ii. 39. (On the sources of 'a prophet like unto Moses', see Y. Heinemann, *Aggadot we-Toledotehen* (Jerusalem, 1974), 109–10.)

Just as Maimonides followed Samuel's conception on the Messianic age as freedom from subjugation to the other nations, so is his view as to the comparison of Moses and the Messiah similar to that of Samuel: 'Rav said, "The world was not created save for David." Samuel said, "For Moses." Rabbi Johanan said, "For the Messiah"' (*Sanhedrin*, 95*b*). It would seem that, with regard to a third question, Maimonides decided against Samuel's opinion in regard to redemption (Hartman, 'Approaches to Messianism', 7). In a tannaitic dispute in *Sanhedrin*, 97*b* it is related 'Rav said, "All the 'ends' have already come; now all depends upon repentance and good deeds." Samuel said, "It is enough for a mourner to sustain his mourning."' The printed texts, however, are confused; the latter statement was made not by Samuel but by R. Joshua b. Levi (as seen explicitly in some MSS and in *rishonim*; Cf. Urbach, *Ḥazal* (Jerusalem, 1971), 614 n. 22).

made Messianic phenomena conditional upon supernatural wonders (as he did, in fact, in the *Iggeret Teman* in the face of an actual crisis),[47] upon a spontaneous and complete repentance of the entire Jewish people, and upon awesome and frightening birth-pangs of Messiah. Yet his halakhic stipulations not only refrained from any such demands, but even went so far as to grant legitimacy to a historical effort which was finally frustrated, and to one whose Messianic character was retroactively refuted: 'If he does not meet with full success, or is slain, it is obvious that he is not the Messiah promised in the Torah. He is to be regarded like all the other *wholehearted and worthy* kings of the House of David who died.' There exists a third historical alternative between a true Messiah and a false Messiah, an alternative which was not invalidated normatively.[48] The preferences of the author are also reflected in his selection and use of relevant talmudic sources. Were he to have wished to deny *ab initiam* the validity of historical Messianism, he could have adopted the Babylonian Talmud's account of Ben Kozba's death, which attributes his execution to the Sages of Israel themselves;[49] however, his own preference was for the version of the Palestinian Talmud, in which his death was brought about by the enemies of Israel.[50] (Cf. *Ta'aniyyot*, v. 3: 'But he fell into the hands of the Romans who slew them all'.) Now, having followed the Palestinian Talmud, one might have expected Maimonides not to ignore another tradition quoted in the same place as to the argument of R. Joḥanan b. Torta against the messiahship of Ben Kozba ('Akiba, grass will grow from your cheeks, but the son of David will not yet have come'[51]), yet his description

[47] In *Melakhim*, xi. 3, we read: 'Do not think that King Messiah will have to perform signs and wonders, bring anything new into being, revive the dead, or do similar things.' On the other hand, in the *Epistle to Yemen*, Maimonides said: 'the wonders and miracles which he shall perform are the sure sign of the truth of his lineage'; 'When he shall appear all the kings of the earth shall be astounded . . . by the miracles performed by him . . . and I do not see that this one who appeared in your land had all of these.' See *Iggeret Teman*, Introd., 28 n. 278. On Maimonides' refusal to make Messianism conditional upon supernatural miracles, and his relating it to a human's capability, one should note his use of the phrase '[he] rebuilds the sanctuary', unlike the opinion of those that 'the future rebuilding of the Temple will be the work of heaven'; *Sanhedrin*, 30*a* (see Rashi, ad loc.), *Sukkah*, 41*b*.

[48] See S. Goren, 'Yesodot ha-Ge'ulah', *Torat ha-Mo'adim* (Tel Aviv, 1964), 312–13.

[49] *Sanhedrin*, 93*b*; cf. Rabad's comment on Maimonides' view.

[50] *TY*, *Ta'anit*, iv. 5.

[51] Ibid. Cf. *Ekhah Rabbah*, ii. 14. See there also regarding R. Eleazar ha-Moda'i and Ben Kozba.

attributes to the Sages of that time a consensus as to Ben Kozba's Messiahship.'[52] It may be that Maimonides believed that, at an earlier stage, when the leader met the basic normative conditions for being 'assumed to be the Messiah', everyone accepted him;[53] it is also probable that, according to him, the failure of the rebellion was not a necessary historical development: a hypothetical alternative activity could have caused different facts ('he was slain in sin'). The Sages did not err in principle, but in their evaluation of certain facts; not *ab initiam* but *post factum*. The same approach is manifested in the tendency recognizable in the *Mishneh Torah* to eliminate the awesome image of the pre-Messianic period[54] ('let him come, but let me not see him')[55] to minimize the catastrophic element with which the redemption is associated in Jewish sources (again compare *Iggeret Teman*, which underlines the 'Messianic travails concerning which the sages invoked God that they be spared seeing experiencing them').[56] This same tendency is also reflected in Maimonides' total ignoring of the personality and image of Messiah b. Joseph, upon whom the

[52] 'He [R. Akiba] and all the wise men of his generation affirmed that the latter [Ben Kozba] was the King Messiah' (*Melakhim*, xi. 3). Cf. *Ta'aniyyot*, 5. 3: 'All Israel, including the greatest scholars, thought [him] to be the King Messiah.'

[53] See the comments of the Radbaz (R. David b. abi Zimra) on *Melakhim*, ibid.

[54] The only comment on this in *Hilkhot Melakhim* states: 'To take the words of the prophets in their *literal sense*, it appears that the inauguration of the Messianic era will be marked by the war of Gog and Magog' (xii. 2). (However, a few lines earlier Maimonides states that one is to take such prophetic utterances 'metaphorically'.) Compare *Epistle to Yemen*: 'that this verse *definitely* refers to the war of Gog and Magog'. See also J. Levinger, *Darke ha-Mahshavah ha-Hilkhatit shel ha-Rambam* (Jerusalem, 1965), 163.

[55] *Sanhedrin*, 98*b*.

[56] Twersky, *Maimonides Reader*, 438. The popular nature of the *Iggeret Teman*, compared with the well-measured statements of *Mishneh Torah*, is not confined to the question of the miracles done by the Messiah and the birthpangs of the Messiah. The far-reaching description of the personal stature of the Messiah in the *Iggeret* does not match the moderate description in *Hilkhot Melakhim* (see Kasher, *Ha-Tequfah ha-Gedolah*, 339); the *Iggeret*'s conception of the level of the Jewish people at the Sinaitic revelation is not identical with that of the *Guide* ii. 33; the use of verses there from Song of Songs (a historical allegory about the destiny of the Jewish people) does not square with their interpretation dominant both in his halakhic and in his philosophical work—a metaphysical allegory on the relationship between God (or the Active Intellect) and man (see *Teshuvah*, viii. 2; x. 3; *Yesode ha-Torah*, vi. 9; *Guide*, iii. 51; iii. 54; iii. 33. Cf. J. B. Soloveitchik, 'U-Viqashtem mi-Sham', *Ha-Darom*, 43 (1978), 67 n. 1, or in his *Ish ha-Halakhah*: *Galuy we-Nistar* (Jerusalem, 1979), 119–20 n. 1. The attitude towards Christianity and Islam is also not identical in the *Iggeret Teman* and in *Melakhim*. In addition: within the *Iggeret Teman* itself the persecutions are, on the one hand, used as actual signs of a forthcoming Messiah and, on the other, as the constant lot of the Jewish people, etc. Only in this context may one adopt G. Scholem's comment about Maimonides, 'the eruption of redemption is to occur by divine decree' ('Towards an Understanding', 31), which indeed matches the spirit of the *Iggeret Teman*. I hope to

catastrophical Messianic element, the struggle and downfall anticipating the redemption, was placed in Jewish literature.[57] Within the limits of the normative stipulations of the laws of Messiah, nothing prevents a continuous, gradual, positive historical process whose conclusion validates its beginning.

III

In light of all the above, we may distinguish three different planes according to which the redemption was treated within Maimonides' text, i.e. the *national*, the *universal*, and the *personal*: the redemption of the Jewish people as a *condition*; the redemption of mankind as a *consequence*; and the redemption of the individual as a final *end*, the ultimate goal of Messianism.

Those conditions which define and direct Messianism in the *Hilkhot Melakhim*, whether necessary or sufficient, are entirely confined to the redemption of the people of Israel and contain no hint of the turning of the nations of the world to monotheism, or of the final universal perfection of the human race. They are confined to the first model, the political, and concentrate on the present historical reality. It is possible for a leader to be 'assumed to be the Messiah' and finally to be proclaimed as 'Messiah beyond all doubt', and yet for the nations of the world to still not accept him and his message.

If there arises a king from the House of David who meditates on the Torah, occupies himself with the commandments, as did his ancestor David, observes

discuss the relationship between *Iggeret Teman* and Maimonides' other writings elsewhere. On the rhetorical character of another epistle, *Iggeret ha-Shemad*, see H. Soloveitchik, 'Maimonides' *Iggeret ha-Shemad*: Law and Rhetoric', *Rabbi Joseph B. Lookstein Memorial Volume* (New York, 1979), 281 ff.

[57] See J. Liver, 'The Doctrine of the Two Messiahs, etc.', *HTR* 52 (1959), 149–85; S. Hurwitz, *Die Gestalt des Starbenden Massias* (Zürich, 1958); A. Heinemann, 'Mashiaḥ ben Efraim wi-ẓi'at Miẓrayim shel Bene Efraim be-ṭerem Keẓ', *Tarbiẓ*, 40 (1971), 450–1. For a summary of the differing opinions about the development of the motif of Messiah b. Joseph, see J. Heinemann, *Aggadot we-Toledotehen*, 131 ff. However, in Maimonides' text, the 'two Messiahs' are: 'the first, namely, David . . . and the later Messiah, a descendant of David' (*Melakhim*, xi. 1). We also read in the *Midrash ha-Gadol*, Balak, 24: 17: 'Balaam prophesied the coming of two messiahs: the first Messiah who was David . . . and the later Messiah, who shall rise from his descendants', and 'when [he] was slain . . . it became known that he was not [the Messiah]' (ibid. xi. 2). As we said above, Maimonides combines the personality of the spiritual–religious teacher and that of the political–military leader into one Messianic figure. On this subject, see my article, 'The Prophet *vis-à-vis* His Society', *Forum*, 32 (1978), 89–103.

the precepts prescribed in the written and Oral Law, prevails upon Israel to walk in the way of the Torah and to repair its breaches, and fights the battles of the Lord, it may be assumed that he is the Messiah. If he does these things and succeeds, vanquishes the nations, rebuilds the sanctuary on its site, and gathers the dispersed of Israel, he is beyond all doubt the Messiah.[58]

Human redemption, in its all-encompassing scope, is posited as a result and as a destiny, but not as a condition or as a part of the halakhic definition of Messiah (as we have said, the final transformation in the religious consciousness of the nations of the world is preceded by preparatory historical processes—but these are not dependent upon the activity of the true Messiah). The normative stipulation is only directly intended for those who are subject to it:[59] the author *instructs* his community as to the conditions of the redemption of the people, and *anticipates* the redemption of mankind. He does not confuse this distinction between normative stipulation and final destiny.[60]

[58] The distinction between the national and the universal is clearly reflected in his attitude to Jesus. From the viewpoint of Jewish history, Jesus was definitely a destructive, negative factor, 'who imagined that he was the Messiah, but was put to death by the court . . . For has there ever been a greater stumbling than his? All the prophets affirmed that the Messiah would redeem Israel, save them, gather their dispersed, and confirm the commandments. But he caused Israel to be destroyed by the sword, their remnant to be dispersed and humiliated. He was instrumental in changing the Torah' (*Melakhim*, xi. 4, uncensored). But from the perspective of the history of the nations, there is found dialectically, a positive factor ('to clear the way for King Messiah'). (See n. 14 above.)

[59] Indeed, it is the task of the king in Israel, in every generation, 'to uplift the true religion and to fill the world with righteousness' (*Melakhim*, iv 9).

[60] In point of truth, the causal process leading to the complete turning of the nations of the world to monotheism is not entirely clear: 'All nations will come to hear him' (*Teshuvah*, ix. 2); 'But when the true King Messiah will appear . . . they will forthwith recant and realize that they have inherited naught but lies from their fathers' (*Melakhim*, xi. 4, uncensored); 'All nations will make peace with him, and all countries will serve him' (*Introduction to Ḥeleq*). However, in the same way the author was obscure as to the process leading to national political redemption, and 'there is no explanation given as to the causes and character of the transition from exile to a political community capable of participating effectively in war, at whose head stands the King Messiah' (see Pines, 'Histabrut Tequmatah', 294; Hartman, *Maimonides*, 249 n. 35). This is connected to the principled uncertainty with respect to the details of possible future occurrences. In any event, our main concern is in Maimonides' attempt to subject these developments to the natural, continuous historical process, and his faith in the power of rational political order to improve man and society. See E. Levinas, *L'Am delà du Verset* (Paris, 1982), 213–15. The direct correlation between improvement of the historical situation of the Jewish people and responsiveness of the nations to the Torah has been commented on by Philo of Alexandria: 'If our situation shall ever improve, how much will the honour of our laws be lifted also. I think then they shall all abandon their gods and neglect their ways and begin to honour these laws, that is, ours, alone, for if the light of the people shall come, so shall their [the laws'] light come.' See Y. Amir, 'Ha-Ra'ayon ha-Meshiḥi ba-Yahadut ha-Hellenisṭit', *Ge'ulah u-Medinah* (Jerusalem, 1979), 65.

However, to these two planes there is added a third level of discussion—the redemption of the individual: spiritual eternity, the World to Come. Indeed, Messiah is he who acts upon the stage of history, and not only on the spiritual, personal level. In fact, there is no difference between this world and Messianic times except a social and political change. However, the final end of redemption, its aim and goal, is not focused upon social structures and the status of the public, but is totally subjected to the supreme human goal—the eternity of the intellective soul.

Hence, all Israelites, their prophets and sages, longed for the advent of Messianic times, that they might have relief from the wicked tyranny that does not permit them properly to occupy themselves with the study of Torah and the observance of the commandments, that they might have ease, devote themselves to getting wisdom, and thus attain to life in the world to come . . . The ultimate and perfect reward, the final bliss which will suffer neither interruption nor diminution, is the life in the world to come. (*Teshuva*, ix. 2)

The sages and prophets did not long for the days of the Messiah . . . (but) that Israel be free to devote itself to the Law and its wisdom . . . and thus be worthy of life in the world to come. (*Melakhim*, xii. 4)

The prophets and the saints looked forward to the days of the Messiah and yearned for them because then the righteous will be gathered together in fellowship, and because goodness and wisdom will prevail . . . and the performance of all of the commandments of the Torah of Moses our Teacher . . . Thus, men will achieve the world to come. The world to come is the ultimate end toward which all our effort ought to be devoted. (Introduction, *Pereq Ḥeleq*)

This threefold structure—*condition*, *consequence*, *end*—does in fact define the relationship among three fundamental concepts in Jewish eschatology: *Messiah* (national) the *End of Days* (universal), and the *World to Come* (individual). (As noted above, a fourth concept, the *Garden of Eden*, may be introduced into this scheme.) However, such a generalization requires a certain deviation from Maimonides' own terminological usages, in which he refrained, for clear reasons, from defining universal redemption as 'the end of days',[61] and stamping the other concepts with the mark of his own personal thought.

The establishment of personal spiritual salvation as the final goal of Messianic times is not only indicative of the posture of future man, but also of the concrete stand and capabilities of the individual in the

[61] See *Moreh Nevukhim*, ed. J. Kafiḥ (Arab. and Heb. trans.), (Jerusalem, 1972), ii. 29 n. 45.

present. The final end posited for Messianic times, although Utopian in the terms of public life and humanity at large, has long been available as a personal goal. The individual in any historical situation may and ought to yearn towards the supreme goal to which the Messianic hope was subjected,[62] towards the final goods of the redemption—Torah, wisdom, the World to Come.[63] The force of such a view as a restraint upon actual Messianic tensions needs no proof.

However, Messianism itself, in contrast with personal, spiritual elevation in present times, is concerned with communal, collective fulfilment, not with the ascent of individuals only: the Torah, which is today confined within the personal domain, is meant to burst forth into the public domain; intellectual apprehensions, which in the beginning of *Mishneh Torah* were defined as exclusive and esoteric ('Because not everyone possesses the breadth of intellect requisite for obtaining an accurate grasp of the meaning and interpretation of all its contents . . . and although they were great men of Israel and great sages, they did not possess the capacity to know and grasp these subjects clearly'[64])—are destined, as he stated at the end of this work, to become the inheritance of the community, even if only in the sense of an infinite goal—'The one preoccupation of the whole world will be to know the Lord. Hence they will be very wise, they will know things that are now concealed and will attain an understanding of their Creator to the utmost human capacity.' That which is today meant only for a small élite is destined in the Messianic expectation for the many, for all individuals.

At this point, we must once again stress the powerful link between

[62] This corresponds to Maimonides' general philosophical outlook, which posits models for the improvement of the public but does not make the excellence of the individual dependent upon that of the many. Maimonides stressed the innate value of personal fulfilment, not only in his discussion of such subjects as individual providence, but also in his discussion of prophecy (his teaching specifies a level of prophecy which is not primarily a mission to the many but an expression of the independent, personal excellence of the prophet), and even in the sphere of mutual relationships between man and his fellow ('The fulfilling of duties with regard to others imposed upon you on account of moral virtue such as remedying the injuries of all those who are injured, is called *ẓedakah*. Therefore it says with reference to the returning of a pledge to the poor: "and it shall be *ẓedakah* to you (Deut. 24: 13). For then you walk in the way of the moral virtues, you do justice to your rational soul, giving her the due that is her right' (*Guide*, iii. 53).

[63] It would appear that such is not the case with regard to the prophetic level. But see A. J. Heschel, 'Ha-He'emin ha-Rambam she-Zakhah li-Nevu'ah?', *Louis Ginzburg Jubilee Volume* (New York, 1946), 159–88.

[64] *Yesode ha-Torah*, iv. 11–13.

Maimonides' Messianic views and his philosophical outlook. In studies by Gershom Scholem and Abraham Halkin we read:

For Maimonides, the task of man since the the Revelation has been clearly defined and man's fulfilling is not dependent upon the coming of the Messiah . . . The Messianic age is no highest good but only a preliminary stage in the final transition to the world-to-come . . . Messianism, in fact, is not a postulate of his philosophical thought. (Scholem)[65]

The days of the Messiah are a transient phase on the way to the world to come, which is Maimonides' primary desire . . . as if he were to say, 'I believe in the messianic days because we have been commanded so by the Torah and the tradition, while I believe in the world to come because my intellect requires it.' (Halkin)[66]

These statements require an important qualification: Messianic faith as such, the belief in the future *realization* of the destiny, is indeed not intellectually dictated. However, the *content* of Maimonides' Messianism, its nature and definition, was clearly stamped in the light of his reason. Both the positive models of Messianism—including the political and apolitical one (see above)—and those which were refuted—new creation, a new Torah, new conciousness, a new man (see below)—are discussed in accordance with his philosophical doctrines. Thus, while his Messianism is not demanded by his mind, but by his faith, it is essentially his mind which directs, defines, and limits the object of his faith. Precisely because man's destiny has been fully delimited from the revelation at Sinai and from the creation—the actualization of the priority of the Torah and the priority of intellect—the philosopher comes to the recognition of the theoretical models which have not yet been collectively realized. It should be noted that the subjection of the social and political goals to the individual and spiritual ones was underlined by Maimonides in his philosophical book. This does not impugn the normative social pattern; on the contrary, it clarifies and substantiates it:

The Law as a whole aims at two things . . . the welfare of the states of people in their relations with one another through the abolition of reciprocal wrong-doing and through the acquisition of a noble and excellent character . . . the soundness of beliefs and the giving of correct opinions . . . the ultimate end [is] . . . the attainment of a world in which everything is well and [the whole of which] is long. And this is perpetual preservation.[67]

[65] Scholem, 'Towards an Understanding', 30–1.

[66] A. Halkin, *Iggeret Teman*, Introd. 27.

[67] *Guide*, iii. 27.

The hierarchy of values which points towards the supremacy of the personal spiritual goal does not reject the political theory. On the contrary, it directs it, both in the philosophical work and in the halakhic. It goes without saying that the impact of this conception is clearly revealed in the final Messianic destiny, the apolitical one: the same philosophical, intellectual inclination reflected in the identification of the traditional concept of the World to Come with the clinging of the soul to divine intelligibles and with eternal intellectual acquisitions is also revealed in the identification of the peak of Messianism with universal knowledge of God; both Jewish eschatological concepts were interpreted in light of Maimonides' philosophical doctrines.

IV

Any attempt to establish the pattern of Messianism for posterity requires personal selection and choice among various alternative viewpoints, concepts, and images widespread in Jewish literature.[68] Just as this effort demands the creative elaboration of existing traditional motifs, it also requires the rejection, restriction, and limitation of others. Maimonides accepted this challenge in a distinctly anti-apocalyptic spirit: Messianic goals are historical, not cosmic; they are concerned with the fulfilment and renewal of human history as it ought to be, and not with the end of days; they do not point towards a new creation but to the realization of that which is potentially inherent in this world, in this given human being, in this given Torah. This critical tendency betrays, of course, the caution of the *man of halakhah* confronting the antinomian dangers of a Messianic vision which overturns the world and its laws, as much as it reflects the responsibility of the *leader* to a community faced with crisis and in danger of both internal and external disintegration. However, on the deepest level it is necessitated by the premisses of the *philosopher* adhering to the fundamental positions of the *Guide*. Just as Maimonides'

[68] See Urbach, *The Sages*, 649: 'The teachings of the Sages concerning the Redemption . . . possibly in this sphere, more than in regard to any other theme, there is evident the independent approach of the Sages, which finds expression in a variety of views and conceptions. At times this diversity exceeds the standards of normal differences of opinions and reaches down to fundaments . . . It is not confined to divergences within the framework of the generally accepted system of concepts, but reaches antitheses that imply the complete negation of one doctrine by the other.'

political philosophy and anthropology guided the positive models of Messianism, so did his ontology and theology dictate the rejection of cosmic redemption and apocalyptics and the limitation of Messianism to human existence, to 'the utmost human capacity'.

Messianic expectation, a doctrine of redemption, a desire for deep change in reality, all imply a negative valuation of existence as given, or of one or another of its strata. They all wish to convert evil to good. However, this critical stance, this negation and rejection, may be aimed against objective reality, against the natural, cosmic givens over which man has no control, or it may be aimed towards the activities of man himself within objective reality, towards his modes of self-creation and shaping his world. One approach may give rise to apocalyptic Messianism, foreseeing the destruction of the present order of existence, while the other may lead towards normative Messianism, destining the fulfilment of history and of man.

Maimonides does not recognize any ontological, objective evil. Being, by definition, is God's attribute of action: '"I will make all My goodness pass before thee" . . . "All my goodness" alludes to the display to him of all existing things' (*Guide*, i. 54); 'Hence this reality as a whole—I mean that He, may He be exalted, has brought into being—is *ḥesed* (loving-kindness)' (*Guide*, iii. 53). The ethical terms, 'good and evil', when used in the ontological sphere, do not distinguish between different kinds of being but between being and its absence: 'All being is good . . . and all the evils are privations' (*Guide*, iii. 10).[69] In fact, ethical concepts would apply properly only to human acts, to man's behaviour, which is subject to normative evaluation and judgement. *Being* itself, by definition, is neither good nor evil; it does not belong to the realm of moral judgement but to that of intellectual knowledge. Ethical terms can be used in the ontological sphere only in a metaphorical sense, borrowed from human action and applied to divine action, to the creation, and to its guidance—that is, to being. Thus, it is self-evident that within this realm the 'evaluation' is given a priori: 'For it may in no way be said of God, may He be cherished and magnified, that He produces evil in an essential act . . . Rather all His acts are an absolute good; for He only produces being, and all being is a good . . . the true reality of the act of God in its entirety is the good' (*Guide*, iii. 10); 'What is primarily intended [by God]—namely, the bringing into being of everything whose existence is possible, existence

[69] See W. Z. Harvey, 'Ha-Rambam u-Spinoza', 174–6.

being indubitably a good' (*Guide*, iii. 25). It is as if there were a metaphysical preference expressed for being over nothingness, for creation and divine action over their privation.

Here, an additional step is required: first, 'being' equals an ordered, permanent being. An existent world means a world which follows immutable natural law, reflecting causal connections and mutual links among its components. Without the principle of order, there is not a universe but chaos, emptiness, and privation. Divine wisdom—his attribute of action in the universe—not only necessitates the very existence of the cosmos but also its being as it is, its paths and ways: 'His wisdom . . . obligatorily necessitated the existence of this world as a whole . . . The particulars of natural acts are all well arranged and ordered and bound up with one another, all of them being causes and effects; and none of them is futile or frivolous or vain' (*Guide*, iii. 25). The overthrowing of natural law and of teleological, causal connections implies the overthrowing of a divine attribute. There is no wisdom but one: 'He created it not in vain' (Isa. 45: 18). In this sense, our belief that the sun will continue to rise in the future is a theological postulate; physical necessity is required in light of the perfection of divine action:

> The statutes of heaven and earth . . . even though created shall not depart . . . These works of the deity—I mean the world and what is in it—even though they are made, are permanently established according to their nature for ever . . . [for] the thing that is changed, is changed because of a deficiency in it that should be made good or because of some excess that is not needed and should be got rid of. Now the works of the deity are most perfect, and with regard to them there is no possibility of an excess or a deficiency. Accordingly they are of necessity permanently established as they are . . . saying, 'The Rock, His work is perfect.' He means that all His works—I mean to say His creatures—are most perfect, that no deficiency at all is commingled with them, that there is no superfluity in them and nothing that is not needed. Similarly all that is being accomplished for and by the created things is absolute justice and follows from the requirement of wisdom. (*Guide*, ii. 28)

> We believe that what exists is eternal *a parte post* and will last forever with that nature which He, may He be exalted, has willed; that nothing in it will be changed in any respect unless it be some particular of it miraculously[70]

[70] Rejection of permanent changes in natural law does not eliminate the possibility of specific miracles, which does not require a new natural order. However, it would appear that Maimonides never gave a consistent adequate answer in the question of the naturalization of miracles. See J. Heller, 'Maimonides' Theory of Miracle', in A. Altmann (ed.), *Between East and West* (London, 1957), 112–27; A. Ravitzky, 'The Anthropological Theory of Miracles in Medieval Jewish Philosophy', in I. Twersky (ed.), *Studies in Medieval Jewish History and Literature*, ii (Cambridge, Mass., 1984), 242.

although He, may He be exalted, has the *power* to change the whole of it, or annihilate it, or to annihilate any nature in it that He wills . . . His *wisdom* required that He should bring creation into existence at the time when He did it, and that what He has brought into existence should not be annihilated nor any of its statutes changed. (*Guide*, ii. 29)

Mention of the divine 'power' to change creation or to annihilate it, a power which is never to be actualized, is only intended to demonstrate that such changes are not *logically* impossible (according to the *Guide* the logically impossible 'has a stable nature . . . is not made by a maker; it is impossible to change it in any way, hence the power over the maker of the impossible is not attributed to the deity'—iii. 15)[71] but physically, metaphysically, or theologically impossible. In the final analysis, there is no being but that which confronts us; the existence of another framework of being would imply the deficiency of that which exists, that is to say, evil, and 'nothing that is evil descends from above'.[72] This is not the *best* of all possible worlds, but the *only* possible world. (By way of sharpening the point one might say: once some elements of physics were included in the *Laws of the Basic Principles of the Torah*, a change in the physical order of the world would also mean a change of one of the fundaments of the Torah, a change in 'the way that will lead to the love of Him and the fear of Him . . . when a person contemplates His great and wondrous works and creatures'.[73]) This is the philosophical reasoning underlying the continuation of the natural order of the Messianic era.[74]

[71] The impossible has a stable nature, one whose stability is constant and is not made by a maker; it is impossible to change it in any way. Hence the power over the maker of the impossible is not attributed to the deity . . . for example, the coming together of contraries at the same instant and at the same place' (*Guide*, ii. 15). However, not all of the examples given there are purely logical impossibilities: the question requires further study. Elsewhere, I hope to deal with the relation between Maimonides' conception and the scholastic distinction between *potentia dei absoluta* and *potentia dei ordinata*.

[72] *Bereshit Rabbah*, lv. 3.

[73] *Yesode ha-Torah*, ii. 2. In another formulation: change in the order of the universe is change in the attributes of action by which God is known to man, of 'an examination of the beings with a view to drawing from them proof with regard to Him, so as to know His governance of them' (*Guide*, iii. 51), which is also needed for attaining prophecy (see Pines, 'The Philosophic Sources', xcvi). In *Ma'amar Teḥiyat ha-Metim*, another epistemological argument is added, on a popular level: a permanent change in nature, as opposed to a passing miracle, will not reveal God's miraculous intervention to the eyes of the beholder who will identify it with original nature.

[74] This is not said only of the physical reality, but also of the biological reality, which is also God's attribute of action (see *Guide* i. 54; iii. 12, 37, 53). This reasoning is that which requires allegorical interpretations of various prohecies: 'The words of Isaiah, "and the wolf shall dwell with the lamb, and the leopard shall lie down with the kid", are

Moreover, in the body of his philosophical work itself, the author repeated at length his rejection of catastrophic and apocalyptic eschatological images and refuted the literal reading of many scriptural passages concerning the days to come: the prophecies of cosmic destruction, the thundering of heaven and earth, the 'great and dreadful day of the Lord', are discussed in detail, and are all allegorically interpreted as referring to historical events from the biblical period, which are all past; the promises of 'the new heaven and the new earth' (Isa. 66: 22) which 'the common people and even some of those who are supposed to belong to the elite use . . . as if it contained information given to us in the Torah about the end of the heavens' were intended by the prophet with regard to Israel's liberation from the domination of the nations, 'with regard to the return of the king of Israel, his stability and his permanence . . . with regard to the permanence of the king that is the Messiah'.[75] The future 'new creation' will be a political creation, not a cosmic one. Maimonides' philosophical position leads him to go quite far in his allegorization of biblical verses: 'it is better to force the limits of

to be understood figuratively, meaning that Israel will live securely among the wicked of the heathens who are likened to wolves and leopards' (*Melakhim*, xi. 2; cf. *Ma'amar Teḥiyat ha-Metim*). R. Abraham b. David of Posquières commented on this, ad loc., 'Is it not written in the Torah, "I will rid evil beasts out of the land".' This comment apparently draws a distinction between the legitimacy of interpreting verses from the Prophets and Writings allegorically, and that of rejecting the literal meaning of verses from the Torah (see *Merkevet ha-Mishneh*, ad loc. Compare the editor's comment in *Milḥamot Ha-Shem of Abraham Maimon*, ed. R. Margalioth (Jerusalem, 1953), 65 n. 79; Funkenstein, 'Political Theory and Realistic Messianism', 86 n. 17. Cf. also several versions of *Midrash 32 Middot* (*Middah* 26): 'And so you find that the prophets spoke parables. In what circumstances? In *divre Kabbalah* [traditions], but words of the Torah and the commandments themselves may not be expounded metaphorically.' See the notes of the editor, H. G. Heiman-Enelow, to *Midrash* 32 *Middot* (New York, 1934), 35–6. However, it is also possible that the Rabad had in mind a tannaitic dispute on this question: ' "I will rid evil beasts out of the land." R. Judah said, "I shall remove them from the land." R. Simeon said, "I shall make them to rest, so that they cause not harm" ' (*Sifra, Beḥukotay*, 2). Thus, neither side of this dispute agrees with Maimonides' allegorization (further on in his Midrash, Isaiah's vision is also mentioned). The view of Y. Gershuni in *Mishpaṭ ha-Melukhah* (New York, 1950), 402, that the removal of wild beasts from the world is not a change in nature does not correspond to the Aristotelian view with regard to the eternity of species, and in any event does not resolve Maimonides' interpretation, which applies this verse to evil *nations*. However, in a recently discovered manuscript of the *Targum Yerushalmi*, this verse is interpreted in the same way as it is in Maimonides (see Kasher, *Ha-Tequfah ha-Gedolah*, 349). Cf. Sa'adyah Gaon, *Book of Doctrines and Beliefs*, viii. 8; R. David Kimḥi, comments on Isa. 11: 6; Ramban, 'Torat Ha-Shem Temimah' (op. cit. in n. 15), 154.

[75] *Guide*, ii. 29.

language than to force the limits of reality' (Samuel b. Tibbon).[76] This problem, which was briefly remarked upon in the *Mishneh Torah*, is discussed at length in the *Guide*, in which the author also does not conceal the polemical and critical context of his words.

From the moment Messianism was removed from the cosmic sphere and confined to the parameters of human existence, it was no longer expected to overcome ontological evil but human evil. 'Human evil' contains a double meaning: an evil which visits man—'the evils that befall man'—and the evil done by man 'by his own action'. Thus, precisely within the framework of the discussion of this subject in the *Guide* did the Messianic goal for the final social and intellectual perfection of the human race appear (see above, the apolitical Messianic model). The normative nature of the discussion is reflected here more than anywhere else: the two evils referred to human being—his evil destiny and his evil act—are one in root and source: 'This hath been to you of your own doing';[77] 'He doeth it that would destroy his own soul'.[78] The actor himself is the one acted upon.

All the evils that befall man fall under one of three species:

The first species of evil is that which befalls man because of the nature of coming-to-be and passing-away, I mean to say because of his being endowed with matter . . . Divine wisdom has made it obligatory that there should be no coming-to-be except through passing-away. Were it not for the passing away of the individuals, the coming-to-be related to the species would not continue . . . The evils of the second kind are those that men inflict upon one another, such as tyrannical domination of some of them over others. These evils are more numerous than those belonging to the first kind . . . In the cases, for instance, when one individual surprises another individual and kills him or robs him by night. The evils of the third kind are those that are inflicted upon any individual among us by his own action; this is what happens in the majority of cases. . . . He who is reached by them deserves truly to be blamed . . . This kind is consequent upon all vices, I mean concupiscence for eating, drinking, and copulation . . . This is the cause of all corporeal and psychical diseases and ailments. (*Guide*, iii. 12)

In light of Maimonides' negation of ontological, objective evil, there is no evil except from a certain point of view, in light of a certain relation, such as in relation to a given individual (egocentric) or in

[76] See Samuel b. Tibbon, *Ma'amar Yiqawu ha-Mayim* (Pressburg, 1837), 17.

[77] Mal. 1: 9. The words 'to you' were added by Maimonides.

[78] Prov. 6: 32.

relation to the human being in general (anthropocentric). Such an evil may visit a person by virtue of his or her being part of nature, of empirical reality ('the first kind of evil'), which is beyond Messianic concern. Change in this reality is, by definition, a privation of being, that is, objective evil. However, there is a sore evil which is not connected to the very status of the human being in the world and his or her portion within objective reality, but upon the individuals' action against their human fellows ('the second kind') and against themselves ('the third kind'). 'All men lament over evils of this kind', and towards them Messianism is directed. Therefore, whatever is not within the capacity of humankind – conversion of the natural order, change within the Torah, *ab initiam* certainty of future success, miraculous verification, a historical break – is removed from the realm of Messianism. Whatever lies within human capacity and human original destiny from Sinai and from creation – the realization of the Law and the actualization of the intellect – became the positive essence of Messianism. Whatever is within human capacity, but not within that of the reader of the *Mishneh Torah* (i.e. the ultimate perfection of the nations of the world), was excluded from the normative, direct definition of Messianism and posited as a result and a goal.

13

Maimonides and Eretz Yisrael: Halakhic, Philosophic, and Historical Perspectives

ISADORE TWERSKY

I

THE subject of this conference, 'Maimonides in Egypt',[1] is multi-dimensional and, I must confess, not entirely clear to me.[2] In any case, although I am supposed to address the focal issue of 'Maimonides in Eretz Yisrael', and not necessarily from Egypt's perspective, let me begin with an item of topical interest which may even be appropriate as a theme for this conference. I have in mind a passage from the *Discorso circa il stato de ol'hebrei et in particolar dimoranti nell'inclita città di Venetia* (Treatise on Venetian Jewry) by R. Simone Luzzatto, the thinker, historian, *shtadlan*, and propagandist of the seventeenth century, who tried to show the world the beauty and vitality of the Torah of Israel, and its culture; and to highlight the great importance of Jews as loyal

[1] This, with minor changes, is the substance of the address delivered at the conference. The text was translated from Hebrew by Jacqueline and Joshua Teitelbaum. Quotations from the *Epistle to Yemen* are from the edition by A. S. Halkin with English translation by Boaz Cohen (New York, 1952). The *Book of Commandments* is quoted from the translation of Charles B. Chavel (London, 1940). Quotations from the Introduction and first two books of the *Mishneh Torah* are from the English translation by Moses Hyamson (Jerusalem, 1965). Passages from the remaining 12 books of the *Mishneh Torah* are from the Yale Judaica Series. (Minor changes have been made when required.) For the *Guide of the Perplexed* the translation of Shlomo Pines has been used.

[2] On the subject of Maimonides in Egypt there is quite a bit to be discussed and considered, although much of it transcends the conceptual context of this volume. For example, Maimonides settled in Egypt despite an explicit *halakhah* against living there (*Hilkhot Melakhim*, v. 8). The debates concerning this astonishing fact and attempts to explain it were numerous (see the autobiographical comment of R. David ibn Abi Zimra, ad loc., and J. M. Epstein, *'Arukh ha-Shulḥan he-'Atid* (Jerusalem, 1973), *Hilkhot Melakhim*, 76–7). It seems that Maimonides himself did not directly address himself to this issue (see, however, R. Ishtori ha-Parḥi, *Kaftor wa-Feraḥ*, ch. 5), nor did he attempt to justify his decision to leave Palestine and settle in Egypt. He writes off-handedly: 'Thus we taught and did in Egypt since we came there' (*Teshuvot ha-Rambam*, ed. J. Blau,

citizens of the states in which they lived.[3] After some partly routine and partly profound remarks on the development of Jewish philosophic thought from antiquity to the end of the Middle Ages (Rabbi Ḥasday Crescas, Rabbi Joseph Albo), the author lauds Egypt's special significance in the annals of Jewish thought. He writes:

no. 218, p. 387). See also ibid., no. 242: 'We are scholars residing in Egypt at this time.' Concerning the close contacts with Alexandria, see no. 233 (p. 424), no. 355 (p. 633) and index, iii. p. 217; S. D. Goitein, *A Mediterranean Society* (Berkeley, 1967), i. 66.

Likewise, one should note various pieces of information on Egypt. For example, in *Hilkhot Tefillah*, xiii. 1, Maimonides mentions the triennial Torah-reading cycle, which was still customary in Egypt, but he writes reservedly, turning a blind eye to the reality of his day ('The custom prevailing through Israel is [that the reading of the Pentateuch is completed in one year]. Some complete the reading of the Pentateuch in three years, but this is not a prevalent custom.')

In his *Book of Travels*, Benjamin of Tudela gives an account of the various practices in Egypt: 'Two large synagogues are there, one belonging to the men of the Land of Israel and one belonging to the men of the land of Babylon. Their usage with regard to the portions and sections of the Law is not alike; for the men of Babylon are accustomed to read a portion every week whilst the men of Palestine do not do so but divide each portion into three sections and finish the Law at the end of three years (trans. M. N. Adler (New York, 1964), 70. Maimonides writes (*Hilkhot Qiddush ha-Ḥodesh*, v. 10): 'Were this matter of observance of a second holiday dependent upon the proximity to Jerusalem, all the Jews of Egypt would have to observe only one day, since the messengers of Tishri could have reached them in time. For the journey from Jerusalem to Egypt by way of Ascalon takes only eight days, or less.' This is precise topographical information befitting even a travelogue.

Although Maimonides was apparently not influenced by territorial metaphysics regarding the relation between the nation of Israel and the Land of Israel (but see *Hilkhot Melakhim*, v. 12 and *Hilkhot Ishut*, xiii. 19), regarding Egypt he repeated just such an assertion: 'because the practices of the Egyptians are more corrupt than those of the inhabitants of all other lands' (*Hilkhot Melakhim*, v. 8). And consider the passage beginning: 'It appears to me': see, however, *Hilkhot Issure Bi'ah*, xii. 25, and, for example, G. Arieli, *Torat ha-Melekh* (Jerusalem, 1958), 159. See also *Hilkhot 'Akum*, i. 3: 'When the Israelites had stayed a long while in Egypt, they relapsed and learnt the practices of their neighbours.' He feared the influence of the surroundings in Egypt, in light of which he cited the well-known *midrash*. Likewise, in the response to Obadiah the Proselyte (*Teshuvot ha-Rambam*, ed. J. Blau, no. 293, p. 549): 'Know that our ancestors, who left Egypt, were mostly idolaters when in Egypt—they mingled with the nations and learned their ways.' See also the *Book of Commandments*, negative commandment no. 46. Research to determine how and to what extent residence in Egypt influenced Maimonides and his work would be most valuable.

[3] See B. Ravid, *Economics and Toleration in Seventeenth-Century Venice: The Background and Context of the Discorso of Simone Luzzatto* (Jerusalem, 1978). See also id., 'How Profitable the Nation of the Jews Are: The Humble Addresses of Menasseh b. Israel and the Discorso of Simone Luzzatto', in J. Rheinharz *et al.* (eds), *Mystics, Philosophers, and Politicians: Essays in Honor of Alexander Altmann* (Durham, 1982), 159–80; and B. Septimus, 'Biblical Religion and Political Rationality in Simone Luzzato, Maimonides and Spinoza', in I. Twersky and B. Septimus (eds.), *Jewish Thought in the Seventeenth Century* (Cambridge, 1987), 399–433.

It should be noted that just as Egypt bestowed fame on the Jewish nation at its beginning, by means of the signs and wonders performed there for its redemption, so it has become famed by virtue of the fact that the three most famous personages of the nation were born and educated there: Moses, first and greatest of the prophets and lawgiver at the beginning of the nation's consolidation; Philo, the learned philosopher, who lived when the nation was still esteemed by other peoples; and Rabbi Moses [Maimonides], whom I have recently mentioned, the luminary of the sages at the time of [the Jews'] decline and subjugation.[4]

The historical evaluation *per se* and the vapid apologetics do not concern us at present, but the last part of the statement, where Luzzatto hints at the enormous challenge of Exile and existence (more precisely, existence in exile), at the mutual relationship between the actual historical reality and spiritual-cultural activity—or, in other words, the influence of the Diaspora on national consciousness and cultural momentum—provides a fitting transition to the topic under discussion. This statement, which accentuates the socio-historical contrast between Philo's time, when Jews still enjoyed independence and consequently respect of the nations, and that of Maimonides, which was characterized by adversity, tribulation, and contempt, reflects an important historical conception deserving attention and analysis.[5]

II

The difficulty of a discussion concerning Maimonides and Eretz Yisrael is threefold: the complexity of the man and the problematic

[4] *Ma'amar 'al Yehude Veneziyah*, Heb. trans. D. Lattes, ed. A. Z. Aescoly (Jerusalem, 1951), 142. Luzzatto says of Maimonides that 'due to his profound erudition in all of the world's sciences, he is considered one of the greatest individuals ever to arise out of the Jewish nation'. The emphasis is on the universal evaluation inherent in Maimonides' general scientific achievement, not on his contribution to the Jewish people.

[5] On p. 138 ibid. we find the following passage: 'The Bible extols the nation's importance, which is greater because of its wisdom than because of its military prowess. However, after Heaven decreed their subjugation, and they fell under the yoke of Roman rule and the Temple was destroyed and the city captured and the religion suppressed and the people taken captive and dispersed—not only was their honor lost and their spirit bowed to the ground, but the light of knowledge nearly flickered out in their midst and the brilliance of their learning grew dim, for virtues are not preserved in a nation unless they live in ease and in comfort.' This notion approximates Maimonides' opinion. See my *Introduction to the Code of Maimonides* (New Haven, 1980), 62 ff.

nature of his teaching; the delicacy of the subject and the importance of its implications; and the scarcity or fragmentation of sources.

1. The complexity of Maimonides and his philosophy is sufficiently well known and does not, therefore, require any elaboration; it is difficult to determine the precise meaning and intent of several aspects of his thinking. Basic components of his philosophy are controversial either because of their intrinsic difficulty or because of the bewildering method of their presentation. As a result of this, the interpretation of Maimonides in general and the question of the unity or diversity of his philosophic teachings in particular are troublesome; many specific themes are ensnared in this general complexity.[6] The understanding of Maimonides and the interpretation of Maimonideanism remain elusive. The problem of Eretz Yisrael—impinging upon such themes as nationalism, territorialism, independence, spirituality, rationalism, even asceticism and the *via contemplativa*, as well as redemption and Messianism (that is, the relationship between the individual and the community and the measure of the individual's dependence on the community necessary for his fulfilment and perfection)—is rooted in the same complexity.

2. The attitude towards Eretz Yisrael raises fundamental problems concerning Jews' national consciousness and historical image, and consequently demands maximum caution and meticulous analysis. It is no easy task to free oneself of the preconceived notions or deep-seated predilections, which do not necessarily stem from conclusions of disciplined study and scholarship. Knowingly or not, any theorist or ideologist of this subject likes to think that he has based his ideas on unimpeachably authoritative sources.[7] Maimonides is obviously a favourite; his authority is great, and everyone seeks his paternity.

[6] The work of Leo Strauss and Shlomo Pines, in particular, is well known. See e.g. S. Klein-Braslavy, *Perush ha-Rambam le-Sippur Beri'at ha-'Olam* (Jerusalem, 1978), 17 ff.; also my *Introduction*, p. 357. Almost every detail of his philosophic system is surrounded by divergent or conflicting assessments. Creation, prophecy, law of nature and miracles, free will and divine foreknowledge, providence, ethical theory, political theory, resurrection and immortality. In other words, there is no consensus concerning Maimonides' views on all the major issues of religious philosophy.

[7] Thus, the Satmar Rebbe, in *Wa-Yo'el Mosheh* (New York, 1978) frequently cites Maimonides as his authority, including Maimonides' *Guide of the Perplexed* and *Iggeret Teman*, in accordance with his own approach and outlook. In general, the subject of different modes of studying Maimonides throughout the ages awaits systematic research, a parallel subject being the ways of using Maimonides. He undergoes constant metamorphosis. A literary-historiographic review would illuminate the various perceptions of Maimonides which represent the range of views (and self-images) of generations—every generation having its own interpreters.

3. Explicit assertions in the total Maimonidean *œuvre* are relatively few and restrained. Biographical data are also fragmentary.[8] Therefore, any attempt to construct a correct and precise framework must, of necessity, be subject to Maimonides' suppositions and not to the assumptions of others. We must follow his lead, be sensitive to his concerns, and work with his directives. Hence, if we come to search out an indubitable proto-Zionist inclination, as Benzion Dinur attempted with respect to the thought and deeds of Judah Halevi,[9] or as it is possible to do with respect to those of Naḥmanides and R. Judah Loew b. Bezalel (the Maharal of Prague)—the two great representatives of pre-modern 'Love of Zion'[10]—we shall ultimately be disappointed. On the other hand, one should not suppose it axiomatic that philosophy stimulated Maimonides to devote himself to improving the individual, to be concerned with ethical-intellectual perfection, and to alienate himself from preoccupation with national values and communal-territorial principles. He should not, in other words, assume that there is a congenital, unavoidable antagonism between the philosopher and society. It is true that ideas and emphases central to R. Judah Halevi's thought, which were influential in some circles, were swept aside in Maimonides' teaching; but they were replaced by concepts of his own, whose significance and implications merit balanced and independent evaluation.

It seems, then, that in order to arrive at a complete and comprehensive system or an overall conception, we must develop an approach of 'precept upon precept, line upon line, here a little and

[8] See e.g. *Hilkhot Melakhim*, v. 9, the most famous and most oft-quoted section. There is no systematic presentation of material as in *Kaftor wa-Feraḥ* and *Pe'at ha-Shulḥan*, and it must be drawn from *Hilkhot Terumot*, *Bet ha-Beḥirah*, *Sanhedrin*, *Melakhim*, etc. The passage quoted in *Sefer Ḥaredim* on his journey to Palestine is well known. As previously mentioned, the biographical-halakhic riddle of his settling in Egypt remains unresolved.

[9] B. Dinur, 'Aliyyato shel Rabbi Yehudah ha-Lewi li-Ereẓ Yisra'el we-ha-Tesisah ha-Meshiḥit be-Yamaw', in *Ma'avaq ha-Dorot* (Jerusalem, 1975), 202 ff. The article was first published in *Minḥah le-David* (Jerusalem, 1935). See the important letter published by S. Abramson, 'Mikhtav Rabbi Yehudah ha-Lewi 'al 'Aliyyato li-Eretẓ Yisra'el,' *Kiryat Sefer*, 29 (1954), 133 ff.

[10] Naḥmanides' attitude is manifested in various places in his writings, primarily in his Commentary on the Torah and his supplements to Maimonides' Book of Commandments, positive commandment no. 4. See Ḥ. Ḥanokh, *Ha-Ramban ke-Ḥoqer u-ke-Mequbbal* (Jerusalem, 1978), 144 ff. On R. Judah Loew b. Bezalel (Maharal), see Martin Buber's well-known essay, *Israel and Palestine* (London, 1952), ch. 3, and B. Gross, *Neẓaḥ Yisra'el* (The Messianic outlook of the Maharal of Prague) (Tel Aviv, 1974). In many respects, R. Judah Halevi, Naḥmanides, and the Maharal constitute a special strand in Jewish thought—threefold, yet unified.

there is little' (see Isa. 28: 13, cited by Maimonides at the end of his *Ma'amar Teḥiyyat ha-Metim*), and extract specific emphases from Maimonides' writings in various contexts. This will enable us to come to conclusions regarding his attitude and attachment to Eretz Yisrael—an abstract, theoretical, conceptual attitude, and a spiritual, existential, emotional attachment, two separate but ultimately interlocking issues.[11]

[11] His well-known comment concerning the sanctity of Jerusalem (*Hilkhot Bet ha-Beḥirah*, vi. 16), quoted below, reads excitingly—and not only as a presentation of an outstanding and shining halakhic concept. We must carefully combine and evaluate all the data and components, emphases and inclinations. Clearly, a simplistic and single dimensional comparison to Judah Halevi or Naḥmanides misses the mark; e.g. there is much to be learned from the well-known fact that Naḥmanides regarded the conquest and settlement of Palestine as a positive commandment and questioned Maimonides' omission of this from his enumeration of commandments. This issue is endlessly considered and reconsidered; great importance is attached to it today, as some construct entire ideologies upon it. An extensive halakhic discussion may be found in R. Shaul Yisra'eli's *Sefer Erez Ḥemdah* (or *Hilkhot Erez Yisra'el* (Jerusalem, 1982). See the most recent exchange between R. Yaakov Ariel and R. Nachum Rabinovitz in *Teḥumin*, 5 (1984), 174–86. However, to avoid a trap of reductionism, one should not be satisfied with conclusions based on a single detail but should rather fit them into a broader framework. Maimonides' passionate comments in *Hilkhot Melakhim*, v. 10–11 (to be cited at the end of this paper), his positive attitude towards kingship and political independence (see *Hilkhot Berakhot*, ii. 4: 'Israel's consolation will only be a complete consolation when the House of David will be restored to sovereignty') and the general historical *Anschauung* concerning Exile, hardship and suffering, adversity and danger expressed in his *Letter on Forced Conversion*, *Epistle to Yemen*, and some *teshuvot*—e.g. to Obadiah the Proselyte—should be taken into consideration. I have always thought it possible to contend that Naḥmanides had a more positive approach to history, a cheerful attitude, to a certain extent, whereas Maimonides was gloomy. For example, the statement in the Talmud (*Rosh ha-Shanah*, 18*b*) on fasts: 'When there is peace they shall be for joy and gladness; if there is persecution, they shall be fast days; if there is no persecution but yet not peace, then those who desire may fast and those who desire need not fast'—has been variously interpreted. Maimonides identified the state of 'no persecution but yet no peace' with the period of the Second Temple, a time that was not all brilliance, power, and independence. He equates 'persecution' with Exile in general (i.e. degradation and submission, persecution and torture), while 'peace' is a thing of the days of the Messiah (cf. also *Hilkhot Ta'aniyyot*, v. 19). For Naḥmanides (see H. D. Chavel, *Torat ha-Adam: Kitve ha-Ramban* (Jerusalem, 1964), ii. 283), peace is equated with the period of the Temple's existence (therefore the fast of the Ninth of Av was not observed during the time of the Second Temple, a period of ascendancy), and 'no persecution but yet not peace' (in other words, a historical reality not entirely sombre) characterizes Exile—and therefore the observance of fasts is not an obligation in and of itself; rather, it is dependent upon national consensus and choice. However, he adds: 'And even now they wanted to fast and were accustomed to doing so and took it upon themselves and surely now because of an increase in our transgressions and Israel has troubles and there is no peace.' His commentary on Deut. 28: 42 is well known: 'But after being in exile in the lands of our enemies, and neither the work of our hands nor our work-animals nor the increase of our flocks, nor our vineyards nor our olive groves have been cursed, but *we are in the lands of the other nations as settlers of that land, or even better off than them*'—quite a rosy perception of Diaspora reality. We are again reminded

I am actually suggesting an indirect approach to the subject (comparable, if you like, to the Maimonidean approach to the study of God), via consideration of a number of central topics in Maimonides' thought, topics which are, in any case, central to Jewish thought in general, and specifically to see what place Eretz Yisrael holds and what its function is in the formation of Maimonides' attitudes. The presence or absence of the Eretz Yisrael factor illumines our inquiry. A tangible, meaningful, and defined picture will thus be drawn, which brings into focus substantive elements and basic ideas. A wide range of topics that are worthy of consideration and will shed light on the subject may be noted:

1. The history of religion, the principle focus being the spread of monotheism.[12]

2. The history of the *halakhah*, particularly the appearance of controversy in the Oral Law and the growth of custom, as well as the compilation of the Mishnah and the Talmud despite the prohibition against writing down the Oral Law.[13]

of things in *Wikkuaḥ ha-Ramban* (*Kitveh Ha-Ramban*, ed. Chavel, i. 310): 'For you are worth more to me than the Messiah. You are a king and he is a King, you rule a nation and he rules Israel, for the Messiah is nothing other than flesh and blood like you. And when I worship my Creator, with your permission, *in exile and under duress, subjugated and abused by the nations who will always abuse us*, my reward is great as I offer my body as a sacrifice to God' (cf. his commentary to Lev. 1: 9). The dialectical nature of his historical thought is complex and sharp.

In addition, the spiritual inclinations and aspirations of Maimonides and Naḥmanides and their influence on historical, political, and social perceptions should not be ignored. The following passage from *She'elot u-Teshuvot ha-Rashbash* (Solomon b. Simeon Duran), (Jerusalem, 1968), para. 3, will serve as an example of the far-reaching possibilities: 'I have seen all that you have written concerning Aliyah to Eretz Yisrael. It is understood from your words that there is no spiritual perfection save by apprehending the intelligibilia, and that 'Aliyah to Eretz Yisrael neither helps nor hinders.' Philosophy and *kabbalah* are tremendously potent forces, and are capable of penetrating all areas of life, shaping thought and action. Immigration to Palestine occupied an important position in kabbalistic thought from the 13th to the 18th cent. (R. Menaḥem Mendel of Vitebsk). See also *She'elot u-Teshuvot ha-Rashbash*, para. 2: 'Also as regards the words of Rabbenu Mosheh of blessed memory, who did not count it as a positive commandment. In any case, if a commandment is not counted as scriptural, it is a commandment of our Rabbis, and this is apart from other extended benefits to one who dwells there.'

Note that since I prepared this article Gerald J. Blidstein has published *Political Concepts in Maimonidean Halakhah* (Heb.), (Ramat Gan, 1983), a rigorous analysis of Maimonides' *Hilkhot Melakhim*.

[12] See *Hilkhot 'Akum*, i; *Commentary on the Mishnah*, *'Avodah Zarah*, iv. 7; *Epistle to Yemen*; *Guide of the Perplexed*, i. 63, etc. *Teshuvot ha-Rambam*, ed. J. Blau, nos. 293, 448 and other responsa.

[13] See Introd. to the *Commentary on the Mishnah*; Introd. to the *Mishneh Torah*; *Hilkhot Mamrim*, i–ii; *Hilkhot Melakhim*, ix. 1; *Guide of the Perplexed*, i. 71; iii. 34.

3. The history of philosophy, and first and foremost the various reasons given for the loss of the philosophic legacy that was, according to Maimonides, part of the Oral Law in antiquity.[14]

4. The history of prophecy, primarily the definition of its essence, the clarification of the reasons that led to its cessation, and the chances of its resurgence.[15]

5. The history of prayer, with special attention to the impetus that led to the consolidation of fixed and stylized prayer in lieu of worship flowing from the depths of the heart, expressed in various unrestrained, and immediate fashions, 'each according to his ability'.[16]

6. The history of the Hebrew language, from the vantage point of the problem of linguistic purism, the relation between biblical and mishnaic language, the loss of considerable segments of 'the Hebrew literature' of the biblical period and the resulting impoverishment of the language.[17]

7. The history of the religious establishment—that is, the nature, authority, and fate of the Sanhedrin, the monarchy, the ordination (*semikhah*) of judges and rabbis, and status of the holy places (the sanctity of the Temple, Jerusalem, and Eretz Yisrael).[18]

In all of these, the influence of the territorial dimension, or the lack thereof, and its replacement by another historical dimension, needs to be investigated.

It is further possible to analyse Maimonides' historical perception in general as reflected in such issues as:

1. The problem of causality in historical process and the understanding of certain significant events in keeping with natural-rational lawfulness or causality.

2. The division of history into periods, even while recognizing historical continuity.

3. The Diaspora experience, the hardship and suffering—the distress of the Jews and of Judaism in the adverse conditions of Exile.[19]

[14] See especially *Guide of the Perplexed*, i. 71; also ii. 11.

[15] *Guide of the Perplexed*, ii. 32 ff.; *Hilkhot Yesode ha-Torah*, vii; *Epistle to Yemen*; also the *Commentary on the Mishnah*, Introd. and *Pereq Ḥeleq*.

[16] *Hilkhot Tefillah*, i; *'Avodat Yom ha-Kippurim*, iii. 11; and cf. R. Maimon's *Iggeret ha-Neḥamah*, ed. B. Klar (Jerusalem, 1945).

[17] See the *Commentary on the Mishnah*, *Terumot*, i. 1; *Hilkhot Nedarim*, i. 16; and the end of *Hilkhot Tefillah*. 1.

[18] See e.g. *Hilkhot Sanhedrin*, iv; *Melakhim*, i. xi–xii; *Bet ha-Beḥirah*, vi, vii, etc.

[19] The most interesting source is the *Epistle to Yemen*; also *The Letter on Forced Conversion* and the *Letter to the Sages of Lunel*. See also *Hilkhot 'Akum*, i; *Melakhim* xi, xii.

Since we are unable to analyse fully all these topics, it is my intention to concretize my approach by means of a discussion of selected topics that represent the entire complex of issues—*halakhah*, philosophy, prophecy, and history—and can therefore illustrate the main points.

III

In the attempt to assess the place of Eretz Yisrael in the history of the Oral Law, one encounters an intricate causal framework. We must distinguish between the various aspects of 'Eretz Yisrael', especially between that of a sovereign state and its institutions (monarchical and religious sovereignty, as in the time of the Temple) and that of settlement of the people in their land without the accoutrements of a monarchy; in other words, historical reality necessitates a distinction between political-statist and territorial-demographic orientation. On the one hand, it is evident that the destruction of the Temple terminated the applicability of certain laws (Temple worship, sacrifices, defilement and purity, etc.), and there is no need to analyse or even itemize them here. The Temple clearly constituted a framework for the implementation of numerous laws that were suspended upon its destruction. One of the accomplishments associated with the King Messiah, after rebuilding the Temple and gathering the nation's exiled together, is that 'all the ancient laws will be reinstituted in his days . . .' (*Hilkhot Melakhim*, xi. 1). In other words, there will be a halakhic restoration alongside and following the restoration of the monarchy, the religious establishment, and the nation; a full-panoplied halakhic observance is part of the fourfold Messianic restoration. 'In the time of the Temple' is a distinct halakhic concept, not only the designation of a historical period from the standpoint of a political situation. Following the destruction of the Temple, some precepts lost their force. Ever since, one may differentiate between precepts that are required during the time of Exile and those that are not.[20] The law did not change but the possibility of observing it *in toto* diminished.

[20] Introd. to the *Book of Commandments* (ed. Kafiḥ, p. 1). The word 'exile' (*galut*) appears in this source as though the Destruction and the Exile were identical, whereas in most contexts they are distinct. In his Introduction to the *Mishneh Torah* Maimonides does not mention this distinction—in one place, discussing books of precepts composed by the *ge'onim*, he says that they were concerned with matters of practical importance—but rather emphasizes the comprehensive scope of his study. See also his *Commentary on the Mishnah*, introd. to *Ṭohorot* (p. 34): 'And such a situation should not cause wonder *in*

On the other hand, there are precepts that were defined in relation to settlement in the Land (*knesset Yisrael* in Eretz Yisrael) without any connection to the political or religious situation; the destruction of the Temple, the loss of independence, is not a deciding factor in this area. The land is the crucial determinant. For example:

According to the Torah, the laws of heave offering and tithes apply only in the Land of Israel, both when the Temple is standing and when it is not. (*Hilkhot Terumot*, i. 1)

Whenever the term 'Land of Israel' is mentioned, it refers to the lands conquered by the Israelite king or by a prophet with the consent of the majority of Israel. This is the so-called national conquest.

If, however, an individual Israelite family, or Tribe, has gone forth and has conquered a place for itself, even if it is part of the land given to Abraham, it is not called Land of Israel in so far as all the commandments would apply thereto. (ibid. i. 2)

At the end of the chapter (i. 26), Maimonides sums up:

In our time the heave offering is obligatory not by the authority of the Torah but by Scribal law, even in places seized by those who had come up from Babylonia, or even by those who had come later in the days of Ezra. For there is no heave offering authorized by the Torah except in the Land of Israel alone, and at the time when all the children of Israel are there, as it is said, 'When ye are come' (Num. 15: 2), implying, when all of you shall have come, as they did at the first settlement, and as they are to do again at the third settlement, not as they did at the second settlement in the days of Ezra, when only some of them returned, wherefore the Torah did not so obligate them.

Likewise regarding the sabbatical year and jubilee:

When the Tribes of Reuben and Gad and half of the Tribe of Manasseh were exiled, Jubilees ceased, as it is said, 'And proclaim liberty throughout the land unto all the inhabitants thereof' (Lev. 25: 40), implying, as long as all its inhabitants are there . . .' (*Hilkhot Shemiṭṭah we-Yovel*, x. 8)

'In our time', in these contexts, is not in contrast to the time of the Temple; it rather signifies the time when the Jewish people left Eretz Yisrael and went into Exile. Even the Second Temple in the days of Ezra and the time afterwards is included within the range of 'our time'.

the time of Galut and the discontinuation of this subject, due to the small number of those who study it, for we find them *in the time of the Temple*.' The Destruction was clearly religious and political—in other words, a blow to the Sanctuary and the monarchy simultaneously—but the *halakhah* was influenced and shaped in a decisive manner by the burning of the Sanctuary.

The demographic-territorial situation, not the political one, determines the *halakhah*.

As far as halakhic institutions and the crystallization of the great literary works (Mishnah and Talmud) in which the Oral Law was stored are concerned, it is certainly noteworthy that it is not the destruction of the Temple that determines, nor is it the political independence of the Second Commonwealth that guides and shapes halakhic reality; the deciding factor is either the continuance of a large Jewish population in Palestine or its dispersion. In other words, we are dealing with fine distinctions concerning Eretz Yisrael—sovereign state or thriving, self-reliant settlement functioning without the trappings of kingship. In Maimonides' description of the chain of oral tradition from time immemorial, and in his discussion of the great and revolutionary turning point in the transmission of the Oral Law, there is no mention of the end of the Second Temple. The great change was the redaction of the Mishnah by Rabbi Judah ha-Nasi (and, prior to that, the decentralization of authority during the life of R. Joḥanan b. Zakkai).[21]

[21] Maimonides' opinion on the decentralization of authority and increased dissension can be reconstructed from two fundamental sources. See *Hilkhot Mamrim*, i. 4: 'So long as the Supreme Court was in existence, there were no controversies in Israel.' He continues with a description of the judiciary process according to the Sages in tractate *Sanhedrin* and concludes: 'After the Supreme Court ceased to exist, disputes multiplied in Israel: one declaring it "unclean", giving a reason for his ruling; another declaring it "clean", giving a reason for his ruling; and there is no possibility of reaching a decision acceptable to all.' (See the Introd. to the *Commentary on the Mishnah*, 20, concerning the saying of the Sages, *Sanhedrin*, 88*b*—'when the disciples of Shammai and Hillel, who had studied insufficiently increased, disputes multiplied in Israel'.) Maimonides suggests an inner-directed explanation that depends upon methods of study, logic, and speculation unrelated to changes in the legal establishment or, as surfaces in *Guide of the Perplexed*, in the status of the Oral Law. He writes:

> But their saying, 'When the disciples of Shammai and Hillel, who had studied insufficiently, increased, disputes multiplied in Israel,' is very clear, as two people of equal understanding, study, and knowledge of the principles to be learned will definitely not have a dispute over any one of the rules. And if there should be, it will be slight, as we found no dispute between Shammai and Hillel except over a few precepts, as their methods of study of the rules were similar, and both observed identical correct principles. And when their students' studiousness decreased and their ways of judgment weakened as compared to Shammai and Hillel their teachers, controversy broke out among them during the proceedings on many issues, as each one ruled according to his intellectual capability and according to the rules he knew. And in this manner controversy started.

In *Guide of the Perplexed*, i. 71, 175–6, Maimonides ascribes the appearance of the dissension to a combination of factors: the termination of the Supreme Court together with the compilation of the Oral Law and its distribution in a book accessible to everyone:

This was the method in vogue till the time of Our Teacher, the Saint. He gathered together all the traditions, enactments, interpretations and expositions of every portion of the Torah. All this material he redacted in the Mishnah, which was diligently taught *in public, and thus became universally known among the Jewish people.* Copies of it were made *and widely disseminated* [emphasis mine—I.T.].[22]

'Why did Our Teacher, the Saint, act so and not leave things as they were?'—that is to say, what historic circumstance spurred Rabbi Judah ha-Nasi into taking such a far-reaching step (literary redaction and publication), which, at first glance, even goes against the *halakhah*?[23]

> You already know that even the legalistic science of law was not put down in writing in the olden times because of the precept, which is widely known in the nation: *Words that I have communicated to you orally, you are not allowed to put down in writing.* This precept shows extreme wisdom with regard to the Law. For it was meant to prevent what has ultimately come about in this respect: I mean the multiplicity of opinions, the variety of schools, the confusions occurring in the expression of what is put down, the divisions of the people, who are separated into sects, and the production of confusion with regard to actions. All these matters should be within the authority of *the Great Court of Law*, as we have made clear in our juridical compilations.

Here the increased dissension is inherent in the transformation of the Oral Law into the possession of the masses as a result of its redaction in books. As long as it was available only to a few individuals it was spared controversy; publication and literary status changed its character. The preferability of learning by heart is stressed in an original argument which is very interesting from a cultural-historical perspective: all studying by heart is superior to the written word. The idea that only with the redaction of the Mishnah did the Oral Law become accessible to anyone wishing to study it is emphasized in the introduction to the *Mishneh Torah.*

[22] See n. 21. This idea that until the compilation of the Mishnah the entire Torah—not just mystical speculations on the Divine Chariot and cosmogony—was the property of a select few is worthy of attention. The *halakhah* is 'exoteric', open, but its study may be closed and restricted.

[23] In other words, as stated in *Giṭṭin*, 60*b*: 'the words transmitted orally thou art not at liberty to recite from writing'. In his Introd. to *Guide of the Perplexed* (p. 16), Maimonides takes pains to justify his bold decision to write a book about the secrets of the Torah and remarks, *inter alia*: 'God, may He be exalted, knows that I have never ceased to be exceedingly apprehensive about setting down those things that I wish to set down in this Treatise. For they are concealed things: none of them has been set down in any book—written in the religious community *in these times of Exile* [emphasis added]—the books composed in these times being in our hands. How then can I now innovate and set them down? However, I have relied on two premisses, the one being [the Sages'] saying in a similar case, *It is time to do something for the Lord* [for they have infringed Thy Law]. This is apparently a parallel between R. Judah ha-Nasi's redaction of the Mishnah and Maimonides' writing the *Guide of the Perplexed.* An exceedingly important parallel may also be drawn between the redaction of the Mishnah and the writing of Maimonides' *Mishneh Torah.* I have dealt with the affinity between Maimonides and R. Judah ha-Nasi elsewhere.

'Because he observed that the number of disciples was diminishing, fresh calamities were continually happening, the wicked Government was extending its domain and increasing in power, and Israelites were wandering and emigrating to distant countries.' In other words, the decisive factors were the general social deterioration, the sclerosis of political, social, and defensive structures, and especially the dispersion of the people—uprooting, wandering, and demographic shifts which influenced methods of study and generated concern that the Jewish people might forget the Law. The political motif—the continuation of disruption of sovereignty—was not a factor in this development.

This demographic refrain surfaces again in Maimonides' comments on the emergence of the Babylonian Talmud, the supreme authority in determining the *halakhah*.

After the Court of Rav Ashi, who compiled the Gemara which was finally completed in the days of his son, an extraordinarily great dispersion of Israel throughout the world took place. The people emigrated to remote parts and distant isles. The prevalence of wars and the march of armies made travel insecure. The study of the Torah declined.

The same emphasis which transfers the centre of gravity from the political-institutional frameworks to the disintegration of a centralized population is operative with regard to another vital issue, namely, the fundamental change in the Jewish calendar—the transition from declaring the first of the month on the word of eyewitnesses who had seen the new moon to determining it according to an agreed calculation. Maimonides weaves the following historical remark into his explanation:

Since when did all of Israel begin to employ these methods of calculation? Since the time of the last Sages of the Gemara; that was the time when [the Jewish community of] Palestine was destroyed and no regularly established court was left. In the times of the Sages of the Mishnah and also of the Gemara, however, up to the days of Abbayye and Raba (*c.*AD 325) the people depended upon the Palestinian courts for the determination [of the calendar]. (*Hilkhot Qiddush ha-Ḥodesh*, v. 3)[24]

[24] In a preceding section, Maimonides spoke about the existence of the Sanhedrin in Eretz Yisrael, even though its powers and authority were limited as it wandered from its place in the Chamber of Hewn Stones (see *Hilkhot Sanhedrin*, xiv. 13, 'Forty years prior to the destruction of the Second Temple, the right of Israel to try capital cases ceased, for though the sanctuary still existed, the Sanhedrin was exiled and no longer held sessions in the place assigned to it in the sanctuary'). See also xiv. 2, where Maimonides states vaguely, without explaining the chronological details, 'Capital charges are tried

Neither the time of the destruction of the Temple nor that of the last generation of Tannaim, whose authority overrides that of the Amoraim, is the decisive-formative component, but rather the last sages of the Gemara. However, the equating of 'the last Sages of the Gemara' with 'when Palestine was destroyed' calls for further explanation; this is an unusual equation. In fact, one does not have to dig too far; this enigmatic formulation becomes clear in light of the above. The phrase 'when Palestine was destroyed' refers to the intensification of the Exile—the accelerated, expanded dispersion of the population and the break-down of the social order which had remained intact after the Temple's destruction—and not to the loss of political independence. In question are the absolute end of the legislative institution (the Supreme Court) and the final decline and disintegration of the Jewish population in Eretz Yisrael, not the final days of the Second Temple. The destruction of the Temple is a matter entirely distinct from the destruction of Eretz Yisrael.

From this we may derive that the phrase 'when Eretz Yisrael was destroyed' appears homonymously—it is an ambiguous expression—and each context requires adjustment to its precise meaning. Thus, for example, Maimonides explains a certain law concerning the time for reading the *Megillah*. The first Mishnah of tractate *Megillah* opens as follows: 'The *Megillah* is read on the eleventh, the twelfth, the thirteenth, the fourteenth, and the fifteenth [of Adar]; never earlier and never later.' The Gemara there adds: 'R. Judah said, When does this rule [reading on different days] hold good? When the years are properly fixed (i.e. are characterized by normalcy) and Israel reside upon their own soil. But in these days, since people reckon from it, the *Megillah* is to be read only on the proper day.' Rabbi Isaac b. Jacob Alfasi quotes another version. In place of 'since people reckon from it' (*mistaklin*), he reads 'since people are endangered by it (*mistaknin*)' (and see Naḥmanides, *Milḥamot*, loc. cit.), and adds by way of explanation: 'That is, in the same time that Israel upheld their religion and were not endangered . . . but in these days when Israel takes risks with its religion, [the *Megillah*] is to be read only on the proper day. In the *Mishneh Torah* Maimonides sums up with utmost brevity: ' "The

only while the Temple is in existence, provided that the Supreme Court meets in the Hall of Hewn Stones in the sanctuary. By tradition it has been learned that capital offences are tried only when the priests bring offerings on the altar, provided that the Supreme Court is in its right place.' In short, the situation in the Land in general, the status of the population, and the measure of social normalcy are what determine the situation.

rule that reading of the *Megillah* might be advanced . . . applied *only when the Israelites constituted a sovereign state* (*Malkhut*). Nowadays it may be read only on the normal date' (*Hilkhot Megillah we-Ḥanukkah*, i. 9). As we see, he concluded with a vague reference to 'nowadays', which is, by contrast, dependent on abolition of the monarchy.[25] However, Maimonides elaborates the point in his *Commentary on the Mishnah*: '[The *Megillah*] was read on different days only in the time when we prevailed and were able to enforce complete observance of the commandments, but nowadays, that is, *from the redaction of the Talmud until the coming of the Messiah, may he soon be revealed*, [the *Megillah*] is to be read only on the proper day. Maimonides here glossed over the issue of danger,[26] and expatiated on the matter of 'when the years are properly fixed'; in other words, the lack of political power and the inability to enforce desirable arrangements.[27] What

[25] See *Hilkhot Megillah we-Ḥannukah*, iii. 1: 'For the Hasmonean family of High Priests won a victory. They set up a king from among the priests, and restored Israel's kingdom for a period of more than two hundred years—until the destruction of the Second Temple.' Here the abolition of the monarchy coincides with the destruction.

[26] R. Menaḥem ha-Meiri explained that imminent danger to the Jewish people exists if Purim celebrations are excessively prolonged and ostentatious. See *Bet ha-Beḥirah* (Jerusalem, 1968), *Megillah*, 15: 'The reason for "since Israel is now endangered" in the observance of their religion is that people object when they see the Jews celebrating their revenge, so the Sages instructed them not overly to publicize their celebrations; it is enough [to read the Megillah] on its proper day. And even though the Ḥannukah celebration lasts eight days, that is a celebration of the miracle of the oil, not of the victory over the enemies.' In other words, Ḥannukah has a spiritual character, whereas Purim has a clearly politico-military one that can arouse jealousy and hatred.

[27] See the phrasing in *Hilkhot 'Akum*, x. 6 concerning the issue of the resident alien (*ger toshav*). There too the ruling depends on the status of the nation and its coercive capability: 'The foregoing rules apply to the time when the people of Israel live exiled among the nations, or when the gentile's power is predominant.' If so, at issue here are two possibilities: exile, or decline while the Jewish people live in their land but do not have the upper hand. He continues: 'But when Israel is predominant over the nations of the world, we are forbidden to permit a gentile who is an idolater to dwell among us.' See also *Hilkhot Melakhim*, viii. 10 ('Moreover, Moses, our teacher, was commanded by God to *compel* (or coerce) all human beings.') Regarding the annihilation of idolatry, the ruling is: 'An affirmative precept enjoins the destruction of any idol, articles subsidiary to its worship, and everything made for its sake. In the Land of Israel, it is a duty actively to pursue idolatry till we have exterminated it from the whole of our country. Outside the Holy Land, however, we are not so commanded; but only that whenever we acquire any territory by conquest, we should destroy all the idols found there (*Hilkhot 'Akum*, vii. 1)' The same double antithesis is suggested by the formulation in *Teshuvah*, ix. 1 where Maimonides addresses the question of the reward for the fulfilment of the commandments and the good to which we will attain if we have kept the ways of the Lord. 'Inasmuch as the reward is life in the world to come . . . what then is the meaning of the

particularly interests us is the identification of 'nowadays', when the Jews lack power, with the era of the compilation of the Talmud, that is, the last Sages of the Gemara, that being the time when Eretz Yisrael was devastated and the remaining foundations of the existing society were undermined. The statements in the *Commentary on the Mishnah* can be understood only in the light of the ruling in *Hilkhot Qiddush ha-Ḥodesh* (and also the description of the social, cultural, and political situation at the time of the Talmud's compilation, which Maimonides put in his introduction to the *Mishneh Torah*).[28] Again, 'nowadays' is not the opposite of the Temple period; rather, it signifies a lack of power, initiative, and stability. The destruction of the institutional and political frameworks serves as a backdrop for further developments.

This is a good place to turn to two significant innovations which also become clear in the context of our discussion:

1. In the detailed and explicated list of 'days which are observed by all Israel as fasts because tragic events happened on them', Maimonides enters the Fast of Gedaliah as follows: 'Tishri 3rd, because Gedaliah the son of Aḥikam was slain on the day, thus extinguishing the last remaining ember of Israel's independence and making her exile complete' (*Hilkhot Ta'aniyyot*, v. 2). We find in tractate *Rosh ha-Shanah*, 18*b*: 'The fast of the seventh month: this is the third of Tishri on which Gedaliah the son of Aḥikam was killed [the fact that a fast was instituted on this day] shows that the death of the righteous is put on a level with the burning of the House of our God.' Differing explanation in Maimonides' formulations is always provocative (and sometimes problematical too), and draws the attention of his students. We need not, at present, delve into the matter and discuss how Maimonides' comments on the subject relate to the talmudic source. It suffices if we stress that the novel emphasis is understood and the implication clear and reflective of Maimonides' perception: the thorough demographic dispersion, the increasing dimming of the light,

statement found everywhere in the Torah that if you obey, it will happen to you thus; if you do not obey, it will be otherwise; and all these happenings will take place in this world such as war and peace, sovereignty (*malkhut*) and subjection (*shiflut*), residence in the Promised Land and exile.' These opposites represent two different conditions.

[28] Regarding the era 'from the redaction of the Talmud until the coming of the Messiah', see *Hilkhot Melakhim*, xi. 4: 'If there arise a king from the House of David who meditates on the Torah, occupies himself with the commandments, *prevails upon* (or coerces) Israel to walk in the way of the Torah and to repair its breaches.' The concept of coercion (*kefiyah*) is multi-faceted.

the last stages of the uprooting of the nation from Eretz Yisrael and its Exile—these are what determined reality. We might say that there is here a concept of 'the end of exile' paralleling 'the end of learning' (*sof hora'ah*)—i.e. the final consummation of a prolonged process. A look at the following section of the same chapter convinces us that the emphasis is not happenstance, but reflects a clear historical perspective. In summing up the five things that occurred on the 9th of Av, Maimonides describes the fall of Bettar and the failure of the Bar Kokhba rebellion:

A great city named Bettar was captured—it contained thousands and myriads of Israelites and had a great king whom all Israel, including the greatest scholars, thought to be the King Messiah, but he fell into the hands of the Romans who slew them all, a calamity as great as that of the destruction of the Temple.

The destruction of the Temple is a general species of calamitous events and not completely *sui generis*. It should be noted that at the end of *Hilkhot Melakhim* as well, regarding Jesus as a false messiah, the principle of the ingathering of the Jewish people as against the dispersion is emphasized, together with the eternal nature of the Torah.

For has there ever been a greater stumbling than this? All the prophets affirmed that the Messiah would redeem Israel, save them, gather their dispersed, and confirm the commandments. But he caused Israel to be destroyed by the sword, their remnant to be dispersed and humiliated. He was instrumental in changing the Torah.

2. It is well known that Maimonides suggested the possibility that the Sanhedrin might be revived. In the *Mishneh Torah* he wrote:

It seems to me that if all the wise men in Palestine were to agree to appoint judges and to ordain them, the ordination would be valid, empowering the ordained to adjudicate cases in involving fines and to ordain others. (*Hilkhot Sanhedrin*, iv. 11)

The logic of his supposition is laid out in the *Commentary on the Mishnah*, where he determines that a revival of the Sanhedrin is bound to take place, as its re-establishment is a prerequisite for the coming of the Messiah, and there is a divine promise to this effect.[29] In any case,

[29] *Commentary on the Mishnah*, *Sanhedrin*, i. 3 (p. 148): 'And I believe that if there were to come about a consensus on the part of all the pupils and sages to appoint someone in the academy by making him its head, provided that this be in the Land of Israel, as we have said above, the academy will be instituted, and He will become

one detail is not yet as clear as it should be, and Maimonides is aware that he must reply to a penetrating question: how can the possibility of reviving the Sanhedrin be reconciled with the tremendous anxiety concerning its abolition? If it is possible to make amends for the abolition of the Sanhedrin, what upset the Sages, and why did they worry and belabour the point that the chain of man-to-man ordination was broken—giving the impression that this break is irreparable? In *Hilkhot Sanhedrin* (iv. 11) Maimonides goes on to answer the question:

> If what we have said is true, the question arises: Why were the Rabbis disturbed over the matter of ordination, apprehending the abolition of the laws involving fines? Because Israel is scattered and agreement on the part of all is impossible. If, however, there were one ordained by a man who had himself been ordained, no unanimity would be necessary.

The dispersion of the Jewish people is a decisive historical factor which makes the revival of the Sanhedrin very difficult, although not impossible. The Jewish nation will have to find a way to overcome this difficulty because a Sanhedrin is a prerequisite for the King Messiah.

IV

We now move to another area: the problem and nature of linguistic purism. We shall see that the corruption and misuse of language too were caused in the first instance by the Exile and by settlement in foreign lands. Moreover, the misuse was so firmly entrenched that the return to Zion in the days of Ezra did not solve the problem (just as it did not restore the status of 'all its inhabitants are there', as we have seen above with regard to laws of tithing). This misuse brought about the formation of a fixed version of prayer:

> When the people of Israel went into exile in the days of the wicked Nebuchadnezzar, they mingled with the Persians, Greeks and other nations.

ordained, and will thereafter ordain whomever he wishes. For if you do not hold this principle, then the existence of the Supreme Court is forever precluded, for all its [judges] must certainly be ordained. And God promised their restoration when he said, "I will restore your judges of old" (Isa. 1: 26). Perhaps you will say that the Messiah will appoint them even though they are not ordained. But this is absurd. For we have already explained at the beginning of our book that the Messiah will not add to the Law nor detract therefrom, neither from the Written Law nor from the Oral Law. And I believe that the Sanhedrin will return before the appearance of the Messiah, and that this will be one of his signs.'

> In those foreign countries, children were born to them, whose language was confused. Everyone's speech was a mixture of many tongues. No one was able, when he spoke, to express his thoughts adequately in any one language, otherwise than incoherently, as it is said, 'And their children spoke half in the speech of Ashdod and they could not speak in the Jews' language, but according to the language of each people.'
>
> Consequently, when anyone of them prayed in Hebrew, he was unable adequately to express his needs or recount the praises of God, without mixing Hebrew with other languages. When Ezra and his council realized this condition, they ordained the Eighteen Benedictions in their present order. The object aimed at was that these prayers should be in an orderly form in everyone's mouth, that all should learn them, and thus the prayer of those who were not expert in speech would be as perfect as that of those who had command of a chaste style. For the same reason, they arranged [in a fixed form] all the blessings and prayers for all the Jews so that the substance of every blessing should be familiar and current in the mouth of one who is not expert in speech.[30]

In other words, Maimonides here sketched halakhic implications of a demographic reality that brought strange and undesirable linguistic phenomena in its wake—'defective' phenomena, from a purist perspective. Exile into foreign lands is responsible for linguistic assimilation and confusion. In order to be extricated from these straits and adjust the prayer of the inarticulate (whose speech was mixed and corrupt) to that of the eloquent, Ezra changed what 'had been ever since the time of Moses' until his own time and instituted a fixed and unified form for prayers and benedictions, a far-reaching change which from a certain vantage point resembles the redaction of the Mishnah and the resultant change in the literary status of the Oral Law. From this we may conclude that both modifications are a forced compromise, as prayer without a prescribed number of prayers, 'a prescribed form of prayer', and a 'fixed time' for its recitation is the ideal type of prayer, service of the heart, 'and this is how it was from the time of Moses until that of Ezra'. Likewise, oral learning that is not

[30] *Hilkhot Tefillah*, i. 4. Maimonides interpreted the text in Neh. 13: 24 in the sense of a confusion of languages and not only as linguistic assimilation or absorption among the nations, which was also reflected in the neglect of the Hebrew language. The corrupt tongue necessitated modification and reform. R. Sa'adyah Gaon also interpreted it in this way (*Sefer ha-Agron*, ed. N. Allony (Jerusalem, 1969), p. 31). On the reform of the fixed version of prayer, see also R. Maimon's *Iggeret ha-Neḥamah*, trans. B. Klar (Jerusalem, 1945), 22; also *Hilkhot Nedarim*, i. 16: 'In some places the people's speech is corrupt, and they debase the language by substituting one word for another.' In *Hilkhot Tefillah*, xv. 1 the word *'illeg* means someone with a speech defect, not someone who corrupts the language by mixing it with many others.

bound to a formulated literary text is the ideal, 'and so it was from the time of Moses to that of R. Joḥanan b. Zakkai'. The previous, pristine practice in both cases was modifed.

We can widen the field and move from a description of negative linguistic consequences coming in the wake of exile to a clear and positive determination that residence in the homeland guarantees proper linguistic development. In an entirely different context, in which Maimonides defends mishnaic language from attack as a deviation from biblical language, we find: 'The basis of every language rests upon what its speakers express and what is heard from them, and [the Sages] were undoubtedly Hebrews in their land that is, Eretz Yisrael.'[31] It is an established claim—as well as a principle acknowledged by perfect sages and expert linguists—that 'Hebrews in their land' guarded the purity of their tongue, while those born in foreign countries confused it.[32]

[31] *Commentary on the Mishnah, Terumot*, i. 1 (p. 269). He adds there, 'And this should be the manner of your response to any of the recent ones [i.e. the recent linguists] who think that Mishnaic language is not pure, and that it inflected some expressions incorrectly.' On purity and precision of language as the loftiest principle, see my *Introduction to the Code of Maimonides*, p. 349. Bernard Septimus's *Maimonides on Language*, to appear shortly, contains an exhaustive discussion of this cultural, historical, and linguistic problem.

[32] I wish that there might be a similar guarantee today that 'Hebrews in their land' would preserve their language. (One scholar has observed that our Semitic language has turned from Semitic into Indo-European.)

The following question needs to be addressed: could such a linguistic decline and distortion have occurred in Eretz Yisrael? Could 'Hebrews in their land', in a hostile environment inhabited by a non-Jewish majority, experience a fate similar to those who went into exile and had their 'language confused'? Maimonides' statement about non-Jewish influences adulterating the authentic philosophic nature of Judaism does not apparently limit this phenomenon to Jews in exile. See *Guide of the Perplexed*, ii. 11, p. 276:

> We have already explained that all these views do not contradict anything said by our prophets and the sustainers of our Law. For our community is a community that is full of knowledge and is perfect, as He, may He be exalted, has made clear through the intermediary of the Master who made us perfect, saying: 'Surely, this great community is a wise and understanding people.' However, when the wicked from among the ignorant communities ruined our good qualities, destroyed our words of wisdom and our compilations, and caused our men of knowledge to perish, so that we again became ignorant, as we had been threatened because of our sins—for it says: 'And the wisdom of their wise men shall perish, and the understanding of their prudent men shall be hid'; when, furthermore, we mingled with these communities and their opinions were taken over by us, as were their morals and actions—for just as it says regarding the similarity of actions: 'They mingled themselves with the communities and learned their works', it says with regard to the adoption by us of the opinions of the ignorant: 'And they please themselves in the children of strangers', which is translated by Jonathan ben Uziel, peace be on him: 'And they walk according

Finally, I should like to note that the dispersion is also the historic cause of the growth of regional custom, whose validity is limited, in contrast to universal law obligating all Jews everywhere. Maimonides writes:

> If a court established in any country, after the time of the Talmud, made decrees and ordinances or introduced customs for those residing in its particular country or for residents of other countries, its enactments did not obtain the acceptance of all Israel because of the remoteness of the Jewish settlements and the difficulties of travel. And as the court of any particular country consisted of individuals [whose authority was not universally recognized], while the Supreme Court of seventy-one members had, several years before the compilation of the Talmud, ceased to exist, no compulsion is exercised on those living in one country to observe the customs of another country; nor is any court directed to issue a decree that had been issued by another court in the same country.[33]

Herein lies the foundation for the autonomy of local custom, every place having its own ways. It is rooted in the loss of independence and the people's dispersion to distant places cut off from each other. More precisely, the people's dispersion, along with some of the inevitable changes triggered by it, is the cause. The principal stages of this development are as follows: (*a*) the start of halakhic controversy in the wake of the break-down of the exclusive central authority; (*b*) the dispersion, and the sociopolitical deterioration in general, which brought about the redaction of the Mishnah and the Gemara; (*c*) termination, after some partial jurisdictional limitations, of the Supreme Court, and the multiplication of controversy (see, in particular, *Hilkhot Mamrim*, i. 4); and (*d*) restriction of the applicability

to the laws of the gentiles'; when, in consequence of all this, we grew up accustomed to the opinions of the ignorant, these philosophic views appeared to be, as it were, foreign to our Law, just as they are foreign to the opinions of the ignorant. However, matters are not like this.

Concerning the cessation of prophecy, see *Guide of the Perplexed*, ii. 36, where there is an explicit contrast between 'exile' and the 'days of the Messiah'; the cessation of prophecy, however, happens even in Eretz Yisrael.

On the other hand, Maimonides, following talmudic statements, attaches special value to the Land of Israel even when the environmental influence is negative; it is best to live in Eretz Yisrael even if the majority of the population is non-Jewish. See e.g. *Hilkhot Ishut*, xiii. 19 and *Hilkhot Melakhim*, v. 12.

[33] *Mishneh Torah*, Introd. The following paragraph emphasizes that the ruling of the Gemarah *obligates* everyone. See *Hilkhot Mamrim*, ii. 2, and its interpretations. Here the question is focused on the issue of the absolute authority of the Mishnah and the Gemarah.

and validity of the all- inclusive and all-obligatory law (incorporated in the Gemara) and the rise of custom alongside universal law. The entire matter bears a dialectical imprint—land and destruction concentration and dispersion of the people—with the shrunken or withered political aspect serving only as a general background.

V

Let us now turn our attention to an important literary feature of Maimonides' work that has ramified implications. The destruction of the Second Temple, as previously mentioned, led to essential changes in the *halakhah*, and Maimonides knew how to be precise in terminology and formulation when he needed to mention these changes. The way in which Maimonides relates to these changes is what is important to us, not the fact they took place. It may be said that the changes did not influence Maimonides' work or its underlying conception of the Oral Law. In his summary codification of the *halakhah*, he did not set up a partition between 'what is required in the time of the exile and what is not', between 'in the sanctuary' (Jerusalem) and 'in the countryside' (i.e. all places outside of Jerusalem). He codified everything without differentiating between applicable law and law for the future (i.e. for the time of the Messiah), currently impracticable. This comprehensive codification was one of his main innovations. As a result of his principled stand that the Oral Law is an organic, indivisible whole—at least as far as studying and teaching are concerned—he restored Eretz Yisrael to the people's consciousness without resorting to metaphysical declarations or fiery propaganda. Anyone who studies *Hilkhot Tefillah* comes across Eretz Yisrael (see especially ch. xiv, which deals with the priestly benediction, where Maimonides presents the details of these laws as they are practised in the time of the Temple and at this time); anyone who studies the description of the Seder night (*Hilkhot Ḥameẓ u-Maẓẓah*, vii) unwittingly crosses into the time of the Temple and delves into the differences between the order of the night preceding the 15th day of Nisan in this time and in the Temple period. It is worth noting that there is apparently no consistently expressed 'preference' that presents the law for the period of the Temple before that of this time; sometimes one comes first, sometimes the other—they are woven into a single fabric. Needless to say, anyone who plunges into the completely new sections of his Great Compilation—*Hilkhot Bet ha-Beḥirah* and *Hilkhot Kele ha-Miqdash*, and so forth—is returned to Eretz Yisrael in general and to Jerusalem in particular. These topics and ideas, of course, were not Maimonides' innovations or inventions, but he revived them and reintroduced them into the house of study. Hence, there is also a special link to Eretz Yisrael embodied within his comprehensive grasp of the Oral Law, which has influence and implications *vis-à-vis* the place of Eretz Yisrael in his philosophy.

I shall comment further on this at the end of this paper. We need to emphasize that Eretz Yisrael does not appear solely as a component of Maimonides' eschatological doctrine; it is turned into a halakhic datum, just as the King Messiah is made a well-known and accepted halakhic detail. The references to the King Messiah are inconspicuously incorporated in various rulings and seem to appear casually, as a natural, ordinary matter. 'Similarly in the days to come, at the third return, when the Israelites shall re-enter the Land' (*Hilkhot Shemiṭṭah ve-Yovel*, xii. 16). 'Now nine red heifers were prepared from the time this commandment was received until the Temple was destroyed the second time. And a tenth King Messiah will prepare—may he soon be revealed!' (*Hilkhot Parah Adumah*, iii. 4). 'King Messiah will receive one-thirteenth of all the provinces to be conquered by Israel' (*Hilkhot Melakhim*, iv. 8). Everything is stated with matter-of-fact, literary simplicity, as though the subject in question were the time of the morning or evening prayer, the shaking of the *lulav*, eating *maẓẓah*, or a wedding celebration. The assertions are vibrant and real, not swept into a dark, esoteric corner or an inert eschatological teaching. We are dealing with a halakhic reality rather than a remote eschatology. Comprehensiveness of his approach also means the natural fusion of its parts.

The subject requires that we note, however cursorily, two more areas. First, let us be attentive to the repercussions our topic has upon Maimonides' conceptions of prophecy—the causes of its cessation and its chances of revival. In the *Guide of the Perplexed* (ii. 36, p. 373), he writes:

> This is indubitably the essential and proximate cause of the fact that prophecy was taken away during the time of the *Exile*. For what *languor* or *sadness* can befall a man in any state that would be stronger than that due to his being a thrall slave in bondage to the ignorant who commit great sins and in whom the privation of true reason is united to the perfection of the lusts of the beast? *And there shall be no might in thine hand* (Deut. 28: 32). This was with what we have

been threatened. And this was what it meant by saying: 'They shall run to and fro to seek the word of the Lord, and shall not find it' (Amos 8: 12).[34]

Maimonides maintains that the political and cultural troubles that influence the individual's perfection—sadness, disease, war, hunger—undermine prophecy, as they preclude intellectual excellence, which is a *sine qua non* for the occurrence of prophecy. As opposed to other sages, who emphasized Eretz Yisrael's precedence and exclusive supremacy and determined that prophecy is possible only there, Maimonides adhered to his theory of the connection between cognitive excellence and politico-cultural stability. The focal point is not geography but rather the oppressive, adverse consequences of the Exile. In keeping with this view he goes on to interpret the verse: 'Her king and her princes are among the nations, the Law is no more; yea, her prophets find no vision from the Lord' (Lam. 2: 9).[35] Following from this principle are the words of encouragement with which Maimonides concludes (ii. 36): 'This will also be the cause for prophecy being restored to us in its habitual form, as has been promised, in the days of the Messiah, may he be revealed soon.' With this emphasis on the divine promise, he complements and extends that which was formulated with considerable restraint in the *Mishneh Torah*. In this case the philosophic context reveals more than the

[34] See the *Commentary on the Mishnah*, Introd. to *Ṭohorot* (p. 33), where Maimonides, following what is stated in tractate *Shabbat* (138*b*), refers this verse to *knowledge of halakhah*: 'The Torah will eventually be forgotten by Israel, as it is said, "And they shall wander from sea to sea, and from the north even to the east, they shall run to and fro to seek the word of the Lord, and shall not find it" (Amos 8: 12). What is meant by they run to and fro seeking the word of the Lord and not finding it? In the future a woman will take a loaf of heave offering, make the round of synagogues and academies to determine if she is first or second.' In the sequel (p. 36) he stresses: 'And consider their statement, "the Torah will eventually be forgotten by Israel". This is because they will overlook laws of impurity and purity. When the Lord commanded the prophet to ask about this, he told him to seek Torah from the priests. Torah *per se* is thus the discussion of purity and impurity and a knowledge of their status. And why not? They are the ladder to the holy spirit.' The 'word of God' is *halakhah* as well as prophecy; they are unified.

[35] Maimonides already alludes to this interpretation in ii. 33 p. 362: '"Yea, her prophets find no vision from the Lord" (Lam. 2: 9); this was the case because they were in Exile.' It is important to remember that prior to the aforementioned passage beginning, 'This is indubitably the essential and proximate cause', Maimonides writes: 'Accordingly you will find that the prophecy of the prophets ceases when they are sad or angry, or in a mood similar to one of these two. You know their saying that "prophecy does not descend [during a mood of] sadness or languor"; that prophetic revelation did not come to "Moses, peace be on him", after the disastrous incident of the spies.' Exile intensifies and deepens these phenomena, which have the power to prevent the occurrence of prophecy in Eretz Yisrael too.

halakhic one, but the underlying concept is unified and consistent in both.

Elsewhere, I reviewed how Maimonides' concept of the correlation between political times of trouble and cultural-intellectual decline is reflected in various areas.[36] For example, his comments on the history of Jewish philosophic thought, or more precisely, the loss of philosophy, belong to this category. 'The many sciences that have existed in our religious community have perished because of the length of the time that has passed, because of our being dominated by the pagan nations' (*Guide*, i. 71, p. 175). Similarly, the time of the Messiah appears in Maimonides' teaching as a socio-political means of intellectual advancement and cultural efflorescence—of service of God which leads to love of God and knowledge of him. Just as oppressive domination by the kingdom of evil prevents us from studying Torah and science, so independence and freedom from hostile realms enables profound and fruitful study. This tranquil and productive period, with its dazzling consequences and repercussions in the field of Torah and science, is described at the end of *Hilkhot Melakhim*:

> The Sages and Prophets did not long for the days of the Messiah that Israel might exercise dominion over the world, or rule over the heathens, or be exalted by the nations, or that it might eat and drink and rejoice. Their aspiration was that Israel be free to devote itself to the Law and its wisdom, with no one to oppress or disturb it, and thus be worthy of life in the world to come.

The reciprocal influence beween the socio-economic situation and cultural-theological development is clearly and emphatically expressed here.

[36] 'The Mishneh Torah of Maimonides', *The Israel Academy of Sciences and Humanities Proceedings*, 5/10 (1976), 11 ff. It is worth emphasizing that social improvement and well-being is a firm foundation of Maimonides' philosophy and is expressed not only in the *Guide of the Perplexed* (e.g. iii. 27) but also in the *Mishneh Torah*. Consider *Hilkhot Rozeah*, iv. 8, 9:

> If one commits murder without being seen by two witnesses at the same time, the rule in all such cases is that the murderer is put into a cell and fed on a minimum of bread and water until his stomach contracts and then he is given barley so that his stomach splits under the stress of sickness.
>
> This, however, is not done to other persons guilty of crimes involving the death penalty at the hand of the court, although there are worse crimes than bloodshed, none causes such destruction to civilized society as bloodshed. Not even idolatry, nor immorality not destruction of the Sabbath, is the equal of bloodshed. For these are crimes between man and God, while bloodshed is a crime between man and man.

VII

Maimonides' entire historical outlook is saturated with tension. There is a clash between the spiritual and the temporal, between divine providence and the influence of natural factors, between a view of history as focused around religion and attention to real political developments. History, according to Maimonides, is a chronicle about religion, a story of belief and those who know and believe in God, not the record of terrestrial events. Periodization of history is constructed according to the evolution of faith, not political independence or loss of sovereignty. While there are systems that divide history into periods on the basis of political, personal, or cultural events, Maimonides' system (in the *Iggeret Teman*) is based on the spread of the true belief, its achievements and failures, victories and defeats. Nevertheless, political reality plays a highly significant role in his conception of historical causation; concrete, terrestrial factors are of considerable weight. The destruction of the Temple illustrates that superstitions lead men astray, and remove them from wise and productive preoccupations that are the mainstay of the body politic. Maimonides' comments on the accursed astrology that prevented the Israelites from training themselves in war tactics are well known. Great significance is attached to natural causality in the historic sphere. The feeling of suffering in Exile, degradation and submission, wandering and sorrow, cruelty, and the sense of precariousness of existence is very powerful in his teaching.[37] As we have seen, intellectual achievement, cultural

[37] See e.g. the definition of 'an apostate with respect to the whole Torah' in *Hilkhot Teshuvah*, iii. 9 (and the criticism of R. Abraham b. David of Posquières ad loc.): 'An apostate with respect to the whole Torah is one, for example, who at a time of religious persecution becomes converted to the idolaters' religion, clings to them, saying, "what advantage is it to me to adhere to the people of Israel, who are of low estate and persecuted. Better for me to join these nations who are powerful."' The precise and emotional phrasing, which gave rise to halakhic debate on various levels, is reminiscent of the ruling on accepting sincere proselytes. See *Hilkhot Issure Bi'ah*, xiv.1 (which is based on the Sages' comments in tractate *Yevamot*): 'When a heathen comes forth for the purpose of becoming a proselyte, and upon investigation no ulterior motive is found, the court should say to him, "Why do you come forth to become a proselyte? Do you not know that Israel is at present *sorely afflicted, oppressed, despised*, confounded and beset by suffering?"'

In the sequel (xiv. 5) we find a very meaningful historiosophy in a highly compressed form: 'Nevertheless, the Holy One, blessed be He, does not bring upon them too many calamities, lest they should altogether perish. Rather, *all the heathen shall cease to exist, while they shall endure*.' This decisive and enthusiastic declaration concerning national immortality complements the passage in the *Guide of the Perplexed* (ii. 29, p. 342) on the

creativity, philosophical and spiritual perfection all depend upon a natural social order. The individual is unable to deviate from this natural, causal framework. It may be said, by extending the principle of *Guide of the Perplexed*, iii. 32 (pp. 525–31), that just as God is assisted by history and takes it into consideration, so the individual must make allowance for historical processes and forces and even take the initiative and sustain a measure of activism.[38] History is designed to attain a lofty aim, a socio-religious reality such as the world has never seen. The Torah outlined the plan for the perfect state (see *Guide of the Perplexed*, ii. 40, pp. 381–5), which simultaneously cultivates

difference between 'seed' and 'name' in the verse 'so shall your seed and your name remain': 'For it sometimes happens that the *seed* remains while the *name* does not. Thus you can find many peoples that are indubitably the seed of *Persia* or *Greece*, but are not known by special name'—the assimilation of the nations as opposed to Israel's perpetuity. Note that in detailing the different stages of accepting a sincere proselyte, Maimonides emphasizes that two matters are to be fully elaborated: 'He should then be made acquainted with the principles of the faith, which are the oneness of God and the prohibition of idolatry. *These matters should be discussed in great detail.*' 'Rather, all the heathen shall cease to exist while they shall endure: *The court should expatiate on this point*, by token of their affection for him.' The theological foundations of the Torah and the permanence of the nation, these need to be elaborated. See also *Hilkhot Mattenot 'Aniyyim*, x. 2 on the great virtue and paramount importance of charity: 'Whosoever is cruel and merciless lays himself open to suspicion as to his descent, for cruelty is found only among the heathens. All Israelites and those that have attached themselves to them are to each other like brothers, as it is said, "Ye are the children of the Lord". If brother will show no compassion to brother, who will? And unto whom shall the poor of Israel raise their eyes? *Unto the heathens, who hate them and persecute them?* Their eyes are therefore hanging solely upon their brethren.' On cruelty as characteristic of paganism, see *Hilkhot Teshuvah*, ii. 10; *Issure Bi'ah*, xix. 17; *Ḥovel u-Mazziq*, v. 10.

[38] Regarding the Messianic era, it appears that those who hold that according to Maimonides' teaching no preparatory activity is necessary (as opposed to kabbalists, who demand practical and spiritual preparation) carried their view to an extreme. Maimonides calls for a revival of the Sanhedrin ('This will undoubtedly be when God prepares men's hearts, when their goodness and desire for God and the Law increase, and they do more good deeds and their desire for God and his righteousness grows *before* the coming of the Messiah'; *Commentary on the Mishnah*, *Sanhedrin*, i. 3.) In the *Epistle to Yemen* (in contrast to the *Guide of the Perplexed*, ii. 36), Maimonides maintains that the return of prophecy precedes the Messiah. Note that while the Messianic era will glorify Torah and wisdom, their glorification is also a precondition for this era. His comments regarding the Mishnah (*Megillah*, iv. 2) should be noted: 'The Temple that was destroyed, grass rose on the site, it is not plucked because of anguish' (and Rashi, for example, *Megillah*, 28*a*, explained that 'they ask for mercy, that they may return to its original state'). In the *Commentary on the Mishnah* Maimonides remarks: 'They are not plucked because of sorrow, that people may grieve when grass is there, and try to rebuild it if they can, or that their hearts submit to God and they return to Him if it is impossible for them to rebuild it.' In the *Mishneh Torah*, *Hilkhot Tefillah*, xi. 10, he writes: 'If grass has sprung up in them, the blades are plucked and left there, so that the people may be stirred to rebuild the ruined edifices.'

intellectual, spiritual, social, and personal tendencies, but this plan has not yet been fully implemented, even during Moses' time. The Messianic state will not only be something reconstructed and restored, but a new reality which will be the first to implement fully the Torah's design and enable a maximum of people to approach the final objective, which is improvement of the soul and intellectual perfection.[39] Eretz Yisrael, the scene of the Messianic vision, is not only the place with which the uniqueness and chosenness of the Jewish people are linked; without it neither the universal vision nor the personal one can be realized. Just as exile intensifies the adverse phenomena that preclude prophecy, and as the Messianic era increases its chances of revival, so it is with intellectual perfection.[40] The Messianic mission is important to the community and the individual, including the philosopher.

Maimonides' Messianic scenario shows that the political dimension was of central importance. Jewish sovereignty—although not aggressive or expansionist—is crucial. While the state is not an end in itself (its

[39] It seems that this is a reply to those who claim that the perfect man, the philosopher, does not need the Messianic era because he can reach the desired goal, 'to know God alone', on his own, and thereby merit life in the world to come. There is a fundamental parallel between the Messianic era and the Torah in its entirety, with its commandments and its wisdom. Both serve as a means to attain life in the next world. His comments at the end of *Hilkhot Melakhim* regarding the Messianic era as the authentic and superior means (as quoted above) should be compared to those in *Hilkhot Yesode ha-Torah*, iv. 13, about the Torah's precepts being another means to the same end: 'For the knowledge of these things gives primarily composure to the mind. They are the precious boon bestowed by God, to promote social well-being on earth, and enable men to obtain bliss in the life hereafter.' The anonymous commentator on this part of the *Mishneh Torah* (R. Yom Tov Lipmann Muelhausen, as recently suggested by Ephraim Kupfer) apparently grasped the connection between the two passages, i.e. the two means, and integrated Messianic terminology into his interpretation of the passage in *Yesode ha-Torah*: 'And all these are for the sake of an orderly society, as in their performance there will be peace in the world, harm will depart, and man will be able to know his Creator and he will attain life in the world to come.' This is a masterful summation of Maimonides' views in *Hilkhot Teshuvah* and *Melakhim*. Consequently, the abstract possibility for an individual to attain life in the world to come exists, but a suitable preparatory reality is lacking; whereas in the Messianic era reality will suit aspiration and the opportunity will be within reach. Indeed, when all is said and done, the same holds true for the individual as for the community (see also *Guide*, iii. 51).

[40] Implicit here is a decisive and instructive distinction between R. Judah Halevi's theory (*Kuzari*, iv. 25) and Maimonides' theory concerning the Torah's ever-increasing influence upon Christianity and Islam and their coming ever closer to Judaism. In R. Judah Halevi's view of the Jewish people's influence on other nations—a kind of theory of Israel's mission, the 'light unto the gentiles'—Exile is given a major role; in Maimonides' teaching the influence is primarily located in Eretz Yisrael in the Messianic era. As it is generally assumed that the views of R. Judah Halevi and Maimonides are identical, I hope to elaborate on this contrast in a separate article.

telos being found in the spiritual realm), it is here an indispensable instrument. Political restoration and social normalcy are prerequisites for national excellence and individual well-being.

VIII

Eretz Yisrael in its various aspects—the Temple and the Sanhedrin, monarchy and sovereignty, the Jewish people dwelling in its land—is a focus in many spheres, halakhic and philosophic, and it does not appear solely in Maimonides' Messianic teaching; it is also revealed in spiritual consciousness. It is a legacy, a fact, a hope and a promise, a fundamental means to prophecy and to spiritual and intellectual perfection. A basic observation concerning this theme in particular and Maimonides' teaching in general is in order here: it should not be assumed that these things are said solely from a talmudic perspective and are less significant from a philosophic point of view. The epistemology of the medieval religious philosophers was based on the assumption that religious tradition is the source of reliable information which complements other sources of knowledge (senses, reason). An axiom of medieval philosophic thought is that the religious and philosophic traditions are intertwined—not without tension or conflict, but it is generally possible, and necessary, to reconcile them.

No one questions the existence in Maimonides' teaching of associations and facts dictated by the tradition, which nothing in the world can dislodge—Eretz Yisrael is the holiest of all lands, and it belongs to the Israelite people, handed down from their ancestors; it is the scene of the realization of the Messianic dream. Maimonides drew upon the words of the Sages, but this was made part and parcel of his doctrine and outlook, either literally or in a changed form. One should not overlook these points of traditional lore that could be sharpened or blurred. Maimonides, in fact, honed and polished, and the emotion or passion of his expression is sometimes discernible. Maimonides' observations on the holiness of Jerusalem are perhaps the most salient, as a result both of their phrasing and of the idea of holiness in them. I have demonstrated elsewhere that in most cases Maimonides attributes holiness to God, and the holiness ascribed to various objects (such as Torah scrolls, *mezuzot*, phylacteries, the holy language) stems from this singular and specific source and is teleological.[41] The sanctity of

[41] See, for example, *Hilkhot Qeri'at Shema'*, iii. 5; *Sefer Torah*, x. 2; *Tefillin*, iv. 14, 25; *Mezuzah*, v. 4; *Ẓiẓit*, iii. 9; etc.

Jerusalem, however, was created in a particular manner by the divine presence; holiness results from the presence of the *Shekhinah*. God's presence renders space sacred.

> Now why is it my contention that as far as the sanctuary and Jerusalem were concerned the first sanctification hallowed them for all time to come, whereas the sanctification of the rest of the Land of Israel, which involved the laws of the Sabbatical year and tithes and like matters, did not hallow the land for all time to come? Because the sanctity of the Sanctuary and of Jerusalem derives from the Divine Presence, which could not be banished.[42]

These words reverberated and left their mark on the link to Jerusalem in particular, and to Eretz Yisrael in general, although Maimonides himself underscored the distinction between them from the perspective of the concept of holiness; the sacredness of the Land is unlike the sacredness of Jerusalem. The following passage is very instructive, for it identifies a common aspect of eternity shared by Jerusalem and the Jewish people.

> He called Jerusalem a legacy because of the permanence of its sanctity and its eternal existence. Of [Jerusalem] the prophet said: 'nor will he forsake his inheritance', as he had already said, at the start, that God chose Jerusalem to be the place upon which the Divine Presence would settle, and He chose Israel for his people, may its virtue be exalted. And then he said that the Lord will not cast off this nation, which he chose for his inheritance, nor [will he cast off] that same place which he chose. And he said, 'For the Lord has chosen Zion: he has desired it for his habitation' (Ps. 132: 13). 'For the Lord has chosen Jacob to himself, Israel for his peculiar possession' (Ps. 135: 4). 'For the Lord will not cast off his people, nor will he forsake his inheritance' (Ps. 94: 14). And he had already made it plain that its sanctity is eternal and said 'This is my resting place forever' (Ps. 132: 14).[43]

In other words—place and nation, inheritance and chosenness.

This determination of Jerusalem's eternal holiness and chosenness on the one hand, and of the Jewish nation on the other, ought to be interwoven into the triple strand which also includes the eternity of the bond between the Land of Israel and the people of Israel. In the *Book of Commandments*, Maimonides develops a comprehensive halakhic theory (concerning sanctification of the new moon), which remains

[42] *Bet ha-Beḥirah*, vi. 16. See e.g. *Tosafot*, *Yevamot*, 82*b* (and parallels).

[43] *Commentary on the Mishnah*, *Zevaḥim*, xiv. 8 (94). The Mishnah says: 'They came to Jerusalem, altars were banned, and they were no longer allowed and it became an inheritance.'

controversial and continues to be discussed frequently; in that context one captivating expression stands out:

Suppose we were to posit by way of illustration that the inhabitants of the Land of Israel should disappear from there—*far be it from the Lord to let it come about, for He has assured [us] that He will not altogether efface the remnants of [our] Nation*;—[suppose, however, further] that no Court should be there, and that outside of the Land of Israel there should be no court which has received Ordination in the Land [of Israel: under such circumstances] our reckoning would prove of no avail whatever to us in any repects. [This is because] we are not to reckon the months and intercalate the years outside of the Land [of Israel] save only under aforesaid conditions, as we have explained; [it being written], 'For out of Zion shall go forth the Law'.[44]

Students of Maimonides exert themselves to find a source or proof of this promise that Eretz Yisrael will never be totally without a Jewish population.[45] Notwithstanding the determination that surfaces relevant to our topic—which may be formulated as 'Jerusalem, the Jewish people, and Eretz Yisrael are one because of God's will and choice'—is unaltered and maintains its significance.

On reading the description of Tu bi-Shevaṭ or the prayer for dew in S. Y. Agnon's *Korot Betenu* (pp. 49, 56), one understands the importance of literary formulation and of historical memory preserved and strengthened by literary description which affords a vicarious experience in the absence of a direct and immediate one. Maimonides' remarks helped to restore the Temple to active historical consciousness. It is also possible to say that remarks like these served as a shield

[44] The *Book of Commandments*, positive commandment no. 53 (ed. Kafiḥ, p. 133). The halakhic issue is so difficult and complicated that Maimonides adds: 'On this point; [that is to say, in their attempt to reinstitute the seeing of the new moon for the purpose of establishing the first of the month], the heretics called Karaites have erred. [It should thus ever be] a principle [with us] not to avow anything but what the Sages [have taught], while the followers [of the Karaites] walk with them in thickest darkness.' Naḥmanides, fully cognizant of the originality of the Maimonidean view, criticizes this at great length; see the superb halakhic discussion of it by R. Joseph Dov Soloveitchik, *Kovetz Ḥiddushe Torah* (Jerusalem, n.d.), pp. 47 ff. (first published in *ha-Pardess*, vol. 17). Maimonides seems to be reacting to Geonic criticism of the centrality of Eretz Yisrael; it is as if he were saying that Ben-Meir is right and not R. Sa'adya Gaon.

[45] R. Kafiḥ's note ad loc., n. 51, does not shed any light on this, nor is there any proof in his comment. On the other hand, see e.g. the book of responsa *Nefesh Ḥayyah*, by Rabbi Ḥayyim Eleazar Wax (para. 1, p. 5), in which he remarks: 'Here, in any case, Maimonides' statement that should the Jewish people disappear from Eretz Yisrael, Heaven forbid, God will be praised as he promised us, in the Torah, that he would not destroy this nation, is enigmatic. *It is not understood.* He only promised us that we would not be completely destroyed; He did not at all promise that we would not disappear from Eretz Yisrael.'

against any spiritualizing exegesis which is liable to find Jerusalem in Lithuania or New York or in the Jewish soul.[46] The divine presence is immovable, the parameters of its sanctity unchangeable, and it is impossible to find a substitute for it.

The tie to Eretz Yisrael is revealed and expressed not only in abstract and complicated laws, not only in traditional ideas concerning the Temple, David's kingdom, the Sanhedrin or Messianic beliefs, but also in certain emotion-laden passages. For example, there is a line at the beginning of the *Iggeret Teman* that is lacking in most editions: 'When we departed from the West to behold the pleasantness of the Lord and to visit His holy place' (trans. B. Cohen, p. i.). Towards the end of the letter, in connection with the Messianic hope, we get another glimpse of his sentiment: 'He will gather our nation, assemble our exiles and redeem us from our degradation' (ibid., p. xv). In the *Book of Commandments*, in explaining the prohibition, 'thou shalt not deliver unto his master a bondman [that is escaped from his master unto thee]', Maimonides stresses the halakhic detail (which for some reason he omitted from the section on the reasons for the commandments in *Guide of the Perplexed*) that the precept is valid only in Eretz Yisrael: 'In no circumstances is [the bondman] to return to his serfdom, seeing that he has come to dwell in the clean (or pure) land, which has been chosen for the exalted people' (trans. Charles B. Chavel (London, 1940), ii. 242). The autobiographical gem in the *Mishneh Torah* (*Hilkhot Ta'aniyyot*, v. 9) describing his behaviour on the eve of Tish'ah be-Av, poignantly conveys a deep sense of Exile and suffering:

The aforementioned rule applies to the general public who cannot endure excess privation. The practice of the pious men of old, however, was as

[46] R. Isaac b. Samuel of Acre (*Ozar ha-Ḥayyim*, in MS) exemplifies another approach to Eretz Yisrael's centrality or exclusivity as regards prophecy: a far-reaching, spiritualizing approach (see above concerning the cessation of prophecy). He interprets the phrase 'Prophecy does not occur outside of Eretz Yisrael' as follows: 'The true meaning of outside the Land and Eretz Yisrael in this case is not land but the souls that dwell in the earth. Land is the habitat of flesh and blood. If the soul dwelling in the land is of Jacob's seed then it surely dwells in Eretz Yisrael. If a soul not of the seed of Jacob son of Isaac son of Abraham our father dwells in the land, it is certainly dwelling outside the Land. Though if [physically] be located in Eretz Yisrael, in Jerusalem, Providence will not impart its presence to it and the spirit of prophecy will not rest upon it, because it is certainly [located] outside the land.' Quoted by M. Idel, 'Eretz Yisrael we-ha-Qabbalah bi-Me'ah ha-Shalosh 'Esre', *Shalem*, 3 (1981), 126 n. 40. He correctly notes that 'Eretz Yisrael is here translated into a term referring to every Jew'. Spiritualization of Eretz Yisrael in its various forms deserves systematic and exhaustive discussion. For a good example of spiritualization, see R. Menaḥem ha-Me'iri, *Bet ha-Beḥirah*, *Ketubbot*, 111*a*.

follows: On the eve of the ninth of Ab, each man in his solitude would be served with dry bread and salt, and he would dip this in water and eat it while seated between the oven and the stove. He would wash it down with a pitcher of water, drunk in sadness, desolation, and tears, like a person seated before his dead kinsman. This procedure, or one very much like it, is the one appropriate to scholars. In all my life, I have never eaten cooked food—even cooked lentils—on the eve of the ninth of Ab, unless this day was a Sabbath.

This sense of personal involvement, this existential posture, may also be at the heart of his quotation of aggadic statements. There was no objective need to cite them; he could not be faulted for omitting them, as he is sometimes criticized by careful students for overlooking or failing to include a certain halakhic detail. Hence the statements concerning the virtue of living in Eretz Yisrael and its magnetic appeal invite careful scrutiny.

The well-known remarks in *Hilkhot Melakhim*, v. 10, 11 are thus appropriate for the conclusion and summation of my paper, implying as they do that Eretz Yisrael has some inherent, intrinsic superiority:

The greatest of our Sages used to kiss [the rocks] on the borders of Palestine. They used to kiss the stones of the land and roll themselves in its dust. The Rabbis said that the sins of him who lives in Palestine are forgiven. Even if one walks four cubits in it, one is assured of life in the world to come. So too, one who is buried there will obtain atonement; it is as though that place [where one lies] were an altar which effects atonement, as it is said: 'And the land doth make expiation for His people' (Deut. 32–43). In [forecasting] punishment, [the prophet] says: 'And thou thyself shalt die in an unclean land' (Amos 4: 17). There is no comparison between one whom Palestine receives while he is living and one whom it receives after his death; nevertheless the greatest among our wise men brought their dead there. Think of Jacob, our father, and of Joseph, the righteous!

These are basically aggadic remarks, and although I am convinced that *aggadah* and *halakhah* cannot be completely separated, they deserve special consideration because of the length, fervour, and selection of these illustrations and perspectives. *Aggadah* is nevertheless relatively rare in this magnificent book of legal decisions and its very presence, even at the end of the fourteen books, signals something to us. It provides guidelines for intellectual or socio-personal orientations. We know that some of Maimonides' ideas are occasionally embedded, explicitly or implicitly, in exegesis. Likewise, we should realize that a clear cohesive point of view may surface from aggadic statements, which are often seasoned with emphases and linguistic effects of his own.

IX

Maimonides' teaching on Eretz Yisrael is marked by tension and dialectic; it is a microcosm of his larger, all-embracing philosophy which is also characterized by tension, conflict, and dialectic struggle. His teaching points to the conflict between rational, spiritual, and philosophic inclinations, and practical, earthly, and national motifs, as well as between individual perfection and societal improvement. One is not dealing with a contradiction but with tension and confrontation.

There is then, a pot-pourri of ideas and emphases. On the one hand, there is Eretz Yisrael with its Sanctuary and holiness. Maimonides' teaching is saturated with Eretz Yisrael on account of its inherent values of tradition, his comments on Jerusalem, and his comprehensive concept of *halakhah*—and all this had an influence in the long run, both directly and indirectly, on how Eretz Yisrael is viewed: not as an abstract entity, but as an absolutely necessary reality and a source of inspiration. On the other hand, a principal focus of his teaching is the people's condition and its bond with Eretz Yisrael and with stable social conditions. From this perspective political independence does not apparently occupy a principal position. 'In the time of the Temple' has multiple meanings. It should also be remembered that he perceived Eretz Yisrael in the broad context of historical and political concepts which need to be carefully assessed and, above all, of his Messianic doctrine and vision of the End of Days.

PART III

HISTORY

14

'At Our Place in al-Andalus', 'At Our Place in the Maghreb'

JOSHUA BLAU

MAIMONIDES frequently speaks of customs and expressions used 'at our place' (*'indanā*, literally *chez-nous*), often being more explicit and speaking of 'at our place in al-Andalus', or usually, 'at our place in the Maghreb'. A. Geiger,[1] the first to deal with these expressions, considered them always to refer to Maimonides' actual place of abode: when in Spain, he wrote 'at our place in al-Andulus', whereas when in North-west Africa he used 'at our place in the Maghreb'. However, H. Kroner[2] claimed that Maimonides wrote his commentary to *Mishnah Pesaḥim* in Spain, since he mentions 'at our place in the island [i.e. peninsula] of al-Andalus'. Yet as in the *Book of Commandments*, which was *not* written in Spain, Maimonides also speaks of 'at our place in al-Andalus', and in his *Commentary on the Mishnah*, alongside with the usual 'at our place in the Maghreb', there is also one instance of 'at our place in al-Andalus', I. Friedlaender rejected the plausibility of Geiger's thesis.[3] He proposed that in writing 'at our place in al-Andalus' Maimonides was referring to his place of origin, while with 'at our place in the Maghreb' (and even 'at our place' alone), he referred to his actual place of abode, that is, to North-west Africa. Not only does Friedlaender's theory postulate two different usages of 'at our place'—one referring to Maimonides' place of origin, the other to his actual place of abode—it also does not explain the very frequent use of 'at our place in the Maghreb', especially in his commentary to the last *seder* of the Mishnah, viz., *Ṭohorot*; although, as attested in the colophon and proved by various references to Egypt, Maimonides

1 A. Geiger, *Moses b. Maimon: Studien I* (Breslau, 1850), 60–1 n. 41.

2 H. Kroner, *Maimonides Commentar zum Tractat Pesaḥim* (Berlin, 1901), 9 n. 19.

3 I. Friedlaender, *Arabisch-Deutsches Lexicon zum Sprachgebrauch des Maimonides* (Frankfurt, 1902), p. xviii n. 1.

finished his *Commentary on the Mishnah* in Egypt. My own proposal is that in using 'at our place' and even 'at our place in the Maghreb' (and of course, also 'at our place in al-Andalus'), Maimonides invariably referred to his place of origin, Spain. Thus, Maghreb, in the usage of Maimonides (as also in the writings of some Arab geographers), may have been applied in both a restricted and in a broad sense. In the restricted sense, it denotes North-west Africa, perhaps even in contrast to Spain; in the broad sense, it includes Spain. It is always in the broad sense that 'Maghreb' is used whenever Maimonides speaks of 'at our place in the Maghreb'. This is demonstrated by the fact that when speaking of Maghrebian customs, for example, Maimonides cites *Spanish* sages as practising them; or, likewise, by his adducing as Maghrebian expressions which are known from other sources as Spanish Arabic. Moreover, only the assumption that 'Maghreb' may include Spain accounts for Maimonides enumerating various countries, including *bilād a-gharb*, 'the Western countries', without mentioning Spain: Spain is included in the Western countries! The fact that 'at our place [in the Maghreb]' invariably refers to Spain also has dialectal importance: words referred to as being used 'at our place [in the Maghreb]' have to be regarded as reflecting Spanish Arabic.

15
The Early Decades of Ayyūbid Rule

JOSEPH DRORY

CLASSICAL and modern historians, both European and Middle Eastern, generally share the opinion that the appointment of Saladin as vizier of the ailing Fāṭimid dynasty and his ultimate rise to the sultanate marked a new era in the history of Egypt and the Middle East. Textbooks speak of Saladin's ascent as giving 'new life to Egypt and the entire Muslim world'. The romantic biographer S. Lane-Poole called Saladin's epoch 'the most glorious in the history of Muslim domination in Egypt',[1] and even A. Ehrenkreutz, a critical observer of Saladin's right to glory and immortality, admits that he brought about 'major changes which decisively affected Egypt's history'.[2]

It is widely known that Saladin's fame and reputation were achieved mainly as result of his military successes in Syria and Palestine against the Crusaders and his political skill in uniting Arab countries against foreign intruders. These achievements, however, can hardly be regarded as having brought 'new life' to *Egypt*. One must look beyond for the facts that made the rule of Saladin and his successors outstanding for Egyptian history and society. Or to put it differently: what did the Ayyūbids really alter in Egypt? Was this anything more than a mere change of policy made by those standing at the head of the Egyptian state?

The conventional reply to this question is that Egypt under the reign of Saladin and his successors returned to the sphere of orthodox (Sunnī) Islam. An appreciation of the different aspects of this new reality may therefore enrich our understanding of the environment with which Maimonides came into contact.

The return of Egypt to the Sunnī circle of influence meant that formal and traditional allegiance was henceforth given to the 'Abbāsid

[1] Stanley Lane-Poole, *A History of Egypt in the Middle Ages* (repr. London, 1968), 190.
[2] Andrew Ehrenkreutz, *Saladin* (Albany, 1972), 234.

caliph, whose seat was in Baghdad. This move, ending the rule of the lightly rooted, almost foreign, Ismāʿīlī dynasty in Egypt, was a remarkable accomplishment for the young ruler in his rise to power and a promising step for the future.[3]

The daily features which characterized Egypt's return to Sunnī Islam were as follows:

1. The external signs (*rusūm*) of Fāṭimid authority were abolished. The clearest signal was the changing of the prayer sermon, in Muḥarram 567 (September 1171). The Shīʿī sermon was replaced by a Sunnī version, acknowledging the ruling ʿAbbāsid caliph and praising past Sunnī heroes.[4] Coins with Fāṭimid verses were withdrawn from circulation, and new coins bearing Sunnī formulas were minted to replace them. Pro-Fāṭimid silver inscriptions in silver in the mosques of Cairo were taken down.[5] The treasures of the Fāṭimid caliphs were sold and their magnificent palaces were allowed to fall into disuse.[6]

2. Buildings that had served the old regime as judicial or penal institutions were turned into Shāfiʿī academies,[7] allowing Saladin to claim that the days of evil and oppression had ended and that a period of learning and knowledge had begun.

3. The judicial system was re-examined. Shīʿī judges were discharged, and new Shāfiʿī *qāḍī*s were given the mandate of chief justices in Egypt.[8]

4. The commitment and loyalty of the new regime to Sharīʿa laws and moral obligations received wide emphasis. Among the steps taken were abolishing illegal and oppressive taxes,[9] rectifying the monetary system by withdrawing coins of doubtful content and circulating coins

[3] Saladin established Sunnism in Egypt under the explicit insistence of his sultan, Nūr al-Dīn. He himself did not favour it. He doubted his own capacity to overcome the expected opposition of the local court and regarded the Fāṭimids as future allies if Nūr al-Dīn were to oust him from office. However, his fear of not fulfilling his overlord's orders was so great that he overcame his hesitations and proclaimed Sunnī norms.

[4] Ibn al-Athīr, *Al-Kāmil fi l-Taʾrīkh*, ed. C. J. Tornberg (Leiden, 1851–76), ix. 241; al-Maqrīzī, *Kitāb al-Sulūk*, ed. M. Ziadeh (Cairo, 1936–58), i. 44, 45; Ehrenkreutz, *Saladin*, 89.

[5] Ehrenkreutz, *Saladin*, 104; K. Creswell, *The Muslim Architecture of Egypt* (Oxford, 1952), pt. i, 37 n. 9.

[6] Al-Maqrīzī, *Khiṭaṭ* (Bulaq, 1853), i. 496.

[7] Ibn al-Athīr, *Kāmil*, ix. 240; al-Maqrīzī, *Khiṭaṭ*, ii. 363.

[8] Ibn al-Athīr, *Kāmil*, ix. 240; al-Maqrīzī, *Khiṭaṭ*, ii. 233; Ehrenkreutz, *Saladin*, 87.

[9] Ibn Wāṣil, *Mufarrij al-Kurūb*, ed. J. Shayyāl (Cairo, 1953), ii. 473, suppl. 8, citing Abū Shāmah, *Al-Rawḍatayn* (Cairo, 1872), i. 205; al-Maqrīzī, *Sulūk*, i. 86; Ehrenkreutz, *Saladin*, 101, 105.

of better quality in their stead,[10] giving half of the Zakāt money to the state treasury for the traditional goals of freeing slaves or financing the war against the infidels,[11] expelling non-Muslims, mainly Jews, from governmental posts,[12] reasserting the ancient discriminatory law forbidding non-Muslims to ride on horses and mules,[13] making public prayer compulsory,[14] cancelling the levies on pilgrims travelling via the Red Sea to Mecca,[15] and limiting the production of forbidden intoxicants to particular breweries (*buyūt al-mizr*) which produced a special kind of beer.[16]

5. The dynasty maintained a positive attitude towards medicine and public health. That policy, undoubtedly an imitation of the Saljūq welfare-state model, is described enthusiastically by the traveller Ibn Jubayr. He portrays the imposing Cairo hospital established by Saladin,[17] its stores of drugs, different sections (including separate halls for the mentally ill and for women), and the male nurses who

[10] Al-Maqrīzī, *Sulūk*, i. 99.

[11] Al-Maqrīzī, *Sulūk*, i. 44; al-Maqrīzī, *Khiṭaṭ*, i. 108; ii. 233; H. Rabie, *The Financial System of Egypt* (Oxford, 1972), 96.

[12] Al-Maqrīzī, *Sulūk*, i. 47.

[13] Ibid. 77; E. Ashtor, 'Saladin and the Jews', *HUCA* 27 (1956), 306.

[14] Al-Maqrīzī, *Sulūk*, i. 47.

[15] Ibn Jubayr, *Riḥla*, ed. H. Naṣṣār (Cairo, 1955), 25–6; al-Maqrīzī, *Sulūk*, i. 64, 74; id., *Khiṭaṭ*, 233; Ehrenkreutz, *Saladin*, 157.

[16] Al-Maqrīzī, *Sulūk*, i. 73; *Khiṭaṭ*, i. 105; Rabie, *Financial System of Egypt*, 119; Ehrenkreutz, *Saladin*, 109.

[17] Maimonides, in a letter to R. Joseph b. Judah, wrote that 'a very high esteem of my knowledge of medicine was developed by important court personalities . . . This led me into spending the whole day in al-Qāhira [he then lived in Fusṭāṭ, about 3 km south] visiting the sick' (*Iggerot ha-Rambam*, ed. D. Z. Baneth (Jerusalem, 1946), 69; S. Baron, *Essays on Maimonides* (New York, 1941) 271). In another letter, he relates that he devotes a considerable part of his time to healing the sick people of the court (*Teshuvot ha-Rambam we-Iggerotaw*, ed. A. Lichtenberg (Leipzig, 1859), ii. 28; Baron, *Essays on Maimonides*, 271.) Ibn abī Uṣaybi'a says that Maimonides served Saladin himself as court physician; for a Hebrew translation of the paragraph, see B. Lewis, 'Jews and Judaism in Arab sources' (Heb.), *Metzudah*, 3–4 (London, 1945) 177. But this fact has not been accepted literally by modern scholars; see id., *Islam in History* (London 1973), 175–6; Ashtor, 'Saladin and the Jews', *HUCA* 27 (1956), 312 n. 25. However, most would agree that Maimonides maintained close intimacy with Ayyūbid rulers and courtiers, and that the 'gates of the Royal Palace were opened to him some years after Saladin left Egypt' (ibid.). On his famous connections with al-Qāḍī al-Fāḍil, see the tract of al-Wāsiṭī, in N. A. Stillman, *The Jews of Arab Lands* (Philadelphia, 1979), 276. (See also below, n. 43.)

It is possible, as S. Muntner has suggested in his edn. of Mosheh b. Tibbon's Heb. trans. of Maimonides' *Commentary on the Aphorisms of Hippocrates* (Jerusalem, 1961, p. viii) that Maimonides was acquainted with the medical institution established by Saladin for public health care, and that he even served there. Cf. his reponse to a colleague who faced similar halakhic problems, in Moses b. Maimon, *Responsa*, ed. J. Blau (Jerusalem, 1957), ii. 302.

cared for and fed the patients.[18] The location of the hospital, in a monumental but dilapidated Fāṭimid hall, was in line with the public relations–oriented policy of the new regime, which was to make use of empty, extravagant, but unneeded buildings as welfare institutions serving the entire population.

6. There was a surge in the construction of Sunnī religious schools or mosques. Large sums were poured into alms-giving, and the state-supported clerical sector of the economy was inflated.

Following this general description of Saladin's activities in the course of 'sunnizing' the country, in all of which he consciously emphasized the gap between himself and the former sovereigns, one must also consider certain elements which inevitably served to balance the equation.

1. Egypt's return to Sunnī Islam did not meet with insurmountable obstacles. The majority of Muslims were Sunnīs. There were no protracted military struggles or cultural conflicts connected with the establishment of the 'new (Sunnī) order'. The Fāṭimid opposition was scant and lacked widespread public support.[19]

2. The undertaking of a series of quick, ostentatious actions aimed at giving public expression to the new political situation created when a new sultan rises to power was a common practice, even when the new ruler did not follow an exceedingly alien dynasty.[20] Saladin's 'sunnizing' moves were wholly in keeping with the tradition of a new Muslim sovereign.

3. The Ayyūbid success in eradicating existing norms and traditions was limited: the Egyptians continued to adhere to their old ways in many areas of activity. The Ayyūbids were not successful in changing the customs practised in the markets,[21] in prohibiting popular festivals,[22] or in implementing the tax reductions introduced by Saladin.[23]

We may sum up by saying that the Ayyūbid rulers, while endeavouring to shape the country according to their tastes and preferences, tried to enforce an accelerated rhythm of orthodoxy. Their efforts were

[18] Ibn Jubayr, *Riḥla*, 20–1. Al-Maqrīzī, *Khiṭaṭ*, i. 407, ii. 203, gives details on the medical and paramedical team.

[19] Ibn Wāṣil, *Mufarrij al-Kurūb*, ii. 276.

[20] For instance, the undertaking of al-'Azīz 'Uthmān, Saladin's son, when the former became ruler of Damascus; al-Maqrīzī, *Sulūk*, i. 135.

[21] Ibid. i. 134.

[22] Al-Maqrīzī, *Khiṭaṭ*, i. 493.

[23] Ibid. i. 105; Rabie, *Financial System of Egypt*, 102, 119.

generally successful. But this was not the only effect of Ayyūbid domination over Egypt. As a result of Saladin's own particular background, education, political tradition, and familial connections, his rise to power had further significant implications for Egypt.

1. Egyptian involvement in the wars against the Crusaders was increased. In the last days of the Fāṭimids, the Egyptian army had practically ceased fighting the Christians, with the exception of those instances in which Egyptian navies were sent to attack European flotillas or Frankish ports.[24] There had even been groups within Egypt which actually turned to the Crusaders for help in their internal struggles,[25] and this practice was now brought to a halt. From now on, Egyptian warriors, following the example of Saladin, joined other Muslim armies in fighting the Franks.[26] The eloquent dispatches calling for military aid were now responded to both positively and efficiently. Saladin's boastful claims in his letters to the caliph that 'not one year elapses [without] a raid on the Franks on land and on sea, on animals and on ships'[27] may not have reflected the entire truth, but it pointed to the new policy of the Ayyūbids and their lofty intentions.

2. The links with other countries conquered by Saladin and ruled by his relatives (Damascus, Aleppo, towns in Mesopotamia) were strengthened. As the rule over Saladin's dominions was divided among his relatives and each was eager to enhance his share at all costs, their dominions often changed hands. The rulers, officers, or policy-makers of Egypt were often former (or future) rulers of Syrian or Mesopotamian towns. Egypt drew nearer to other Islamic states, not out of noble intentions but for sound political reasons. Its sovereigns did not restrain themselves from an 'unending tale of plots, revolts, ephemeral alliances, treacheries, calculated perfidies, dethronements'[28] typical of the Ayyūbid political tradition.

[24] Historians blamed the (Fāṭimid) Egyptians for not attending to the Franks, and praised Saladin for his devotion to the *Jihād* and reconquest of Muslim territories; see e.g. Ibn Taghrībirdī, *Al-Nujūm al-Zāhira* (Cairo, 1935), 179–80.

[25] The Fāṭimid vizier Shāwar called them in against Nūr al-Dīn (Ibn al-Athīr, *Kāmil*, ix. 197, 222) or Shīrkūh (Ibn al-Athīr, *Kāmil*, ix. 213), the Cairenes who sought to restore a Fāṭimid dynasty (al-Maqrīzī, *Sulūk*, i. 53), a group of Egyptian notables against Shāwar (Ibn al-Athīr, *Kāmil*, ix. 211), and others.

[26] In 583 (1187), the troops of Saladin's brother al-'Adil conquered Majdal Yābā and Jaffa on the Palestinian coast (Ibn al-Athīr, *Kāmil*, ix. 356, 357; al-Maqrīzī, *Sulūk*, i. 94, 95).

[27] Ibn Wāṣil, *Mufarrij al-Kurūb*, ii. 25.

[28] H. A. R. Gibb, 'The Achievement of Saladin', *Studies on the Civilization of Islam* (Boston, 1962), 95. Al-'Ādil was deputy in Egypt when Saladin was in Syria: the years 570/1174 (al-Maqrīzī, *Sulūk*, i. 58), 573/1178 (ibid. i. 65), and 578/1182 (Ibn al-Athīr,

The effect of opening the window towards the East was twofold. On the one hand, new economic opportunities were opened up for merchants, dealers, and financial investors. Egyptian trade with Eastern countries increased. No less important, the movement of 'Eastern' jurists, religious scholars, theologians, writers, and 'pen aristocrats' to and from Egypt also increased. At the same time, the all-too-frequent changes of rule destroyed the feeling of security, permanence, or stability that a civilian population needs. It increased the already great mistrust and indifference felt by an unconcerned population towards its rulers' actions.

3. Egypt gained a predominant position in Yemen. Saladin, seeking a place of aṣylum (*'iṣma*) for his family from the anticipated wrath of his overlord Nūr al-Dīn, sent his brother Shams al-Dawla Tūrān Shāh to conquer Yemen, including the port of Aden, in 569 (1174).[29] Following the successful effort, governors, officers, and troops were sent from Egypt to maintain both order and Ayyūbid sovereignty over that country. The Yemen's later rulers were sons of the Ayyūbid family.[30] This political annexation, apparently carried out for selfish motives, increased Saladin's credit with the 'Abbāsid caliph, since by this act he imposed Sunnī Islam in Yemen and removed a false prophet[31] who had claimed to be the *mahdī*.

4. Egypt adopted the modes and style of government that had prevailed in the Muslim East ever since the middle of the eleventh century. The Ayyūbid rulers introduced Saljūq models. In the words of Bernard Lewis, 'While creating a new political power in Egypt, Saladin was at the same time restoring and tightening the bonds that bound Egypt to Eastern Islam.'[32] That tendency had various ramifications, the most obvious of which was a widespread penetration of soldiers and officers of Turkish origin into the army, while non-Turkish units (e.g. Armenian, Sudanese) were disbanded.[33] The

Kāmil, ii. 323; al-Maqrīzī, *Sulūk*, i. 79. But in 579/1183 he moved to Aleppo, and his seat in Egypt was taken by Saladin's ambitious nephew, Taqī al-Dīn 'Umar, who was the guardian of the former's son, al-Afḍal 'Alī (Ibn al-Athīr, *Kāmil*, ix. 331; al-Maqrīzī, *Sulūk*, i. 82). In 582/1186, al-'Ādil came back to rule Egypt, this time as guardian of another nephew, Saladin's son, al-'Azīz 'Uthmān (Ibn al-Athīr, *Kāmil*, ix. 345; al-Maqrīzī, *Sulūk*, i. 91). The list of examples of these recurrent substitutions can be easily extended.

[29] Ibn al-Athīr, *Kāmil*, ix. 261, 310; al-Maqrīzī, *Sulūk*, i. 52; id., *Khiṭaṭ*, ii. 203–4.

[30] See further in al-Maqrīzī, *Sulūk*, i. 72, 74.

[31] Maimonides refers in his *Epistle to Yemen* to a Jewish false prophet who appeared in the Yemen at the same time.

[32] B. Lewis, 'Egypt and Syria', in *Cambridge History of Islam* (Cambridge, 1970), i. 205.

[33] Ibn Wāṣil, *Mufarrij al-Kurūb*, ii. 27; 489, suppl. 15; 479, suppl. 10.

Turks now gained predominance not only in the army but also in the upper echelons of the political establishment, whereas under the Fāṭimids the leading posts had been held by people qualified by their skills rather than their origins.[34]

The new reality was reflected in other ways too. 'Ayyūbid rule saw the construction of huge military forts, castles, and fortifications—Alexandria,[35] Damietta, and the Castle of Cairo.[36] Law and order was strictly enforced—for example, bedouin intruders were driven back into the desert,[37] and the system of granting concessions for the right to collect taxes (*iqṭā'*) was modified on the basis of the Zangid model. The right to a concession was now granted only following military service.[38] Similarly, the state was now active in promoting education. The state financed, controlled, and fostered a broader scale of teaching activity and enabled more people to enter educational institutions. Ibn Jubayr relates that in Alexandria he saw, for the first time, mature students streaming to governmental colleges (*madrasas*). Such students were now entitled to accommodation, instruction, and 'pocket money' at the state's expense.[39] Another major change was that mystical Ṣūfī orders, which appealed to popular religious sentiments, were granted a freer hand to operate. The seat of the last Fāṭimid viziers, Dār Sa'īd al-Su'adā, became a Ṣūfī convent (*khānqāh*) in 569 (1173–4).[40]

What effect, if any, did the rapid modification of Egyptian society have upon Maimonides' views, social relations, or range of influence? Was the new political, cultural, and social situation a relevant factor in his private world? It appears that the influence was limited, at least in so far as it gained explicit expression in his writings.

I would argue that Maimonides' contact with other Jewish communities, with wealthy Karaites, or with Islamic civilization as he observed it in Egypt was little influenced by the political, economic, or cultural transformation of the larger society.[41] Neither in his halakhic responsa nor in his philosophic writings do we find reference to the

[34] Ibn al-Athīr defines Saladin's revolution as 'transfer of authority from Shāwar and the Egyptians to the Turks' (Ibn al-Athīr, *Kāmil*, ix. 191).

[35] Ehrenkreutz, *Saladin*, 168.

[36] Al-Maqrīzī, *Sulūk*, i. 63.

[37] Ibid. i. 47, 54, 71, 73.

[38] Rabie, *Financial System of Egypt*, 29.

[39] Ibn Jubayr, *Riḥla*, 8.

[40] Al-Maqrīzī, *Khiṭaṭ*, ii. 415.

[41] See Maimonides' firm reply to Obadiah the Proselyte (*Responsa*, ed. Blau, ii. 726), in which he rejects the paganism of the Muslim pilgrimage rituals. Instead he stresses the pious, monotheistic intentions of Muslim pilgrims and lauds some of their scholars' monotheistic interpretation of these ancient customs. See also H. Lazarus-Yafeh, 'The Religious Dialectics of the Ḥadjdj', in her *Some Religious Aspects of Islam* (Leiden, 1981), 37.

political or military situation of this period. One fails to see how Maimonides' Messianic expectations or reflections upon the fate of cultures, religions, and nations were affected by current events. The mentality, language, and facts of civilization reflected in his writings are Muslim, but they might just as easily have been composed decades before or after, even in different Islamic countries. Although the 'guide of the perplexed' lived in Egypt at the time that such momentous events as the defeat of the Franks at Ḥiṭṭīn or the fall of Jerusalem to the Muslims took place, we hardly find any reference to these events in his works. The fact that Muslim rulers with whom he was acquainted[42] reconquered Palestine is not mentioned in any of his books or letters. If he were asked to state his preference between a Muslim and a Frankish Palestine, he would, I believe, have preferred Islamic rule,[43] but we have no record of an expression of jubilation at Muslim successes; his attitude was apparently one of indifference. Should one explain this by his natural cautiousness, which led him to stay the expression of premature joy? Or should one assume that as long as the Jews were only a minority in the Land of Israel, Maimonides simply did not care who ruled there?[44]

The significance, it seems, of studying the period in which Maimonides worked lies not in its capacity to explain his decisions, reactions, or social ties but in the fact that presenting the background against which he worked re-creates the authentic context for the Egyptian phase in his biography.

[42] In one of his letters, he related that 'It is unavoidable for me not to see him [the Ayyūbid sultan of Egypt] at the beginning of every day' (*Teshuvot ha-Rambam we-Iggerotaw*, ii. 281.

[43] Ibn al-Qifṭī mentions that Maimonides refused an invitation of the king(?) of the Franks in Ascalon to serve as his private doctor. On this, see Lewis, *Islam in History*, 173. On the other hand he did serve Ayyūbid rulers in Egypt. For his protector, al-Qāḍī al-Fāḍil, he composed a treatise on poisons and protection from deadly remedies. This little treatise was called, because of the dedication, *al-Risāla al-Fāḍiliyya*. He likewise dedicated two treatises to Saladin's son, the Sultan al-Afḍal 'Alī, in whose service he worked: *On the Regulation of Health* (*Fī Tadbīr al-Ṣiḥḥa*) and *Discourse on the Explanation of Symptoms* (*Maqāla fī Bayān al-A'rāḍ*). To another relative of Saladin, Taqī al-Dīn 'Umar, who was given full authority in Egypt when his uncle was in Syria, Maimonides dedicated an epistle on sexual intercourse (*Fil-Jimā'*).

[44] It is in this vein that we should relate to the forged letter, attributed to Maimonides, in which Saladin admits that 'even I, as well, do not have the right to rule in God's domain, because I know that the king [of the Jews] will come now and will take the countries from me and from them [the Franks]. But I had better luck, because from me the king of the Jews will take it in peace and not in war, [thus] I might find grace in his eyes.' See Neubauer, 'Une pseudo-biographie de Moïse Maïmonide', *REJ* 4 (1882), 176–7.

16

Saladin's Egypt and Maimonides

ANDREW S. EHRENKREUTZ

WHEN Maimonides settled in Alexandria in 1165, he could hardly have expected to witness so many dramatic events that would in subsequent decades decisively affect the course of Egyptian history. Interestingly enough, the rise of the great Jewish philosopher, physician, and social activist to public prominence in Egypt coincided chronologically and geographically with that of his famous Muslim contemporary, Saladin (born in 1137 or 1138, the year of Maimonides' birth),[1] whose career in Egypt opened a new chapter in the history of the Eastern Mediterranean. To be exact, of these two celebrities, Saladin was the first to set foot on Egyptian soil. In 1164, he distinguished himself during the expedition of a Syrian army commanded by his uncle Shīrkūh and sent to Cairo by Nūr al-Dīn, the Zangid ruler of Syria, to help the cause of Shāwar, an ousted Fāṭimid vizier. Once restored to power, Shāwar reneged on his financial promises, provoking a military reaction on the part of Shīrkūh. To save himself and the tottering Fāṭimid regime, Shāwar successfully appealed to the Crusaders for direct military intervention.

The fact that Maimonides was not dissuaded from moving to Egypt might have been because the 1164 confrontation, which ended in a deadlock at Bilbays, was resolved by means of negotiations that resulted in the simultaneous evacuation of Egypt by the Syrians and the Crusaders, and another lease on life for the Shī'ite caliphate of Cairo. In 1167, Shīrkūh led another army to Egypt. Once again Saladin played a decisive part in the operations of the Syrians, but as in

[1] This date is taken from S. D. Goitein, 'Moses Maimonides, Man of Action: A Revision of the Master's Biography in Light of the Geniza Documents', *Hommage à Georges Vajda: Études d'histoire et de pensée juives* (Louvain, 1980), 155–67, which has served as a source of other factual and bibliographic information concerning Maimonides' career in Egypt. Details concerning the career of Saladin are based on A. S. Ehrenkreutz, *Saladin* (Albany, NY, 1972).

1164, they had to return empty-handed because the Crusaders rushed to defend Shāwar's interests. This time the Christians were allowed to leave a token garrison in Cairo, manifesting their concern about Egypt's vulnerability.

As for the status of Jewish communities, in 1164 the Jewish community of Bilbays may have experienced some hardship because of the fighting between the Syrians and the Crusaders; and from May until August of 1167, the Jews and other civilian groups of Alexandria must have suffered privations during the tenacious defence of that city by Saladin against the superior forces of the Crusaders and the Egyptians. On the other hand, Fusṭāṭ, in the Fāṭimid capital, remained unharmed, and may have been one of the motives behind Maimonides' move to its Jewish quarter.

This did not prevent the war which engulfed the Nile delta in the fall and winter of 1168/9. This time it was the turn of the Crusaders, supported by a Pisan naval contingent, to launch a large-scale invasion of Lower Egypt. On 5 November 1168, the Crusaders captured Bilbays, which suffered plunder and conflagration, while civilians who failed to escape were either slain or enslaved. On 14 November the Crusader army laid siege to the Fāṭimid capital. Quarters that lay outside the city walls, including Fusṭāṭ, were put to the torch and looted. The Fāṭimid caliph al-ʿĀḍid appealed to Nūr al-Dīn, who hastily sent yet another army, once again under the command of Shīrkūh accompanied by Saladin. The arrival of the Syrians in January 1169 compelled the Crusaders to withdraw to Palestine, but not without some 12,000 captive men, women, and children.

To ransom the Jews among the captives, Maimonides carried out an intensive fund-raising campaign by means of fervent personal letters to Jewish communities in Egypt and Palestine. It was this action which established his reputation in Fusṭāṭ as an outspoken communal leader (*ha-rav ha-gadol*).

This time the Syrians, more specifically Shīrkūh and Saladin, were determined not to be deprived of the spoils of their intervention. On 18 January 1169 Saladin treacherously disposed of Shāwar, and in his place Shīrkūh, a Sunnī Muslim, emerged as the new vizier of the Shīʿite caliphate of the Fāṭimid. On 26 March 1169, three days after the death of Shīrkūh, Saladin was proclaimed as vizier and commander-in-chief of the Syrian forces.

Once in power, Saladin introduced a number of administrative, military, economic, and pro-Sunnī religious reforms which weakened the Fāṭimid establishment, while at the same time effectively emancipating himself from his Syrian overlord, Nūr al-Dīn. He was ably and vigorously assisted by his father Ayyūb, by his numerous brothers and other relatives, as well as by the outstanding Egyptian statesman of Palestinian origin, al-Qāḍī al-Fāḍil. In September 1171, in refusing the enthronement of a Fāṭimid successor on the death of al-ʿĀḍid, he terminated the once glorious Fāṭimid dynasty and thus closed a chapter in Egyptian history. Sunnī Islam had triumphed over its Shīʿite challenger, and the era of the Ayyūbids in Egypt had begun.

The abrupt termination of the Fāṭimid caliphate, under whose relatively tolerant and commercially oriented regime the non-Muslim minorities had experienced a period of prosperity, did not immediately have an adverse effect on the Jewish community of Fusṭāṭ. It must have welcomed Saladin's fiscal decree of 1171, which included an incentive to traders in the heavily populated metropolitan area. That clause exempted the people of Cairo and Fusṭāṭ, as well as all exporters and importers in those two centres and those passing through the Nile ports of al-Maqs and al-Minya, from all customs dues and formalities. As for Maimonides, shortly after the abolition of the Fāṭimid caliphate he was recognized by the new regime as the *reshut*, or official authority, and was even acclaimed as *ra'īs al-yahūd* (head of the Jews).

However, on his way to absolute power over the country of the Nile, Saladin had to overcome a number of internal and external dangers of which the people of the delta must have been quite aware. In August 1169, he ruthlessly suppressed a rebellion of the Fāṭimid palace guards. The burnt-out houses along the main street of the capital, the smouldering ruins of the barracks housing the rebels, and the massacre of those who naïvely surrendered illustrated the kind of retaliation the new ruler would mete out to those who challenged his authority.

Towards the end of 1169, Saladin foiled a major attempt by the Byzantines to capture the industrial town of Damietta on the coast. In 1172, a military expedition was needed to repel a Nubian attack against Aswān. In March of 1174, a serious pro-Fāṭimid plot was discovered and mercilessly liquidated. For several days beginning 6 April, the residents of the capital witnessed a gruesome spectacle, where many of Egypt's former élite were crucified and their corpses strung up in the central square of Cairo. Then, toward the end of July 1174, Saladin defeated a strong Norman attack on Alexandria.

It was in that same year, 1174, that Saladin embarked on a new foreign policy that was to have serious consequences for the status of Egypt. Prior to that date Saladin had seen Egypt as the focal base supporting the nascent Ayyūbid power in the face of growing impatience of Nūr al-Dīn. To shore up this base, territorially and economically, the Ayyūbid leader had sent military expeditions to North Africa, Nubia, and Yemen. Moreover, the death of Nūr al-Dīn on 15 May 1174 provided Saladin with a chance to expand his power by reaching out for Syria. On 28 October 1174, he established control over Damascus and initiated a long series of campaigns against both the Crusaders and his Muslim rivals in Syria and northern Mesopotamia —a strategy ultimately rewarded with the subjugation of Aleppo in 1183 and Mosul in 1186. On 4 July 1187, in the battle of Ḥiṭṭīn, he dealt a nearly fatal blow to the Crusader Kingdom and followed it up with the recapture of its capital, Jerusalem, on 2 October 1187. Only the Third Crusade (1189–91) prevented Saladin from eliminating the Crusader Kingdom. Although he retained Jerusalem and many of the recaptured places in Palestine and Syria, he had to accept a truncated Crusader state on the Palestino-Syrian littoral.

Except for his stay in Egypt in 1167/7 and 1181/2, during that entire period until his death on 4 March 1193, Saladin delegated his authority over Egypt to vice-regents selected from among his brothers, nephews, and sons, while effectively administration remained in the hands of the experienced and prestigious chancellor and vizier, al-Qāḍī al-Fāḍil. Now subordinated to Saladin's expansionist dynastic ambitions Egypt was reduced to a quasi-colony, with the usual adverse consequences: economic exploitation, increased taxation, interference with freedom of trade (in 1183, following a Crusader naval raid in the Red Sea, Saladin declared that sea closed to non-Muslims), acceptance of European commercial ascendancy in Egyptian ports, and a disastrous increase in military expenditure.

Saladin's death did not reverse this negative impact on Egypt's political, social, and economic conditions. Its resources continued to be wasted on the hectic diplomatic, political, and military contest for supremacy among Saladin's Ayyūbid successors. Between 1193 and 1204 the office of the sultan in Cairo passed from al-'Azīz, who ruled for five years (1193–8), to the ten-year-old al-Manṣūr, who ruled from 1198 to 1200 (with al-Afḍal performing the function of regent from 1199), and finally to al-'Ādil (1200–18). Furthermore, Saladin's transformation of Egypt into a potent military establishment compelled the Crusaders, from Palestine as well as from Western Europe, to focus their offensive on Egypt. This strategy was implemented following the destruction of the Egyptian fleet during the Third Crusade, rendering the Mediterranean coast of Egypt with its industrial communities vulnerable to Christian naval attacks. In the spring of 1200, for example, a Crusader fleet sailed up the western branch of the Nile and sacked Fūwwa, a sensitive commercial canal link to Alexandria.[2]

But these dramatic events do not appear to have affected Maimonides' professional and social status. Although a few years after Saladin's departure for Syria he ceased to serve as *ra'īs al-yahūd*, he lost neither in prestige nor in influence with the Ayyūbid circles in Cairo. He wrote: 'I must tell you that in the practice of medicine I have achieved much fame among the great, such as the chief judge, the amīrs, the house of al-Fāḍil, and other great ones of the city.' He passed much of his time at the court of sultan al-Afḍal. 'Every morning I must call on the sultan . . . Even when there is nothing special I never get home before the afternoon.'[3]

How rich in international events Maimonides' life in Egypt turned out to be! He was witness to the overthrow of the Fāṭimid caliphate and the suppression of Shī'ite Islam in Egypt; the collapse of Nūr al-Dīn's political legacy and the rise of the Ayyūbid sultanate; the recapture of Jerusalem by Islam and a drastic truncation of the Crusader Kingdom; and, in 1194, the extinction of the once-powerful Saljūqid sultanate of Iraq. Shortly before his death, news reached Cairo of yet another stunning event which shook the foundations of the Mediterranean world. In April 1204, the Fourth Crusade, diverted by the Venetians from its original Egyptian destination, stormed and looted Constantinople. The proud capital of the Byzantine empire was thus turned into a centre of a new, expansionist Crusader state. Behind this façade the Venetians escalated their commercial operations, a decisive phase in the Italian bid for mercantile hegemony in the Mediterranean. Its success ultimately sapped the economic vein which had long sustained the flourishing urban society of medieval Egypt. For many centuries to come, the stern citadel on the Muqaṭṭam mountain, legacy of Saladin and his Ayyūbid successors, replaced the dynamic Fusṭāṭ as the main symbol of the lifestyle of the capital of the country of the Nile.

[2] Ibn Wāṣil, *Mufarrij al-Kurūb* (Cairo, 1953–60), iii. 161.

[3] These quotations are taken from B. Lewis, 'Maimonides, Lionheart, and Saladin', in *L. A. Mayer Memorial Volume* (*Eretz-Israel*, vii), (Jerusalem, 1964), 70–5.

17
Saladin's Religious Personality, Policy, and Image

MICHAEL WINTER

THE PROBLEM

THE discussion of Saladin's religious personality, policy, and image is important because religion was one of the main social markers in the Middle Ages. In that religious age, a person's religious devotion, certainly a ruler's attitude to religion, determined his character in the view of his contemporaries. It was believed that one could not be honest, kind, or upright without being pious, although it was well understood that the reverse was possible, then as nowadays.

The charismatic personality of Saladin, the great Ayyūbid sultan, still fascinates historians—as it impressed his contemporaries, friend and Crusader enemy alike—and all the Orientalists who have studied the period have concerned themselves with the question of Saladin's religious devotion. H. A. R. Gibb, E. Sivan, and A. Ehrenkreutz have, in fact, devoted considerable attention to this aspect of Saladin's life.[1] Ehrenkreutz holds that Saladin's image as portrayed by his court historians and in Gibb's studies is too perfect to be true, and his book, *Saladin*, is an attempt to remove the layers of romanticism that have been piled upon the historical Ṣalāḥ al-Dīn. Ehrenkreutz thus judges Saladin critically, mainly by his actions and not by the praises of panegyrists.[2]

In *From Saladin to the Mongols*, R. S. Humphreys states the dilemma convincingly: 'The problem of Saladin's personal sincerity may well be

[1] See H. A. R. Gibb, 'The Achievement of Saladin', in *Studies on the Civilization of Islam* (Boston, 1962), 91–107; id., 'The Rise of Saladin', in M. W. Baldwin (ed.), *A History of the Crusades* (Philadelphia, 1955), i. 563–89; E. Sivan, *L'Islam et la croisade* (Paris, 1968); A. Ehrenkreutz, *Saladin*, (Albany, 1972).

[2] Ehrenkreutz stresses this point most explicitly in the Introduction and in the last chapter of *Saladin*.

insoluble. Motives are hard to fathom in any case, and with Saladin the difficulty is all the greater because the duty implied by his professed goals coincided so closely with the policies which mere selfish ambition might have suggested.'[3]

The question of Saladin's sincerity in religious and other matters is indeed hard to resolve, and it may be added that it is only of limited historical relevance (notwithstanding our natural and legitimate curiosity). For a superb statesman and political leader like Saladin, the main thing that matters is his public image, and this is also the only subject upon which we have reliable and solid evidence.

SALADIN AND THE JIHĀD

Saladin's zeal for holy war (*jihād*) is the aspect of his religious image that has been most subject to scrutiny. It is natural that the victor of Ḥiṭṭīn is presented by his biographers primarily as a great *mujāhid*. The most impressive description of Saladin's dedication to holy war is found in Ibn Shaddād's *Al-Nawādir as-Sulṭāniyya*.[4] Bahā' al-Dīn b. Shaddād, Saladin's secretary and confidant, relates that he compiled for the sultan's use a collection of laws and regulations concerning holy war. He also relates that the sultan was very much attached to his family, but that he did not hesitate to endure separation from his loved ones whenever the call of duty made this necessary.[5] The author recounts with admiration mingled with horror how Saladin, facing the stormy sea, expressed his wish to renounce all his power after reconquering the *Sāḥil* (the Syro-Palestinian coast), and then to set out to sea in pursuit of the infidels and to fight till no unbeliever remained on earth or to die in the attempt.[6]

Sivan, in his study of *jihād* propaganda during the Crusades, describes Saladin's period as the climax of the anti-Crusade propaganda campaign.[7] Ehrenkreutz, however, questions whether Saladin, who spent most of his career fighting against his co-religionists, thereby clearly giving the 'unification' of Islam under his command priority

[3] R. S. Humphreys, *From Saladin to the Mongols: The Ayyūbids of Damascus* (Albany, 1977), 22.

[4] Bahā' al-Dīn b. Shaddād, *Al-Nawādir al-Sulṭāniyya wal-Maḥāsin al-Yūsufiyya*, ed. J. al-Shayyāl (Cairo, 1964), 21–3. The introduction to Ibn Shaddād's biography of Saladin is translated by F. Gabrieli, *Arab Historians of the Crusades* (London, 1969), 57–113.

[5] Ibn Shaddād, *Al-Nawādir*, 27.

[6] Ibid. 22–23.

[7] Sivan, *L'Islam et la croisade*, esp. 95–106.

over warfare against the Franks, could claim in good faith to be an idealistic and selfless champion of holy war.[8]

SALADIN'S PERSONAL FAITH

There is unanimous agreement in the sources about Saladin's general religious image and policy. Even the critical and sometimes hostile historian Ibn al-Athīr does not dispute that Saladin was a devout and personally modest ruler,[9] and from the descriptions and sayings that abound in the chronicles he certainly radiated intense piety.

While according to the prevailing values it was only to be expected that great piety would be attributed to the victor of Ḥiṭṭīn and the liberator of Jerusalem, there must nevertheless have been a grain of truth around which such an image might develop. Saladin's achievement as a great *mujāhid* is not in itself sufficient to account for his religious reputation. A comparison with al-Malik al-Ẓāhir Baybars, founder of the Mamlūk sultanate, will help clarify this point.[10] Baybars was an abler and more successful soldier than Saladin as well as a more efficient ruler. Moreover, like Saladin, he publicly pursued an impeccably Islamic orthodox policy. Yet, unlike Saladin, Baybars did not have a religious aura. While Baybars is reputed to have had a cruel streak, Saladin was, or at least was perceived as, a noble man endowed with compassion for all human beings. The biographer explicitly lauds his love of all mankind (*maḥabbatuhū li-jins al-bashar*), which includes not only Muslims but even Christian enemies. Some quite touching anecdotes demonstrate Saladin's humanity, lenient treatment of subordinates, generosity, and forbearance.

Ibn Shaddād recounts how Saladin compassionately ordered that the daughter of a Christian woman who had been carried away by Muslim raiders be located and brought back. We are told that a frightened Frankish prisoner of war was calmed merely by looking at

[8] Ehrenkreutz, *Saladin*, 175, 185, 193, 207, 236.

[9] See e.g. Ibn al-Athīr, *Al-Kāmil fil-Ta'rīkh*, ed. C. J. Tonberg (Leiden, 1871), xii. 63.

[10] An outline of a comparison between Saladin and Baybars, concerning their military policies and strategic approach (but not religious policy) is given in *Ayyubids, Mamluks and Crusaders: Selections from* Tārīkh al-Dawla wal-Mulūk of Ibn Furāt, ed. U. and M. C. Lyons and J. S. C. Riley-Smith (Cambridge, 1972), vol. ii, pp. xi ff. On Baybars' reputation for cruelty, see *The Theologus Autodidactus of Ibn al-Nafīs*, ed. M. Meyerhof and J. Schacht (Oxford, 1968), 141.

Saladin's kindly countenance.[11] His generosity is too well known to require detailed demonstration. He is generally depicted as a soft-hearted, sentimental man.[12]

As we know from Ibn Shaddād's lengthy introduction to his biography of Saladin, the sultan's personal piety was considered flawless by the most strict Sunnī standards. He studied religious subjects with leading *'ulamā'*. His faith was free of the taint of heterodoxy. Shaykh Quṭb al-Dīn al-Nīsābūrī compiled a catechism (*'aqīda*) for his use, and Saladin studied it and taught it to his children. Ibn Shaddād assures us that Saladin believed in the resurrection of the dead and hated philosophers (*falāsifa*), heretics, and materialists.[13] He enjoyed listening to the recitation of the Qur'ān and was often moved to tears by it.

A salient feature of Saladin's piety is his passion for *ḥadīth*. This aspect of Islamic devotion was immensely popular at the time and betokened the Sunnī orthodox resurgence.[14] Saladin went to such unprecedented extremes in his admiration of *ḥadīth* that he ordered *ḥadīth* texts to be recited on the battlefield. He sought the company of men who were renowned authorities on *ḥadīth* in order to study it directly with them. He insisted on travelling to Alexandria to meet al-Ḥāfiẓ al-Iṣfahānī, a distinguished *ḥadīth* scholar, thus emulating the 'Abbāsid caliph Hārūn al-Rashīd, who had also travelled great distances to study *ḥadīth*.[15] Saladin's stress on *ḥadīth* was an appeal to popular piety intended to counterbalance the influence of Shī'ī institutions of learning in which other religious and intellectual aspects of Islam were taught.[16]

Despite all the services Saladin rendered for Islam and his reputed personal piety, he failed to perform the *ḥajj* to Mecca, which is incumbent upon every Muslim at least once in a lifetime. This failure to do so inevitably raised questions. Ibn Shaddād, who in his introduction to the sultan's biography specifies how faithfully Saladin

[11] Ibn Shaddād, *Al-Nawādir*, 32–3, 158–9; Gabrieli, *Arab Historians*, 110–11.

[12] Gabrieli, *Arab Historians*, 9.

[13] Ibid. 7, 10.

[14] Ibid. 9, 10, 20.

[15] Ibn Shaddād, *Al-Nawādir*, 9; Jalāl al-Dīn al-Suyūṭī, *Ḥusn al-Muḥāḍara fī Ta'rīkh Miṣr wal-Qāhira*, ed. M. Ibrāhīm (Cairo, n.d.), ii. 19. On the popularity of *ḥadīth* generally and on Hārūn al-Rashīd's patronage of it, see al-Sam'ānī, *Die Methodik des Diktatkollegs (Adab al-Imlā' wal-Istimlā')* ed. M. Weisweiler (Leiden, *c.*1952), 18–23.

[16] See I. Goldziher, 'Education (Muslim)', in *Hastings Encyclopaedia of Religion and Ethics* (New York, 1925), v. 198–207.

adhered to Islam in general and to the 'five pillars' (*arkān*) in particular, says apologetically that Saladin was too busy fighting the infidels, and adds that he could not go to Mecca as he did not have the material means to go on the *hajj* in a manner befitting someone of his rank.[17]

Ehrenkreutz, who tends to dismiss Saladin's piety as a product of propaganda, is very sceptical about this and asserts that Saladin could have gone on the *hajj* had he really wanted to do so.[18] But it is surely true that Saladin did not have much spare time, as his administration was very dependent upon his presence, both for political and military reasons. Last but not least, even the most cynical observer must admit that Saladin, who clearly wished to be *seen* as a deeply religious man, could have used a pilgrimage as an impressive demonstration of piety and power. Muslim rulers were often reluctant to perform the *hajj* not on account of religious laxity but precisely because of the reasons which Ibn Shaddād cited in the case of Saladin.

SALADIN AND THE ṢŪFĪS

Saladin's attitude towards, and relations with, the Ṣūfīs are worthy of review, since in his time Ṣūfism was clearly a rising force. It had not yet become the common religious 'addiction' of rulers, which it became in later times, notably under the Mamlūks and the Ottomans. Following the policy of Nūr al-Dīn and his Saljūq predecessors, Saladin revered and patronized Ṣūfīs, and contributed donations to Ṣūfī centres (*zawāyā* and *khawāniq*), but he did so as a patron, not as an active participant like some later rulers. Ibn Shaddād recounts an encounter between Saladin and a Ṣūfī shaykh who was also an *ʿālim* (religious scholar). The man was a son of the ruler of Tabrīz, but he renounced worldly power and wealth (following an old Ṣūfī pattern) and became an ascetic. This saintly person came to see Saladin and to thank him for the services he had rendered Islam. After seeing the sultan, the Ṣūfī left abruptly without taking leave. When Saladin found out, he was furious with his retainers for releasing the man before he could give him presents in token of his veneration. He made Ibn Shaddād recall the Ṣūfī so that the latter could benefit from the sultan's beneficence. Thus the two men played their respective roles according to the prescribed convention: the man of God shuns the presence of

---

[17] Ibn Shaddād, *Al-Nawādir*, 9.
[18] Ehrenkreutz, *Saladin*, 225–7.

the ruler, while the just, God-fearing sultan insists upon honouring him.[19]

Although Saladin was favourably inclined towards the Ṣūfīs, he was only a sympathetic outsider and never actually participated in their rituals. A short episode throws light upon this. After the battle of Ḥiṭṭīn, Saladin visited his nephew, Taqī al-Dīn ʿUmar, who was then the ruler of Ḥamāt. The host entertained Saladin generously and arranged for him a Ṣūfī recital of religious melodies (*samāʿ*) as a special treat. This Ṣūfī concert was obviously meant to be part of the hospitality granted the sultan; the latter, in return, did not disappoint his host, and conferred upon him the districts of Jabala and al-Lādhiqiyya in Syria.[20]

In his patronage of the Ṣūfīs, Saladin in fact continued the policy of his predecessor, Nūr al-Dīn. We have Ibn Jubayr's lively description of the flourishing state of the Ṣūfīs in Syria, whom even the religiously observant Maghribī traveller considered to be good Sunnīs. They lived there like 'kings in castles'; according to Ibn Jubayr, it was Nūr al-Dīn who had given them these castles, which had belonged to an inebriate Turkish prince.[21]

It goes without saying that Saladin's patronage was extended only to orthodox Ṣūfīs. He ordered his son al-Malik al-Ẓāhir, the lord of Ḥalab, to put to death the important Ṣūfī writer and illuminist mystic, Shihāb al-Dīn al-Suhrawardī ('al-Maqtūl'), who was accused of heresy and disobedience to the Law.[22]

SALADIN AS A HOLY, SAINTLY MAN

Saladin is occasionally depicted not merely as a deeply religious ruler but as an ascetic and virtually a saint. It is reported that he scrupulously abstained from anything morally tainted (*ḥarām*) and was careful to use only permissible (*ḥalāl*) things. He refused to wear clothes that were regarded as contravening Islam (such as silk, for example), limiting himself to cotton, wool, and the like.[23]

[19] Ibn Shaddād, *Al-Nawādir*, 31–2. On relations between rulers and Ṣūfīs see my *Society and Religion in Early Ottoman Egypt: Studies in the Writings of ʿAbd al-Wahhāb al-Shaʿrānī* (New Brunswick, NJ, 1982), 262–72.

[20] Ibn al-Athīr, *Al-Kāmil*, xii. 63; Ibn Taghrībirdī, *Al-Nujūm al-Zāhira* (Cairo, n.d.), vi. 42.

[21] Ibn Jubayr, *Riḥla*, ed. M. de Goeje (London, 1907), 284–5.

[22] Ibn Shaddād, *Al-Nawādir*, 10.

[23] Suyūṭī, *Ḥusn al-Muḥāḍara*, ii. 21.

No cheap laughter was allowed in his presence, and he was always surrounded by *'ulamā'* (religious scholars). He never listened to astrologers' advice but always relied upon God alone. Ibn Shaddād reports Saladin's behaviour during a serious crisis when the Franks were besieging Jerusalem and the situation of the Muslims seemed desperate. At Ibn Shaddād's suggestion, Saladin decided that reliance on God remained his only hope. He prayed at the al-Aqṣā mosque, gave alms incognito, and then recited the following beautiful *ḥadīth* as an invocation: 'My God, all my earthly power to bring victory to your faith has come to nothing: my only resource is to turn to you, to rely on your help and trust in your goodness. You are my sufficience, you are the best preserver.' Afterwards a quarrel broke out among the Franks concerning their next steps. They finally withdrew to the region of Ramleh.[24] With his considerable literary talent, Ibn Shaddād merely insinuates that the relief was caused by supernatural intervention, leading us to think that Jerusalem was saved by a miracle (*karāma*) which befell the pious sultan.[25]

Ibn Shaddād also alludes to Saladin's *baraka* (holiness) in his report of the Muslim reconquest of Jerusalem. The coincidence of the event with the twenty-seventh day of Rajab, which is Laylat al-Mi'rāj (the nocturnal ascension of Muhammad from Jerusalem to the seven heavens), is inevitably interpreted as a miracle.[26]

Some sources state outright that Saladin was a saintly man. One writer states that the sultan was one of the 300 *awliyā'*, saints or favourites of God (a Ṣūfī term which denotes a group of anonymous saints whose existence is vital for the right order of the world).[27] Ibn Khallikān notes correctly that although Saladin built many religious institutions, hardly any of them were attributed to him or named after him: thus, the *madrasa* in the Qarāfa cemetery of Cairo was named after al-Imām al-Shāfi'ī; another near Ḥusayn's mosque was simply called al-Mashhad; the *khānqāh* (Ṣūfī convent) Saladin established was known as Sa'īd al-Su'adā; the Ḥanafī *madrasa* was named al-Suyūfiyya, and so on. The writer concludes: 'And this is the real

[24] Ibn Shaddād, *Al-Nawādir*, 10–12; Gabrieli, *Arab Historians*, 92–3.

[25] It was believed in Islam (particularly on the popular level) that every person in authority was in a sense sacred, even magically so. The prayer of a ruler is heard so long as it is made for the sake of others. See S. D. Goitein, *Studies in Islamic History and Institutions* (Leiden, 1966), 204.

[26] Ibn Shaddād, *Al-Nawādir*, 82.

[27] Suyūṭī, *Ḥusn al-Muḥāḍara*, ii. 22, citing the Ṣūfī writer al-Yāfi'ī.

meaning of secret charity' (*wa-hādhihī ṣadaqat al-sirr ʿalā al-ḥaqīqa*), i.e. generosity without ostentation.[28]

SALADIN IN IBN JUBAYR'S RIḤLA: A MAGHRIBĪ VIEW

The evidence of the Spanish traveller Ibn Jubayr, who passed through Saladin's territories just before the battle of Ḥiṭṭīn, is particularly valuable. It helps us realize how effective Saladin's religious policy was and how strongly he projected his pious image throughout the East. Like many Maghribī travellers, Ibn Jubayr was strictly, even fanatically, religious. He writes in the Maghribī tradition, which measures Eastern (*Mashriqī*) Islam by the standards of the Maghreb and finds it wanting: 'There is no Islam except in the lands of the Maghreb, since they are on a main road which has no sidetracks; whereas other lands, such as these Eastern (*Mashriqiyya*) regions are full of heretical tendencies, innovations, and erroneous sects.' Ibn Jubayr continues his tirade, claiming that only the Almohades (*al-Muwaḥḥidūn*) rule with justice and piety. All other kings at the present time oppress the Muslim merchants by imposing the taxes incumbent on the *dhimmīs* and seek all kinds of stratagems to rob them of their money. Ibn Jubayr concludes by saying that the only just ruler is Sultan Saladin.[29]

Saladin's immense popularity is demonstrated in Ibn Jubayr's impressive description of the service in the holy mosque of Mecca. As was customary, the preacher said the blessings for the rulers and mentioned the name of Caliph al-Nāṣir li-Dīn Allāh, then that of Mukthir, the ruling amir of Mecca. Only when he came to the blessing (*duʿā'*) of Saladin's name the public started to cheer and to thank God for the popular love and praise he bestowed upon this just sultan.[30]

It should be emphasized that Ibn Jubayr was not close to Saladin's circles, as were some of the sultan's biographers. Furthermore, like most Maghribis, he was not afraid to speak his mind. His enthusiastic praise of Saladin cannot therefore be viewed as flattery; it rather reflects genuine admiration for the sultan, whose public religious policy and good works spoke louder than words. Since Ibn Jubayr was widely travelled, he was in a position to judge and compare. He quotes Saladin as saying, '[In my lands] religious justice is open to everyone

[28] Ibn Khallikān, *Wafayāt al-Aʿyān* (Cairo, 1948), vi. 205–6.
[29] Ibn Jubayr, *Riḥla*, 78.
[30] Ibid. 103–4.

(*lil-khaṣṣa wal-'āmma*) and its ordinances and prohibitions are obeyed. I am only the servant and constable of the Law.'[31]

Ibn Jubayr repeatedly stresses that the sultan's name, Ṣalāḥ al-Dīn ('the welfare of religion'), suited him perfectly, since he enhanced the cause of religion by funding *madāris* (colleges) in Egypt (where until then there were only Shī'ī institutions of learning), Ṣūfī centres, Qur'ān schools, a hospital, and a lunatic asylum.[32]

The first city which Ibn Jubayr visited in Egypt was naturally Alexandria. He lauds the sultān for the numerous and generously endowed religious institutions which flourished there, to which foreign scholars and devotees were attracted. Ibn Jubayr estimated that there were between 4,000 and 8,000 mosques in Alexandria, each with imāms who were paid by the sultan a salary of five Egyptian dinars (equalling ten *mu'minī*, i.e. Almohade dinars).[33]

Ibn Jubayr's impression of Cairo is just as favourable. The famous Qarāfa—the cemetery with its saints' sepulchres—the mosques, and the various Islamic monuments were all frequented by foreign and local *'ulamā'*, Ṣūfīs, and pietists. Ech of the religious monuments was endowed by the treasury with a regular allowance. Ibn Jubayr discovered that the daily expenditures on the religious institutions in Cairo exceeded 2,000 Egyptian dinars; the mosque of 'Amr b. al-'Āṣ alone received 300 dinars daily for the salaries of its personnel and Qur'ān readers. Ibn Jubayr mentions in particular the sanctuary (*mashhad*) of al Imām al Shāfi'ī, which was administered by Shaykh al-Khabūshānī, whom Saladin encouraged to spend more on the shrine in order to adorn it further. The writer concludes: 'There is no Friday-mosque (*jāmi'*), regular mosque (*masjid*), cemetery garden, Ṣūfī centre, or college (*madrasa*) that does not benefit from the sultan's generosity and from the expenditures of the treasury.' The sultan also ordered to arrange and to support financially assemblies (*maḥāḍir*) to study the Qur'ān, especially for orphans and poor children.[34]

Ibn Jubayr likewise approves of the sermons (*khuṭab*) held in the mosques of Cairo, which he regards as blamelessly Sunnī, and which included blessings for the Prophet's companions (*ṣaḥāba*), their followers in the next generation (*tābi'ūn*), Muhammad's wives and his uncles Ḥamza and 'Abbās, in contradistinction to the now-abolished Shī'ī sermons, which of course omitted all these blessings.[35]

[31] Ibid. 298.
[32] Ibid. 48, 241; Ibn Taghrībirdī, *Al-Nujūm al-Zāhira*, vi. 59.
[33] Ibid. 42–3. [34] Ibid. 52. [35] Ibid. 50.

Doubtlessly, a major reason for Ibn Jubayr's ardent support of Saladin was the sultan's special generosity towards Muslim foreigners generally and North Africans (*maghāriba*) in particular, with whom our author naturally identifies.[36]

According to Ibn Jubayr, Saladin devoted special attention to Maghribī wayfarers (*abnā' sabīl*), who arrived in Alexandria, most of them as pilgrims to Mecca. He founded a *waqf* to provide for each of them two loaves of bread daily, the total quantity occasionally adding up to 200 loaves. Ibn Jubayr sharply denounces an unnamed adviser who tried to convince Saladin to stop feeding the Maghribī pilgrims in order spare the expense. Yet when Saladin realized the extent of the hardships the Maghribīs had endured before arriving in Egypt, he contemptuously rejected the bad advice.[37]

In Cairo, Saladin transformed the mosque of Ibn Ṭūlūn into a shelter for Maghribīs. He fixed a monthly allowance for them. Moreover, he granted them full autonomy by appointing one of them to be their chief, ordering that they turn only to him to solve their disputes and problems. Saladin decreed that no one should have authority over them, so they would enjoy the necessary peace of mind to worship God as they wished.[38]

By helping these strangers, Saladin expressed a sentiment of Islamic solidarity. The Maghribīs, as already noted, have always been renowned for their ardent religiosity. Demonstrating kindness to them could enhance a ruler's reputation throughout the Muslim world. It is well known that many *'ulamā'* and Ṣūfīs in Saladin's milieu were of Persian extraction. We do not know of Maghribīs who attained similarly high positions at the time in the Ayyūbid state, but nevertheless they were a highly visible and not uninfluential community.

It should be pointed out that in patronizing the Maghribī community in the East, Saladin again followed in the footsteps of Nūr al-Dīn, the great Zangid ruler in whose service Saladin rose and whose dynasty he replaced by his own. Ibn Jubayr reports that Nūr al-Dīn had spent large sums of money to ransom Maghribī prisoners of war, preferring them to the natives of Ḥamāt, who were his own subjects, because he understood that, unlike the Maghribīs, the former had relatives who could ransom them. Ibn Jubayr also learned from a member of the Maghribī community in Damascus that Nūr al-Dīn had established

[36] It seems that Ibn Jubayr in *Riḥla* deliberately plays on the similarity beween the word *ghurabā'* (foreigners) and *Maghāriba* (Maghribīs, North Africans).

[37] Ibid. 43.

[38] Ibid. 52.

generous *waqfs* for the benefit of the Mālikī section of the great mosque of Damascus. These *waqfs* yielded 500 dinars annually. In this way Nūr al-Dīn created conditions that enabled the Maghribīs to come to the East and devote their time to learning.[39] This was not the only thing in which Saladin emulated his predecessor: his entire religious policy is heavily indebted to Nūr al-Dīn's ideological foundations, even if in some things Saladin surpassed him.

SALADIN'S PROMOTION OF THE ḤAJJ

Saladin promoted the *ḥajj* and thereby won immense prestige and popularity. Modern scholars have discussed in detail this side of his religious policy.[40] When Saladin was still nominally a Fāṭimid vizier and a subordinate of Nūr al-Dīn, he conquered Ailah on the Gulf of 'Aqaba from the Franks. The pilgrims of the Damascus caravan, who until then had had to go through Frankish-controlled territories, could now pass through that newly conquered strategic stronghold.[41]

Equally famous is Saladin's shrewd abolition of the special toll of seven and a half Egyptian dinars which each pilgrim was obliged to pay on his way to Mecca, which was intended to support the holy cities of the Ḥijāz. Instead, Saladin committed his treasury to supplying Mecca and Medina with food and cash.[42] What has received less attention, however, was the fact that travellers were not exempted from paying custom duties, which under Saladin's orthodox-minded administration were called *zakāt*, the legal poor-tax. Saladin was lauded for abolishing religiously objectionable custom duties and other illegal taxes (*maẓālim*), but his bureaucracy replaced them with the *zakāt*.

It is astonishing yet perfectly in accord with the medieval Islamic perception of the ruler that he gets full credit for all the good deeds carried out in his realm but is never held responsible for the blameworthy or unpopular actions committed by his subordinates. Ibn Jubayr, whom as we have seen keenly extols Saladin, gives a bitter description of the cruelty of his customs officials, piously called '*zakāt* collectors', at the Egyptian borders, both in Alexandria and in the Upper Egyptian towns of Ikhmīm, Qūṣ, and Minyat b. al-Khaṣīb.

[39] Ibid. 284–5.
[40] Ehrenkreutz, *Saladin*, 53, 210; Sivan, *l'Islam et la croisade*, 99.
[41] Ehrenkreutz, *Saladin*, 54.
[42] Ibn Jubayr, *Riḥla*, 29, 55, 77; *Suyūṭī, Ḥusn al-Muḥāḍara*, ii. 17.

Ibn Jubayr relates in an eyewitness account that passengers of both sexes, mostly Maghribī pilgrims and merchants, were subjected to a humiliating body search. Sometimes they were compelled to swear by the Qur'ān what the value of their possessions was, lest they conceal some money or goods. Ibn Jubayr expresses his conviction that Saladin knew nothing of the cruel actions of 'the fiendish assistants of the *zakāt* collectors', otherwise he certainly would have forbidden them just as he had abolished more serious offences.[43]

The fifteenth-century historian al-Maqrīzī repeats Ibn Jubayr's description of the way the travellers were searched, stating: 'Such is the practice in the whole land of Egypt since the period of Salāḥ al-Dīn b. Ayyūb.' Al-Maqrīzī says that Saladin was the first ruler of Egypt who collected *zakāt*, but it was the Ayyūbid sultan al-Malik al-Kāmil who appropriated the money which had been collected since the times of Saladin under the name of *zakāt*, for the sake of its legally prescribed purposes, including stipends for *'ulamā'*, jurists, and devout men.[44]

SALADIN'S FLEXIBILITY

We can assume that Saladin was personally religious, or at least he wanted to appear in that light. There are indications, however, that compared to Nūr al-Dīn, for example, his religious sentiments never had the upper hand over his discretion and caution. Nūr al-Dīn pressured Saladin to abolish the Shī'ī *khuṭba* immediately, but Saladin was in no hurry and acted only when the moment seemed opportune for the coup.[45]

Saladin's postponement of the *jihād* until he had dominated almost the entire Islamic East has already been mentioned. Indeed, this theme is a central thesis of Ehrenkreutz's *Saladin*. The sultan's settlement with the fanatical, heretical sect of the Assassins is also indicative of his flexibility. He probably regarded them as a security problem and a nuisance more than an ideological and a religious threat, and he established a *modus vivendi* with them—again unlike Nūr al-Dīn, who had relentlessly persecuted them.[46]

Sometime we are entirely dependent on the evidence of Ibn

[43] Ibn Jubayr, *Riḥla*, 62–4.

[44] Al-Maqrīzī, *Al-Mawā'iẓ wal-I'tibār fī-Dhikr al-Khiṭaṭ wal-Āthār* (Beirut, 1959), i. 193.

[45] Ehrenkreutz, *Saladin*, 84–7.

[46] Ibid. 148, 152.

Shaddād, who is certainly a biased source. This biographer either interpolates or overemphasizes religious motives to interpret Saladin's actions. A case in point is the conquest of Yemen. In Saladin's time, as often in the history of Egypt, the strategic and economic interests of Egypt favoured control of Yemen. Yet Saladin's expedition to conquer that land, carried out under the command of his brother al-Malik al-Mu'aẓẓam Tūrān Shāh, is presented as religiously motivated. The conquest is presented as a liberation of Yemen from a usurper who called himself 'Abd al-Nabī b. Mahdī (!), and who presumably cherished ambitions to conquer the world.[47]

Ibn Shaddād reports how the notorious Reynald of Châtillon broke the truce by attacking a Muslim caravan which was passing by his territory in Transjordan. Reynald tortured his captives and imprisoned them in narrow dungeons. When the Muslim prisoners protested, reminding him of the truce, he reportedly said: 'Call upon your Muhammad to rescue you.' Ibn Shaddād says that when Saladin learned of this, he vowed that when God put the man in his power he would kill him with his own hand. Saladin, in fact, fulfilled his vow after the battle of Ḥiṭṭīn.[48] Ibn Shaddād makes us understand that it was Reynald's disparaging words concerning the Prophet that caused Saladin's wrath more than anything else.

CONCLUSION

In concluding his stimulating book, Ehrenkreutz says that Saladin's religious behaviour conforms too closely to the injunctions formulated in the standard Islamic manuals for princes (*Fürstenspiegel*)—that is, too closely to be credible. In other words, Saladin's biographers attributed to him characteristics and behaviour that suit to perfection the ideal Muslim prince rather than describing him realistically.[49]

Some of Saladin's biographies were undoubtedly written by dependent admirers in whose writings a strong element of propaganda was present. Yet, Ibn Jubayr's unbiased and lucid description attests to the impressive record of Saladin, at least in his public religious policy. Ibn Jubayr was an independent and honest observer (who did not even hesitate to commend the Franks for their tolerant treatment

47 Ibn Shaddād, *Al-Nawādir*, 46.
48 Ibid. 33.
49 Ehrenkreutz, *Saladin*, 237.

of their Muslim subjects and the respect they showed to the Ṣūfīs).[50] It seems that Saladin, who was a shrewd political leader constantly aware of his image and surrounded by professional men of religion, did actually live up to the standards stipulated in the Islamic *Fürstenspiegel* and other classical sources, or at least tried hard to look as if he did.

Saladin not only succeeded in bringing Egypt back to the Sunnī–'Abbāsid fold after two centuries of Fāṭimid rule; he also created a superstructure of Islamic institutions and an atmosphere of vigorous Sunnī Islam, sure of itself and therefore reasonably tolerant of the religious minorities. It can be asserted that Maimonides' rather sympathetic view of Islam, and the extent that it is so, owes much to the fact that he met Islam in Egypt at its best, in large measure because of Saladin's dynamic leadership and vision.

[50] Ibn Jubayr, *Riḥla*, 287, 301–2.

Index

ʿAbbās (uncle of Muḥammad) 317
ʿAbbāsid caliph, ʿAbbāsids 295–6, 300, 312, 322
Abbayya 269
ʿAbd al-Nabī b. Mahdī (Yemenite usurper) 321
Abigail 212
Abrabanel, R. Isaac 59, 229 n. 15, 231, 234
Abraham 235, 266
  Abrahamic teaching 218
Abū Bakr al-Rāzī 31, 50
Abu l-Ḥasan al-ʿĀmirī 13
Abū Hāshim (al-Jubbāʾī) 109
Abū Marwān b. Zuhr 199
Abulafia, Abraham 5
Abusch, R. Abraham 211
Account of the Beginning 53, 55, 57, 60, 65
Account of the Chariot 53, 55–62, 65–6
Adam 19, 22, 25, 230–1, 235
  Adamites 43
Aden 300
al-ʿĀḍid (caliph) 304–5
al-ʿĀdil (sultan) 306
al-Afḍal (sultan) 74, 306–7
aggadah 214
  and *halakhah* 289
Agnon, S. Y. 287
Ailah (pl.) 319
Akiba, Rabbi 56, 65, 238, 240, 243
Alain of Lille 187
Albo, Joseph 172, 258
Aleppo (Ḥalab) 299, 306, 314
Alexandria 301, 303–5, 317, 319
Alfarabi 5, 13, 19, 21, 23, 25, 34, *et passim*
  Attainment of Happiness 19
  Catalogue (Enumeration) of the Sciences 23, 86–9, 97
  Commentary on the Ethics 23–4
  Introductory Epistle (Treatise) on Logic 24, 81–2, 85, 87–90
  Kitāb al-milla 93–4
  al-Madina al-Fāḍila 93–4
  Paraphrase of Aristotle's eight books on logic 102
  al-Siyāsa al-Madaniyya 91, 93–4
Alfasi, Isaac b. Jacob 270
allegory, Maimonides' use of 72, 230, 254
All, the (Universe) 125
Almohade(s) 8, 316–17
Altmann, A. 71
Amalekites 211, 219
amān (safe conduct) 216
ʿAmr b. al-ʿĀṣ mosque 317
ancients, the 85
al-Andalus, Andalusī 8, 83, 293; *see also* Spain
angels 88
anger 28
anthropology 221, 251
anthropomorphisms 136
antiquity 258
apocalypse 254
apologetics 259
apostasy *see shemad*
apprehension, intellectual 231, 248
  of God 41, 66
al-Aqṣā mosque 315
Aquinas, Thomas 187, 189
Arab(s), Arabic 77, 79, 98, 116–17, 143, 179, 189, 200–1, 294
arguments:
  demonstrative 102
  dialectical 102, 104
  rhetorical 102, 104
Aristotelian(s) 4, 6, 14, 22, 29, 30, 127, 138, 159
  cosmology 6, 170
  ethics 86
  logic 24
  natural philosophy 160
  neo-Aristotelian 144
  notion of eternity 113
  philosophy 149–50
Aristotle 4, 15–17, 20, 27, 29–30, 46 n 36, 50, 84, 89, 94, 102, 119, 167
  De Anima 87

Aristotle (*cont.*):
Ethics 2, 13–17, 20, 31, 84
Metaphysics 84, 86–7
Politics 20, 94–5, 100
arithmetic 87
Armenian(s) 300
art 82, 84–5
logical 89
productive 84
syllogistic 85
theoretical 84
Ashdod, speech of 275
Ashi, Rav 269
association, political 95
astrology 164
astronomer(s) 159, 162, 171–2
astronomy 87, 160–2, 166–7, 173
Aswān (place) 305
Averroes (Ibn Rushd) 6, 13 n. 3, 14, 23–4, 31, 113 n. 28, 160, 170, 184, 201
Commentary on Plato's Republic 34–5
Decisive Treatise 176
Epitome of the Categories 178
Avicenna (Ibn Sīnā) 3, 13, 24, 69, 96, 113 n. 28, 114, 185
Ayyūbid(s), Ayyūbid dynasty 8, 295, 298–301, 305–7, 309, 318, 320
al-ʿAzīz (sultan) 306

Baghdad 83, 296
Bar-Sela, A. 204
bedouins 301
Being (Plotinus) 120
Ben Kozba 238–9, 243–4
Berman, L. V. 3, 70–1, 110–11
Bilbays (place) 303–4
al-Biṭrūjī 6, 160, 173–4
Blau, J. 8
Blidstein, G. 7
Blumenthal, D. R. 64
Butterworth, C. E. 79
Byzantine(s), Byzantine empire 305, 307

Cairo 75, 297, 301, 303–5, 307, 315, 317
Canaanite(s) 211–12, 216, 219
causation 118, 121–2
Chariot, vision of the 72
Ezekiel's vision of 59
Isaiah's vision of 59
Christian(s) 83, 99, 235, 299, 304, 307, 311
Christianity 228, 242
Christology 145
city (*polis*), cities 91–2, 94–5, 100
commandments (divine) 25, 36, 63, 73, 99–100, 134, 137, 210, 226, 247
ceremonial 25, 26
ethical 27
generally accepted 21
political 27
rational 25
Ten 25, 136
traditional 26
confederacy (*symmachia*) 94
Constantinople 307
contemplation 52, 67
contradiction, self- 146–7
Corcos, Solomon 171
Cordova 8
cosmology 71, 168, 170
courage 153, 179
creation 111, 113, 123, 130, 138, 147, 150, 233, 249, 251
Creator 113, 123, 230, 232, 248
Crusades 295, 307
Crusader(s) 299, 303–4, 306–7
culture, transmission of 28

Damascus 299
great mosque of 319
Damietta 301, 305
Dār Saʿīd al-Suʿadā (Ṣūfī convent) 301, 315
David (King) 212, 227, 234–6, 288
House, dynasty of 235, 243–5
deism 145
demonstration 89
determinism 121
deterministic theories 118
dhimmīs (protected peoples) 316
dialectic(al) 4, 5, 85, 103, 111, 147, 155, 157
dialectical theologians 87; *see also* Mutakallimun
Diaspora 142, 216, 259
Dinur, Benzion 261
divination 151, 153
divine:
attributes 51, 175–9, 181, 184–9; *see also* God
matters 63
names 175–9
overflow 143–6, 152–3, 155–6; *see also* emanation
Presence 67–8, 73, 138, 286, 288

things 37, 87, 99
will 128–30, 132–3, 138, 150
wisdom 133, 152
)rory, J. 8
)uran, Profiat *see* Efodi

:ast (Eastern) 318, 320
countries 300
Mediterranean 303
ccentres, eccentric (orbs) 6, 151, 161, 168–9, 173
conomics 90, 96–7
:fodi, Isaac b. Moses (Profiat Duran) 54, 59, 169, 172–3
:gypt 114, 161, 257–8, 295–6, 298, 300, 306–7, 317, 322
Lower 304
Upper 319
:gyptians 299–300, 302–3, 305, 319–20
:hrenkreutz, A. 8, 295, 309–10, 320–1
lite, the few 31, 33, 42, 175, 225
manation 124–5, 127, 139, 146, 155
intellectual 139
process of 120
:nd of Days 290
nlightened, the 51; *see also* élite
nlightenment 176–7, 180, 182
picycles, epicyclic 6, 159, 161, 163, 168–70, 172
quant 161
rgon (function) 16
schatology 250, 254, 279
soteric(ism), exoteric(ism) 5, 55, 106, 110, 113, 147–8, 248
ternity 150
a parte ante 112–13
thics 14, 90, 95–6, 99
Europe, Western 295, 299, 306
evil inclination 21
evil(s) 40–1, 95, 121–2, 255, 281
exegetes, biblical 180
Exile 144, 223, 232–3, 259, 265, 270, 274, 279–80, 282
exile of man 233
existence 185
necessary existence, notion of 190
exoteric(ism) *see* esoteric(ism)
Ezra 266, 274–5

al-Fāḍil, house of; *see* al-Qāḍī al-Fāḍil
falāsifa (Islamic philosophers) 69, 73, 89, 102, 312; *see also* philosophers
fate 119
Fāṭimid(s) dynasty 8, 295–6, 298–9, 301, 303–5, 307, 319, 322
Fez, Morocco 8
fiqh see jurisprudence
First Cause 123
foods, forbidden 6
fish 203–4
game 197
meat with milk 197–8, 206–7
poultry 201–3, 208
Fox, M. 29
France, southern 164
Franks 195, 299, 302, 311, 315, 319, 321; *see also* Europeans
freedom
Divine 129
human 118, 122
Friedlaender, I. 293
Fusṭāṭ (Old Cairo) 73–4, 304–5, 307
Fuwwa (place) 307

Gad (tribe) 266
Galen 197–8, 200–1, 204, 207–8
Galston, M. 71
game (animals) 197
Garden of Eden 230–1, 233
Gaunilo, lost island of 69
Geiger, A. 293
Gemara 269–70, 278
Genizah, studies 52
geometry 87
Gersonides 185
Gibb, H. A. R. 309
Giqatilla, Joseph 64 n. 64
God 88, 112, 124–5, 127, 130, 133–4, 144, *et passim*; *see also* divine; the One
actions of 17, 26, 43, 66
attributes of 51, 175–7, 179, 181, 184–9
corporeality of 176
doctrine of 146
essence of 65, 190
existence of 101, 113
first cause of 118
freedom of 132
governance of 3, 43, 59
incorporeality of 184
intellectual apprehension of 37, 40
judgment of 44
knowledge by 131, 164
knowledge concerning 51, 101, 225
known through nature 29
love for 38, 40, 101

God (*cont.*):
mind of 132
nearness to 36, 73
non-corporeality of 26
transcendence of 145
unity of 26, 101, 113, 176, 183, 212
will 59
wisdom of 45
Goitein, S. D. 47 n. 3, 52
good, the (Aristotle) 50
Good, the (Plotinus) 120, 123, 128
governance 91, 96, 100
of the city 97, 103, 223
divine 58, 59
political 44–5, 103–4
self- 95–6
of the solitary 33
grammar 83
universal 83
Greek(s) 117, 122, 142, 274
non-Greeks 95
translation into Arabic 13
Greek Sage, the 117 n. 1, 118, 126, 129, 132; *see also* Plotinus
Gruenwald, I. 5
Gulf of ʿAqaba 319
Guttmann, J. 149

ḥadīth (tradition) 312, 315
al-Ḥāfiẓ al-Iṣfahānī 312
Halevi, Judah 31, 116, 261
Kuzari 115
Halkin, A. S. 8, 249
Ḥamāt (place) 318
Ḥamza (uncle of Muhammad) 317
Ḥanafīs 315
Ḥaninah, R. 190
happiness, flourishing 2–3, 14, 15–17, 49, 96
political 24
presumed 97
true 86, 97
harmonization 146–7, 154, 209
Harūn al-Rashīd 312
Harvey, S. 3–4
Harvey, W. Z. 4, 71
Hasday Crescas 258
heaven(s) 6, 121, 162, 164–5
ascension to 143
bodies of 159
heavenly spheres 152, 167, 170
Hebrew(s) 41, 75, 79, 98, 179, 200–1, 264, 275–6
Heinemann, I. 210
Hekhalot, writings 63
Heller, R. Hayyim 219
Heschel, A. J. 1, 47 n. 3, 72
ḥesed (loving-kindness) 43–4, 46, 133, 251
Hezekiah 234
Ḥijāz (place) 319
Hipparchus 173
historians 295
history 233, 265, 282–3
Ḥiṭṭīn (battle of) 302, 306, 311, 314, 316
Hobbes, Thomas 107
human:
knowledge 23
perfection 2–4
society, ideal 222
humours, Galen on 201, 204–5
Humphreys, R. S. 309
Ḥusayn mosque 315
Hyman, A. 5

Ibn ʿArabī 5
Ibn al-Athīr 311
Ibn Bājja 6, 14, 17, 23–4, 160, 168–9
Tadbīr al-Mutawaḥḥid (Governance of the solitary) 34, 48
Ibn al-Furāt (vizier) 83
Ibn al-Haytham 170
Doubts on Ptolemy 161
Ibn Jubayr 314, 316, 318, 320–1
Ibn Kaspi 56
Ibn Khallikān 315
Ibn Miskawayh 13
Ibn Sabʿīn 5
Ibn Shaddād, Bahā'al-Dīn 310–12, 315, 321
Ibn Ṭufayl 6, 69, 160
Ḥayy b. Yaqẓān 34, 69
Ibn Ṭulūn mosque 318
idolater(s) 212, 215
idolatry 35, 211–12, 215–16, 218, 229
ignoramuses, the ignorant 36, 63, 165
ignorance 125, 133
Ikhmīm (place) 319
imagination 19–20, 73, 134
imaginative faculty 22, 152–4
imitation of God (*imitatio Dei*) 17–18, 20, 29–30, 41–4, 70, 110
infidels 310, 313
intellect:
Active Intellect 48, 128, 141–5, 152
as bond between man and God 68

human 19, 38, 83, 124, 141, 143–5, 151
and imagination 105
ıtellection 143, 150, 155
ıtellectual apprehension 45
ntelligence, universal (Plotinus) 119, 122–3
ntelligible(s) 38, 81–2, 95, 231
raq 307
slam 23, 142, 228, 242, 300, 307, 311–13, 321–2, 316
Eastern 316
Shīʿī 139
slamic(ate) 216
civilization 13–14, 301
intellectual tradition 13
philosophers 4
thought 4
world 14, 115
smāʿīlī 4, 8, 115–16
dynasty 296
srael
great men of 248
Land of (Eretz Yisrael) 8, 211, 216, 257–90, 302
people of (Israelites) 91, 210–11, 213, 221, 225–7, 232, 237, *et passim*
sraeli, Isaac 171
sraelite, non- 211
talian 307
vry, A. 4

abala (place) 314
acob 182, 286, 289
his dream of ladder 44, 61–2, 72
acobite(s) 83
erusalem 278–9, 285–6, 288, 302, 307, 311
esus 228 n. 14, 229 n. 15, 242, 246 n. 58
ew(s) 90, 98, 100, 185, 210, 215–16, 259, 275, 297, 304
ewish 212, 230, 258, 303–4
calendar 269
community 269
eschatology 247
literature 245, 250
people 210, 216, 226, 240, 243, 269, 274
population 267, 270
scholars 242
thought 263
world 115
ohanan b. Torta, R. 243
Joḥanan b. Zakkai, R. 267, 276
Jonathan b. Joseph of Ruzhany 166 n. 27
Joseph b. Judah 36, 87
Joseph b. Kaspi 231
Joseph 289
al-Jubbāʾī, Abū ʿAlī 109
Judah ha-Nasi, R. 267–8
Judah Loew b. Bezalel (Maharal of Prague) 261
Judaism 90, 210, 235
and philosophy 106
Jupiter 161
jurisprudence 86
justice 97

Kafiḥ, J. 59, 198, 201, 205
Kalam (*kalām*) 4, 86, 105, 107, 108–10, 114; *see also* theology, dialectical
Karaites 301
al-Khabūshānī, Shaykh 317
al-Kirmānī, Ḥamīd al-Dīn 115, 128
knowledge 124, 150–1
concerning God 18 n. 13, 66, 235
men of 67, 73–4
Koran 176
kosher, non-kosher 6; *see also* forbidden foods
Kraemer, J. L. 111
Kroner, H. 204, 293

al-Lādhiqiyya (place) 314
Lane-Poole, S. 295
Langermann, T. 6
language 135, 181–3
about god 183
Mosaic 138
negative 189
religious 175–7, 190
and religious law 78
Latin 143
Law, law(s) 35, 38, 41, 148–50, 156, 195, 224, 242, 249, 269
civil 80, 100
divine 100–1, 224, 228
on idolatry 215
Jewish 138, 201, 221
Mosaic 134, 149, 223
natural 252
Noahide 210–11, 213, 217, 219
nomic 97–101, 228
Oral 227, 246, 263–5, 267, 275, 278
rational 26

Law, law(s) (*cont.*):
religious 31–2, 77–8, 80, 83, 100, 134
Scribal 266
Sharīʿa 296
talmudic 197, 214
Lerner, R. 3
Levi b. Gerson 169, 172
Levinger, J. 6
Lewis, Bernard 300
life-style
active, practical 2, 18, 51–2, 72
contemplative, theoretical 2, 16, 50–1, 260
logic (*manṭiq*) 4, 36, 63, 78, 80, 83, 85, 87–9, 175, 184
logos 80, 119
love 127, 133, 143
intellectual 125
Luzzatto, R. Simone 257

madrasa (college) 301, 315, 317
Maghreb 8, 293–4, 316
Maghrebian(s), Maghribī(s) 294, 314, 316, 320; *see also* North Africans
Mahdi, M. 80
mahdī (redeemer) 300
Maimonides:
Book of Commandments 6, 212, 219, 286, 288
Commentary on the Mishnah 6, 14, 22–3, 25, 135, 145, 165, 175, 201–2, 205, 227, 271, 293–4
Fuṣūl Mūsā (*Pirqe Moshe*) 198–200, 204
Guide 4–7, 14–15, 17, 19, 22–6, 30–1, 33, 41, *et passim*
legal writings 6
Letter on Apostasy 240
Letter to Yemen 240, 243–4, 282
life of 47
Maimonideanism 148, 260
medical works of 7
Mishneh Torah (Code of Law) 6–7, 14, 22–3, 30–1, 35, 46, 67, *et passim*
as philosopher and philosopher-statesman 105, 108
philosophic writings of 209
Regimen of Health 197, 199, 201, 203, 204, 206
Responsa 6, 31
Treatise on Asthma 199, 204
Treatise on the Art of Logic 24, 77, 79, 104, 175, 180–5
Treatise on Poisons and their Antidotes 7
Treatise on Resurrection 237, 262
al-Malik al-Kāmil 320
al-Malik al-Muʿaẓẓam Shams al-Dawla Tūrān Shāh 300, 321
al-Malik al-Ẓāhir 314
al-Malik al-Ẓāhir Baybars 311
Malikī 319
Mamlūks 313
Mamlūk sultanate 311
man:
end purpose of 2, 66
morally strong 20–3
a political animal 33, 69
of practical intellect, wisdom 20, 23, 2 28
righteous (*ẓaddiq*) 40
Manasseh (tribe) 266
al-Manṣūr (sultan) 306
al-Maqrīzī 320
al-Maqs (Nile port) 305
Marseilles 214
mashhūrāt (*endoxa*, accepted beliefs) 25, 103
masses, multitude 36, 39, 52, 69, 176, 18
mathematics 36, 63, 85–9, 101, 167, 173
Mattā b. Yūnus 83
matter (*golem*) 87, 119–21, 166
intelligible 119
mean, middle path 27–9
meaning 185
figurative 53, 55, 58
Mecca 297, 312–13, 316, 318–19
Medina 319
Mediterranean world 307
Mercury 161, 178
Merkavah (*merkavah*) mystics (mysticism) 5, 98, 176
Mesopotamia 299, 306
Messiah 212, 218, 265, 273–4, 278, 280–1, 220–55
Messiah b. Joseph 244
Messianic (era, days) 7, 144, 220–55, 284, 288, 290, 304
Messianism 260
apocalyptic 251
restorative 233–4
Utopian 233–4
metaphors, metaphorical 153, 156, 237
metaphysics 5, 23, 57, 86–8, 122, 142, 150, 184, 221, 252
Middle Ages 150, 258, 309
Midrashim 237

Mind, World (Plotinus) 123–4, 127, 131; *see also* Intelligence, universal
al-Minya (Nile port) 305
Minyat Ibn al-Khaṣīb (place) 319
miracles 150, 155, 252 n. 70
Mishnah 142, 202, 263, 267–9, 275
monotheism, monotheists 98, 215–16, 218
Moses 20, 23, 26, 39, 65, 72, 134, *et passim*
Moses b. Tibbon 206
mosques 317
Mosul 306
Muʿtazilite(s) 25
Muḥammad 23, 228 n. 14, 317, 321
al-Mukthir (amir of Mecca) 316
Munk, S. 59
Muqaṭṭam mountain (Cairo) 307
music 87
Muslim(s) 83, 99, 178, 184–5, 215, 298, *et passim*
  East 300
  non-Muslims 297, 305
  predecessors of Maimonides 33
  world 295
Mutakallim(ūn) 4, 87, 102, 105, 108–10, 112, 114, 138; *see also* dialectical theologians
mysticism, mystics 5, 115, 141–3
  of Maimonides 64 n. 64

Naḥmanides 262 n. 11, 270
Naḥmias, Joseph 173
al-Nāṣir li-Dīn Allāh (caliph) 316
nation(s) 90, 92–5, 227
  ancient, pagan 90–1, 100
  great 90
  national independence 7
nature 37, 121, 170–1
  Nature (Plotinus) 131
Nebuchadnezzar 274
necessity 119, 122, 130
negations 187, 189–90
Neoplatonic, Neoplatonism 4–5 115–16, 125, 137–8, 144
  Neoplatonized Aristotelianism 5
Nile 305, 307
  delta 304
  ports 305
al-Nīsābūrī, Quṭb al-Dīn 312
Noahide laws 7, 210–11, 217–18
Normans 305
North Africa(ns) 8, 293, 306, 318
Nubia(ns) 305–6
Nūr al-Dīn (Zangid ruler) 300, 303–5, 306–7, 313–14, 318–20

One, the (Plotinus) 4, 120, 122–4, 126–30, 132–3
  transcendence 124 n. 39
ontology, ontological 131, 184–5, 221, 251
opinions, necessary 103
orbs (*galgalim*) 162–3, 166, 170
ordination *see semikhah*
Orientalists 309
Ottomans 313

Palestine 267, 269–70, 289, 295, 302, 304–6; *see also* Israel, Land of
parable(s), prophetic 52, 57, 62, 75, 156
paradox 71, 146
  of Maimonides' life 47–50, 52, 68–9, 72
Pardes 65
particularization 190
Patriarchs 39, 45, 72
perfection(s) 18, 40
  highest 70
  human 19, 39, 47, 87, 143, 151, 225, 229, 232
  of human history, final 232
  individual 33, 72, 97
  intellectual 30, 44, 68–70, 224
  political 33
  social-political 223
  of the soul 71
  theoretical 71–2
  ultimate 68–9, 71–2
perplexity 26, 58, 103
  true 159
Persians 274, 318
Philo 259
philosopher(s) 19, 21–2, 30, 44, 49–50, 56–7, *et passim*
  books of 98
  Jewish 48
  imitatio dei of 43
  Islamic 48
  non-philosophers 180
  philosopher-king 20
  religious 145
philosophy 4–5, 26, 78, 83, 85, 138, 142, *et passim*
  aim of, ultimate 103
  demonstrative 85

philosophy (*cont.*):
Graeco–Islamic 5
history of 264
human 85–6
and *kalām* 105
and the Law 148–50, 152
natural 161
political 5, 91, 221, 251
practical 84–6, 96, 102, 251
religious 145
theoretical 26, 84–7, 101
phlegma, phlegmy humour 204–5
physician(s) 197, 205–6, 208, 303
physics 6, 24, 57, 85–9, 101, 150, 172, 221
pig, swine 196, 198, 200
pilgrimage (*ḥajj*) 312–13, 319
Pines, S. 18 n. 13, 23–4, 43 n. 26, 51, 59, 71, 94–5, 108, 111, 115
Pisans 304
Plato 18, 94, 119–20
cave allegory of 49, 51, 70
city of 35
Gorgias 110
Laws 20, 99
Platonic-Alfarabian tradition 3–4
political philosophy 51, 222
Republic 20, 70, 99, 107
Plotinus 4, 127–8
Arabic corpus 118, 122, 123, 126, 128, 137
Enneads 116–33
'Long Theology' 117
Theology of Aristotle 117 n. 5
poetry 85
poets and preachers 190
politics 90, 96–7, 99; *see also* governance of the city
political activity 51
political state 18
polity:
civil 92
religious 92, 99
practical life 31
practical reason, wisdom (*phronēsis*) 2, 17, 24, 28
prayer 177, 179, 264
predeterminism 119
predication, amphibolous 182
privation 187–8
proof (*burhān*) 124
prophecy 5, 20, 142–3, 147, 150–2, 156, 224, 264–5, 279–80
books of 52
Mosaic 135, 138, 148
Prophet *see* Muhammad
prophet(s) 37, 40, 59, 142, 145, 135, 152–4, 223, 247, 281
prophetic:
experience 142
inspiration 142
revelation 44
visions 137
prophetology 101
prosneusis, lunar 161
Protagoras 110
providence, divine 4, 6, 39–40, 43–4, 65, 117, 121, 139, 145, 282
Psyche (Plotinus) 119
Ptolemy 159, 172
Almagest 159, 161
Planetary Hypotheses 159
Ptolemaic theory 6, 161–3, 170, 173–4

al-Qabīṣī, 160–1
al-Qāḍī al-Fāḍil 8, 74, 305–7
Qarāfa cemetery (Cairo) 315, 317
quadrupeds 196
qualities, moral 95–7
quiddity (*māhiyya*) 185
Qur'ān 312, 317, 320
Qūṣ (place) 319

ra'īs al-yahūd (Head of the Jews) 8, 47 n. 3, 305, 307
Raba 269
Rabbis 29, 274; *see also* Sages
rabbinic literature 22, 28
rational faculty 82–3, 101, 152
Ravitzky, A. 7
Realism, philosophical 138
reason 24, 28, 122
reason (*nous*) 2
reason (*qiyās*) 123
redemption 239
cosmic 251
of man 235
national 7, 225, 232–3, 235–8, 242, 245–7, 260
Red Sea 297, 306
regimes 97
religion 52, 83
Near Eastern 31
principles of 37
true 211

  universalistic 83, 91, 99–100
repentance 22
reshut (official authority) 213, 305
responsibility, individual 118
resurrection 234, 312
Reuben (tribe) 266
revelation 26, 135, 249
  progressive 6
Reynald of Chatillon 321
rhetoric 5, 85
Romans 273
Rosin, David 15

Sa'adya Gaon 15, 275
sage 28
  the sage and the saint 30
Sages, the talmudic 21–2, 38, 59, 142, 195, 242, *et passim*
saints (*awliya'*) 315
Saladin (Ṣalāḥ al-Dīn) 8, 74, 295, 297–9, 303–4, 309–22
Saljūq(id) 300, 313, 341
Samuel, R. 234
Samuel b. Tibbon 48, 73–5, 255
Samuel b. Ẓarẓa 231
sanctifying the Name 198
Sanhedrin 264, 274, 285, 288, 290
scholars, Maimonidean 105
Scholem, G. 233, 249
science(s) 50, 89, 281
  classification of 85
  demonstrative 102, 104
  divine 24, 37, 55–8, 65, 85–6, 88, 101
  of the Law 42, 77
  natural 36, 55–7; *see also* physics
  philosophic 78, 84
  political 14, 78, 85–6, 90, 93, 95–7, 101–2
  practical 89–90
  productive 84
  propaeduetic-mathematical 87
  religious 85
  speculative 154
  theoretical 84, 89, 104, 110
  true 40
scientists, men of science 37, 160
Scripture 6, 41, 135, 181–2, 190
seal(s) 63–4
Second Commonwealth 7, 267
secret(s) 57
  of the Law 53
  teachings 56
Seder night 278
semikhah (ordination) 264, 287
seven 60–1
al-Shāfi'ī 315, 317
  school of 296
Shāwar (vizier) 303
Shem Ṭov Falaquera 50
Shem Ṭov b. Joseph 33, 231
Shem Ṭov b. Shem Ṭov 54
Shemā' prayer 39
shemad (apostasy, persecution) 241
Shī'ī(s), Shī'ite(s) 4, 8, 115, 296, 303–5, 307, 312, 317, 320
Shī'ism 116
Shīrkūh (vizier) 303–4
silence 183
Simon b. Gamliel, R. 21
Sinai, Mt., Gathering at 135–7, 233, 236, 249
al-Sīrāfī, Abū Sa'īd 83
Sivan, E. 309–10
society, societies:
  ideal 224
  imperfect 92
  perfect 92
Socrates 110, 184
solitude (*khalwa*) 3, 33–4, 38, 47, 51, 66, 68–70, 73–4, 96
Solomon 189, 227, 235
sophistic(al), sophists 85, 110–11
sōphrosynē 20 n. 21
soul:
  ascent of the 144
  individual, human 118–19, 125
  rational 40
Soul, World (universal) 120, 122, 124–5, 131
Spain 8, 161, 293–4
Spanish 160, 164, 204, 173–4, 316
  Arabic 8
  Aristotelian school 6
speculation (*theōria*) 84
speech 124
  articulate 81
  inner 81–2
  external 81–2
  of God 137
  ordinary 136
Spinoza 100
state:
  civil 90–1
  religious 91
statements, poetical 102
Strauss, Leo 1, 4–5, 53 n. 26, 56, 60,

Strauss, Leo (*cont.*):
78–9, 91, 96, 98–100, 106, 110–11, 180
Sudanese 300
Ṣūfī(s), Ṣūfism 5, 301, 313–14, 317–18, 322
al-Suhrawardī, Shihāb al-Dīn 314
sultan(s) 63, 74–5, 306
palace, parable of 3, 35, 60, 62, 66
Sunnī(s) 8, 296, 298, 304, 312, 314, 317, 322
Islam 295–6, 300, 305
Supreme Court 270, 277
Suyūfiyya (Ḥanafī college) 315
symbols 153
Syria(ns) 295, 303, 305–6, 314
Syro-Palestinian coast (Sahil) 310
syzgies 173

Tabrīz (place) 313
Talmud 7, 65, 142, 197, 212, 243, 263, 267, 269, 277
Tannaim 270
Taqī al-Dīn ʿUmar (nephew of Saladin) 314
Temple 265–7, 270, 272–3, 278, 282, 285, 288
Thābit b. Qurra 161, 169
theologians 25, 115, 300
theology 221
dialectical 86; *see also* Kalam
natural 88
Tishʿah be-Av 288–9
Torah 42, 67, 79, 91, 99, 135, 180–1, *et passim*
tradition 25, 42
transcendentalism 145–6
Transjordan 321
true:
perfection 40
realitites (*ḥaqāʾiq*) 52
worship 3
truth, apodictic 24, 27
Türker, Mubahat 177
Turks 300–1
Twersky, I. 1, 7, 25, 47 n. 3, 148–9

ʿ*ulamāʾ* (religious scholars) 315, 317–18, 320
understanding, human 165
unification 144
with Active Intellect 143
mystical or quasi-mystical 142
Utopia(n) 224, 230, 233–5, 248

Venetians 307
Venus 161
virtue(s) 16, 95–6
virtuous city 34, 49
viziers 75
Voice, divine 136–7

waqf (s) (pious foundation) 318–19
war:
commanded 211, 213, 216
holy 7, 209–20, 310–11, 320
normative 217
permitted 215, 213–14, 216–17
welfare:
of the body 69
of the soul 69
West, the 288
Winter, M. 8
wisdom (Wisdom) 17, 40–3, 128
divine 133, 252
ḥokhmah 41
sophia 16
Wolfson, H. A. 79, 84, 99
World to Come 144, 247–8, 250
world, intelligible 125
worship 35, 38, 40, 45, 66–7
intellectual 67
true 37
ultimate 66

Yaḥya b. ʿAdī 83
Yemen 300, 306, 321

zakāt (legal poor-tax) 319
collectors 319–20
Zangids 301, 303, 318
zedaqah (righteousness) 40, 44
Zion 286
return to 274

Index compiled by Joel E. Kraemer